Spitfires

Off the Cliff: How the Making of Thelma & Louise
Drove Hollywood to the Edge

*Saturday Night Widows: The Adventures of Six Friends
Remaking Their Lives*

Spitfires

The American Women Who Flew in the Face
of Danger during World War II

Becky Aikman

BLOOMSBURY PUBLISHING
NEW YORK · LONDON · OXFORD · NEW DELHI · SYDNEY

BLOOMSBURY PUBLISHING
Bloomsbury Publishing Inc.
1359 Broadway, New York, NY 10018, USA
50 Bedford Square, London, WC1B 3DP, UK
Bloomsbury Publishing Ireland Limited, 29 Earlsfort Terrace,
Dublin 2, D02 AY28, Ireland

BLOOMSBURY, BLOOMSBURY PUBLISHING, and the Diana logo
are trademarks of Bloomsbury Publishing Plc

First published in the United States 2025

ISBN: HB: 978-1-63557-656-6; EBOOK: 978-1-63557-657-3

LIBRARY OF CONGRESS CATALOGING-IN-PUBLICATION DATA IS AVAILABLE

Library of Congress Control Number: 2024942519

2 4 6 8 10 9 7 5 3 1

Typeset by Westchester Publishing Services
Printed in the United States by Lakeside Book Company, Harrisonburg, VA

To find out more about our authors and books visit www.bloomsbury.com and
sign up for our newsletters.

Bloomsbury books may be purchased for business or promotional use. For information
on bulk purchases please contact Macmillan Corporate and Premium Sales Department at
specialmarkets@macmillan.com.

For product safety–related questions contact productsafety@bloomsbury.com.

For my mother, the bold and curious Barbara Aikman,
one of the few who remembered

CONTENTS

PROLOGUE

March 2, 1943
Collingbourne Kingston, England

Second Officer Raines streaked across the sky, blissfully alone at the controls of a Spitfire Mark IX fighter. A puff of cloud popped up on the horizon. Nothing alarming at first, but the pilot took note.

The Spitfire had just rolled off an assembly line near the southern coast of England. Raines scrambled into the air to make sure German bombing or strafing didn't take the valuable aircraft out, then headed toward a maintenance unit of the Royal Air Force near Oxford. Ground crew there would load up the fighter with arms and other military gadgets to prep it for strikes against Germany.

Raines knew that ferrying such an advanced aircraft was one of the most dangerous jobs of World War II. The most obvious peril was the unpredictable nature of English weather. Ferry pilots flew without using instruments, so a sudden appearance of overcast skies raised the risk of losing one's bearings, losing one's altitude, and smashing into a church steeple or a hill. The specter of death lurked behind the gauzy curtain of every cloud.

There were other threats as well. Only four decades after the invention of mechanical flight, this war rained down unprecedented destruction from the air, yet the aircraft of the era were still unreliable machines that often failed. Fuel lines leaked. Parts rattled apart. Gauges conked out. Engines sputtered or stopped. Pilots like Raines strapped themselves into barely vetted planes just out of the factories or clunkers on the way to repair after being shot up in battle. Too many ferry pilots took off on flights from which they wouldn't return. Nearly one in seven of them died during the course of the war.

For now, though, the path directly ahead looked serene. As Raines gazed out from the clear acrylic canopy of the Spitfire, the midday landscape unspooled a thousand feet below. Pastureland shimmered green and peaceful under the sun, and the glossy water of the slow, meandering Bourne River reflected silver glints of light. Storybook cottages clustered in villages along the banks.

The twenty-six-year-old aviator smiled, reveling in the opportunity to command one of the most state-of-the-art aircraft in the world. Like most pilots who had the chance to fly one, Raines loved the Spitfire for its power and grace. Capable of exceeding a blistering four hundred miles per hour, the compact, single-engine fighter was sleek, like a fish slicing through water, and responsive, like a well-trained horse. Intuitive, like an extension of the pilot's own body.

"Mother, if you could know how happy I am when I fly a plane!" Raines had written in a letter home. "I never feel so completely close to God as when I'm up in the blue. So if you ever get a message that I've been in a crackup and have been killed, don't grieve for me any more than you can possibly help. Just know that I died the way I wanted to."

Minutes passed. Unusually short for a pilot, Raines hitched up to take another look over the nose. The cloud loomed larger up ahead, closer now and moving fast. With luck, there would be an easy way around.

The engine made a quick series of choking sounds. What was happening? It wasn't clear. The dial on the rpm gauge swung back and forth; lights flickered on the instrument panel. Raines banked left, making for the nearest aerodrome. The choking stopped in the middle of the turn.

Silence. The engine was dead.

Raines tried to restart. Nothing. Again—nothing.

The pilot's first thought was superfluous: *There's not much time to think.*

Next thought: *Too low to parachute.*

Raines wondered if the disabled Spitfire could glide to a forced landing. It might be possible to find a flat field and pray that training, instinct, and luck could get the fighter down in one piece. Raines lowered the nose to maintain a viable speed of about a hundred miles an hour and continued turning, hoping to complete the maneuver before piercing the looming cloud.

Too late. A last beam of sunlight vanished as the cloudbank towered above the Spitfire and swallowed it up. Raines hurtled into a whiteout, where the act of flying felt like wallowing in a bowl of milk. All spatial awareness disappeared. Amid the vast, impassive void, Raines couldn't judge left from right, up from down, earth from sky. It was nearly impossible to keep the plane on an even keel, let alone maintain the proper angle to complete a turn. Already tilting left, the Spitfire soon slipped too far from level, the air no longer passing across the wings to hold the plane aloft. The nose buffeted, heaving violently up and down, a warning that the Spit would shortly fall out of the sky, a helpless hunk of plunging metal in the shape of an aircraft.

Raines entered a sickening vertical spin. It felt like being sucked headfirst into a whirlpool. The corkscrew tightened, the speed accelerated. Centrifugal force drove the pilot hard against the seat. Nausea swelled. Yet Raines dug deep to concentrate. The last hope rested on earth and sky more than a pilot's talent. Would the plane emerge from the murk in time to regain control?

When the Spit finally broke free from the haze, Raines, stomach heaving, bore down with grim resolve and kicked the right rudder, hard, to break the momentum of the spin. The ship righted. But again, too late. Too low. Too close to the ground. Too little time to pull up.

I've had it, Raines thought.

Small country cottages, getting bigger fast, rose in the windscreen to meet the plane.

TWO LITTLE BOYS, Derek Palmer and Gordon Lee, had been sitting on the stoop of a picturesque thatched-roof home in the southern English town of Collingbourne Kingston. They were hoping for a handout from Mrs. Merrifield, who made candy next door. All the nearby houses were crowned with at least two feet of wheat straw that provided insulation as well as the occasional nesting place for birds and mice.

In the eerie quiet, the Spitfire careened out of the sky. The ground shook. The boys saw the neighbor's roof explode in a cloud of thatch and dust, pushed clear off the walls by the force of the impact. Broken furniture trailed across the yard. What was left of the fuselage rested, hissing, in a garden across the street. Both wings wound up who-knows-where in the debris. The boys saw an aviator's leather helmet slumped over the joystick.

Derek's mother sprinted from a shop, but she didn't have the strength to wrest the body from the cockpit. Two broad-shouldered farmers ran from the closest field with the bleak intent of digging the dead man out. But when they pried away the canopy, the pilot, shockingly small, popped up, blood pouring from a nasty forehead gash. The farmhands couldn't believe it. The dead man was alive. Even more shocking, the dead man was . . . a woman. An American woman.

Following crash protocol, Hazel Jane Raines called out in the honeyed accent of the American South, "London! Guard that plane!" Then she fainted clean away.

HAZEL JANE RAINES, a former flight instructor and stunt pilot from Macon, Georgia, served as one of twenty-five American women who ferried planes for England during World War II. She was part of a little-known corps that shook things up wherever they landed. They had crossed the perilous wartime Atlantic in 1942 because the United States military, in all its wisdom, refused to accept women pilots, no matter how courageous and skilled. A newspaper back home once praised Hazel's loop-de-loop aerobatics under a headline that read: LOCAL GIRL AIR INSTRUCTOR DESIRES TO BE U.S. BOMBER PILOT DESPITE MALE SNICKERS.

But the British weren't laughing. Beset by death, blackouts, deprivation, and a perfectly rational fear that Hitler might wipe the nation off the map, the United Kingdom was so desperate for ferry pilots that it accepted some who had lost arms, legs, or eyes. It took pilots who were too old for the Royal Air Force, along with foreigners, members of any race, and yes, even women. Together they formed a civilian offshoot of the RAF that went by the rather pedestrian name of Air Transport Auxiliary. The ragtag flyers of the ATA cooked up nicknames that better suited the arch spirit of the organization: Ancient and Tattered Airmen. Anything To Anywhere. Always Terrified Airwomen. Atta-Girls!

The Atta-Girls got the ride of a lifetime. Joining up was a bold choice, but any woman who had the audacity to learn to fly back when flying was a risky gamble was already breaking a whole string of conventions. The group of young Americans leaped at the chance to fly up to 147 different models of the most advanced aircraft in the world, aircraft like the Hurricane and Spitfire fighters and the Wellington bomber. With little training and even less advance notice, the flyers took on whatever missions were thrown at them each day, often taking command of planes they'd never seen before with only a few minutes to read the instructions. For women who often had to scratch and beg in their homeland to command single-engine puddle-jumpers made of fabric and wood—or to find any kind of job behind the controls of any kind of plane—this was an opportunity beyond their dreams. It made them the first American women to fly such military aircraft, let alone a whole slew of them, and in a war zone no less.

These pilots had answered a distress call that ricocheted around the world once Germany overran Western Europe by the summer of 1940. Since then, the United Kingdom had stood alone, with only the English Channel, twenty-one miles across at the narrowest point, to provide protection. During the four-month aerial Battle of Britain that year, British pilots in fighters like the Spitfire won the gratitude of the nation for repelling the German Luftwaffe, but the cost was dear. More than 1,500 aircrew and 1,700 British aircraft were lost trying to protect the country from German bombs, which killed 43,000 civilians in 1940 and terrorized countless more. Throughout the war, the losses mounted: 70,000 British civilians killed, another 70,000 aircrew dead, and at least 20,000 British aircraft destroyed.

By the time the American women arrived in 1942, the RAF needed ever more aircraft to fend off continued bombing as the country ramped up to take the fight to Germany. Every replacement plane, and every pilot trained to fly one, was precious.

Well paid and well respected for their work, the Atta-Girls lived ahead of their time, carrying on the way ambitious women aspired to behave decades later. Professionally, they mastered jobs that demanded technical expertise, physical strength, steely valor, and quick judgment, all while serving a cause greater than themselves. And privately, the wartime circumstances set them free. Far from home and released from the expectation of settling down in "proper" marriages, they delighted in making their own choices. They pursued their personal lives with gusto, on their own terms. Some kept an eye toward marriage, especially an advantageous one, but others seized the opportunity for same-sex partnerships or brazen out-of-wedlock affairs. For a crazy instant during the chaos and epic change of a world war, they defied every tenet of what was expected of a woman in the 1940s and beyond.

The freethinking, freewheeling Americans also cut an exuberant swath through British society, just as the war was beginning to break down class distinctions and social mores. It made for a fizzy mix. Many British women who served as ferry pilots were daughters of privilege whose wealth had allowed them to indulge the newly fashionable pursuit of winging from ski slopes to garden parties in their own planes. They assumed the Americans enjoyed the same status. And it was true, a few had sprung from the pinnacle of American society. Virginia Farr, twenty-three years old when she joined, was celebrated as "the flying socialite," groomed to play the part of a debutante in the family of the Western Union fortune. Yet Roberta Sandoz, twenty-four, had worked for rock-bottom pay as a crop duster. She scraped together money for flying lessons by performing a mock striptease at an air show, tossing layers of clothing out of the cockpit with each pass over the field. Mary Webb Nicholson, one of the oldest at thirty-six, had bartered for classes by parachuting out of a plane for a publicity stunt without so much as a practice run. And Dorothy Furey grew up in poverty, but she passed in England as a wealthy American heiress at the age of twenty-three by acting imperious and recycling a single red dress.

Others who made a spirited impression included Hazel Jane Raines, who crashed into that thatched-roof house. When she joined up at the age of twenty-five, she aspired to prove that she had the chops to fly for the U.S. military if she would ever be allowed. Helen Richey, thirty-two, was one of America's most famous stunt flyers, while Ann Wood was a relative novice at twenty-four. A college graduate, she hoped to parlay wartime contacts into the kind of high-powered career in government or business that was considered out of reach for women at that time. Winnie Pierce, an incorrigible twenty-five-year-old party girl, carried on without regard to caution both on duty and off, while Nancy Miller, twenty-three, a minister's daughter, lived a squeaky-clean existence on the ground but learned to tear it up in the sky. Mary Zerbel, a twenty-one-year-old romantic, risked her happiness to marry a bomber pilot with long odds of survival. She had been acclaimed in the United States as the youngest American woman flight instructor.

Their former identities didn't seem to matter. In England, they invented new ones. The brave young flyers were so admired and looked so dazzling in their sharp Savile Row uniforms that lords and ladies invited the Americans to parties, where they shocked the company with boisterous behavior. They danced and drank champagne behind the blackout curtains at Claridge's and the Savoy as buzz bombs barreled overhead. The international expatriate community that gathered in London couldn't get enough of the flyers, either. They mixed with a heady scene full of diplomats, journalists, generals, and spies.

By the last year of the war, one third of the twenty-five American Atta-Girls still served. Along the way, others failed to make the grade or lost their nerve. Some married, and several returned home for other work. A few flamed out in crashes that led to injury or death. The stakes were high. Someday, the women all knew, if they survived the war, the door to modernity that had opened for them might close again. They had a few short years to prove themselves, to notch the experience and connections that might allow them to them remain independent and original after the war. To test how far and high they might soar into unknown terrain. Flying without instruments—it was their way of life.

The mission of the American pilots began not in the sky but on ships, rolling across an ocean menaced by German submarines. Adventure beckoned. They were women in flight, and they were going to make the most of it.

CHAPTER I

The North Atlantic Passage

March 3, 1942
On board the SS Beaverhill

T he passage across the North Atlantic had just begun, and already
Dorothy Furey was breaking the rules. The 5 female pilots and 130
male recruits who packed onto the SS *Beaverhill*, a ponderous coal carrier
converted for transporting troops, had received strict orders: Sleep in
your clothes.

At that time, any ship bound from Canada's Gulf of St. Lawrence to
the British port of Liverpool faced forbidding odds of a nighttime torpedo
strike from a German U-boat. Temperatures in the lifeboats would be
deathly cold.

Dorothy Furey went her own way, as she usually did. Assigned a stifling
hot berth next to the boiler room, she lay very still on top of the sheets,
entirely in the nude. The bunk sat below the waterline, she reasoned, so
she was unlikely to make it out of the sinking ship anyway. If the end
was near, she chose to be comfortable instead.

Few who traversed the Atlantic in 1942 could maintain her level of
sangfroid. The Germans would sink some 720 Allied ships during the
months from March to August, when the Americans traveled to England,
one of the heaviest tolls of the war. Dorothy had heard that the last convoy

on the *Beaverhill*'s route had lost six out of ten ships. Unscathed vessels wouldn't stop for survivors, as the Germans would be looking to pick them off. The Air Transport Auxiliary split up the twenty-five American pilots, placing the first five on the *Beaverhill*, to escape the fate of eleven male American flyers who had sailed together the year before on the SS *Nerissa*—all of them drowned.

As the ship groaned and heaved across the waves, the claustrophobic cabin reminded Dorothy of her childhood in New Orleans. She would stretch out there at night in a thin-walled house, glistening with sweat, her sheets flung aside in the soggy bayou heat that she despised, listening for a distant train whistle. "Someday," she vowed, "I'm going to be on that train, and I'm never coming back." A ship would have to do.

Legend had it that Dorothy Furey was the daughter of a wealthy banana importer. Legend had it that her family lost a fortune in the crash of 1929. None of it was true.

While it was hard to sort out truth from fiction about Dorothy Furey, what no one ever doubted was the irrefutable fact that she was a great beauty. Even as a child, slender in a thin cotton dress, her sisters gave her the nickname of Stunny. What stunned observers first were her eyes. They were such a mind-bending shade of blue that people sometimes misremembered them as green or violet, whatever seemed most vivid and extraordinary.

Her gaze was level, but when she chose to deploy her full, captivating attention upon admirers, of which there were many, those eyes contained vistas. They enhanced other natural gifts—symmetrical features, a brilliant complexion, porcelain skin against shiny black hair—but her allure also lay in presentation. She wasn't vain, in that she didn't care what people thought of her. That chilly detachment only goaded conquests to want to please her. Already, her companions on the voyage had made assumptions, which she didn't bother to correct, that she inhabited some higher plane. Dorothy's aloof, intimidating façade helped to ensure that they never learned the secrets of her childhood.

Born in 1919, Dorothy was the youngest of five children in a second-generation Irish Catholic family, eight years younger than the next oldest sibling. The others grew up and moved away from the small, boxy clapboard house in the Fourth Ward, leaving her the lone child in a chaotic family drama. She believed she was a mistake, unwanted, and grew to hate her mother, Edna, who drilled a religious education into her brood while failing to lead by example. Church was mandatory every Wednesday and twice on Sundays, yet in between, Edna disappeared into her bedroom for days with bootleg alcohol. Brandishing a ferocious temper, she veered between fretfulness and indifference, once refusing to help when Dorothy suffered stomach pains that turned out to be a bursting appendix. An older sister took the child to a hospital just in time.

Dorothy's father, Michael Furey, didn't figure much in her memories. He probably steered clear of the whole contentious scene when he could. A purchasing agent at the Standard Fruit & Steamship Company, he supported the family well enough until he was pensioned off in the Great Depression around 1930. After that, money grew scarce. He was the more soft-spoken parent, but once, when he was reading a newspaper at the kitchen table, he became enraged at some sharp words from his wife. Michael leaped at her, pinned her to the table, and held her there, squeezing her throat. It took of all the panicked children to pull him off. Dorothy saw everything, the drinking and the fights, the creeping undercurrent of violence, but she learned to keep her feelings to herself.

At first, the girl embraced religion. She so admired a nun who taught at the Catholic school that she daydreamed of taking vows herself. But one day when she was giving confession, a priest got his hands all the way up her skirt, probing her, and she bolted, screaming. Overnight she abandoned her faith, declaring herself a strict atheist for the rest of her life.

The family crumbled entirely when her father contracted tuberculosis of the kidneys. Dorothy couldn't escape the sound of his screams, especially when he endured the amputation of a gangrenous leg right there in the house. His labored breathing lasted for days. He died in 1934, when Dorothy was fifteen. Afterward, she escaped what she called the "Gothic dysfunction," moving in with an older sister and embarking on a lifelong quest to rise in the world. But the damage was done. For years afterward, Dorothy projected a look of wariness or outright mistrust whenever she met anyone new, particularly a woman.

A small weekly newspaper hired Dorothy at fifteen as a "girl Friday." She made herself useful, putting the paper to bed on Friday nights and even writing articles. She rarely made it to school, and she never gradu-ated, but her innate intelligence served her well. Dorothy read widely—Shakespeare, Tolstoy, history, current affairs. The more she learned, the more she burned to *do* something, to make something of herself. She became incensed at the racial discrimination so prevalent in New Orleans, which made her all the more determined to leave the city behind. And when Hitler sent troops into the Rhineland in 1936, his persecution of Jews made Dorothy seethe. Unlike most Americans before the U.S. entry into the war, she felt that she personally should do something to stop him. She wrote an ardent editorial criticizing other countries for failing to intervene and predicting that the United States would be pulled into a world war. She was only seventeen years old.

By now she had a new goal: to become a heroine in a righteous cause. "I felt this would be the only justifiable war in my lifetime," she later wrote, "so I began to think of ways in which I could be useful." She settled on the most dramatic role she could imagine—a pilot, taking to the sky, often alone, righting wrongs like a knight-errant of old. "I didn't envision flying combat," she wrote, "but thought women would be useful in transporting the wounded to hospitals and in general helping trans-port planes wherever they were needed." This was a pipe dream—well under a thousand women in the country held pilot's licenses at the time. Many women didn't even drive cars. Besides, the United States wouldn't enter the war for a few more years, and women were not permitted to fly for U.S. forces anyway. But Dorothy wanted to prepare should the chance arise.

Another trauma settled it. Dorothy wasn't physically strong—five feet five inches tall but weighing only 110 pounds. Late one night at the newspaper, an editor sexually assaulted her. She pushed that from her mind, too, and never shared the details with anyone. She was determined: Never show weakness, never look back. Soon after, at the age of twenty, Dorothy quit the job and drove out to the New Orleans Airport. It consisted of a three-thousand-foot field and an Art Deco terminal perched on a man-made peninsula that jutted into Lake Pontchartrain. She spotted a sign: MAYNARD SCHOOL OF AVIATION.

It wasn't easy for any woman to talk her way into flying lessons in that era, let alone a woman who couldn't afford them. But Dorothy knew well the effect she had on men, and it gave her remarkable self-assurance. She approached the owner with cool reserve and told him she wanted to learn but couldn't pay.

"Is that your car?" he asked, pointing outside to a beat-up Ford sedan she had bought with her newspaper salary.

"Yes," Dorothy said. "And it's free and clear."

He gave it a glance. "Well, you give me your car," he said, "and I will teach you to fly."

Two years later, without a car but with a commercial pilot's license in hand, she broke through as the school's only woman teacher under a new government project called the Civilian Pilot Training Program. It was intended to boost the number of pilots in case of war by offering college students fifty hours of free instruction. Almost to a woman, Dorothy's future colleagues in the ATA first took up flying for sheer love of the pursuit, but she saw it as a means to an end. Not only to shake off the past and save the world from Hitler, but to provide steady work in a field with potential. "A lot of the women who flew, they did it for fun," said a member of her family. "Dorothy needed the money."

As it turned out, her unflappable demeanor supplied just the right mojo for a pilot in a rudimentary plane—double for someone training a nervous student to fly one. Schools mostly used aircraft like the Piper J-3 Cub, a single-wing, single-engine workhorse about as substantial as a modern-day go-cart and not much heavier. The steel frame supported a shell of lacquered cotton. In flight, the student and instructor, sitting one in front of the other, bobbed along at a plodding eighty miles an hour, tops. This basic flying machine was simple enough for a beginner to operate but noisier than a gas-powered lawn mower, tipsy in crosswinds, and prone to stalling at low altitudes. Learning takeoffs, landings, and recovery from spins could bring on all kinds of side effects, from flop sweat to vomit.

If Dorothy felt distress about any of this, she didn't show it. For a final test, she directed her students, all men save for one, to climb to a safe altitude. Then, without a word, she'd cut the engine. Dorothy always wore sunglasses and would turn casually as if looking out the side, but she actually shut her eyes, trusting her life to the students' ability to make a forced landing. After they returned to the airstrip with a case of rubbery legs, she would finally speak. "You passed," she would deadpan. "And by the way, I had my eyes closed the entire time. I wasn't watching a single thing you were doing."

Later she explained, "I had the confidence that I had trained them properly, that they would know what to do." Dorothy always said that nothing scared her. Only in sleep did she feel terror in frequent nightmares, full of religious images and heat, but she told almost no one.

Dorothy's ticket out of New Orleans appeared in 1941, in the form of two British military men who visited the airport to learn American tactics. Chatting them up, she learned that the Air Transport Auxiliary would shortly be giving flight tests to North American pilots in Montreal. It was all hands on deck—women weren't out of the question. The officers planned to head there themselves following a ten-day stopover in Washington, D.C. Dorothy offered to pick them up there and drive them the rest of the way. Procuring the transportation wasn't difficult. She asked a man she considered her fiancé, a besotted medical student from a prominent family, if she could borrow his "snappy little Studebaker," as she often did for a day. Quite a few days later she picked up the British officers, then stopped in New York to see the town and sample the fried chicken in Harlem. On arrival in Montreal, she sold the car. "I'll pay you back for it someday," she wrote to the fiancé, adding, it goes without saying, that the marriage was off. There were more important matters in the world.

IN THE FALL of 1941, Dorval Airport on the outskirts of Montreal teemed with officious commotion in support of the war in Britain. The United States had not yet entered the contest, but factories all over Canada and the U.S. were churning out new aircraft for the British war effort and sending them through Dorval. It offered a perfect jumping-off point for crews to ferry them across the sea because Montreal sat at the western end of a great circle that followed the curvature of the earth to the British Isles, the shortest distance between the two continents. Mosquito and Hudson bombers flew in and out of the field at all hours, and the headquarters buzzed with functionaries from the Canadian and British air forces. They slotted in flight checks for aspiring ATA pilots when they could.

Taking that test gave the willies to flyers accustomed to poky planes. After only three hours of practice with an instructor, Dorothy was expected to solo in a Harvard AT-6, a zippy number designed for training combat pilots and one of the first American military planes ordered in bulk by the RAF. The Harvard's top speed of more than two hundred miles per hour felt like hyperdrive compared to civilian rides. "It was a big jump to this 600-horsepower noisy beauty, especially after 65-horsepower trainers," wrote the American Nancy Miller, who took her shot at it a few months later. "My goodness," she added, "the gadgets!" Gadgets the young flyers had never encountered before—retractable landing gear, radios, wobble pumps, carburetor heat controls, inertia starters. A kaleidoscope of bewildering dials and gizmos threatened from the instrument panel. Scariest of all to the uninitiated were the landings, which called for coming in hot and then applying another alien innovation, flaps that lowered from the wings, to reach a more reasonable speed just before touching down. Trainees called the brightly colored plane "the yellow peril." On the day of her test, Nancy Miller wrote, "My stage fright was tremendous."

Even former RAF pilots who tried out on a Harvard critiqued its "perfectly dreadful noise" and concluded that the aircraft "possessed all the features of a flying death trap." Add to that the tricky Dorval crosswinds and, for Americans, the unfamiliar British terminology. Practice runs consisted mostly of repeated takeoffs and landings, known to the Brits as "circuits and bumps." And yet, however difficult, flying a completely alien aircraft was an appropriate trial for someone joining the Anything To Anywhere service, where pilots routinely had to hop into models they'd never flown before and figure them out literally on the fly.

Undaunted, Dorothy mastered the technicalities, but there was another obstacle still in the way—Captain Harry Smith, an instructor tasked with training all the applicants. He made it known that he didn't like pushy women and thought that most women, pushy or not, belonged at home. Ultimately, he rejected about a third of the American flyers who tried out, but word got around that taking him out for a drink improved the odds. As the first American to encounter Captain Smith, Dorothy Furey didn't benefit from a heads-up, but she figured out the score on her own. Within a week, she was calling him Smitty, and she passed with ease.

Dorothy didn't think of herself as a trailblazer, although she was the first American woman cleared to fly during World War II, before her country even joined the fight.

With the attack on Pearl Harbor on December 7, 1941, the United States committed to entering the war, but it would be many months before significant numbers of American troops would deploy to Europe. Dorothy was eager to get there ahead of them, but she had to cool her heels until five other American women turned up for their ATA tests in February 1942, when they could take transport to England together. The British government put the newcomers up in grand style in Montreal's Mount Royal Hotel, a luxurious 1,100-room affair festooned with rococo swags and cornices. One of the five soon washed out, but the other four followed Dorothy to put the Harvard through its paces, pass their physicals, and await news on when they would ship overseas. Too excited to settle down, they carried on in the interim like the young women they were, throwing raucous parties and setting a pattern of burning off tension with full-throttle carousing.

Dorothy sometimes joined them for cocktails, but she mostly kept her distance. An old boyfriend from back home, now working at Dorval, helped her find her own apartment. She also found a new boyfriend, who turned out to be married. Otherwise, she spent her days steeping herself in books about her destination, the better to sparkle in conversation on arrival. "When I got to England I knew more history than the Brits did," she said. "I could tell you every king and prime minister from Alfred"—a monarch in the ninth century—"right up to the present time."

Despite her formidable mind, it was inevitably her sensual allure that made the strongest impression on the others. Dorothy "was extremely feminine and had a slight, unathletic figure with the kind of walk men follow with their eyes and whistle," wrote Winnabelle Pierce, a pilot known as Winnie, who kept a witty diary. "She had been around and knew the value of sex. She was the kind of pretty girl that most men liked to show off to their competition."

Still, the source of this power was hard to square with Dorothy's difficult history. "One thing remains a complete mystery to me among her many extreme contradictions," said a member of her family. "Where did she acquire her aristocratic, worldly, sophisticated, glamorous appearance, as she is described as having already in 1942? I really don't know. For someone who came from a broken, alcoholic home and didn't finish school, it seems extraordinary. But I think she realized at some point that her beauty was her ticket to the bigger, more cosmopolitan life that she wanted."

As Dorothy herself put it later, "There wasn't anybody to compare with me."

Orders finally came through. On March 2, 1942, Dorothy and the four other Americans boarded an overnight train to the port of Saint John in New Brunswick, where the *Beaverhill* awaited to carry them to war. Dorothy had filled her allotted luggage with gear recommended for flyers in the harsh British climate—warm socks, long underwear, some canned goods. But she also made space for a single red evening dress that showed off a bit of leg. She called it her *Gone with the Wind* dress, thinking it would see her through a gamut of wartime drama. Dorothy planned to wear it in England with a black velvet choker around her neck, because she had no jewels.

No one would know her there. No one would know the truth. They might see what she wanted them to see. By projecting the woman she hoped to become, a woman of consequence, a woman with jewels, she might make it true.

CHAPTER 2

A Cobra in a Hurricane

March 5, 1942
Halifax Harbor, Nova Scotia

F or most of the women, the first inkling of this opportunity had appeared in the form of a telegram delivered out of the blue. "Confidential," it began. "On behalf of the British Air Transport Auxiliary I am wiring all the women pilots whose addresses [are] available to ask if you would be willing to volunteer for service . . ." At a time when the appearance of any dispatch from Western Union signaled big news, this one topped all expectations. The recipients couldn't believe their luck. They read on as the wonders continued. Paid work for eighteen months' service, transportation to England, a promise of "experience with combat planes." Perhaps most surprising of all was the sign-off at the bottom: "Cordial regards=Jacqueline Cochran."

The Jacqueline Cochran. Everyone who flew knew that the brash and flashy Jackie Cochran reigned as the most celebrated American aviatrix since Amelia Earhart disappeared over the Pacific in 1937, and as hands down the most ambitious. From a dirt-poor background in Florida, Jackie had propelled herself to astounding heights of wealth and fame when she made a fortune as the founder of a cosmetics company, married a millionaire, bought her own plane, and learned to fly. She proceeded to conquer the world of the air through the late 1930s. Jackie won prestigious races and set one speed record after another, her platinum hair a beacon on the front pages of newspapers, her trophy room a gleaming shrine in her Upper East Side Manhattan apartment.

Jackie's triumph capped a decade of public fascination with air shows and air racing, when one hundred thousand people at a time would gather at fields across America to gasp at the exploits of death-defying pilots. Women who flew, in particular, held the public spellbound, trailing hints of glamor and peril in their wake. Shows regularly featured a range of pilots performing loops, spins, and figure eights, but watching a *woman* hazard such maneuvers was something else. Celebrated aviatrixes posed for newspaper photos and magazine covers in lipstick, heels, and ruffled skirts, mounting the phallic fuselages of early planes. They participated in "powder-puff" races for "girl flyers" and headlined ticker-tape parades.

Jackie Cochran didn't see herself as performing stunts for entertainment; she aimed to carry out serious advances in aviation. In 1937, she set the world's unlimited speed record for women. The next year she triumphed as the second woman ever to win the country's most prominent cross-country competition, the Bendix race from Burbank, California, to Cleveland, Ohio. One of the highlights of her trophy collection was a gift from her husband, a cigarette case bedazzled with rubies and emeralds that traced her winning route. But she was after more than treasure. Once she secured the Bendix victory, Jackie flew at speeds of more than three hundred miles per hour to top another record, then followed up by smashing Howard Hughes's flight time between New York and Miami. Back to back in 1938 and 1939, she won the renowned Harmon Trophy, previously bestowed on pioneers like Hughes, Charles Lindbergh, and Amelia Earhart, sealing Jackie's status as the world's outstanding aviatrix. In the competitive arena of ceiling-shattering women's flying, Jackie Cochran led the field.

By 1941, with rumblings about the United States entering the war, Jackie, now thirty-five, nursed an ambition to command a flying force of American women. To promote this quest, she lobbied connections from President Franklin Roosevelt and his wife, Eleanor, to Major General Henry H. Arnold, chief of the Army Air Corps. Careful not to overstep, she conceded that women shouldn't fly in war zones, but she argued that they could ferry aircraft within the United States and therefore free up men for more important duties. Even so, through 1941, Jackie failed to wear down the resistance to women in U.S. military cockpits. She decided to pivot and prove her point by offering to lead an American women's arm of the British Air Transport Auxiliary, always with an eye to how it would play in Washington. The ATA was game. It deputized her to choose the pilots who would serve in Britain under her command. There, on a distant island, under siege in the crux of war, they would become the first American women to fly military planes, although they would have to leave their own country to do it.

Since Jackie's master plan was to parlay the ATA gambit into a trail-blazing role in the United States, she sought pilots who would stand up to scrutiny. She lined up everyone with the exception of Dorothy Furey, who had skipped the line to sign on by herself. First, Jackie sent telegrams to seventy-six women who had earned more than three hundred hours of flying time. Then she interviewed everyone who responded, ruling out anybody who didn't conform to her ideals of airborne moxie and ladylike comportment. Tacky clothes or makeup, for example, might move an applicant to the bottom of the list. Race may have played a role as well. All of Jackie's finalists were white, even though the ATA accepted pilots of other races, and there were two Black American women who held pilot's licenses in 1942. Willa Brown of Chicago had earned a more advanced commercial license by 1939, while Janet Harmon was denied that certification until 1943 even though she had qualified. Jackie may not have considered them because of lower total flying hours or other factors, but it seems likely that she wouldn't have taken them regardless. She knew that if her plan to start a women's ferrying unit succeeded, the fully segregated U.S. Army Air Forces would not accept Black pilots. Jackie was only willing to challenge one barrier at a time.

Once she had made the selections, Jackie traveled to England by air while the first contingent of her recruits enjoyed the dubious honor of a three-week cruise on the *Beaverhill*. Back in New York, her assistant, the stunt pilot Mary Webb Nicholson, took over deploying the rest of the recruits until she could join the final shipload herself. She wrote cheery letters advising everyone on questions ranging from what documents they needed to what shoes they should wear (black with low heels). Following the first five women in March 1942, Mary spaced the rest out to arrive over five months—four women in April, three in May, six in June, two in early August, and four at the end of that month. There would be six ships in total, twenty-four recruits in all, and one more counting Jackie herself.

IN EARLY MARCH 1942, the first five women ever to board the *Beaverhill* shivered under a canopy of stars as they passed through the mined channel into Halifax harbor. After a couple of days hugging the coast at sea, they stopped at this last North American port to pick up the contingent of Canadian Royal Air Force pilots who would share the old coal freighter for the rest of the voyage before they joined forces with the RAF. It was three o'clock in the morning, but the women wouldn't miss the spectacle. Eyes wide, they gawked at ships with huge holes in their sides. Aircraft searchlights sent long fingers into the sky. "We were full of apprehension," Winnie Pierce wrote in her diary. Nevertheless, she added, "It was so beautiful!" This was real. They were cutting the last ties to home. The grand, dangerous, and improbable adventure had begun.

On bracing but clear days at sea that March, the women on the *Beaverhill* clung to the railings and looked out over their strange surroundings. "What a sight!" Winnie Pierce wrote about their first impressions of the ship. The vessel bristled with armaments—four-inch guns fore and aft, five machine-gun turrets, antiaircraft weaponry. It was one of five nearly identical Canadian sister ships that had operated on the same route, but in the last two years, all four of the others had sunk at the hands of Germany. "It's not bad," Winnie wrote, noting that at least this ship had made several tours intact. "She's had no trouble up to now."

For this crossing, the *Beaverhill* claimed a position second from starboard in the front row of the twenty-two-ship convoy. Across the waves, other vessels remained in sight most of the time, with a cruiser patrolling out front and several destroyers offering added protection. Tankers loaded with fuel made up most of the rest. For the passengers, gas mask training and lifeboat drills broke up the monotony. On March 12, the sea rang out with thunder as the ships put on a show with gunnery practice. One beautiful sunny day, a raft of life preservers floated by. On rough days and most every night, the women played poker on the bridge with the captain and crew.

Their accommodations were far from deluxe. Coal dust stirred in every corner of the ship. After the first night or so, everyone scratched at itchy ankles from the flea-infested bunks in the single cabin the women shared, where the others were surprised to find Dorothy sleeping without nightclothes. Each bunkmate took a turn—or two or three—at seasickness. And there would be no baths until London, because the two sinks in the cabin served up nothing but cold saltwater for minimal washing. The hardship fostered camaraderie, but the women were sizing each other up, too. When Louise Schuurman smashed her fingers in a door, Winnie noted, "She had ten stitches without anesthesia and really has what it takes." No one else, Winnie presumed, "has any guts."

But each member of the pack had already shown her steel to make it this far. "We were a remarkable group," said Roberta Sandoz, who qualified a few months later. "We were all mavericks, outspoken, dominant." These first five set the tone. Jackie Cochran assumed that her choices would serve as ambassadors as well as pilots, so she had chosen them with particular care, especially the most famous of the group, Helen Richey.

AT THIRTY-TWO, HELEN was the oldest and by far the most experienced of the five, with 1,800 hours of flying on her record. She'd been everywhere and knew everyone in the world of stunt aviation, having served as copilot with Amelia Earhart in the 1936 Bendix race, placing fourth. Along with Earhart, Helen was an early member of the Ninety-Nines, an organization that promoted the advancement of women aviators, started by ninety-nine of them in 1929, back when women made up 1 percent of licensed pilots.

Newspapers had gushed for years about Helen's exploits, including international records for speed, altitude, and endurance. In 1933 she and another woman stayed aloft for ten consecutive days over Miami. When fuel ran low, it fell to Helen to climb onto the wing to attach a refueling line from an airborne supply plane. She described the task as "wrestling a cobra in a hurricane." Later, fabric tore on the wing, and Helen crawled out with a needle and thread to sew up the gap in a vicious wind. The press inevitably described how she looked, which was short and slight, with clear, gray-blue eyes. Photos captured excited children thronging her for autographs at an airport.

Helen had grown up middle class in McKeesport, a town near Pittsburgh. Her father, a school superintendent, wanted her to become a teacher, but her mother convinced him to let Helen follow her passion. They even helped her to buy an open-cockpit biplane. She enjoyed some widely publicized success. In 1935, she became the first woman pilot of a commercial carrier when Central Airlines assigned her to fly the route from Washington, D.C. to Detroit. "Yes, she's a girl. She's young. She's pretty. She's a good flyer," wrote *Collier's* magazine. "But she's more than that . . ."

It was the "more than that" that Helen strove to emphasize. "My getting this job was constructive, not sensational," she told a reporter. "It makes it easier for other women flyers." Until it didn't. Male pilots objected that the woman who had famously clung to a wing to repair it in a gale wouldn't have enough strength to control a tri-engine aircraft in rough weather. She was rarely assigned to fly, and so she resigned. Prominent feminists spoke out in her defense, but Helen preferred to keep her head down and find new work as a pilot.

By the time Helen signed on to the ATA, her brown hair was graying a bit, but her younger colleagues still saw her as the one to beat when it came time to master British warplanes. Maybe that achievement would finally prove her ability to fly the most advanced aircraft and, postwar, gain the secure position in the air that she hoped for.

On board the ship she was funny and cheerful, yet she also gave off an occasional air of melancholy. She'd paid a price for her struggles to succeed. By the time the ATA offer arose, she was earning a meager salary as a flying instructor. "Helen was reluctant to leave for so long a time, but instructing was dull, and money didn't come easily to a girl who'd always worked for everything," Winnabelle Pierce wrote. "Here was a chance to send money home to her mother in Pittsburgh and still have a time for herself overseas."

IF ANYONE WOULD have a time for herself, it was Winnie Pierce. Some of the pilots had learned to fly because of where it would take them.

Winnie flew for the thrill of it. She was an exuberant twenty-five-year-old with an active social life and a showboating way with a plane. Always up for a laugh, and usually up for a flirtation, she'd been the driving force of the parties in Montreal. She didn't let up aboard ship.

Winnie described herself as "a chubby, five-foot-four, brown-eyed athlete with a long scholastic record." Raised by a well-to-do family in Des Moines, she'd enjoyed every advantage, including a bachelor's degree in English literature from Wellesley. At a time when only 4 percent of women graduated from four-year colleges, Winnie knew she was fortunate to have the opportunity. She followed up with a certificate from the Katherine Gibbs Secretarial School, as was customary for educated women who had any desire for employment. Unfortunately, from her parents' point of view, they had also treated her to a plane ride around Boston harbor for her fourteenth birthday. Ever since, she'd wanted nothing so much as to fly, despite their objections. She wrote in a journal, "Conservative Middle-Western families were not inclined to let their children do the unorthodox."

Her mother's early death when Winnie was seventeen left only a stepfather to curb her nonconformity. Stories about air races and transatlantic flights fired her enthusiasm to perform aerial exploits rather than settle for office work. After college, she baffled prospective employers by seeking a secretarial job that would also involve piloting planes, despite the fact that no such job existed. Damned if she didn't ultimately create one.

First, she used an inheritance from her mother to buy a fifty-dollar Model A Ford, which she drove to Nebraska to take flying lessons at Charles Lindbergh's alma mater, Lincoln Aviation. Returning to Des Moines, Winnie lived rent-free with her stepfather so she could afford to rack up flying time in lieu of pay from a typing job at the airport. She saved up to buy her own plane, a used Lambert Monocoupe, a sporty fabric-covered two-seater. "I get an aesthetic pleasure from flying," she said at the time. "When you are up there, the world seems so pretty. Worries and problems seem to disappear. Everything is so much bigger than you and your problems."

She didn't consider herself a feminist, often repeating her belief that women needed to cultivate enough drive to prove themselves. But she was well aware that she was blazing a trail. "Flying is about the last activity where men have things pretty much to themselves," she told the local newspaper when she was inducted as a "Petticoat Pilot" into Des Moines's Ladies' Afternoon Flying Circle. "I get a kick out of busting in where women are supposed to be inadequate. Flying is about the last frontier. It's the pioneer spirit in me, I guess." It was notable that the article ran with language in the subhead that Winnie didn't use in the story: "Gets a Kick Out of 'Annoying Men.'"

On a flight to Texas in 1940, she landed in Blackwell, Oklahoma, where a flying school offered Winnie a job as a flight instructor. The newspaper there took note, calling her "23 and Comely," and "exactly the opposite of the grease-stained flying type." She parlayed that position into a better job in New York, as a secretary at a Wall Street firm that happened to have business with the Monocoupe airplane company. Winnie pushed until her boss granted permission to combine office duties with ferrying planes to new owners. It was the dream job she'd been seeking all along—a flying secretary! Her firecracker personality won her a promotion to salesperson and demonstrator.

Winnie's base became fashionable Roosevelt Field on Long Island, the takeoff point for many historic flights. Both the flying action and the social whirl that flourished around it appealed to her thirst for excitement and attention. In August 1941, she got both when she dove a plane repeatedly over a burning mansion near the airport to direct the fire department to the scene. But eventually Winnie's upward trajectory hit a snag. She made a sale to Argentina, anticipating the expedition to deliver the plane, until her boss ruled it out—the trip would be too dangerous for a woman. Jackie Cochran's telegram arrived at the right time. With 850 hours of flying under her belt, Winnie easily made the cut.

Winnie Pierce was twenty-five and on the cusp, always pulled toward the new and eager to stay on the move. She was also deeply interested in falling in love and, better yet, being in love. But how to strike a balance, when the traditional norms of relationships didn't sync with a flying career? On her twenty-fifth birthday before she left for England, Winnie wrote a letter to herself, full of conflicted feelings. She confided that she enjoyed the company of "lovers, but never the marrying kind—I like the absence of ties and obligations." Yet she sometimes envied her sister, a "normal" wife and mother. In the end, Winnie couldn't resist the unconventional choice. "No dull domesticity for me," she wrote. "Rather the wind in my hair, the skyway my road, and the unquenchable desire for change my constant guide, leading me to new adventures, new faces, new dawns, and ever-changing sunsets."

On board the *Beaverhill*, she filled her diary with yearning for Bill, an older pilot she knew from Long Island, declaring that she would stay true to him in England. But that didn't stop her from canoodling with Mac, the *Beaverhill*'s first mate. After several increasingly steamy interludes, she followed up in her diary with contradictory declarations about her guy back home. "I am convinced that Bill is the man for me, and I shall definitely be faithful to him," she wrote late one night. On the other hand, she mused, "I wonder if Mac is right in his analysis of me—that I would leave Bill when he is old because I need the physical."

WITH WINNIE AS the spark plug, laughing uproariously at the onboard bar, some of the women formed a bond. Helen Richey often joined her, as did Louise Schuurman, a friend of Winnie's from Roosevelt Field. Only twenty-one, Louise was tall, well-traveled, and worldly, a resident of the United States and a citizen of the Netherlands, the daughter of a Dutch consul in the United States. She and Winnie often dished about their busy love lives. Back home, Louise had been living with a married flying instructor. "She saw a chance to meet someone new," wrote Winnie, "and further her aviation ambitions by going overseas." Love and flying—although not necessarily in that order—pretty much summed up the ambitions of Winnie Pierce as well.

As the convoy rolled toward its destination, one of the five women remained the odd one out. She was the flyer with the loftiest social pedigree, a solid pilot from one of the wealthiest and most well-connected families of the era. And yet this outsider status was nothing new to her. She'd been the odd one out all her life.

CHAPTER 3

Fly Anywhere, Anytime

March 18, 1942
Approaching the Coast of England

The ships entered the range of German bombers without incident after two weeks at sea, but then German submarines prowled all morning and again at night. A destroyer charged with defending the ships countered by dropping depth charges and firing its guns. Everyone except the nonchalant Dorothy slept in their clothes or stayed up all night on deck. "We expect them to get some of the convoy tonight," Winnie wrote in her diary on March 21. "I wore my good suit in case!" The tension continued for two days, but none of the ships were hit. Liverpool was still another two days away.

By then, the novelty of five women sharing a ship with more than a hundred men had long since worn off. At the beginning of the voyage, the callow Canadian pilots who shared the *Beaverhill* had practically fallen over themselves to escort Dorothy Furey around the dingy deck. But the Americans mostly kept their distance; those boys seemed impossibly young. The women weren't much more senior, and they mostly referred to themselves as girls, but they'd already broken through enough barriers so that they felt older, or at least more mature.

As the passage neared its end, though, Dorothy surprised her colleagues when she accepted a marriage proposal from a fellow passenger, Richard Bragg, a pilot in the British RAF. He had been sent to Canada to enlist the recruits and hobnobbed with Dorothy in Montreal. She had told the others she was set on marrying a rich Englishman, but Bragg wasn't rich. At twenty-four, he was tall and not particularly handsome, Furey said, yet he fit the bill, a few years older and more authoritative than the others. She wasn't in love. She chose him to keep the rest at bay. "I just wanted to be married," she said later.

Marriage was the default position for a woman in those days. It was a given—marriage, children, housekeeping, done—the prevailing course of female adulthood. After a traumatic youth, Dorothy might be forgiven for choosing the most powerful man in her field of vision so soon after she left home. Lieutenant Bragg would keep her safe. Whether she loved him or not didn't seem to be the point.

SUCH CALCULATIONS WERE more complicated for the fifth member of the party, Virginia Farr. She had emerged as the misfit of the group despite her enviable perch at the peak of American society. By the age of twenty-three, Virginia knew well the pressure for a young woman in 1942 to marry. Her photo had been a fixture on society pages since she was a toddler, first as a flower girl and later as a bridesmaid at family weddings that bound her cousins with other descendants of the Gilded Age crowd. As a bona fide American aristocrat, she was expected to attend the tea dances where wealthy young girls met wealthy young boys and the debutante parties that launched the latest contenders into the marriage market.

The Farr family connections were impeccable, their options seemingly unlimited. Yet Virginia wanted nothing more than to leave them behind.

Virginia's father, Barclay Farr, was the son of a Wall Street fixture who was a noted polo player. Barclay grew up in comfort in West Orange, New Jersey, but it was his sister, Georgiana, who positioned the Farrs at the height of New York nobility. Beautiful, intelligent, and socially adept, Georgiana Farr was considered the debutante of the year upon her introduction to society. In 1908, when she was twenty-one, she fulfilled her destiny by making a glittering marriage to Harper Sibley, the grandson of the founder of the Western Union telegraph company, one of the first monopolies in the field of technology. When the couple settled in the birthplace of Western Union, the thriving industrial city of Rochester, New York, Georgiana's glamour and Harper's wealth made their home a gathering place for leading movers and thinkers of the day. Eleanor Roosevelt, Anne Morrow Lindbergh, and Helen Keller attended salons where Georgiana presided in couture gowns by Worth of Paris. Rockefellers and Roosevelts filled out her circle.

Despite having six children who went on to stellar marriages of their own, Georgiana Farr Sibley threw her energy into local and international philanthropy, all made possible with the help of battalions of upstairs and downstairs maids and other servants. The Sibleys traveled on a private train that conveyed them between various homes, including a farm in Illinois, a ranch in Canada, and two more ranches along the prime California coast.

Georgiana's brother, Barclay Farr, rode her coattails into Rochester society. He married the daughter of the rector of the city's fashionable St. Paul's Episcopal Church and founded the private Allendale School. Their net worth was not as stratospheric as the Sibleys', but the Farrs still basked in plenty. Their daughter Virginia, born in 1918, shared her childhood with her Sibley cousins, enjoying the same status and privileges. An active, athletic child, Virginia dominated baseball games at the Sibley farm outside of town. In summers, she traveled with them to their California ranches, forming idyllic memories of sweeping views to the Pacific, whales breaching off the shore, and sea lions barking outside the windows of the house. The children did everything the cowhands did, riding horses, rounding up cattle, and baling hay. After dinner Virginia helped wash the dishes by kerosene lanterns in houses that were simple by the Sibleys' standards. Virginia was in her element.

Later she attended the exclusive Chatham Hall boarding school in Virginia, where she excelled in hockey, soccer, basketball, golf, and baseball. "She was a large person, about five foot ten, muscular and physically strong," said a third-generation cousin.

The flip side of this charmed existence was that social expectations began at an early age. Teenagers in Virginia's milieu made their first impressions at "card dances" sponsored by a ladies' group called the

Chatterbox Club, where attendees were handed dance cards listing pre-assigned partners of the opposite sex. Sometimes boys hid in the bathroom when they didn't like the choices. Later, the same smart set attended the Symphony Ball, deb parties, polo matches, and endless dances at various private clubs.

Virginia did everything she was asked to do and did it with good humor, but this life was not for her. Photos on the society pages captured her looking acquiescent but large, awkward, and out of place. In some ways she resembled her celebrated aunt, with dark hair, a classic face, and steady brows. Yet in every shot she stood in stark contrast to her peers, social butterflies decked out in dainty heels and delicate dresses trimmed with flowers. Virginia wore sober tailored jackets and pants modeled more on menswear. In 1934, when she was sixteen, a newspaper photo spread featured local society girls modeling the outfits they were packing for boarding school. All of them except Virginia posed in skirts, heels, and expensive furs, described in the captions as "smart" and "jaunty." Virginia chose a double-breasted dark blazer and men's-style cap. The caption said, "Miss Virginia Farr's equipment for Chatham Hall, Va., will lean more to sport clothes." At a Junior Assembly dinner dance the next year, other girls wore low-cut gowns held up with slender straps. Virginia's boxy, long-sleeved, high-necked, black velvet dress made her look more like a chaperone than a party girl.

It was apparent for everyone to see. The niece of the former debutante of the year wasn't playing the game, which was to capture the prize of a wealthy husband by projecting high-end feminine grace and charm. "It must have grated on her, because this clearly wasn't her interest," another third-generation cousin, Harper Sibley III, explained. "She obviously took a different path."

The way she dressed wasn't the only issue, her relatives agreed. Virginia's manners were impeccable, but she could come across as blunt and abrupt, certainly never simpering or demure. She made no effort to charm or flirt. "She had something of a heavy personality compared to all the gracious people she was surrounded with in Rochester," said her cousin. "She was more direct. She wasn't going to put on airs and pretend she was something she was not." Whatever anyone else thought, she was comfortable in her own skin.

"She must have hated it," added another cousin, "but she lived with it. She knew how to deal with it. She didn't let it get in her way."

It gradually became clear to Virginia that she was attracted to women rather than men. She was nothing like her Aunt Georgiana, nor any of her more traditional cousins. But they loved her and supported her nonetheless. Her aunt's politics were progressive for the time; she supported causes like international human rights, and later racial equality. But in the 1930s, there was no substantial public movement on behalf of people who didn't conform to the conventions of gender and sexuality. Sexual acts between men were considered criminal in many parts of the world. As for women, there was little popular acknowledgment that such acts even existed. Virginia's family didn't condemn her, but it didn't provide her much guidance, either.

She was a young lady who was born into an enviable world, but it groomed her for only one option, to be a certain kind of girl and marry a certain kind of man. She knew she was not that girl. But where did that leave her? There was no obvious alternative. As her graduation from Chatham Hall approached in 1936, Virginia Farr selected a quotation from the stoic philosopher Epictetus for her yearbook entry: "Difficulties are things that show what men are."

SET TO ENTER Vassar in the fall of 1936, Virginia stumbled across another possibility. One day, she spotted a sign at Rochester's Municipal Airport: FLY YOURSELF ANYWHERE ANYTIME. After one free plane ride, she envisioned an entirely different future for herself. Aviation was becoming the latest rage among American high society, but Virginia decided that flying could offer more than an amusing Sunday afternoon pastime. It could provide a vocation, especially for a woman who lived outside the norms.

"My family was dead set against the idea," she said, "and when I asked my instructor to talk to them about the future of women in aviation, he told them he didn't think there *was* a future for women in flying. I could have died."

Yet she kept at it, and suddenly the newspapers featured very different coverage of the girl they now called a "flying socialite." The Rochester *Democrat and Chronicle* followed every step of her progress: Her first solo flight in 1936 at age eighteen. Her pilot's license six months later. "She believes there is 'something in the future of aviation for women,'" said an article headlined "Blue Book Miss Up in the Air, Would Teach Girls to Fly." "Fresh from the perfumed atmosphere of a girls' finishing school," it continued, "she invaded the pronouncedly masculine surroundings of grease and wrenches."

In almost every story, Virginia laid out her case. "More and more women will want to learn to fly and they'll want a female instructor," she argued as early as November 1936. "Women can make a living out of flying. You wait and see."

There were no more stories about her clothes now that they mostly consisted of functional overalls. Yet whatever her attire, she looked like a new person. The leather flying helmet and the goggles balanced on her head framed a face that was radiant and joyful. At the airfield, she smiled as widely as any of her cousins did on the church steps at their weddings.

Virginia abandoned all thoughts of college and reveled in the class-free society of the airport. The local paper wrote that a "society girl" was hanging around with such fellow pilots as a saxophone player, an auto dealer, an old-time war pilot, and a fur trader who swooped into the wilderness to bargain for pelts. Virginia had found her place. As she worked toward a commercial license that would allow her to teach, she glowed. Flying for a living meant flying for a new life.

Hoping the notion would pass, her parents packed her off on a five-month tour of Europe in 1939. This technique had done the trick for the family before, when a young lady chose a love interest who was considered less than appropriate. Virginia noted that people in Holland, Belgium, and France scoffed at threats of war and felt themselves to be in no imminent danger. She gave little thought to impending war, either. She headed straight for the airport upon her return.

By this time, her parents had relocated back to New Jersey, where Virginia took a teaching post at an airport near Princeton. Although she talked her way into the job with the rationale that the school would lure more women if they could train with a woman, it turned out that most of her students were men. "There was competition," Virginia said about the men. "They thought if I could fly, well, certainly they could fly. And the women preferred the male instructors. That was more romantic."

In February 1941 *Junior League Magazine* ran a photo of the flying socialite with her head tipped back, looking skyward. Then in May of that year, *LIFE* ran a full-width picture of her in profile, kneeling on a grass runway to guide a student plane to landing. She looked robust, confident.

She was also cautious and deliberate about her flying, in contrast with some thrill-seekers of the time. One day when planes were grounded at the airport because the weather was cloudy, rainy, and foggy—"filthy," as Virginia called it—she heard engine noise and saw wheels appear below the murk. It was the madcap Winnie Pierce coming in for a landing in a Monocoupe, the first time they would meet. "She gassed up and was on her way," Virginia said with disapproval of her future colleague. "We listened for a crash, but there wasn't one." The encounter was fleeting, forgettable. There was no way to know that the two women would share a ship to England a year later. Or that their differences would feed a rivalry that would drive them to new heights in the ATA.

Given Virginia Farr's social register connections, Jackie Cochran recognized her as an ideal pick to help the squad make a positive impression, while Virginia grabbed at the chance to advance herself professionally. She recognized that civilian teaching jobs were drying up as the armed forces took over training for military flyers. And personally? She might find a better way forward living an ocean away from the pressures of her illustrious family. For the runaway debutante, this dangerous journey was her single best hope to escape a gilded cage.

VIRGINIA PRESENTED HERSELF on board the ship exactly as she always did, serious about the coming mission yet otherwise making little effort to conform. She'd packed pants and twenty-four identical blue oxford button-down shirts as the basis of a simple wardrobe that would suit her taste, but once again her choices set her outside the circle of her peers. While the others shared confidences and dallied with the crew, Virginia often stayed in the dreary cabin, alone. The extroverted social arbiter Winnie Pierce had barely noticed Virginia when they crossed paths before the war, but now she triggered an instant hostility. Winnie considered the heiress "sullen" and recorded a cutting description in her journal: "A tall, heavy-boned, mannish girl with large feet and hands." If Virginia held herself apart with the intention of protecting her secret, it didn't work. "She was an awkward, introspective girl," Winnie continued, "born to wear trousers instead of dresses; and utterly disinterested in men."

MOST OF THE passengers stayed awake through dawn the morning of March 22, nearly three weeks after their departure. Then the sun rose, the sky cleared, and Ireland appeared out of the mist, gleaming in the distance like Brigadoon. Everyone exhaled. They had reached the far side of the ocean, through the gauntlet of German planes and ships, alive and afloat. Drinks all around.

On the following day, the pilots encountered a more sobering sight. The ship slipped from the Irish Sea into the sludgy tidal estuary of the Mersey River and slowly proceeded through a veil of fog to the massive docks of the port of Liverpool. Enormous barrage balloons like silver blimps, filled with hydrogen and tethered with heavy steel cables, bobbed overhead to deflect attacks from the air. They framed a frightening scene of destruction. The *Beaverhill* wound through buoys that marked safe channels to glide by specters of sunken ships, their masts and upturned hulls jutting like shark fins above the waterline. On shore, there were countless buildings boarded up or in shambles. Long minutes passed when no one spoke. Winnie wrote in her diary, "Much of the city is gone."

For those who hadn't given much thought to it before, it was inescapable now: Whatever their personalities or motives, the five young pilots had committed to service in a country devastated by war.

CHAPTER 4

A Foreign Legion of the Air

March 23, 1942
Liverpool

———

W hen the first batch of American women disembarked to meet the top brass of the Air Transport Auxiliary, the Americans and the British were both in for a rude shock. Pauline Gower, the upright British head of the women's branch, turned up to pay tribute to the new Atlantic alliance by performing the rare honor of greeting the recruits in person. She and a top aide stood stern and erect in full-dress uniforms trimmed with gold stripes. They looked like police officers from back home, marking a point of authority amid the chaos of the quay.

Known for being tactful, gracious, and rather prim, Commander Gower wore her standing lightly as an experienced pilot and the daughter of Sir Robert Gower, a member of Parliament. Her background was typical of the British women who had joined the ATA in its early years. Many belonged to the upper crust, able to afford to fly for pleasure, who stepped up to put their skills to use for king and country. The daughters of peers, landed gentry, elected officials, and successful businesspeople, they assumed that the Americans, as women who flew, hailed from similar backgrounds and therefore behaved with similar decorum.

Not a chance. It took all of Gower's composure to withstand the spectacle of five rowdy ladies sashaying to the bottom of the gangplank. The captain and crew, drunk and disorderly, lined up to cover the women's faces with farewell kisses. Dorothy Furey clinched with her new fiancé in a shameless embrace. Winnabelle Pierce, flushed and flurried from making out with Mac while waiting on board to clear Customs, acted giddy as usual. "So overjoyed was everyone to get ashore and actually be at Liverpool after the long dangerous trip," Winnie wrote, "that no one gave a damn or thought to who was meeting them and what impression they would make." She realized too late that their new commander saw "what carefree loose women these Americans were."

If the Americans hoped to give the appearance of nobly riding to the rescue of a beleaguered Britain, they had blown their entrance. It set a tone that would color their early relations with the service.

The cultural disconnect continued. Commander Gower stepped forward to shake hands. "I know you are probably tired," she said in measured tones, "but come round and join us at the hotel for dinner tonight. That is, if you feel like it?" To anyone fluent in the purse-lipped communications of the British upper class, this clearly meant "I am your commanding officer, and I expect you at dinner."

The Americans answered along the lines of, "How nice, yes. We will if we feel like it." Which translated as "No, we are crazy tired, and you seem awfully dull. But nice of you to ask."

Hours later, the two ATA officials sat steaming, alone at a table for seven, and relations tumbled further. "British reserve! American bewilderment! Not the best mixture for a good beginning," noted Alison King, a British officer who worked with Gower. The commander and her aide escaped that night on an early train to London, leaving a lower-ranking officer to escort the riffraff the next day.

King saw that the Americans had blundered, but she felt sympathy for them in this foreign milieu. "They had come with much experience and many flying hours, and they had taken a big and voluntary decision to leave their own wide shores for what might be a tottering island," she wrote. "They had come to fly unknown aircraft in treacherous weather that was reputed to be mainly fog." It was little wonder, she continued, that "when they finally docked and were ready to step on English soil, they had the feeling of walking the last mile to another world of which they knew nothing."

Oblivious to their crass behavior, the Americans grappled with shock of their own. They had never seen such wreckage—buildings collapsed like matchsticks all around the port, a church with the windows blown out. The streets looked bleak and grimy, the people poorly clad. Taken to Liverpool's best hotel, the Adelphi, the group found it glacial and bare, "a ghastly marble-pillared, high-ceilinged cold edifice," according to Winnie. There were no drinks at the bar except for a few obscure liqueurs, no cigarettes to be found anywhere. Mac took Winnie and Louise out to show them what remained of the town. "In peacetime a dull, dirty factory city," Winnie wrote, "Liverpool in the blackout, many times bombed, was no place to wander in." Streetlights, headlights, and illuminated signs were extinguished to discourage bombers, and black curtains covered the windows. The three heard their footsteps clicking on empty streets. Everything seemed strange, ominous.

American colleagues who arrived over the next five months felt the same dislocation. "We saw bombed-out areas, whole blocks gone," observed Nancy Miller. On her first night in the hotel, an air raid siren startled her awake. She ducked under the covers and then under the bed. "Never have I heard such a wailing," she wrote, "and the fact that it was associated not with fire trucks at home but with possible bombers made my heart pound furiously." Finally, she threw on her bathrobe and raced to the basement, where other residents in nightclothes were already drinking at the bar. It was an introduction to wartime compartmentalization—taking pleasure in the midst of terror, because in the moment there was nothing else to be done.

By now, Liverpool was accustomed to the weird juxtaposition. As one of the country's most important ports, it was a prime target for German bombing in 1940 and 1941 that aimed to sever the supply lines of food, people, and military equipment arriving from North America. The damage and casualties in the city ranked second only to those of London. Bombing had already killed more than four thousand Liverpudlians and destroyed ten thousand homes.

The stark evidence of this assault brought home to the Americans the extent to which the air war had been carried out on British soil. Before their arrival, they had understood the country's perilous position only in theory. Ever since Hitler had launched his offensive against his European neighbors in 1939, the British people had been bracing for the full power of the German military machine to be turned against them. One by one, the Nazis overtook Poland, Norway, Denmark, Belgium, Holland, and ultimately France as Germany's blitzkrieg strategy proved brutally effective. It called for quick ground attacks that encircled the enemy and then bombing that trapped the soldiers from the air. Yet Hitler delayed a land invasion of the British Isles so he could begin with relentless bombing to weaken the country's infrastructure and disable the RAF. The resulting Battle of Britain, begun in the summer of 1940, was the fiercest air confrontation in history to date, remaking British daily life into a recurring ordeal that revolved around air raid shelters, sirens, blackouts, fires, building collapses, and evacuations from cities.

The Germans dominated the skies and inflicted punishing damage. But they failed at two key goals: weakening British morale and permanently crippling the country's air power. The public dug in and rallied in the face of hardship, and the RAF managed to turn the tide by sending pilots up in one-man fighter planes to bring down German bombers in dramatic one-on-one aerial combat. The American women had heard the ringing rhetoric from Winston Churchill that expressed the gratitude of the nation: "Never in the field of human conflict was so much owed by so many to so few."

The Germans scaled back the intensity of their attacks in the fall of 1940 as Hitler turned more attention toward the Soviet Union, but bombing against Britain's civilian and military targets continued beyond the time when Jackie Cochran's women reached England in the spring of 1942. The aerial attacks still spread terror, hitting a range of targets that included historic cities like Exeter and Canterbury. The Germans called this phase the Baedeker Blitz after the series of tourist guidebooks.

Within hours of the Americans' arrival, the battered condition of Liverpool had awakened them to a dreadful reality. World War II had expanded the concept of an air war to a scale never before seen. And any outcome was possible.

★

IF LIVERPOOL DISAPPOINTED, the trip to London the next day delivered a shot of adrenaline. A taxi took the group from the damaged train station to the Park Lane Hotel on Hyde Park, spinning them past sights like a montage from a travelogue. Big Ben, Parliament, Trafalgar Square, and Buckingham Palace—all still standing under barrage balloons. Signs of the war were less apparent in this part of town than in districts along the Thames that looked more like Liverpool. Still, the odd convergence persisted between wartime blight and a zest for normal life. The women came down on the side of taking in all that they could.

After a delicious hot private bath at the hotel, they plunged into what the city had to offer. Austin Reed, a renowned made-to-order tailor on busy Regent Street, took their measurements for the ATA uniforms. To the pilots' delight, it was a surprisingly chic ensemble topped by a belted, sharp-shouldered navy wool jacket with a pinched waist that flattered a woman's figure. It came with a matching skirt, pants, and a zippy side cap. The women would pick up the hand-tailored outfits in a few weeks. Otherwise, their walkabout revealed that half the shops were closed, and restaurants open for dinner were scarce. But cinemas were packed in the moonlit blackout. The group cheered to *Captains of the Clouds*, an up-to-the-minute release set during the war. It starred Jimmy Cagney playing, of all things, a Canadian transport pilot called upon to sacrifice his life to save his crew. The Americans thrilled to hear "God Save the King" played before the show. Winnie Pierce effused in her diary, "God, but it's swell to be here in England at last in the midst of this."

The next morning, duty called them to a westbound train at Paddington Station, which was crowded with passengers despite gaps in the roof from repeated bombing. Forty-five minutes later, they arrived in the town of Maidenhead in Berkshire, home of the ATA headquarters. Not far from Windsor Castle, Maidenhead was a charming town known for picturesque inns that hosted weekend boaters along a scenic stretch of the Thames. Centuries-old stone bridges spanned the river, and rowing clubs lined the banks. On the outskirts was the ATA aerodrome, called White Waltham, a former flying school that the military had requisitioned for use in the war. Situated on a broad, flat sweep of land, the base provided space for a long grass runway and a collection of utilitarian, single-story buildings that ringed the field. They housed an operations center and classrooms where the group would spend a few weeks taking ground courses like airplane mechanics, map reading, and navigation. But what turned the ladies' heads was the tantalizing variety of camouflage-painted aircraft parked around the periphery. Winnie reported: "What a thrill it will be—I want to get at them!"

This was a second opportunity for the group to introduce itself, and it didn't go any better than the first. The workers at the aerodrome, mostly men, lined up to gawk at the arriving Americans and made no effort to hide their disappointment. "Hollywood had given them a picture of American womanhood, and it was all blonde, and glamour, all singy and dancy," wrote the British Alison King. The guys were expecting Ginger Rogers or Betty Grable but got reality instead. Virginia Farr remembered "the walk past the windows filled with silent male faces, all dropping as they saw the travel-stained girls arriving. You could feel their thoughts— 'why, one's fat, and one's definitely strapping'—no glamour, no glamour anywhere."

Anglo–American relations didn't progress any better at a meeting with the top men who ran the ATA. The women felt insulted when Commodore Gerard d'Erlanger warned them against behaving like "ill-mannered Americans," based on his experiences with some of the hard-drinking men who had joined the service. But Virginia Farr committed the greatest faux pas. When asked why she had joined the ATA, her answer was characteristically forthright but undiplomatic. "To get flying experience," she said, "and because civilian flying has stopped at home." Once again, Virginia's manner grated on Winnie, whose animosity toward her colleague grew. Winnie wrote in her diary that the others were "furious" that Virginia didn't think "of pushing the 'help the war effort' angle."

That night the women moved into the Riviera Hotel, Maidenhead's finest, where they proceeded to throw themselves an ill-mannered welcome party. "Dubious, resentful Britishers," according to Winnie, "were out *en masse* at the hotel bar to look them over with a critical, unsympathetic eye." Everyone got good and tight except Virginia, who stopped after two or three vermouths. "I often wonder if the ATA will ever get over their first impression of us," Winnie wrote in a letter. "We indulged in a bacchanalian orgy our first night in Maidenhead. Our identification photographs taken at the local police station the morning after that night tell the whole story and remain a constant reminder to us. Never again!" At least until the next time.

IF THERE WAS a chance that the Americans might eventually fit in, it was because the Air Transport Auxiliary was an organization where renegade behavior was part of the DNA. In the service's short, dramatic history of flying Anything To Anywhere, it had established itself as a seat-of-the pants operation that sometimes tolerated, or even celebrated, eccentrics. Near the outbreak of the war in 1939, Gerard d'Erlanger, a banker in civilian life who was also a director of the British Overseas Airways Corporation, cobbled together the first thirty ATA pilots from men who didn't qualify for military service due to their age or health. They included Stewart Keith-Jopp, a fifty-year-old who had emerged from the first world war with only one arm and one eye. There was also an innkeeper, a race car driver, an antique expert, and various avid adventurers. Frederick Ellam, another World War I vet, said his friends expressed surprise "that his Majesty's Government, even in its extremity, should consider allowing middle-aged physical wrecks to use its aircraft for the purpose of committing suicide."

The need to ferry aircraft to frontline squadrons was so great that there was often a slapdash, improvised quality to the mission, a "making do and patching elbows" attitude. Officers briefly considered buying some out-of-work circus elephants to repair the runway when earth-moving equipment was in short supply. Some of the aircraft were in such disrepair that the equipment officer stripped one plane almost entirely for spare parts. Then, unable to account for this loss of property, he waited until Germans attacked the field to drag the metal carcass outside the hangar and dump it in a bomb crater. Some prospective pilots showed up for interviews and wound up being dragooned that very day into ferrying planes they had never seen before, while wearing their civilian clothes.

This band of laymen enjoyed the leeway to decide when, where, and how to make their deliveries. There were legendary stories of their exploits. Pilots flew through smoke trails past ongoing dogfights. They delivered Hurricanes to squadrons that were waiting to take off until the new planes arrived to replace those that had just been destroyed. As France was falling, a group of new ATA pilots made their way across the Channel to collect three Hurricanes before they were lost to the Germans. The only map available to them was torn out of an atlas. They arrived to learn that one of the aircraft had no brakes, another no serviceable landing flaps, and the third's engine depleted its oil by spraying it all over the windscreen. It was the first time that the pilot Peter Mursell, who had been a farmer in Sussex only weeks before, had seen the inside of a Hurricane cockpit. "It shows the straits into which our Country had fallen," he said, "that it became necessary to trust complete amateurs with the very few fighter planes which were available at the time."

Desperate times called for such desperate measures. With more aircraft and men lost every day, more and more replacements were needed, not only to defend the homeland but to carry out a new offensive strategy, bombing German-held territory in hopes of one day winning the war.

As each phase played out, the RAF needed not only new fleets of bombers but also the fighters that flew alongside to protect them. The United Kingdom produced 131,549 aircraft during the war, surging from less than 8,000 during 1939 to more than 26,000 each year in 1943 and 1944. U.S. production eventually added more than 300,000 planes deployed throughout the world. This aspect of the war was conducted on the factory floors and in the ferry service, where it was understood that the project of manufacturing and delivering a steady stream of aircraft was as crucial to the war effort as any confrontation on the field of battle. The ATA grew, ultimately deploying 1,250 pilots from 25 countries, a sort of Foreign Legion of the air.

The mix of cultures and personalities added to the multifaceted nature of the assignment. Like the RAF, the ATA accepted pilots of all races, even though many militaries around the world at the time were fully segregated, including the United States, until 1948. Among those who served in the ATA were South Asian pilots from India and Ceylon, a Central American pilot from Nicaragua, a Black pilot from South Africa, and Olive Ramsey, a part-Maori woman from New Zealand.

Early on, Pauline Gower called on her connections to convince the ATA to give women a role. Eight of them were allowed to join in January 1940 under her guidance, despite some objections in the flying community. Even the Nazi radio propagandist Lord Haw-Haw weighed in, disparaging the flyers in a snooty voice as "decadent and unnatural women." C. G. Grey, the editor of the magazine *Aeroplane*, scoffed at women performing vital war work: "The trouble is that so many of them insist on wanting to do jobs which they are quite incapable of doing. The menace is the woman who thinks she ought to be flying a high-speed bomber when she really has not the intelligence to scrub the floor of a hospital properly, or who wants to nose round as an Air Raid Warden and yet can't cook her husband's dinner."

Not that the original eight had devoted much time to cooking. Most were experienced flying instructors from middle-class homes or wealthy and titled families. Like many people who are called upon to be the first at something, they realized that nothing short of perfection would advance their cause, so that's what they delivered. At first, the eight were restricted to operating light, open-cockpit biplanes used for training. Without complaint, they flew those drafty aircraft north to Scotland in bitter winter weather. Once there, they hauled their parachutes and heavy flying suits onto night trains back to base. The women completed two thousand such deliveries without even a minor accident, a record perfect enough that the Air Ministry decided to let more women join. The female contingent would grow to 168 over the course of the war. By the time the Americans arrived, women had proved they could fly the latest fighters and bombers.

So far, the debut of the American women's squad hadn't inspired such a favorable response. Intervention from their leader, Jackie Cochran, only made matters worse.

PILOTS WERE THE rock 'n' roll guitarists of their era, admired for their swagger if they had the technical skills to back it up, and none flaunted it more than Jackie Cochran. She had just touched down at the Savoy in London to a blast of coverage in the British papers when she got word that the new recruits at White Waltham were being asked to submit to medical exams in the nude. Determined to defend her girls, she sped to headquarters to shut this travesty down. Jackie pulled up at the wheel of a Rolls-Royce borrowed from a wealthy friend and emerged decked out in a mink coat, her signature makeup and Jean Harlow hairdo

Hollywood-ready. Here was American glamour in spades. But while the other pilots' deficits of style had disappointed, the ATA didn't know what to make of Jackie Cochran's startling entrance.

The truth was, now that Jackie had recruited her pilots for the ATA, the higher-ups couldn't figure out a proper role for this brighter-than-life creature. She expected to swan about leading her contingent of Americans from the ground, but the ATA assumed she would fly like everyone else—even Pauline Gower sometimes ferried aircraft. The service already had officers to oversee all the pilots, so the job of leading the American wing would be relatively meaningless in reality, an empty title. And there was a war on—the British needed aviators with Jackie's ability. But she quickly set herself up in London, where she saw her role as a mover and shaker, whipping up publicity to promote her dream of a women's service at home and hosting soirees for American officials at the lavish digs she was lining up in Chelsea. She also played mother hen to her girls. On their first day off, she invited them back to town for tea in her suite at the Savoy—"too, too swank," said Winnie.

Days into Jackie's tenure, it was already becoming clear that she and the English weren't a good fit. Despite her efforts to choose pilots with tasteful appearances, her own bottle-blond curls, robust physique, and all-around flash turned heads in the gloomy wartime city. Everything about Jackie was too much—too much makeup, too much attitude. Her manner of speaking, too pushy. While others made do with meager food rations, Jackie's parties featured the best menus the black market could provide. Even her girls, the Americans, sometimes wished she would scale it back. "She had a loud way of speaking, was intolerant—loud profanity," said the American Roberta Sandoz. "We were in awe of her and kind of embarrassed by her."

The British found her unpolished but high-handed. They might not have stated their most hurtful judgment out loud, but they were thinking it: Vulgar.

Jackie commuted to White Waltham in the Rolls and tried to exert some authority. "She messed about and gave us hell for drinking the first night," said Winnie. And Jackie looked askance at Dorothy Furey's "eye on the men." Yet the famous aviator also chafed at the ATA's requirement that she take ground classes with the rest of the pilots. The others thought she made a fool of herself, interrupting in navigation class.

The Americans plowed their way through ground school, but it didn't change their hosts' opinions. "Most of them resented our presence because they figured we wouldn't last out our contracts," said Nancy Miller, "that we would go home as soon as we had some hard work, that we looked upon the job entirely as an adventure and a lark."

The situation wasn't hopeless. Other Americans who might prove more diplomatic were passing tests in Montreal. In the meantime, though, it looked like there was only one way for the first group of Jackie Cochran's ladies to shake off those first impressions. It was time to prove themselves in the air.

CHAPTER 5

The Concrete

April 11, 1942
Luton, Bedfordshire

W innabelle Pierce pressed the throttle forward, and within eight seconds the lightweight Miles Magister single-engine plane skipped into the air. A blast of cold hit Winnie in the open cockpit, chilling her clear through. She'd trussed herself up in layers of long underwear and street clothes under a one-piece heavy cotton Sidcot flying suit, accessorized with extra socks, gloves, and a hood. Unlike the snazzy, figure-skimming lines of the ATA uniforms, the dull, tan Sidcot, with its sagging behind and ample supply of pockets and zippers, lent its wearer the bulky proportions of a well-fed bear. Still, Winnie shivered.

The British-built aircraft, used for training pilots, felt similar to other planes Winnie had flown, but everything else was another dimension. In the United States, she was accustomed to navigating across wide-open spaces marked with landmarks that were easy to spot. Here, she squinted down through her goggles onto a maze of twisting roads and crisscrossing rail lines as she tried to identify aerodromes where she would soon be expected to make deliveries. Just when she thought she'd spotted a hangar behind some camouflage netting, clouds or whiffs of industrial smoke conspired to muddle her view. "The weather got terrible in a rush,"

Winnie wrote. She knew she was lost. Yet after six weeks without flying, she felt elated to be in the sky again. "Flew today!" she wrote in her diary on April 11. "Eureka!"

The tradeoff was that she and her colleagues had to move from the pretty country retreat of Maidenhead for aerial training in industrial Luton, thirty miles north of London. Winnie found the city grim. There were bomb shelters everywhere, and smoke pots choked the streets to mask the locations of former auto factories that now produced army tanks. At night, she went to the movies because she couldn't find many places to eat, drink, or carry on her usual social life. Like most ATA pilots throughout the country, she was assigned to bunk with a family in a private home. Winnie considered herself lucky to score a billet with a warm bath, but the house was so cold that she could see her breath when she dressed in the morning.

The ATA paid women 20 percent less than men, but the American women still made $150 a week, with added payment for travel expenses and a $500 cash bonus after a year. That was a respectable sum in those days, an amount that would allow them to live well in Britain. They didn't expect pay parity with men at a time when inequality was the norm, although Pauline Gower was working to change that. But despite salaries that the pilots considered ample, their daily lives were subject to deprivations. Food rationing limited them to one egg a week and minimal meat. Fish was more plentiful, while boiled cabbage and potatoes—combined as the redoubtable bubble and squeak—were available in monotonous rotation. The women ate so many brussels sprouts that some vowed never to choke one down again. They turned over their ration cards to their hosts, who did their best to provide adequate meals. Clothing purchases were limited, too—finding stockings was hopeless—and there were shortages of other products. Winnie grumbled that she couldn't find shampoo or chewing gum.

All this was worth it for the chance to fly. With the move to Luton, the American pilots entered the first tier of the ATA flight training program, designed to get them up to speed on aircraft designated as Class 1: light, single-engine models like the Miles Magister, nicknamed the Maggie. After soloing in one, the pilots practiced flying cross-country to learn how to find their way through the bewildering geography. Over the course of some thirty trips, they were expected to absorb the locations of railway lines, rivers, and roads that led to aerodromes. Once they completed more cross-country drills back at White Waltham, the women would perform a brief stint of ferrying Class 1 beginner planes. Then they would tackle Class 2, the much-anticipated single-engine fighters like Hurricanes and Spitfires—they tingled with excitement at the thought. The cycle would repeat though Class 3, twin-engine bombers; Class 4, larger, faster, trickier two-engine bombers; and Class 5, massive four-engine bombers like the Lancaster or Liberator. No women had been approved for Class 5 yet, although Pauline Gower was pushing, and they were never assigned to Class 6, seaplanes, because there were no accommodations for women on board ships.

One of the features that made ferry piloting so dangerous—and the mastery of it so impressive—was that each student learned to fly only one aircraft in each category during training. Afterward she was expected to ferry any number of planes belonging to that class with little or no notice. Each time she encountered a new type, as they were called, it was like sliding behind the wheel of an unfamiliar car—only one that was dismayingly more powerful, convoluted, and deadly than your everyday ride— then taking it high in the sky where any mistake could be lethal. For such moments, the ATA provided a lifeline, a flip-pad called the *Ferry Pilots Notes*. It was a no-frills guide to the essentials of each type of aircraft— laying out which knobs and gauges did what and what the parameters were for air speed, takeoffs, landings, and so on. It was so terse that the whole thing fit in the pocket of a uniform. Pilots could, and often did, riffle through the pages on an airfield in the minutes between finding out what aircraft they'd been assigned and taking off.

This was nothing like other branches of military flying. Most pilots who flew in combat were expected to fly a narrow range of planes, or usually just one. ATA pilots could fly as many as 147 different types of aircraft during their careers. When a member of an RAF ground crew led one of the women to a model and asked how many times she'd flown it, he often gulped when she answered, "Never saw one before. But I'll read the instructions before I start!"

The Class 1 Miles Magister lesson was the first step. On day one, an instructor joined Winnie Pierce for twenty minutes and then let her loose to solo. On the third day, she performed her first cross-country flight with the instructor on board, following a route card and hitting every aero-drome on the dot. From high above, it seemed as if hundreds of airports were under construction, hundreds of runways being paved, as if the war would never end. At first, they all looked alike. Winnie repeated the cross-country exercise the next day on her own, despite a strong wind. Only in her diary did she admit: "Was scared stiff."

This kind of flying was nerve-racking, less under a pilot's control than anything the Americans had done before. They weren't familiar with the plane, the weather, or the geography, and many felt the strain. Winnie acknowledged an undertow of fear, but she wasn't rattled by it. It sharp-ened her focus; it gave her a thrill. "Had a swell time, and oh it was wonderful to be back up there where I belong," she wrote. "I enjoyed every minute of it."

Others didn't breeze through as easily, struggling to get the hang of not so much the Maggie as this new environment. They fought the chill by adding so many layers they could barely move. Winnie carried on despite catching a cold, but Virginia Farr lost days on sick leave, and Jackie Cochran missed even more time due to sinus infections. Jackie was already annoyed that the training required her to pilot a beginner plane, and now she complained that the open cockpit aggravated her condition. After a few weeks, Winnie wrote of Jackie: "She put up a big fuss and refuses once and for all to fly these open ships."

The diva in Jackie once again flummoxed the ATA, which expected everyone, however elite, to follow the customary drill. Given her level of skill, it might have been reasonable to start her on a more complex aircraft, but the Maggie's slower speed and open cockpit were better suited to the task of learning the layout of the country. Officials sat on Jackie's request while she sat out more weeks in London—a stalemate.

Meanwhile, everyone floundered finding her way. Dorothy Furey got lost twice. That was to be expected of new recruits. The stunt ace Helen Richey, sure of herself at first with all her aerial experience, excelled at piloting the Maggie. But once she got so lost that she meandered among the barrage balloons over London, at risk of striking the cables, before finding her way home. The constant spatial confusion played with the pilots' minds. A strong wind so unnerved Louise Schuurman on her first solo that it shattered her nerves, and she wound up badly off course.

Throughout their service, the women often considered what qualities made for a successful ferry pilot. Was it a steady, careful temperament or a daring one? Experience and wisdom versus heedless youth? Winnie was wild outside of a cockpit, but as a pilot she hadn't slipped up yet. The gregarious twenty-six-year-old flew with assurance, blasting through obstacles without giving them much thought. Flying made her feel alive in the best way, and she took that fuel to power the rest of her life. While some might rest after a trying day, Winnie forgot about work and headed out almost every night, pumping up and down hills on a bicycle she'd bought or taking a train to London for dinner, a show, drinks, or tea with Jackie Cochran. Winnie speculated about marrying her boyfriend Bill back home while corresponding with Mac, her conquest from the ship, and making eyes at her new navigation instructor. When flying gave her a fright, Winnie didn't brood. After performing two cross-countries one day despite a ninety-degree crosswind, she confided to her diary, "God, my nerves." But doubt didn't slow her down—in the air or anywhere else.

She'd heard conjecture that there could be poison gas attacks in the summer, and she saw a British propaganda film about how a Nazi invasion would play out. "Perhaps I shall live through it and perhaps not," she wrote, "but I wish I might be with Bill once more."

Virginia Farr, who already irritated Winnie, gave her another cause for resentment as training progressed. The stolid Virginia notched an equally sterling record, although she followed an entirely different template. She was cautious, conscientious, and parsimonious about drinking, another approach that seemed to be working so far. Then again, it was also possible that temperament or even ability weren't the only factors relevant to success. Everyone came to recognize that much came down to luck.

FOG SOCKED IN the Luton airfield on April 21, 1942, so the school took the opportunity to deliver a lecture on accidents. "Usually deaths," Winnie noted in her diary afterward. Then she put the subject out of her mind while she mowed the lawn at her billet, cycled to see the movie *Dr. Jekyll and Mr. Hyde*, wrote a wire to Bill, and washed her hair before bed.

But there was no distraction so great that it could obscure the danger of a crash when flying for the ATA. The Americans were well aware that one week before their arrival in March, three ATA pilots had taken off from the airfield despite gusty winds and heavy rain in a Fairfax, an air taxi intended to take two of them to ferrying jobs elsewhere. Once airborne, the pilot thought better of it and turned to set back down. The aircraft stalled and smashed into a house near the field. All three pilots died, including two British women. Three other men died in separate accidents elsewhere on that day, all of them flying into craggy high ground in Scotland, blinded by clouds. Six dead. It was the worst single-day toll in ATA history.

By that time, seventy-nine pilots had died in the service. Weather was most often to blame. Unfortunately, the ATA's own rules made it harder to cheat death when conditions turned south. Radios would have helped pilots to seek safer pockets of clear sky and figure out locations when they were lost, but ATA pilots flew without radio contact to keep their whereabouts secret from the Germans, and radios were not installed until after the aircraft were delivered to maintenance units. The ATA also forbade pilots from using cockpit instruments to steer through heavy weather and offered no training on how to navigate with them. Officially, this policy was intended to discourage pilots from taking off unless conditions were fine. But it also saved the ATA the cost and effort of instrument training. That some would die as a result seemed to be factored into the equation.

Mechanical failure was another likely cause of fatal accidents. The first woman to die, and the third ATA death overall, was Elsie Joy Davidson. She was flying a closed-cockpit trainer with an ATA instructor in July 1940 when the plane went into a spin over a base in Wiltshire. It plummeted to the ground as aerodrome workers looked on in horror. An investigation determined that carbon monoxide fumes had seeped into the cabin until both pilots passed out.

By far the most shocking crash to date involved England's most famous aviatrix, Amy Johnson. In 1940 the thirty-six-year-old Amy had joined the ATA as a regular working pilot despite her standing as the Amelia Earhart or Jackie Cochran of her nation. She had made her name ten years earlier when she became the first woman to complete a grueling solo flight from England to Australia. Since then, press coverage had turned her into an icon of inspiration through the Depression as she performed more long-distance international feats. She inspired a popular song, "Wonderful Amy," and a rousing movie version of her life, *They Flew Alone*. It premiered in London one week after the first Americans arrived, with Jackie Cochran and Pauline Gower posing for photos along with other celebrity guests. The box-office draw Anna Neagle starred as Amy.

Amy Johnson had established herself as a legend well before Jackie, setting an early example of a woman from ordinary beginnings who rode aviation to unexpected heights. A slight figure with a wavy light-brown bob and almond-shaped eyes, she earned a bachelor's degree in economics and worked as a secretary until she caught the flying bug. Amy wasn't a natural—her landings were rough. But a year after her first solo in 1929, she cooked up the audacious plan of flying to Australia alone at the age of twenty-six. She hoped the notoriety would make flying a paying occupation.

The journey played out as a series of near calamities. Her aircraft was frail, an open-cockpit biplane made of fabric over a plywood frame with a top speed of ninety miles an hour. The hand-operated fuel pump leaked and made her nauseated. A dust storm near Baghdad drove her off course and forced her down in a hard desert landing that fractured a strut of the under-carriage. A bolt broke during another thumping stop along the Persian Gulf. In India, she snapped a wing while putting down on a parade ground. Forced to land during a monsoon in Rangoon, she wound up in a ditch amid a scrapyard of broken parts. Each time, Amy made repairs and perse-vered. In Java, when bamboo stakes punched holes in the cloth of the wings, local women cut up their shirts to sew replacements.

Each peril boosted readership for reporters who covered the drama, which jacked up the price to sell Amy's exclusive story to the *Daily Mail*. She finally turned up, exhausted and sunburned, in Darwin, Australia, on May 24, 1930. She had covered 8,600 miles in nineteen and a half days.

Amy Johnson scooped up the Harmon aviation trophy that Jackie Cochran would collect eight years later, and King George V named her a Commander of the Order of the British Empire. Best of all, she realized her goal of making a living by performing other novel exploits while selling rights for the publicity. By the time Britain came under attack, though, the public had lost its appetite for aviation stunts. Amy hoped for a leadership post in the war effort. But when the better-connected Pauline

Gower won the job heading the women's ATA, Amy settled for serving as a regular pilot. Others who idolized her were agog when they encountered Wonderful Amy in a waiting room before a flight. The last article she wrote described her feeling "frozen and frightened," flying "in an open cockpit with wind and rain, snow and hail."

Those elements would bring the great Amy Johnson down. Snow, fog, and bitter cold kept most pilots on the ground on January 4, 1941. But Amy had an assignment to deliver an Airspeed Oxford, a twin-engine workhorse used for training bomber crews, to an RAF field near the city of Oxford. She chose to defy the appalling visibility and take off from an aerodrome on the west coast near Blackpool. Waiting for a change in the weather didn't sit well with a person driven to risk her neck for glory.

Confronted with a wall of cloud, Amy faced two choices: try to fly under it, with the danger of winding up too low and smacking into a hill, or "go over the top." This meant ascending above the clouds and gambling on the chance of finding an opening to duck back down. There was the risk that no such window would appear in the white expanse that pilots called "the concrete." In that case, the aircraft would eventually run out of gas and tumble from on high. For this reason, the ATA forbade going over the top as the greater of two risks. Some pilots preferred to take that chance and defy the order. Amy had said she would if given the choice.

Another pilot who flew that day on a similar route, the South African Jackie Sorour, tried staying under the concrete by clinging to valleys, but at the end of a gorge, she feared hitting a wall. "I rammed open the throttles, pulled the control column back and climbed steeply," she later wrote. At four thousand feet, she reached sunshine, but below her, "the clouds stretched to all horizons like a soft woolen blanket." As her fuel gauge sank toward empty, she forced herself to descend blindly into the folds, knowing she might not have long to live. "The clouds embraced me like water around a stone," she wrote. Finally, with only a few hundred feet of altitude left, she broke through and used the last precious drops of fuel to find an aerodrome. She was lucky. Amy Johnson was not.

Amy Johnson's flight should have taken ninety minutes. Instead, she ground on for four hours, seeking an escape. With fuel running out, there was only one option. She strapped on her parachute and bailed out into the white abyss, falling through the cloud and snow without knowing where she would land. Chance was against her. She had drifted seventy miles off course, over the freezing winter waters where the sea met the broad mouth of the Thames. The cold could kill someone in minutes.

As it happened, a convoy of ships was passing through and spotted a figure falling from the sky. The HMS *Haslemere*, a steamer that transported barrage balloons, churned toward her from half a mile away. Amy was still bobbing on the surface when the ship reached her. The crew threw lines to reel her in, but she couldn't grasp them. The ship's captain, Walter Fletcher, dove in to assist. Versions differ about what happened next. Some say Fletcher held her until he lost his grip, and she disappeared. Others remember that she drifted toward the stern of the *Haslemere*, where a large wave raised up the ship and brought the hull down on top of her. Still others thought she was drawn into a propeller. Sailors pulled Fletcher back on board, but he died later from exposure. Amy Johnson's body was never found. British weather had claimed an idol.

AT THE ACCIDENT lecture in Luton in April 1942, the ATA tried to drum into its pilots the policy that flying in poor weather was strictly prohibited. No one should take off into clouds lower than eight hundred feet or visibility less than two thousand yards. WE PAY YOU TO BE SAFE, NOT BRAVE, warned a sign posted in waiting rooms. Beyond that, pilots made their own calls. Yet all pilots were expected to push the limits when aircraft were labeled "Priority 1," meaning they were needed so badly in battle that pilots should make the delivery that day.

Headquarters issued one of the most urgent priorities of the war on April 5, 1942, while the Americans were still in training. A German siege threatened the British-controlled island of Malta, a critical location in the Mediterranean. Malta barely held on against daily drubbing from German bombers based in Sicily, and the island's supply of serviceable fighters had dwindled to single digits.

The call went out for Priority 1 Spitfires. Crews would load them onto an aircraft carrier ship, the USS *Wasp*, on loan from the United States, for delivery to Malta from the River Clyde in Scotland. The ATA was tasked with bringing the aircraft there, but conditions were impossible. A temperature inversion smothered the entire country with heavy mist on the ground and clouds above with barely a gap in between—the concrete again. Snow cover over fields and forests added to the sense of a visual blank. Pilots from an all-woman base on the southern coast waited for a break, taking refuge in a hut with melting snow dripping through the walls. Minute by minute, they weighed the weather and the risks.

On the third day, one English pilot, Ann Welch, set off on the first leg of the journey, toward a maintenance hub less than fifty miles away. She threaded her way between a cloud base of only three hundred feet and fogbanks on the ground, afraid to blink or take a quick peek at the map on her lap. If she lost sight of the fuzzy landmarks below, she would likely lose her life. The tension was nearly unbearable. At such a low altitude, traveling at the Spitfire's lowest speed of 120 miles per hour, what little Ann could see flitted by too fast to process. At one point, when the rail line she followed circled around in two loops, she circled precisely above them, afraid to stray. Ann eventually touched down, white with fear, her voice on the phone back to Operations bleached and expressionless. "It was very bad indeed," she reported to the officer on duty. "Worse than I've ever known."

Forty-seven Spitfires made it north to set off for the Mediterranean on April 13. But the last leg of the delivery went awry. Germans struck the field as soon as the aircraft arrived, disabling all but six—a humiliating end to the effort. The *Wasp* turned around to make a second journey while the ATA delivered another forty-seven priority Spits to Scotland through another course of iffy weather.

One of the British ATA women best known for unshakable nerves, Lettice Curtis, flew one of them. She described the emotions of those who accepted the challenge: "There can be few things more frightening than finding oneself committed to chasing through the sky, in an aeroplane . . . pressed down by a vast greyness, knowing that if reference with the ground is lost even for an instant, one's chances of a safe return to earth are not worth the proverbial row of beans."

When the second batch made it to Malta on May 10, they scrambled into the air within minutes to take down enemy fighters. The delivery was credited with saving the island and turning the course of the war. When much was at stake, the mission to Malta had tested the ATA and found it up to the job.

WHILE THE MALTA crisis played out, the first five Americans passed their Class 1 flight checks and returned to White Waltham for more practice finding their way around the country. Dorothy Furey and Virginia Farr mostly kept themselves apart, while Winnie, Helen, and Louise once again lit up the Riviera bar at night. Afterward, the friends cycled back to billets in local homes, stopping to pee under a tree and laughing hysterically. They mostly socialized with American men, groaning that the English ones were "dull and sticky." Winnie wrote, "I am glad I have no desire of any sort of sex. Guess I must be working it off in my old age." Yet she also groused, "Funny how *not* having a man affects one's disposition. I shall curb that!"

In the first week of May, the Americans' reputations took another hit. Word came down from the top brass that no one was exempt from the rigors of ATA training: The great Jacqueline Cochran had washed out; she would no longer serve as a pilot. The reason given was that her sinuses interfered with flying open ships. Jackie was granted the honorary title of Flight Captain going forward, but it was clear that her leadership was mostly redundant. It was another black mark for the Americans. Amy Johnson died a hero, while the supreme American aviatrix of her age was the first U.S. woman to be barred from flying for the ATA.

The other Americans didn't seem to care what the Brits thought of them, which was just as well. Some felt that the respected British pilot Lettice Curtis looked at them as if they had a bad smell, while Curtis concluded that Jackie "was altogether too high-powered for ATA."

By May 1942, the first group of Americans, experienced pilots all, had made quick work of the Class 1 training, but so far they were mostly known for their silly behavior. Luckily, reinforcements were already steaming to the rescue—more Americans, united in nationality but poles apart in personality. They were primed to put up some competition and make their own marks.

CHAPTER 6

Leftover Parts

May 13, 1942
Maidenhead, Berkshire

W hen the second group of American women turned up at White Waltham air base in May, the early arrivals hosted the four of them for lunch at Skindles, a fashionable Maidenhead hotel where diners watched the Thames flow by through a bank of windows. Suzanne Ford, a society girl familiar to the others from New York flying circles, received a warm welcome. Not so much the others, more provincial women from rural states. "Horrors!" Winnie Pierce wrote in her diary. "We thought every one of them was awful . . . all fat but Sue, and none had eaten lobster before. Imagine!"

Hazel Jane Raines from Macon, Georgia, would have chosen fried chicken and a Coke over lobster and champagne any day. She should have commanded respect if only for her number of flying hours—one thousand—and a well-established finesse at precision aerial acrobatics. But she had built her career in the south, well outside the worldly sphere of the ladies who made up the fast crowd in New York. On the ground with them in a posh restaurant, the accomplished pilot looked out of her element. Hazel was graceful in the air and awkward everywhere else.

She had demonstrated this quality a month before in Halifax harbor, when she and the other three in her group steadied themselves on a small, flat-bottomed barge, which usually carried cargo from the docks, that was taking them toward a sorry-looking ship.

"What's the matter, Miss Raines, you aren't getting homesick already?" teased the sailor guiding their boat.

Hazel smothered her disappointment and spoke through a knotty throat. "Oh, no," she said lightly. "But is that the ship we are sailing on?"

She had her answer when someone flung a rope ladder over the side. Hazel gamely mounted it, although she was dressed more for an entrance on the gangplank of a luxury liner, or at least a proper troop ship, than a climb up the side of the SS *Tetela*. The five-thousand-ton former banana boat towered above. Slowly, she crept from one shaky rung to the next without winding up in the drink, but by the time she reached the top, her dignity had taken a tumble. Or as Hazel put it, "my too-tight girdle and scratchy wool skirt had also done a bit of climbing."

"Cheerio, miss," said a whiskered seaman who appreciated the view. "I say we are lucky to have you fair lassies coming aboard."

Hazel tugged frantically to cover her thighs, produced a false smile, and managed a chipper "thanks."

If anyone could put a cheery face on drawing a short straw, it was Hazel Jane Raines. She was plucky out of all proportion to the luck she'd been handed in life. Her one true ambition was to work as a professional pilot, preferably in the war. Right now, the only place for a woman to find that work was in the ATA, whose doctors in Montreal had already looked askance at her fragile health.

Pale and delicate, her round face framed by fine, silky curls, Hazel had suffered all her life from asthma and a heart condition. At twenty-five, she was often fatigued. Exercise, even a bit of walking, left her winded, and her weight fluctuated along with her condition. In March 1942 she weighed 150 pounds, twenty more than usual, although she was only five feet tall. Her height presented a challenge in reaching the rudder pedals of planes and seeing over the controls through the windscreens. Hazel had never crashed, not even a minor propeller-bender. It would have surprised her to know that a year later she would spin to earth in a Spitfire and smash into a thatched-roof house. Yet the possibility that she might someday meet an early death wasn't entirely foreign to her, either.

All of the women who had signed on with the ATA were driven, but Hazel, with much to overcome, was driven more than most. Her flying went against everything her middle-class Georgia family wanted for her—a husband, children, a tidy home—the example set by her two older sisters, both of them hat-and-gloves housewives in the mold of their mother. The youngest of three, Hazel might have been indulged as the baby or coddled through so much illness that her mother tolerated such an utter rejection of her pedigree.

This made for close but complicated mother-daughter relations. Born in 1916 in small-town Georgia, Hazel, although sickly, embarked on a childhood of comfort, the ladies in the family serving as models of southern womanhood. They were churchgoing women, genteel and gracious, who spoke in soft Georgia drawls. Her mother, Bessie, although she lived to be eighty-six, never learned to drive. Hazel Jane—within the family, it was always Hazel Jane—followed the ladylike example, until she didn't. She played the piano by ear and studied music at a conservatory at Wesleyan College near home in Macon, graduating in 1936. Around that time her father died from a stroke, and Hazel found herself stranded in an office job and still living at home. Some friends dared her to take a flying lesson at an airport outside Macon. "She started disappearing in the afternoon," said a niece, Regina Hawkins. "The family was horrified when it learned."

With undeniable talent, in 1938, at the age of twenty-two, Hazel became the first woman in Georgia to earn a pilot's license. By 1940, she had added a commercial license, another Georgia first, and right away broke with the norms of her background in a move that must have given her mother the vapors: Hazel Jane Raines started touring with a flying circus called the Georgia Air Races and Show. This was no sedate instructor's job guiding hobbyists through the fundamentals. She was executing aerobatic maneuvers, pushing little aircraft to their limits to dazzle the crowds. A highlight of her act was taking an open-cockpit biplane plane up five thousand feet to perform a series of loops. Pulling this off meant climbing vertically and curving backward until she was upside down at the top of each loop and then plunging down the other side until upright at the bottom, like a passenger on a 360-degree roller coaster, without the rails. Once Hazel reached a lower altitude, she topped that feat by placing the plane in a spin and pulling out at the last minute, chillingly close to the ground.

The act was thrilling, but these thrills were created with meticulous skill. Stunt work required a private inner certainty rather than pure daredevil recklessness. Steady hands on the stick, steady feet on the pedals, steady eyes on the horizon. Total physical and mental engagement. To perform a loop, for example, Hazel would first dive to gain speed, then pull the stick back to crest at the top. There she would relax the stick, calibrating carefully to avoid a stall, and float upside down until she let gravity pull her back toward level flight. Many pilots learned this straightforward method to execute loops. But to trace a perfect geometric circle, as Hazel did in a show, took an intuitive feel for the air, a melding of pilot and plane, not to mention an iron stomach. Hazel made constant small, instinctive adjustments to pull the right amount of G-force and maintain height amid changing conditions of wind, humidity, and altitude. An added complication was that once the nose left the horizon on a loop, a pilot could see only sky. It was necessary to look out the sides of the cockpit to stay oriented, something Hazel often did anyway because she was too short to see out the front.

When it all worked perfectly, when Hazel made a plane dance in the sky, she felt euphoric. All of the women who joined the ATA expressed similar emotions. Setting them loose from the bonds of gravity, flying granted them exhilaration and freedom. For Hazel, particularly, movement on terra firma taxed her breathing and heart, while movement in the air released a jolt of pure joy. That was why Hazel later wrote to her mother that she never felt so close to God as when she was up in the blue. It was why she asked her mother not to grieve more than she could help if Hazel cracked up, knowing that she had died the way she wanted to. Hazel had always been musical, playing the piano, bugle, saxophone, cornet, drums, and harmonica. "She could get music out of anything," said her niece. "She could hear music from the wind whistling through the struts of the wings of an airplane."

★

AS AIR SHOW work faltered before the war, Hazel racked up flying hours delivering Taylorcraft planes, small aircraft similar to Piper Cubs, from a factory in Ohio to the south. She also taught at a Civilian Pilot Training Program in Fort Lauderdale, Florida. She still performed aerobatics at shows when she could.

The petite pilot provided an appealing novelty act for the press, which often ran photos of Hazel in her standard flying attire of a short-sleeved white blouse, jodhpurs, and knee-high leather boots. Newspapers referred to her as the "pretty Macon aviatrix," with "clear blue eyes." She could spin an engaging yarn for reporters, too. Papers all over Georgia covered the story when crosswinds blew several pilots off course on the way to a banquet the night before an air show. Hazel, her motor gone dead, made an emergency landing in a wheat field, only "to come face-to-face with a farmer, about ten kids, and a double-barreled shotgun pointed directly at me." Once she explained the situation, he hitched his mule to a buggy and delivered her to a nearby train. Hazel strolled into the banquet with three minutes to spare.

The press took shots at Hazel for being a woman, and a small one at that. One article said, "She gets plenty of kidding about her size-four shoe, but for working she wears fours-and-a-half so that the extra length will reach the rudders in an airplane." She disputed the article that said she drew "male snickers" for wanting to pilot a bomber. Hazel told the paper she was submitting a questionnaire to the war department to apply to fly, "as English women are doing at present."

HAZEL'S TELEGRAM FROM Jackie Cochran arrived out of nowhere in March 1942, asking if Hazel would consider exactly that. "Me, a two-bit Flight Instructor, and a gal trying to make her way in Aviation," Hazel wrote in a journal, "and Bang—Outa the blue comes a telegram, of all things, from the top aviatrix, asking me, quote—'Can you fly to New York Thursday, March 5th for interview—transportation will be reimbursed, answer Western Union.' Even tho it was my last eighty-five cents until payday, I dashed into town and sent a quick—'Arrive New York Thursday 6:45 pm.'" Although her only dress suit "was fast growing too small for my expanding 'fuselage,'" she hurried to pick it up at the cleaners.

Hazel made a point of acting unimpressed by prominent people, so she maintained a matter-of-fact air when she was ushered into Jackie's opulent apartment at the River House on the Upper East Side. Like most visitors, she was steered first through Jackie's overstuffed trophy room with an inlaid compass on the marble floor. Hazel found Jackie to be "a grand person," even though Jackie, ever conscious of the refined image she imagined for the American ATA flyers, noticed the too-tight suit and commented on it. But Hazel won the day with her enthusiasm and record. Jackie picked up the tab for Hazel to spend a week amusing herself in New York. Then she returned to Macon to await another telegram, this one instructing her to catch a train to Montreal on March 15. The cable added, "300 Lbs Baggage Allowed STOP Bring Own Helmut Goggles STOP." There was barely time for Hazel to tell her mother before she left Macon for war, promising to write.

Her mother mourned. "It is a wonderful thing to have a daughter who is capable of working in our first line of defense," Bessie told the *Atlanta Journal*. "But it seems to me it would be an unnatural mother who could work up enthusiasm over such an undertaking."

As Bessie related the story, Hazel had said to her, "If you tell me I cannot go, Mother, I'll give up the thought, but it will break my heart."

Bessie didn't say no. "I just didn't say 'yes.'"

WITHIN TWO DAYS of checking into Montreal's Mount Royal Hotel, Hazel's health put her flying future at risk. Doctors picked up on her irregular heartbeat, a disorder that likely would have crushed her chances to join an outfit with higher standards than the ATA. Hazel wrote a desperate letter to her mother, asking if her physician from home would weigh in. "It would surely help if he could make a casual statement in the report to the effect that there is absolutely nothing organically wrong with my heart, but it is just a fast-beating ticker." She pleaded: "Please impress on Dr. Richardson how much this means to me, my whole future and life—so tell him to make it sound good, if such is possible . . ."

While she crossed her fingers and waited for decent flying weather, Hazel and the other recruits had picnics in their rooms and listened to American radio broadcasts. Hazel, frustrated, felt she looked as healthy as anyone else. In a low moment she wrote to her family, "I think I must have been made out of 'leftovers' and it has just taken me twenty-five years to get them to fit properly. I do know that up until the flying bug bit me, I was a 'Miss-fit,' physically and socially—but now I believe I am on the right track—who knows?"

The others kept up a giddy social pace, but Hazel visited the hangar repair shop every morning, helping to work on Harvards to understand how they ticked. "The rest of the girls," she wrote, "have been going the way ninety percent of the females go, after the tall, dark, and handsome pilots. They can have them—just give me a big shiny aeroplane!"

The skies cleared, and so did her prospects. Hazel made quick work of passing her flight test and, to her even greater relief, winning medical clearance. Some of the gals visited a fortune teller, who delivered more good news: Flying in Britain would make Hazel famous and successful. She would marry a wealthy Englishman, who—*abracadabra*—would boost her flying career with his money. Hazel wrote home that this might ease her relatives' "fear of being disgraced with an old maid sister."

The crossing to England had given Hazel time to reflect. More than most of her colleagues, she was drawn to the military purpose of the mission ahead. The sense of discipline and focus appealed to her. She saw Americans as naïve about the demands of war, "still carrying on with that true American spirit of 'it can't happen to us.' We were going to England to do our bit—our part, all because America, the land of the free and the home of the brave, would not give us a chance to prove our worth for our own land." She saw all the machinations to join the ATA as "what we needed to get us to our destiny, to [a] place where we could serve our country, even if our country didn't want us." The note of bitterness was uncharacteristic of the usually buoyant Hazel.

WHEN THE GROUP moved to Maidenhead the second week of May, the town looked lovely with spring tulips and sweet peas in full bloom, but the aerodrome was busier than ever. The band of thirty pilots who had started the ATA in 1939 had grown to 536 by early 1942, and ground staff expanded to 1,300. The congestion played a role in an accident two days before Hazel reached the base, when two Blenheim bombers collided shortly after takeoff, then crashed and burned. One ATA instructor was killed. Two others were injured.

Hazel found a warm welcome at a billet in the home of a couple named the Littlehales. Mrs. Littlehales doted on Hazel, knitting a blue wool sweater to fit under Hazel's uniform as they eased into a wartime mother-daughter dynamic. The landlady read American newspapers that Hazel's family sent from home, then traded them at the shops for extra butter. Hazel excelled in flight training, unsurprising given her experience. By June, she was told she would soon catch up to the pilots who arrived before her, now preparing to advance to what she called "sure 'nuff stuff"—Class 2 fighters. She seemed to be following the triumphant path set out by the fortune teller in Montreal. Soon, Hazel wrote home, she "would be not only qualified but capable and experienced in flying any machine ever built." Jackie Cochran had promised her an excellent job in aviation after the war, Hazel wrote. "I never intend to grow up and settle down."

So long as she stayed healthy. But the damp and cold, the exertion in a challenging environment, placed a greater strain on Hazel than it did on her fellow pilots. She was happy to lose twenty pounds and look slim in her uniform, and she emerged from cockpits tanned and freckled from the sun and wind. But while she occasionally tried to join her colleagues at night, drinking a Singapore sling and playing the piano at the pub, Hazel wrote that most evenings, "I am so tired all I can do is go to bed." She drained her strength when she biked to the airfield like everyone else. "It almost killed me at first." In June, just when she hoped to step up to the next level of aircraft, the chief medical officer ordered her to take two days' leave to rest. She stayed in bed and returned to the air as soon as she was cleared.

Every time she flew, Hazel carried a silver dollar in the pocket of her flight suit. Before each takeoff, she touched her fingertips to the words "In God We Trust" and repeated them to herself. *In God We Trust.* Maybe the talisman would keep her aloft; maybe it would not. Having always felt like a misfit made from leftover parts, Hazel had learned that her dreams were at the mercy of chance. She could master any plane they threw at her, if only she could keep her body together.

CHAPTER 7

The Impossible Turn

June 1942
Maidenhead, Berkshire

In June the exultant moment arrived when the pilots from the March shipload of Americans took their first shots at the fabled Hawker Hurricane fighter, which shared credit with the Spitfire for winning the Battle of Britain. For Winnie Pierce, rocketing along at 280 miles per hour was just the sort of thrill she'd signed up for. Nowhere else in the world would women have this chance to command the speed and power of the celebrated British fighters and snatch a share of the glory they had earned in battle.

Since the two most iconic models were both single-seaters, the women began by practicing for a few days with instructors on two-seat trainers that they used as stepping stones—the Miles Master and the dreaded Harvard that they knew from Montreal. Winnie shared classes with Joan Marshall, a twenty-eight-year-old from South Africa. On June 20, Winnie watched from the White Waltham airfield as Joan took the Master up for a solo run. When she came in for a landing, the aircraft stalled above the airfield, and Joan couldn't maintain control. Suspended for an agonizing instant, she twisted into a spin that drove the aircraft into the ground.

Joan was killed instantly. Winnie felt compelled to walk to the street where the wreckage rested between some houses, the aircraft now a scattering of broken pieces, reduced to "a heap of scrap." Winnie made no further comment in her diary.

The ATA didn't coddle pilots with a decent interval to recover their nerves. The next day it was Winnie's turn to step into the cockpit of the same model plane. Winnie tuned out the emotional noise and muscled through. Two days later, she served as a pallbearer at Joan's funeral. While Winnie had managed to get back in the cockpit without losing her composure, it infuriated her that the British pilots sat through the service without visible emotion. "It took ten minutes, and the preacher just rolled off lines and didn't give a damn," Winnie fumed. "I am more than ever against church and will write myself a eulogy for fear of having the same type of noncommittal farewell."

Whatever happened to Winnie, she expected—she demanded—to be noticed. She was frustrated that two other Americans won first crack at the Hurricane on June 21, the day after the crash. She understood why the experienced thirty-three-year-old Helen Richey got the nod. But so did the pilot Winnie most disdained, the young but reliable twenty-three-year-old Virginia Farr. Virginia did fine, but Richey flubbed it, bouncing on landing and then dropping a wing into the ground. The fighter was damaged and Helen was blamed.

It became clear that the Hurricane wasn't a docile craft. Intimidating, combat tested, with wings spanning forty feet, the fighter could reach 340 miles per hour at twenty-one thousand feet. But it was an aircraft that had to be actively flown. Aside from its astounding speed, and horsepower that topped a thousand, the fighter had a tendency to pitch back and forth, both in the air and on the ground. This presented a particular problem for takeoffs from White Waltham, where the rough grass airfield served up bump after bump that had a nasty way of corresponding with every oscillation of the plane. All the pilot could do was find a balance by pushing the throttle forward while pulling gently back on the stick. "It was a horrible way of bumping and skidding across the ground," said Nancy Miller, one of the later recruits. Once airborne, the pilot would switch hands so the right could let go of the stick and release the safety catch to bring up the wheels. "It was an entirely different feeling from trainers," Nancy continued. "The feel of power, the tug at the leash as if the Hurricane wanted to fly away on its own."

BY NECESSITY, PILOTS took their first spin in the single-seat Hurricane solo. Winnie celebrated hers on June 25, four days behind her colleagues. After takeoff, she felt the rush of sudden, effortless altitude. Her head swelled and her ears popped. The flight was everything she had imagined: "The excitement of stepping into a fighter. The roar of power on the takeoff, and then wheels up, the speed at cruising, to the final heart in the throat and fearful approach to land not knowing just how the plane would react." She aced it. The ATA cleared her to ferry fighters as well as simpler aircraft from White Waltham, catching up with Virginia Farr.

Several days passed with assignments on lesser planes and delays due to haze. Winnie flew a Master to Prestwick, Scotland, one day, feeling cocky and cheating by going over the top of the clouds and following instruments on the way down, both violations of the rules. On the Fourth of July, she gladly skipped a party at the American embassy in London, because she had secured her first Hurricane delivery that day. She declared the trip "swell" and returned to Maidenhead to get "stinko" for the holiday that evening. She made another short hop in a Hurricane the following day, then a grand, sunny long haul to Prestwick the next, flying in tandem with her buddy Louise. Winnie's ears rang from hours of speeding on high.

On July 11, feeling like an old hand, Winnie won another Hurricane assignment. This one was a shiny new ship from a Hawker factory encircled by barrage balloons at Langley Airfield, not far from ATA headquarters in Maidenhead. Everything checked out on the ground. She delighted in the bone-shaking roar on takeoff. But no sooner had Winnie launched the plane when the ferocious sound went silent.

It took a beat for the disaster to register. The Hurricane's engine had failed.

Winnie was barely off the ground. No leeway to recover. Momentum shot her forward toward the town, but she wouldn't make it far.

This was only Winnie's sixth flight on a Hurricane, but she didn't need more to understand the severity of the emergency. Every pilot knew.

Engine Failure After Takeoff—EFATO—was widely considered to be the worst situation one could face, the most stressful and frequently fatal.

It was one thing to lose power up high, with space available to glide and choose a spot for a forced landing. "Altitude is your friend" was the truism. The inverse was "Low altitude is your enemy." Traveling so close to the ground at the Hurricane's climbing speed of 140 miles per hour left Winnie with no good alternatives.

She knew the ATA rules for EFATO. Continue straight ahead and land as soon as possible, no matter what might be in the way—trees, buildings, ditches, preferably not people. At the moment of failure, Winnie was pointed straight toward all of them. The Hurricane would likely wind up among homes on a residential street, smashed to pieces, and the pilot with it. This was the outcome that had killed her classmate Joan Marshall three weeks before.

Winnie appreciated the reasons for the directive. Whatever the obstacles, plowing straight ahead supposedly offered the best chance of survival. To turn around toward the airfield introduced a series of dangers that the ATA, along with most pilots, considered even worse.

The act of circling back was so widely regarded as the wrong choice that it had a nickname known by everyone in aviation: "The Impossible Turn." It was impossible for a long list of reasons. At a low altitude without power, maintaining the proper speed to glide back to the runway would be a formidable feat. Too slow and Winnie wouldn't make it. Too fast and she might hit the runway with deadly force. Besides, the pilot would have to adjust for the changing crosswinds at each point of the circle, skewing the plane's trajectory and altering the speed. Chances were high of tipping too far one way or another, stalling, and spinning to the ground. Or losing too much speed, stalling, and spinning into the ground. It was all too reminiscent of Joan Marshall's fatal crash.

Even if Winnie managed a turn, lining up with a runway under these conditions would feel like threading a needle. And landing with a tailwind could wreak havoc with the velocity. Under such conditions, Winnie couldn't be sure how and when to deploy the flaps that she had only just learned to use. All valid reasons to gamble on gliding forward, wherever she wound up.

There was no time to spare before Winnie would lose too much speed and the chance to make any choice at all. She was well aware that the ATA had set the rules with the reasoning that it was better to make it back to solid ground by the most direct route, accepting the likely battering of a low-speed impact in order to live. Better than risking the likely stall, spin, and crash of the Impossible Turn.

Winnie understood the rules. In a snap, which was all the time she had, she decided to break them.

It would take a computer to calculate the variables of speed, altitude, wind, and distance that Winnie had only seconds to consider. Instinct might have lured her into keeping the nose up to maintain altitude, but training dictated that she drop the nose to sustain the speed she needed. Pushing through shock and trembling hands, she banked carefully. She chose a path to teeter back to the field before her glide speed trickled to nothing. Somehow, she wobbled past balloon barrage cables and aligned with the runway. She took advantage of the Hurricane's flaps to decelerate.

She held her breath. Winnie hit the field without a swerve.

Witnesses on the ground exhaled when they saw the touchdown. Winnie Pierce had risked everything to bet that she possessed extraordinary skill. The turn had been impossible, but she had made it.

Winnie had often disparaged the stiff-upper-lip attitude of the British. Now it was her turn to follow the dictum. Officers determined that the aircraft was unharmed, simply in need of a new engine. As there were more Hurricanes to deliver, another was produced for her and she followed orders to take off, still unable to breathe for fright.

"Angels were with me today," declared the irreligious Winnie in her diary that night. "I will never forget how I shook all over!" She'd only just begun to pilot these muscular aircraft, and now she wondered when her time would be up.

On her return to headquarters, Winnie realized her place in the hierarchy had shifted. Most pilots who are technically accomplished have internalized the principles of physics that govern the process of flight, but there is a rarer breed with something extra that can't be taught. Could it be that the impulsive Winnabelle Pierce was one of that breed? Everyone she encountered at the airfield, from Jackie Cochran to people who generally rolled their eyes at her antics, looked at her with new respect. British colleagues who had never spoken to her before had to acknowledge that the rash American might have actual talent in the air. They told her they were proud of her "and all that rot about 'good show,'" as she put it.

She was still the same mischievous Winnie Pierce, but this fine act of airmanship had altered her reputation in the eyes of others if not herself. "Lord but I was lucky," she wrote in her diary under the heading, "Horrible Day!"

WINNIE DRANK HERSELF silly that night with her pals "to celebrate my escape." Same old Winnie. She had always balanced her daylight flying with wild escapades after dark. If anything, the trauma of the engine failure only encouraged more drinking and reckless off-duty behavior. If the rules were to be believed, what was an impossible turn but arrogant recklessness?

During the summer, expressions like "binge," "buzzed," "plastered," "boozed," "got an edge on," "poured them down," and "knocked cold" appeared almost daily in her diary. One night she tumbled off her bike a dozen times on the way back to her billet and fell asleep by the side of the road. "Didn't get home until 1:30," she confessed. "What a life!" Other times, she boasted that morning ferry flights helped dispel hangovers. "Heigh-ho, must get over this yen for drink," she pledged with little effect.

Her commanding officer at White Waltham warned her that drinking and flying didn't mix. Winnie hadn't yet suffered a scratch while flying, but sometimes she made it home from the pubs black and blue from falls. One morning she wondered how she had gotten a bloodshot eye and a cigarette burn on her hand. A few weeks later, she got "tight as a tick" at a cocktail party and smashed her finger.

She pursued her love life with similar daredevil energy. Letters dwindled from Bill, her lover at Roosevelt Field on Long Island. Friends wrote Winnie that he was drinking heavily and broke. She sent him a hundred dollars and still dreamed of a future together. In the meantime, Mac, the amorous first mate from the Atlantic crossing, paid her a visit in

Maidenhead. Winnie also pursued a flight instructor in Luton, and once she returned to White Waltham, she mooned over her commanding officer there. She plotted a prolonged campaign against his shyness and switched her nightly carousing to the Plough or Sonny's, hangouts he was known to frequent. Winnie won a victory of sorts after an evening at the Plough, when he invited her to his house, undressed her, and put her to bed. She sighed, "I wish I could have remembered all that happened."

Her escapades weren't unusual in the ATA. Alcohol and sex offered welcome distractions from dangerous duty. The same held true throughout the war zone, where air raid sirens signaled the population to go for broke because they were living on the edge of annihilation anyway. "There was this inexplicable pressure to live our lives to the maximum," the British ATA pilot Mary Wilkins Ellis wrote. Most everyone cut loose during downtime in London, where nightlife still sparkled amid unrelenting darkness. "Because one never knew," Dorothy Furey said. As sirens howled through smoking debris, the pilots on their days off weaved to bars and clubs through pitted streets rendered sinister by blackouts that lent any rendezvous a clandestine cast. This was the inverse of contending with whiteouts in the air. For the pilots, to carouse in defiance of the dark and danger was thrill-seeking of another sort.

CHAPTER 8

The Whole Glorious Feast

June 1942
Luton, Bedfordshire, and Maidenhead, Berkshire

A lthough the United States announced it was entering the war after
the attack on Pearl Harbor in December 1941, there was still little
sign of an American presence in Britain as the summer of 1942 arrived.
The American ATA pilots rarely saw their fellow citizens at work. A few
emissaries from the U.S. Army Air Forces had arrived in the winter and
spring to coordinate a massive mobilization of aircrew that was set to
begin in the coming months. Germany still controlled the Continent,
leaving the United Kingdom as essentially the sole active defender of
European democracy.

The Allies knew that eventually they would have to claw back land
from the ground if the war was to be won, but they believed that the
advances of modern aviation offered an efficient path toward that end.
Together, the two nations would wage a new kind of warfare, an aerial
war. It inflicted terrible suffering but was believed to be the means to ultimate victory.

The Royal Air Force was already carrying out a campaign to bomb
the fight out of German-occupied territory, soon to be multiplied with the
powerful new American partner. This form of combat was still so new that

the British were feeling their way. At first, bombing raids were intended to be strategic, aimed at destroying manufacturing hubs that built military equipment, like ships, submarines, and aircraft. Other targets included the basic infrastructure of the economy, like power, transportation, and oil production. The early results were disastrous for the British. A report in August 1941 concluded that, on average, only one in three aircraft made it to within five miles of its target. Almost half of all bombs fell uselessly on open country. The raids seemed nearly pointless.

RAF Bomber Command concluded that technology wasn't up to the job of precision bombing and shifted more toward what was called area bombing, hitting cities where industrial workers lived, destroying their lives and homes. Many considered the strategy morally indefensible. But with improved targeting technology, raids in March and April 1942 were considered more successful. By June, Bomber Command began to throw more and more aircraft into each raid, hundreds at a time, with the hope that sheer numbers would overwhelm German defenses. The United Kingdom produced an unprecedented aerial arsenal that year, nearly 24,000 new aircraft, three times the number in 1939. The buildup from the United States was even more striking—from 5,800 in 1939 to almost 48,000 in 1942.

The British had witnessed the devastation of being on the wrong side of such an aerial campaign. They understood how breakthroughs in aviation could unleash destruction and horror unlike any yet seen. They were using it for their side now.

AMID ALL THE fraught escalation of the fight, the American ATA women, a tiny outpost of their nation in an alien land, knew they hadn't made the most serious impression yet. If they wanted to find their place in the war effort, it would help if someone stepped up and smoothed the way, someone with the social polish to get along with a wide cast of characters, from the grab-bag of big American personalities to their chilly British colleagues. Jackie Cochran hadn't bridged the gap. The Americans would benefit from a more informal leader, sophisticated enough mix it up in the larger world, able to hold her own with the big thinkers and top military brass in London, but likable enough to befriend the folks in the most remote aerodromes. This leader appeared on the third shipload of Jackie Cochran's Atta-Girls in the unlikely person of Ann Wood.

Twenty-four years old, with barely the minimum hours in her logbook, Wood didn't make the first cut of recruits. But her poise impressed Jackie in an interview, and when others washed out in Montreal, Jackie slotted Ann in. The relative beginner made landfall in Liverpool on May 25, 1942, and advanced quickly through the early training, mostly because the weather was fine. She was already flying by early June, although not without some bumps. "[I] am vaguely lost most of the time—which is a ghastly feeling," Ann recorded in her diary. "Sometimes wonder how I ever started in this racket or how long I may last."

Ann hadn't hit her stride yet, but that would change. "She absolutely lapped it up, every minute of it," recalled a member of her family. She adored flying, and over time she learned to do it well. But she also had a knack for placing herself at the center of the action, which was where Ann Wood truly excelled.

ONE NOTABLE FEATURE of the American women's tenure in England was that, cut off from their pasts, they could be whoever they appeared to be. Dorothy Furey appeared as an upper-class beauty, and it was so; Winnie Pierce as a vivacious party girl, which was essentially true; Virginia Farr as a workaday pilot rather than a privileged debutante; Hazel Raines as a sparky Southern gal with a healthy future before her.

Ann Wood was often described by those who knew her in England as a Philadelphia socialite. The illusion was understandable. She had in fact been born in Philadelphia. Long-limbed, sporty, with high cheekbones and the clipped diction and no-nonsense demeanor of Katharine Hepburn, Ann moved easily in any circle. Everyone liked her, from the persnickety Winnabelle Pierce to the haughty Dorothy Furey to the outcast Virginia Farr. Ann liked all of them in return. She arrived with trunks full of well-chosen clothes—a gray silk suit, a yellow suit styled with a cheery red hat, a gold cocktail dress, some red heels. All of them were stylish but also conveyed a message of authority, like the wardrobe of a career girl in a 1930s screwball comedy. That her family made its humble home in rural Maine rather than along the Main Line didn't register with anyone abroad.

Like the other women who accompanied her, Ann Wood hoped the ATA experience would set her up for an aviation career after the war. But while her colleagues mostly aspired to work *in* aviation, Ann seemed more likely to wind up *in charge of* aviation. The others knew they had to fly better than any man to find work flying. Ann banked on making connections that would pay off at a higher level. She liked a cocktail as well as anyone, or better yet champagne, but when others partied with a rowdy airport crowd, she sought out a more influential set. Ann leaned toward smart conversation with smart people—reporters, ambassadors, high-level officers, even a deposed European prince. She was a master at sending flowers with a thoughtful note. Ann Wood networked before anyone thought to use the word as a verb. She knew exactly why she had gotten into this racket.

ANN WAS TWELVE when her father died in 1929 from an obstruction of the hernia. He had owned a modest photo album business, and his wife Mary was left without income to support five children. In desperation, Mary sold her only asset, the family's old stone house in Philadelphia. This nest egg provided enough to afford the Catholic education Mary envisioned for the children, but only if she applied an unusual strategy. She ordered each child to pack a trunk and herded them onto a steamer bound for Belgium, where she placed them under the tutelage of the nuns at the Institut Notre Dame, a bargain compared with options at home.

The second oldest, Ann emerged as the family manager, overseeing money, buying food, and keeping up appearances on a budget. Stretching every dollar, the Woodses hopped to Biarritz in the South of France and Madrid in the midst of political upheaval, then back to Belgium. It was quite an education. They finally settled in a home of their own when they inherited a furnished house from some cousins in Waldoboro, Maine, a small fishing and farming town along the Atlantic coastline. Ann returned to America a citizen of the world, competent beyond her years and worldly beyond her station. From then on, nothing rattled her. "She spent the rest of her life flying right over problems," said a member of her family.

Ann enrolled in D'Youville College, a Catholic women's school in Buffalo. At five feet ten with a patrician bearing and square jaw, she was impossible to miss. The well-traveled coed studied just well enough to get by, but mostly she stood out for her popularity and an overstuffed schedule of extracurricular activities, from glee club to sports. Classmates elected her president of the student body, calling her "our genial, all-round and born leader, unruffled in manner and savoir-faire."

After graduation in 1938, Ann faced reality head-on. She needed to support her family with a job. Her mother, ever alert to bargains, suggested signing up for the free Civilian Pilot Training Program at the all-male Bowdoin College in Maine. Ann had never shown any interest or aptitude for aviation, yet the prospect of free tuition was irresistible. The college initially rejected her because she was a woman, only slipping her in when it failed to fill a twelfth position with a man. The hope was that no one would notice her at the airfield. But Ann tackled the coursework with her trademark competence and won attention anyway in the local paper: WOMAN HIGHEST RANKING STUDENT IN AVIATION CLASS.

She began instructing, but with war approaching, she wanted in on what was sure to be a momentous event. Ann wrote to correspondents at the *New York Times*, hoping for an entrée, but without success. Jackie Cochran's telegram presented a welcome alternative. "My mother was very pleased . . . that I was going to do a useful job," Ann said. "She was very keen about the war."

ANN'S ARRIVAL IN England coincided with the Royal Air Force's first thousand-bomber raid on Germany on the night of May 30, 1942. Forty-one British bombers were lost, yet 898 hit the target of Cologne. They wiped out 90 percent of the central city, killed almost 500 people, and left 45,132 homeless. Many more fled to the countryside as incendiary bombs ignited thousands of fires. "Terrible thing," Winnie Pierce wrote in her diary. Still, this was a propaganda victory for the RAF, improving on its previous spotty performance while showing the public that the service could take the fight to the German homeland.

On a one-day leave the following morning, Ann debated whether to head into London as the city braced for retaliation. Ever the social creature, she couldn't resist. "Somehow these jaunts to London fill me with utter glee," she noted. She joined English friends from her ship for lunch at the

Cordon Bleu. All the barrage balloons were up, and bedsprings lined the Piccadilly tube station, where residents brought mattresses during raids. On her way back to Luton, St. Pancras station looked like a shell from previous assaults, the glass shattered in its tremendous ceiling. But instead of seeking revenge on London that night, the Luftwaffe hit Canterbury, a cultural target of the Baedeker Blitz, killing forty-five people and destroying eight hundred buildings. Canterbury Cathedral survived thanks to fire marshals who put out incendiaries as they landed on the roof.

From the bedroom of her billet as she tried to sleep that night, Ann heard the RAF stream over Luton in droves—en route to another mass bombing, this time hitting Essen. In the morning, the airport bustled with purpose. Seeing that Ann was a quick study, the ATA moved her through ground school faster than other arrivals and got her into the air on June 3, six days after she reached the country. The other Americans at the aerodrome embarrassed her, filling the waiting room with noisy gossip about their pay while English ears on all sides strained to hear every word. Ann approached the English pilots and introduced herself.

On her first solo cross-country on June 9, however, Ann's usual confidence gave way to dislocation. Crosswinds rocked the Maggie while towns loomed up unexpectedly, and she failed to see the narrow roads and railroad lines until she was upon them. "I managed to lose myself just cruising around," she wrote, "and what a hapless feeling." In a frazzle, she spotted a town and glanced at the map to identify it. But a Sterling bomber, or maybe a Spitfire fighter—she wasn't sure which—zipped by in a close call, so she stopped map-reading and kept an eye out for aircraft instead. Inevitably, she lost all track of where she was, back to square one. Her relative lack of flight hours compared to the other Americans cost her, as her brain overloaded with details. In her second week, she landed at the wrong aerodrome by mistake, then had a dreadful time getting the plane to start again. Ann had no desire to join the rivalries of her colleagues to advance more quickly. She was satisfied to keep her own pace.

Word got around about fellow trainees' failures, which added to the stress. One of Ann's new British friends got the sack, leading Ann to wonder how long her own luck would hold. "People are getting the gate every day," she worried. "Instructors too often fail to realize when they down one it crashes one's entire world—at least now when the ATA is the last hope for anyone wanting to fly." Dorothy Furey attracted the wrong kind of attention by damaging not one but two aircraft when she taxied a lightweight Tiger Moth trainer into the wind, colliding with another plane. An accident report held her responsible, a black mark on her record: "bad airmanship." No one knew how many such findings could lead to dismissal, and no one wanted to find out.

A COUPLE OF weeks in, Ann Wood started to find her groove. "Lots of fun jazzing about," she enthused. She summoned the courage to fly through rainstorms or relax when she got lost, knowing or at least believing that she'd sort herself out. "Putting in at new aerodromes is [the] best part of this business," she decided, "because you are continually running into new faces and new ventures, all of which fit into my idea of things as they should be perfect."

The ATA granted her one day off every Monday for new ventures on the ground. Sunday mornings, she woke up earlier than everyone else, wherever she was, and made her way by bus or foot to early mass. Then she put in a day's work before catching an evening train to London, where she started moving and shaking, building out her first social contacts into a lively and increasingly interesting gang. "I have terrific desire to meet all kinds of people," she declared, "and love it when conversation revolves around interesting topics so that you can find out what makes people tick."

Before she collected friends, Ann listened alone to political orators in Hyde Park. She attended church at Westminster Cathedral, got her hair done at Harrod's, and took in plays and musical revues. Her taste in movies would hold up decades later. *Mrs. Miniver* was "splendid," *Flying Fortress* a piece of propaganda. At the end of the day, she walked through London blackouts to a bleak housekeeping flat she rented to save money on hotels. "My every footstep resonated far and wide," she wrote in her diary, "and I felt as though I were walking on the tombs of the dead."

On her second leave, Ann bought flowers for Jackie Cochran and left them with a note at the Savoy. The gesture paid off. Jackie called with an invitation to dinner the next week. Military leaders, members of Parliament, journalists, and diplomats ringed the table at the new flat Jackie had rented in Chelsea, but Ann Wood had done her homework, hoping to hold her own. She read the important political writers of the day and tuned in to Roosevelt's United Nations Day speech. She even monitored German radio to hear the other side, finding the blatant spin of Lord Haw-Haw hilarious. Ann didn't hesitate to share her opinions, blaming British strategy for the debacle that week at the Libyan port of Tobruk, which had fallen to General Rommel's German and Italian forces as part of the land campaign in North Africa.

One guest found the cheeky young pilot amusing. Air Corps Major Peter Beasley, age fifty-seven, had been an executive at the Lockheed Aircraft Company before the war. He joined the military to serve as one of the first six American staff officers in England to coordinate the buildup of the U.S. air power in Europe. There were colossal logistics to be managed, but he also shouldered the task of bustling about London, gathering scuttlebutt on everything and everyone of note. Evenings found him hosting tables of influential people at the American Stork Club or the Gay Nineties, and Jackie Cochran leaned on him for advice on navigating politics with the U.S. Army Air Forces to boost her plan for a women's branch. Major Beasley had already emerged as a man who could procure favors or fix messes. Ann had little information to trade, but he liked her tart wit and started inviting her for dinners at the Carlisle. Peter was an ideal source of gossip for Ann, although he once told her, "Invitations to dinner consist merely of people wanting to pick your brains for information and not wanting to have the same done to them."

ANN WALKED ON clouds after the dinner at Jackie's. "Such a tremendous thrill to see honest-to-goodness Americans, and I was so proud to be one," she confided to her diary. "For me, the men top all. Here [in England] the puny type is predominant."

In her diary, she often groused about the English. She found them poorly dressed, ill fed, and disorganized. She expressed little patience that they left bomb wreckage in a jumble rather than sorting it out straight away. It irritated her when she heard excuses for the failure at Tobruk or grumbling that the United States wasn't doing its part. At first the British tendency to downplay drama riled her, too. When she shared a train with an upper-class British ATA pilot named Hugh Taylor, she learned that he had been in Singapore when it fell to Japan in February. "What was it like?" she asked.

"The golf was good" was his flippant reply.

But slowly Ann began to feel more empathy for the British plight. On a visit to St. Paul's Cathedral the week after Jackie Cochran's dinner, the scope of the surrounding ruin shocked her. "Damage is ghastly, entirely flattened for several block radius," she wrote. "Crews tearing down— immense job." She warmed to the reticent Hugh Taylor and joined his crowd for trips to the pubs. "Not such a bad apple after you know him," she decided. Another catch to add to her widening net.

And why not stay open to the whole glorious feast of people and possibilities that lay before her? In a few short weeks, Ann had come to appreciate that England, and especially London, was the international epicenter of the most significant happening of the century. She had won a place at the table. Maybe by the end of war she would earn a more prominent seat, and the career to go with it. In the meantime, she decided to lap up every delicious tidbit.

Smoke pits burned every night in late June to obscure ripe targets from German bombs. The smog hung so thick on July 3 that Ann turned back on a cross-country assignment toward Bristol. She reasoned, "Always wonder if I'm being a bit of a sissy, but then it is my neck."

Besides, the next day, the ATA's American women were invited to join the crush at the Fourth of July party thrown by the American embassy. Some of the biggest names of the Allied war effort would be there. Ann Wood, the ersatz Philadelphia socialite from Waldoboro, Maine, was jazzed and ready to join them.

CHAPTER 9

Behind the Façade

July 4, 1942
London

———

Ann Wood chose her most professional gray suit for the July Fourth event at the American embassy on Grosvenor Square, where she planned to forge contacts both useful and amusing. Other flyers who had the day off had arranged to meet in advance for a drink at a hotel, but by the time Ann arrived, the pre-party was fully swinging. They voted to keep it up rather than endure the tedium of a formal affair.

Ann would not be deterred. She felt conspicuous going alone but wouldn't let it stop her. There were dignitaries to meet, dignitaries galore. On the reception line she shook hands with Ambassador John Winant and the top military leaders of the American war effort in Europe, Major General Dwight Eisenhower and Admiral Harold Stark. The strains of a band lured her down a staircase flanked with marines toward the garden, where she made a solo pass around the buffet in search of conversation. Ann saw that the ambassador devoted himself to Crown Prince Olav of Norway, who'd been exiled to England since the German invasion of his country, so she made a point of engaging him, too. He was her kind of guy, an Oxford grad who'd distinguished himself at ski jumping and yachting. "I was much infatuated," she admitted in her diary. She allowed herself to flirt a bit with men from back home. Ann emerged with a patriotic glow, a new list of contacts, and engagements in her datebook.

The deeper Ann entered this milieu, the more she found herself included in Jackie's circle. The world-renowned aviatrix often entertained the American pilots as a group, but Ann made the cut for events with more illustrious guests. During her time off, she started camping out at Jackie's overnight. The closer they became, the more Ann discovered about Jackie that was unexpected, layers and layers of bravado masking weakness and insecurity that she didn't reveal to the public at large.

For one thing, Jackie had little to do with the ATA now that she'd been grounded from flying. She greeted the rest of the trainees as they arrived over the next two months, soothing their homesickness by serving them favorite foods, like fried chicken for the southerner Hazel Jane Raines. Jackie provided a well-dressed shoulder to cry on when the war, the stress, and the distance from family sapped their resolve.

But Jackie spent the rest of her time campaigning for a women's ferrying service in the United States, exerting the same single-minded tenacity that powered all her pursuits. She compiled evidence to send to Washington about the success of women in the ATA and made presentations to U.S. military officials in London. She enlisted the youthful Ann as an informal aide-de-camp, organizing Jackie's schedule and accompanying her to appointments. Jackie, for all her bluster, was wary of gossip when she met with important men; she avoided seeing them in private. "Ann, can you be here at the Statler by five-thirty?" she would call to say. "So-and-so is coming by and I need you here." The young protégé came to serve as a chaperone, third wheel, and student of politics as Jackie conducted business, all lessons Ann would apply as she strove to become a mover and shaker herself.

Ann was getting an education, but she was giving one, too. It began when she was asked to wait outside in the back of Jackie's car while Jackie attended a meeting at a government ministry. When Jackie slid back into the seat, she tossed over a pocket dictionary that she always carried in her handbag. "Annie, you went to college," she said. "Look these words up for me." She proceeded to reel off terms and phrases the officials had used that she didn't understand.

That was the moment when Ann became one of the few people to realize that Jackie Cochran didn't know how to read. She couldn't even recognize the alphabet. Ann explained a half dozen expressions, and they practiced them together. The next time Jackie had a chance, Ann said, she "would fling those words about as though she had known them all her life." They continued the vocabulary lessons from then on, and Ann kept the illiteracy of the aviation legend to herself throughout Jackie's lifetime.

Jackie trusted the young protégé enough to let her see behind the glamorous Cochran façade. But it was unlikely that anyone at the time understood just how far Jackie had traveled in her journey to success, how much she had overcome to fill that trophy room in New York. Even those she trusted most never knew the full story—that Jacqueline Cochran was almost entirely an invention.

Even the famous name wasn't real. Jackie's parents—a father who traveled to work in sawmills and a mother who picked up jobs in cotton factories—named their daughter Bessie May Pittman when she was born in 1906. They raised her mostly in Florida and Georgia, in houses without electricity, on unpaved streets where she sometimes stole food from neighbors' gardens in order to eat. "I was the youngest and a regular little ragamuffin running wild, doing exactly what I pleased," she acknowledged in one of her two published autobiographies, both produced with coauthors who masked her inability to write.

By the time Bessie May was eight she had left school to work in a cotton mill for six cents an hour, fending off sexual molestation from older men. She worked twelve-hour shifts amid grinding noise, her face gray with dust, her hands strong and rough from moving heavy rolls of fabric on the looms. But Bessie was ambitious even then. The meager money she earned gave her hope for independence and a better life. She bought her first shoes from a peddler's cart, a ridiculous pair of high heels—she already coveted glamour. "I'm going to be rich," she told anyone who asked. "I'll wear fine clothes, own my own automobile, and have adventures all over the world." After one year at the mill, when she was nine, she won a promotion to supervise other children as they sorted cloth and folded bolts for shipment. She sought out the peddler again for flashy clothes, a blouse here, a skirt there, like the finery she saw in store windows.

A year later, during a factory strike, Bessie found better work with a family that ran a small chain of beauty parlors. She did odd jobs while learning how to dye hair and give shampoos. A traveling salesman tipped her off to a position at a department store in Montgomery, Alabama. It hired her to create permanent waves for a fancier clientele. Only fourteen, she moved there alone and found a rented room. She entertained the customers with buoyant chatter.

Jackie liked to tell people later, "I passed through the School of Hard Knocks of which there are no real graduates, because you simply keep on learning until you die." The next knock was one of the hardest, omitted from any tale she told of her life: Bessie May Pittman became pregnant at the age of fourteen.

The father of her child, Robert Cochran, was probably in his early twenties, but there is little on record about him. Later, Jackie Cochran never spoke about this period, at least not with any accuracy. Bessie wasn't yet fifteen when she married Cochran and bore a son, Robert Jr., in 1921. It seemed there was little substance to the marriage, and Bessie didn't take to being a mother, either. She later claimed that when she was seven, she had once acted as a midwife to a teenager giving birth. "I was no fool even then, and I knew that hers wasn't the life for me."

Bessie left the child with her parents in Florida to return to her beautician job in Montgomery. Four years later, the boy was playing with a match in his grandparents' yard when he lit some paper on fire. The flames spread to his clothing, and later that day he died from severe burns. Bessie came home to bury him under a heart-shaped stone. She and Robert Cochran Sr. divorced, and the fabrication of Jackie Cochran began in earnest.

She began by changing her name and erasing the Pittman family from her past. The way Jackie told the story from then on, she had been an orphan taken in by foster parents who didn't care for her. Now in her early twenties, running a salon in Pensacola, Florida, she said she felt free to choose a new name, supposedly from a phone book—*Jacqueline Cochran*. It combined her married name with one that better reflected her fantasies. From that point forward, while she supported the Pittmans and bought them gifts, she refused to acknowledge the relationship to anyone outside the family or ever speak about her son.

The next stage in her metamorphosis: New York. In 1929, when she was twenty-three, she sold a Model T she had bought with her beautician's earnings and made her way to the city with the beguiling new name as her calling card. Her curly blond hair styled to perfection, her wide brown eyes and clear complexion enhanced by expert makeup, Jackie talked her way into a job at Antoine de Paris, an elite salon at Saks Fifth Avenue. She pleased the fashionable clients so well that the salon sent her to Miami for the winter season. By then, Jackie had modeled herself enough on the ladies she served that they invited the former Bessie May Pittman to parties.

Floyd Odlum entered her life on one such occasion. A married millionaire fourteen years her senior, Floyd was new money, a self-made tycoon who started out digging ditches and performing other manual work not much higher in station than Jackie's. He eventually made a fortune speculating in stock. Floyd told brokerage industry friends at the Miami party that he would like to meet a woman who worked for a living and didn't engage in mindless chitchat. They introduced him to Jackie as cocktails were served.

"Are you really a beautician?" he asked.

"Yes." Jackie wouldn't be cowed. "You want to make something out of it?"

Their connection was immediate. Each recognized a like-minded scrambler, someone who had earned every bit of the self-taught sophistication they tried to affect. Each strained to suppress the little giveaways, the uncultured speech or lack of polish, that broke the illusion.

"I've been thinking about leaving Antoine's to go on the road selling cosmetics," Jackie told him when they settled at a table. "I love to travel. I want to be out in the air." By that, she meant the outdoors.

Floyd considered her comment about the air and gave it a more pointed interpretation. "There's a Depression on, Jackie," he advised. "If you're going to cover the territory you need to cover in order to make money in this kind of economic climate, you'll need wings. Get your pilot's license."

Jackie had mused about flying in an idle way, drawn to the celebrity and potential riches of women pilots she'd seen in the news. She promised Floyd that she would earn a license over her next six-week vacation, a time frame that seemed impossibly tight. Floyd proposed a wager. If she earned the license that quickly, he would pay for the cost. Jackie handily won the bet, acing her flight test in just three weeks. The only obstacle was her inability to read and write for the written exam. She convinced officials to give her an oral one instead.

All Jackie's inflated dreams of fame and fortune came true in the 1930s. One by one, she ticked them off the list. She won her pilot's license in 1932 at the age of twenty-six. Backed by investments from Floyd, she went on to make her own fortune in cosmetics. She joined the tony set as a member of the Long Island Aviation Country Club, where the members often regarded her the way the British would, as an awkward, showy upstart who tried too hard to stand out. But Jackie could not be denied as she waged her successful campaign to become the queen of air races and aviation records. She became a media star, always applying her lipstick and touching up her hair before stepping out of a plane. By her thirtieth birthday in 1936, Floyd divorced his wife and married Jackie.

From the moment of their marriage, Jackie used the name Mrs. Floyd Odlum only when she wanted to flaunt it. Otherwise, she went by the name she had chosen: Miss Jacqueline Cochran.

Once Jackie started lobbying for a U.S. women's ferrying service, she worked all of the connections she and Floyd had accumulated through his business and her record-breaking flying. First Lady Eleanor Roosevelt and General Henry H. "Hap" Arnold, chief of the Army Air Corps, warmed to the plan. To put it over the top, Jackie, who understood the power of celebrity, proposed a publicity stunt. In June 1941, with General Arnold's approval, she made headlines as the first American woman to fly a bomber, a Lockheed Hudson, across the Atlantic to supply the British. The male pilots of Ferry Command opposed giving her the controls, so she had to compromise by flying on the route but not performing the takeoff or landing. Nevertheless, flashbulbs popped as the flight attracted the limelight she sought. It wasn't enough to push her American idea over the top, not yet, but it got her to England, where she launched her collaboration with the ATA.

"She was a woman who wanted to make something happen all the time, and she knew the very people to make it all possible," Ann Wood said. "She always did have that uncanny ability to envision where she wanted to be and then get there. There was something absolutely magical about her."

Part of that magic was to curate exactly what the public saw—and what it didn't.

JACKIE WAS SECURE enough to develop a fondness for the women under her command who were intelligent, sure of themselves, and, above all, interesting. On July 20, she hosted a dinner with some high-level military connections, including an American general and Gladys d'Erlanger, the wife of the head of the ATA. That man about town, Major Peter Beasley, naturally made the list, because he now served as Jackie's ongoing informal advisor for promoting her plan for the U.S. women's ferry service. Among the pilots, Jackie selected Ann Wood along with Virginia Farr, likely chosen for her social position, and Dorothy Furey, who despite her lack of formal education could enliven her end of the dinner table with her glamorous appearance and self-taught intellect. In England, Dorothy's aloof, imperious demeanor helped create an impression of rank wherever she went, although it won her few friends among the pilots.

Ann Wood, on the other hand, appreciated Dorothy as one of the pilots who took an interest in books, theater, and higher culture. Most guests left early, but they stayed on, chatting with Jackie until midnight. It was a rare display of camaraderie by Dorothy, who rarely palled around with other women. The subject of matrimony came up, as Dorothy had gone ahead with her marriage to Richard Bragg, the British pilot she'd met in Montreal. Their ceremony took place on June 8 at the registry office in his hometown of Nuthall in Nottinghamshire. His parents attended, but none of her colleagues from the ATA did. While Ann hadn't known Dorothy then, she commented in her diary when she heard about it. "Some speed," she noted dryly. "Hope it's the real thing."

It wasn't. Less than two months in, Dorothy already seemed to regard Bragg as her first husband. She made no pretext about loving him. The newlyweds rarely saw each other, because Bragg was now performing one of the RAF's most life-threatening jobs, piloting a heavy four-engine Halifax bomber on night missions over Europe. On the home front, Dorothy continued to attract queues of suitors, not bothering to discourage them. She was ambitious, and she didn't need Jackie Cochran's example to know that at a time when few professions were open to women, aligning oneself with the right man offered the best shot at an elevated destiny.

Those two shared many similarities—childhoods scarred by poverty, poor education, and sexual predation from men, followed by trying to pass as adults from more privileged strata. But perhaps those very similarities kept them at a wary distance. Dorothy, who was rarely kind to other women, didn't mind telling anyone that she thought Jackie "had the face of a dog." For Jackie's part, she thought Dorothy's love affairs hurt the image of her girls, and she likely resented Dorothy's blasé attitude toward flying. But most of all, each probably found it harder to keep her secrets while in the company of someone with the expertise to spot the truth.

The following morning, Dorothy and Ann toured the ornate Catholic Brompton Oratory before they joined some of the other pilots at a packed restaurant for lunch. Jackie marred the occasion when she made a scene over a forty-minute wait for a table. The fuss was typical of Jackie. "She wanted to cause a riot," said Ann. "She loved it. She just did it."

It pained Ann to witness Jackie's missteps in England. "She felt inferior to the British, and she'd pick fights that were silly sometimes." Ann said later. She and Dorothy both felt that Jackie's objection to the ATA's nude physicals was a prudish overreaction. For Jackie, who had faced her share of sexual assailants, the medical officer's request was deeply offensive, while Dorothy, who had experienced her own sexual assaults, and the self-assured Ann shrugged it off. "If he wants you to strip, strip," Ann said. "I can handle it from there."

It was beginning to appear that the drama surrounding Jackie Cochran would be moving to the United States soon anyway, as her political maneuvers with the air force paid off. Ann told her diary after their late-night chat, "I gathered that this American setup would come off, and it was just a matter of time." By then, she thought, the Americans in the ATA could surely take care of themselves.

CHAPTER 10

The Legendary Spitfire

July–August 1942
Maidenhead, Berkshire

T he first three shiploads of Jackie's charges had progressed enough in mid-July to be sent simultaneously to the ferrying unit at White Waltham Aerodrome in Maidenhead. This was bound to spark both friendships and rivalries. It was not surprising that a band of strong-willed personalities, all of them gunning to establish careers in aviation, would tussle for dominance at the airfield. They sparred to be the first to conquer new aircraft, and it wasn't always pretty.

ATA pilots could be posted to any one of fourteen aerodromes (called "ferry pools") throughout the country, but newcomers usually started at White Waltham. The Americans converged there in July because the first group, including Winnie Pierce and Virginia Farr, had started ferry duties for Class 2 aircraft, while more recent arrivals, like Hazel Raines and Ann Wood, were beginning deliveries on Class 1. On any given day, the ATA might ferry as many as five hundred aircraft from the various pools.

Hazel Raines's first day of ferrying was typical. The petite Georgia pilot assembled with others in the break room at nine in the morning. By nine thirty, she received a chit spelling out her assignment for the day—two lightweight, open-cockpit Tiger Moths, the simplest category of aircraft. Hazel dashed off to collect her flying suit and parachute from a locker. She stopped at the meteorology office, known as "the Met," to assess the weather. Finally, she popped into the maps and signals for a heads-up about obstacles like barrage balloons bobbing along her routes and maps she would need to find the way. She heard her name called over the public address system, which everyone called the blower. Hazel ran to a waiting taxi plane, tossed her gear inside, and almost fell in after it.

She took a moment to appreciate the unusual circumstance. There were seven other pilots seated in the back—all women. She glanced up front to the pilot's seat—*my goodness, another woman.* Hazel grinned. "It was quite an odd scene for me," as she later described it. "Eight females starting off on a day's work and no men to worry about." Twenty minutes later, she circled the aerodrome where she would collect her first ship, newly assembled at a factory. After putting on her flying suit and chute, she crawled aboard, feeling "terribly important."

The aircraft put her in her place. Its rudder bars were so far from her size-four feet that she couldn't reach the pedals. She lay down on her back, her full five-foot frame completely prone. She stretched out her toes and poked her head up just enough to manage the takeoff. Once airborne, Hazel spotted her first checkpoint and settled back for the thirty-minute flight. Halfway in, she twisted her head up and checked again: twelve miles off course. After some more contortions, Hazel corrected her trajectory and brought the plane down only forty minutes late.

Later she learned that other short pilots hiked themselves up by bringing their own pillows or sitting on their parachutes. Following her second delivery, a taxi plane scooped Hazel up, and she was home by five. Pilots weren't always so fortunate at the end of the day. If weather interfered, they could be caught out at a distant aerodrome and forced to scrounge for a place to stay, often in a local pub.

THE RESORT TOWN of Maidenhead showed at its best in the summer, with a riot of flowers and crowds of fashionable tourists. They filled the narrow river with boats and packed the pubs and restaurants with revelry, never minding a war in full bloom. By mid-July, the American pilots created their own hive of activity as they crossed paths at work and play. Old cliques solidified and new ones formed. Ann Wood went to work, applying her class-president energy to creating some cohesion among them.

On the first weekend after all the Americans rolled into town, she joined Virginia Farr, Hazel Jane Raines, and a couple of the other more serious-minded pilots for a traditional Maidenhead outing, a low-speed two-hour boat ride up the Thames. They observed picnickers along the banks and ogled the Astor estate that presided over the landscape from a high promontory. The pilots repaired to Virginia Farr's billet for evening drinks and conversation. She had scored a private cottage along the banks of the Thames, where she could boat and fish in privacy during her free time.

With a different mix of women now combined at Maidenhead, Virginia finally had an opening to make some friends and escape the ill will of the pilots who arrived with her. "I gather she has been the outcast of the first group," wrote Ann, who sometimes walked along the river with Virginia. "So she is more than glad to see us and generally pal around with us. [I] gather that cliques are definite—sort of a boarding school idea, which is a tragedy."

Most gravitated toward one of two camps. There were the low-key pilots like Virginia and Hazel who indulged in friendly gatherings and cultural excursions when they weren't in the air. The party girls—including Winnie Pierce, Helen Richey, Louise Schuurman, and Suzanne Ford—carried on love affairs and late-night carousing with the same gusto they applied to flight. Ann tried her best to blend with both and overlook the frictions. "You would think at our age," she wrote, "they could be avoided."

The divide extended to the aerodrome, where pilots angled for shots at the most powerful aircraft, never sure how the instructors decided who would advance or when. "The atmosphere is really hysterical as Sue & Hazel rush madly to beat one another to the Hurricanes," Ann Wood wrote. "I wonder if it is worth it."

Those two were friendly about it, but Winnie didn't always feel that way. "More American girls began to arrive," she remembered about that summer. "All were antagonistic to each other and tried to compete, which made their delivery of aircraft records very high, but friendships low."

She rooted for her closest pals but allowed the competition to feed hostility toward anyone else. That went double for the pilot who emerged as the leading contender, Winnie's archrival—the careful, focused and determined Virginia Farr.

From the time of their voyage to England, Winnie had disparaged what she considered Virginia's "mannish" ways and laughed about her estrangement from the man-crazy social life of Winnie's clique. Jackie Cochran had learned that she couldn't invite the two of them to her home together or the air would be thick with spite. Winnie considered herself someone who flew with panache, while Virginia, Winnie wrote, "was slow and pedantic over technicalities, had no imagination." It galled her that Virginia, only twenty-three, was chosen in June along with the vastly more experienced Helen Richey to fly the first Hurricanes. In early July Winnie thought she had proved her own mettle by pulling off the extraordinary save when her Hurricane engine failed on takeoff, and she tried to gain a further advantage while pursuing her latest romantic interest, the commanding officer of White Waltham. As he escorted Winnie home after some beers, she pushed him to speed the advancement of her crowd. "He is going to fix Helen and Dutch and me on our final reports," Winnie wrote in her diary. She added, "To hell with Farr."

Virginia Farr didn't need a finger on the scale. Only days later, she was poised to retake the lead. She and Helen were chosen again to take first crack at a fighter they'd all been waiting for—the legendary Spitfire.

The unflappable Virginia was flying from strength to strength. And the volatile Winnie couldn't bear the thought that the woman she had mocked since the beginning of this adventure could be first to conquer Spitfires, the fighters that stirred envy in flyers around the world.

THE ATA HAD first allowed British women take the controls of Spitfires in October 1941, and a love affair was born. "Gosh, it felt like someone had kicked me in the rear end and the next thing I knew I was at a thousand feet!" the English pilot Freydis Sharland once said.

If the nifty single-seater captivated British citizens who felt it saved them from defeat in the Battle of Britain, it held a more intimate place in the hearts of women pilots. Its graceful, tapered form complemented a woman's physique. Tucked into a cockpit barely wider than her shoulders, feeling the deep thrum of the powerful engine, she could make the aircraft respond to the lightest touch. Jackie Sorour described her first Spit encounter with near-erotic ecstasy, writing that she "felt exhilarated by the eager, sensitive response. Singing with joy and relief, I dived and climbed and spiraled round the broken clouds, before turning on to course."

Even the all-business British pilot Lettice Curtis fell under the spell. She described the Hurricane as dogged and masculine while the Spit "was altogether more feminine, had more glamour, and threw its wheels outward in an abandoned, extrovert way."

Among the Americans, it was Helen Richey who called the Spitfire a fish in water, a sharp knife through butter. Roberta Sandoz compared flying it to riding a well-trained horse. The stylish New Yorker Suzanne Ford was one of many who said that you didn't fly a Spitfire, you wore it.

The Spit fulfilled the ultimate sense of command that drew them to flying in the first place, that feeling of freedom—freedom from gravity, freedom from the limitations of slower, bulkier planes, freedom from the mundanity of life on the ground. For most every pilot, the Spitfire felt like *her* plane. It felt like her.

The Spitfire still ranks among the sleek, modern achievements of British design, like the Aston Martin sportscar or the miniskirt. Even painted in camouflage, the Spit had style for days, but substance, too. Its thin, slim, backswept wings were not only chic, they rendered the aircraft nimble, able to dive at high speeds and execute whiplash turns. In dogfights, these capabilities allowed the aircraft to defend itself by eluding the less agile enemy Messerschmitt or attack it unawares from behind or above, zipping in close to take it by surprise, striking, and streaking away. The roar of the Rolls-Royce Merlin engine, named for a bird of prey, intimidated with a daunting, low-pitched growl that detracted from the Spitfire's delicacy even as it added to the sensation of menace.

The fighter's maker, Supermarine Aviation Works, named the aircraft after a term of affection for the daughter of the man who ran Supermarine's parent company, Vickers-Armstrongs. Like everything else about the plane, the name was a flattering fit. In the popular culture of the time, the term "spitfire" had taken on the connotation of a feisty female. Katharine Hepburn starred as a mountain girl named Trigger in the 1934 pre-code movie *Spitfire*, and Lupe Velez played a sexier, hotheaded *Mexican Spitfire* in 1940.

The Spitfire Mark IX, probably the most common model flown by the Americans in the ATA, went into service from the fall of 1941 through 1944, although other models progressed through 1954. The cockpit sat well back on the Mark IX's thirty-one-foot fuselage, and the wings spanned nearly thirty-seven feet. With only a single propeller, the ship could whip along at 408 miles per hour at 25,000 feet, thanks to horsepower that surged from 1,475 to 1,650. Some wartime Spits, diving from on high, approached the speed of sound.

Despite its feminine flair, the Spitfire remained a consummate weapon of war, typically armed with a row of Browning machine guns and two Hispano cannons, "raining revenge from the wings of a fighter that really did spit fire," according to a lyrical history of the aircraft.

The Hurricane was the Spitfire's predecessor by a year or so. The earlier fighter, developed in the mid-1930s, continued to serve throughout the war and had its advocates, too. They noted that the record in combat for the two aircraft was nearly equal, and the Hurricane performed better against bombers. The Hurricane was fast, if not quite as fast. A simpler design made it cheaper to manufacture. But for the fickle pilots, always seeking the next thrill, the Hurricane didn't pack the same sensual punch. Steady, reliable performance was no match for Spitfire pizzazz.

VIRGINIA FARR COULDN'T help but notice the chief drawback of the Spitfire on her first assignment to ferry one to an RAF maintenance unit late in July. The Spit was like Virginia's friend Hazel Raines, graceful in the air and awkward on the ground. It was tough to taxi. The nose poked up so high when earthbound that the pilot, no matter how tall, had to zigzag her head from left to right to see the runway through the side windows of the canopy. But once Virginia got it underway, the speed kicked in, the Spitfire leveled off, and she felt that unmistakable acceleration, that avid response to her every move, almost as if it anticipated her intentions. The flight went like a charm.

Veteran Helen Richey, on the other hand, stumbled on her first foray in a Spitfire, just as she had on her first Hurricane flight one month before. Rattled at landing without any previous experience in the Spit, Helen touched down too far along the runway. She ran off the end, banged into various obstructions, and piled the plane into a ditch. Helen walked away unscratched, but she'd violated one of the cardinal tenets of the ATA: Don't Break the Plane.

It was rough going when she was summoned to explain the damage before the fearsome ATA Accident Committee that investigated all crashes and assigned blame, which could range from a defect in the aircraft to pilot error. The findings went into each pilot's personnel record. Some flyers got the sack after a couple of negative rulings, while others continued as before, oppressed by the feeling they were operating under a cloud.

The committee wasn't there to hold a pilot's hand or reassure a jumpy beginner. Probing Helen's Spitfire mishap, the members showed no mercy, lighting into her for cracking the plane despite her years of experience. Then they hit her with questions.

"Where was your judgment?"

"Why didn't you go around again when you saw you were overshooting?"

The damning verdict marred Helen's record for the second time: "Bad airmanship." "Aircraft overshot and hit various objects." "*Pilot held responsible.*" Helen was crushed. Winnie and her other friends offered support, but the ruling couldn't help but dent Helen's hotshot reputation.

Winnie got her own chance at a Spitfire nine days after Virginia and Helen. She delivered the fighter without incident, and doubled down the next day with different versions of the aircraft. "Had two myself—a Mark V and a Mark IX—and they were hot." But a week after that, she couldn't resist spiking the ball when she tried her first Defiant, an earlier-generation fighter. Coming in low to White Waltham, she buzzed her billet in Maidenhead to give a noisy thrill to the children of her hostess—strictly against the rules.

Winnie's incorrigible flying may have been cocky, but her friend Louise's Spitfire debut was worse. She put on an embarrassing display after a late night at the Plough, collapsing the landing gear and crumpling the plane to the ground when all she was doing was taxiing. The Accident Committee was not pleased, deciding that she had activated the undercarriage control by mistake. "Error of judgment on the part of the pilot, who IS responsible."

Meanwhile, rock-solid Virginia Farr shrugged off the crowd that resented her and earned nothing but accolades. She didn't crow about her ATA achievements, once describing her work as "flying anything and everything of two motors or less, and trying desperately to keep them all in one piece." But reports on her progress that summer told a different story. Most written evaluations of ATA pilots stuck to the basics—brief, unremarkable, and almost comically reserved in the best British tradition. If a pilot performed her duties without a hitch, her supervising officer would throw her a bone and note, "pilot of average ability." But Virginia Farr won uncommon raves as she wrapped up her stint in Class 2 fighters by mid-August. "An above average pilot," the report said. Virginia, it continued, "is recommended for conversion to Classes 3 and 4 having quickly completed all her Training Pool work exceptionally well. A keen and hardworking pilot who will make a good officer." A triumph, in other words.

Virginia didn't make a show of besting her colleagues, but her performance served notice that the supposedly flighty Americans might have some serious chops. Even Britain's Lettice Curtis, known for treating them all like an unwanted smell, began to come around. The U.S. women, she later wrote, were "for the most part, happy to take the ATA as it was—to accept the rather uncomfortable conditions of wartime living in Britain." She even conceded, "Amongst them were some of the best women pilots in the ATA."

The organization's flyers generally ferried Class 1 and 2 aircraft for weeks or months—or even years—before moving on to the heftier two-engine aircraft of Class 3 and the even larger two-engine bombers of Class 4. With Virginia's strong evaluation, she was cleared to skip the customary interval and jump the line. This inspired particular envy among the others, because two-engine planes most closely resembled the commercial passenger aircraft that might provide job opportunities in peacetime. On completion of the training, Virginia would wear the two wide gold stripes on her uniform that signaled her status as a first officer, a rank many never achieved.

Second Officer Winnabelle Pierce steamed. "Farr is doing Class 3 and 4, and we are mad."

WOMEN FROM THE second and third ships were coming up fast from behind on Hurricanes. The dreaded Accident Committee had actually given another Helen, the Canadian Helen Harrison, a roommate of Ann Wood's from the third ship, a rare official commendation back in June for her handling of a nasty episode in a Miles Magister with a bad carburetor. When it failed in the air, Helen had kept her head and successfully force-landed on the small sloping field of a farm. She walked to the farmhouse to call into headquarters, tied the plane down safely in the grass, told the farmer to keep an eye on it, and took the train back to Luton. The aircraft had to be dismantled to be recovered from the tiny field.

But Helen's first performance in a Hurricane toward the end of the summer once again demonstrated that one day's victory in the ATA offered no guarantee of another. On the flight check before takeoff, she found that the flaps on her Hurricane wouldn't go down.

"No problem," said a mechanic on the scene. He gave the flaps a good kick, and they fell into place.

Helen made an uneventful flight until she circled the field at her destination to choose one of two runways for landing. She lowered the gear and pulled a lever to lower the flaps. Nothing doing.

Well, I'll just have to come in a little faster, Helen determined. She headed down as best she could for a flaps-up approach.

Racing toward the field and realizing how fast she was traveling, Helen looked down to try the flaps again. Still no luck. When she looked back up, the runway was *right there*—no time to change course. She hit the ground hot, but managed to pull off "a real greaser," a smooth touchdown with the wheels hitting first and the nose gently following.

She was pleased with herself until she saw that she was still zooming—and running out of runway fast. It seemed she had wound up on the wrong one, too short for a making a stop even at normal speed. Thinking fast, Helen turned onto the grass. It slowed her down, but she hit a muddy patch and flipped the Hurricane up on its nose.

"To say I was mortified was to put it mildly," Helen acknowledged afterward. "Broken prop, horn blowing, etc."

Unsparing, the Accident Committee called Second Officer Harrison on the mat.

"Miss Harrison, I would think with your experience you would have known what to do," the committee chairman began. "What is it, two thousand hours?"

Helen kept her chin up and defended herself without any "yes-sir, no-sir" deference. "*Of course*," she said, "I knew what I should have done. *Of course* I should have chosen the correct runway. *Of course* I'm sorry."

The committee wasn't having it. "Endeavored to make flaps-up landing but approached too fast on wrong runway." This was only the first negative report for Helen Harrison, but it ended with the words no one wanted to hear. "Pilot TO BLAME."

CHAPTER 11

Playing Chicken with a Violent End

August 1942
Luton, Bedfordshire
June 1942
White Waltham, England

WHhile the pilots from the first three ships mixed it up in fighters, six more who joined the women's ATA roster in June played catch-up in early training at Luton. Sent over on the fourth of the six ships that transported the Americans, the women were mostly younger and less experienced than Jackie Cochran's first selections, yet they managed to make their own splash. That was especially true for one the youngest Americans, Mary Zerbel, who captured the public imagination in Britain before the summer was out.

Mary was only twenty-one, but she had attracted outsized attention much of her life. She didn't make headlines as an air show performer as some of her colleagues did, nor was she a member of high society as others were, yet countless newspaper articles had covered her progress as the country's youngest woman flight instructor, an exceptionally outspoken and pretty one.

The shy, insecure daughter of a movie theater manager in Iron City, Michigan, Mary had felt overlooked in her childhood. "What irony then," she wrote later, "that fate led me into the most exciting, glamorous, romantic life that anyone could wish for." She also often found herself at the center of one drama or another, acknowledging, on a darker note, that her many experiences "both enriched and tore apart my life."

As a teenager, Mary fantasized about professions that would allow her to say, as she wrote in a journal, "Look at *me*! See what I've done! I'm a *real* person." A relative pointed out, "She wanted to excel, to do something better than anyone else in the world." Mary settled on three possibilities, all out of reach to most women at the time: pilot, brain surgeon, or movie actress. Unlike most little girls with heady dreams, she made a stab at all three. Mary moved to a cousin's home in Los Angeles to enroll in UCLA for a premed degree, then quit to study acting in Hollywood. Flying won out when she joined a Civilian Pilot Training Program.

Once Mary began to fly, newspapers ran her photograph whenever they had a chance, over captions like "Angel Seeks Wings" and "These Women! What will They Get Into Next?" She became well known for the achievement of becoming a flight instructor at the age of nineteen and running up more than seven hundred hours ferrying planes and teaching. The camera loved her dark, gently wavy hair, clipped back at cheekbone level to show off a pale, heart-shaped face. Long lashes framed her light green eyes. At nearly five feet seven, she had the slender figure of Norma Shearer—"slim, but not too slim," as the Associated Press described her. Mary could even make a flying suit look chic. It was easy to speculate that whether or not she had the talent, she had the looks to follow the path of her acting classmate Veronica Lake. After the war, Lana Turner would play Mary in a film about her life, *The Lady Takes a Flyer*.

Fame built on fame. Eventually, reporters trailed along with the photographers, and stories appeared presenting Mary's views on flying, womanhood, and careers for women. She expressed herself with florid emotion. "One short venture above the earth," she said about flying, "one brief interlude of separation from our everyday material world—and your heart is lost forever to today's greatest adventure." The accompanying picture showed her standing high on a fuselage in a short skirt and espadrilles.

In these articles, she didn't say much to advocate for professional opportunities for women. They "were more likely to go to pieces in an emergency," she claimed. Her greatest ambition, she said, was to marry and have five children. Yet she never hesitated to critique the U.S. military for banning women pilots. "They won't let us fly in the States," she told a reporter. "They will in England, so we didn't want to pass this up. It's the chance of a lifetime, and we're taking it."

Mary Zerbel shared a youthful idealism with her sweetheart from flying school, Wes Hooper, a tall, gangly blond with an animated Adam's apple. The U.S. Army Air Forces had turned him away at eighteen because he was too young, but he was still eager to fight for democracy before his country entered the European war. He joined some 244 men in what was known as the Eagle Squadron, made up of Americans who volunteered for the RAF. Before signing on, he had earned only a private pilot's license and logged only 125 hours in the air, a fraction of his girlfriend's experience and less than half the minimum hours for American women who joined the ATA. Yet beginning in August 1941, Wes piloted a two-engine Lockheed Hudson bomber that attacked submarines in the North Sea for the RAF Coastal Command. When he heard that the ATA accepted women, he wrote to Mary suggesting she join up and marry him before the end of the conflict. She would test the premise that a young woman could succeed in dangerous war work without sacrificing marriage.

Mary was just learning Class 1 Magisters and Tiger Moths in Luton when the couple realized that August 17, 1942, would mark their first simultaneous leave. They planned a quiet wedding at the medieval stone Luton Parish Church, attended only by her landlady, who gave the bride away, and Una Goodman, Mary's roommate from the trip over, designated as "best man." Instead, they made news around the world when her landlady's sister tipped off the London press. It went crazy for the story of the first American servicepeople to wed in England. News outlets in America, including the *New York Times*, the *Chicago Sun*, and Associated Press, jumped on the story of young love in wartime. The groom on that day was nineteen, too young to legally marry without written permission from his parents. Mary was twenty-one.

Reporters lavished description on Wes's navy RAF uniform and Mary's knee-length yellow wool dress and black coat. They commented on the time of the service—eight thirty in the morning, because Una had to report for flying later. They mentioned that the acclaimed Jacqueline Cochran drove the couple to the Savoy in London after a wedding breakfast. Wes, puffing out his chest like a guy who had picked a Derby winner, told the journalists that his wife "is just as good a pilot as he is." Tabloids tried to stir up controversy by headlining the fact that Mary omitted "obey" from her vows. Photos captured the newlyweds' shy, hopeful smiles.

Mary had saved up canned orange juice that she'd brought from home as a treat for their honeymoon, a week of compassionate leave spent in the Lake District. They bicycled, visited Wordsworth's grave, and picnicked alongside impassive grazing cows next to a running brook. Mary sent her parents a Western Union telegram: MARRIED LIFE IS SUPER COLOSSAL. ALL OUR LOVE. MARY AND WES HOOPER.

UNTIL THEN, MARY's husband had been an oddity as an American man in the military in the United Kingdom, but suddenly they were everywhere, much to the delight of some of the ATA women. In the spring of 1942, Brigadier General Ira C. Eaker had set up shop in a requisitioned country mansion in High Wycombe, Buckinghamshire, near RAF Bomber Command headquarters, to lay the groundwork. Only five men accompanied him, including Jackie Cochran's ally, the logistical expert Peter Beasley. By summer, troop carriers were disgorging waves of servicemen, "oversexed, overpaid, and over here," as the British liked to say. A few women turned up, too, as part of the Red Cross and the Women's Army Corps. These were among the first of more than two million Americans who would serve in the United Kingdom during the war, half a million of them in the air force at its peak. They transformed the country with their sheer numbers. Ground troops wouldn't see action for a while, and the Eighth Air Force under General Eaker wouldn't begin intensive bombing until 1943, but the tsunami of arrivals threw its energy into a vast mobilization. The British initially allotted fifteen air bases to the Americans. They performed a few isolated missions, but the learning curve was steep. On a first joint bombing raid with the RAF over enemy-occupied territory in Holland, launched symbolically on July 4, 1942, only two of twenty-six bombers reached the targets.

The men were elated when American ATA women started swinging into bases that August. At RAF fields, the women flyers were no longer considered out of the ordinary. But they knew things had changed when their first appearance at Aldermaston, an RAF airfield that converted over to the U.S. in that month, brought forth a fanfare of whistles.

"Flying is quite gay now as we jazz over to Aldermaston and beat the place up," Ann Wood practically chuckled in her diary. "All the boys come running, and if you land, a jeep comes to meet you."

The servicemen paid return joyrides to White Waltham, often stopping in at a new American Club near the river in Maidenhead, complete with a swimming pool. Some American boys landed in a DC-3, a passenger plane converted for transport in the war, to show it off to the ladies. The men came supplied with chocolate and other goodies. "Took us flying (by way of wasting petrol) and zoomed their aerodrome," according to Ann. "It was fun, but felt guilty about the petrol." There were fun and games aplenty for a carefree interlude, before they all settled down to the business of war.

The women pilots who had been missing their countrymen now only had to drop by the American Club to find them. When a U.S. colonel stopped in one night, Suzanne Ford won the skirmish to land the prize, according to Ann. "Amused myself watching Sue go to town on him and how he capitulated," Ann wrote. "Sue isn't even subtle, but such is life." Ann marveled at her colleagues' stamina. "It will forever be a mystery to me how they can burn the candle at both ends and get away with it—much less enjoy their debaucheries," Ann mused, "but the more I see of the ATA the more I realize that that is common practice."

NOT EVERYONE COULD maintain the pace. Ten days after Mary Zerbel's wedding, the "best man," Una Goodman, ground-looped on a landing, one wing of a biplane flipping too high while the other struck the ground. The Accident Committee was damning: "Faulty airmanship." Worse, her instructor weighed in, saying that the thirty-nine-year-old aviator was "unlikely to become an efficient ferry pilot." Six days later, in early September, the ATA fired her, the first American woman to be sacked for subpar flying. The action confirmed the jitters of those who had already received one or two negative accident reports as the fear of dismissal hung over their work. Meanwhile, in August, the service had already discharged Polly Potter, a former shipmate of Ann Wood, for eyesight that wasn't up to standard. She was the second American to wash out after Jackie Cochran. Una was third, and a fourth soon followed. Virginia Garst from the second shipment wound up in the hospital with appendicitis. When she didn't recover quickly, the ATA terminated her contract, too. The group of twenty-five was already down by four.

As Ann often said of service in the ATA, "It's a great life if you don't weaken."

THERE WERE WORSE fates, of course, than leaving the ATA in one piece, as the flyers were too often reminded. During the summer, a student was killed after his engine failed on takeoff, and a popular teacher on board suffered serious wounds. The pilot had followed protocol by trying to glide forward when the engine stopped, but when trees loomed, he stalled and flipped over. "It takes just such a thing to pull us up by our bootstraps and make us wonder if we're next," Ann Wood commented in her diary.

The usual toll of fatal crashes reached a peak when the weather turned in September. Four pilots died during the single week of September 12. They included one of the more unusual foreign volunteers to the ATA, Prince Suprabhat Chirasakti of Siam. He flew a Hurricane into a hill in Scottish fog. The Accident Committee, unsparing even of the dead, concluded that the prince had "persisted too far into hilly country in bad weather, contrary to orders." Others who died that week were well known to the pilots based at the White Waltham pool. "No more 'Hiya Toots,'" Winnie Pierce noted in her diary about Captain Donald Kennard, a founding member of the ATA. "I prayed all day and thought of life and how near at hand death is at all times." By now, Ann Wood had adopted a more guarded perspective, writing dryly, "It had a rather odd effect on people in pool in general." Then she spilled a bottle of ink on the carpet in her room. Accidents happened.

WHEN TRAGEDY STRUCK among the Americans, it came from an unexpected quarter. Mary Zerbel Hooper often took a train to Scotland on her days off to visit her new husband. Otherwise, they got on with their work. For someone so young, his job was remarkably responsible—piloting a sizable two-engine aircraft to bomb and machine-gun German submarines that preyed on shipping lanes. Now that his home country had entered the war, Wes filled out paperwork to shift from the RAF Coastal Command to the U.S. Army Air Force. Marriage didn't dim the couple's zeal to serve. "Right now, I want to be as close to the front lines as possible," Mary once told a reporter.

On the two-month anniversary of their wedding, Wes and the crew of his Hudson bomber took off on a routine reconnaissance flight from the Shetland Islands, the remote northern region of Scotland, surrounded by an inky, subarctic sea. For two days, Mary had no idea that anything was amiss. On October 19, she spent the daylight hours training on a Harvard for advancement to fighter planes. She returned to the White Waltham aerodrome to find a brief telegram from the leader of Wes's squadron: DEEPLY REGRET TO INFORM YOU THAT YOUR HUSBAND P/O R W HOOPER REPORTED MISSING ON OPERATIONAL DUTIES 17/10/42. PLEASE ACCEPT MY PROFOUND SYMPATHY.

It was a message so cryptic, so lacking in detail, that at first the full import escaped her. Once it registered, Mary wanted to scream into the night. She wrote to the group captain of Wes's unit, begging for the full story. He sent a letter telling what he knew, but asked that she keep the contents secret.

Wes and the Hudson's crew of five had failed to return from patrol by the afternoon of October 17, the letter said. The base received no signal from the aircraft. Coastal Command launched a search by air and sea over the next two days, but no trace appeared over an expanse of unusually calm water. Just before dark the first night, a pilot thought he spotted a flashing light on the surface, and a high-speed launch raced to the area. Nothing. "It can only be presumed that the aircraft crashed into the sea and sank immediately," the commanding officer reported to Mary.

He went on to lay out some theories. Enemy patrols, known to be in the area, could have shot the aircraft out of the sky. Or the Hudson might have attacked a U-boat that fired back. Or the aircraft might have sustained damage by dropping bombs from too low an altitude, so that a blast blew back and brought the plane down. Less likely, a rare simultaneous failure of both engines might have hobbled the Hudson before it could signal for help. Least likely of all, Wes could have wound up as a prisoner of war. There was one rare precedent. The year before, a German submarine had picked up the lone survivor from a crash in the area. If Wes had been captured, Mary might receive notice after four to six weeks. "But I can only offer a very slender hope of that being the case," the letter concluded. Mary was a romantic at heart, but logic dictated that her idealistic young husband was lost forever beneath the shifting surface of the northern sea.

TO BECOME A widow at the age of twenty-two was to exist outside the natural order of the human timeline. To become only a *probable* widow, without so much as the recognition granted by a funeral, added more profoundly to the dislocation. While Mary's colleagues packed the pubs, clubs, and dance floors each night in search of connection and release from the oppression of constant danger, Mary resided in a torturous limbo for which there was no relief. Her very presence in the waiting room at the aerodrome served as a living memento mori, a grim reminder that everyone in the flying game was playing chicken with a violent end. Almost as if her condition could be contagious, her colleagues offered sympathy but kept their distance, while Mary kept to herself. A likely widow, much too young—she found no comfort in the knowledge that such aberrations were becoming commonplace throughout the world.

Only the examples of other widows of the lost or dead suggested a path forward. Many ATA pilots kept their heads down, continuing their jobs with stoic resignation as friends, husbands, lovers, and brothers disappeared. And so did Mary. Two days after she received the telegram, she moved up a rung in training from the Harvard to the Miles Master, performing circuits and bumps, circuits and bumps, hour after hour. Five days later, she soloed in her first Hurricane. Commander Pauline Gower advised her to "keep busy as long as necessary." Another one of the Americans in training, Peggy Lennox, weighed in at the airfield: "Keep your chin up, Baby." The trace of warmth was too much. Mary lost her composure and ran to the privacy of the ladies' room.

She took a few days off at the new Red Cross Club in London, which offered Americans on leave a place to stay along with the added comforts of Coca-Colas and hamburgers. Surrounded by revelers, Mary rested and reminded herself that what she still had left—the structure she needed—was meaningful work. She returned to base and took to the air again with oddly steady nerves, weighted now by hard reality.

CHAPTER 12

Coming and Going

August 30, 1942
London

———

T he last of the American women made it to England only days before
a farewell party for Jackie Cochran. The final two ships brought
another six pilots in August 1942, with four of them reaching Liverpool
on the thirtieth. That would bring the total of Jackie's recruits to twenty-
five, although only twenty-one would be left after her departure. The
newest additions would have to make their way on their own merits,
free from the hubbub and baggage that Jackie brought to the corps,
which might have been just as well. The rapid advancement of pilots like
Virginia Farr, Winnie Pierce, and Hazel Raines was already helping
the Americans establish a reputation for aerial competence that balanced
some of the sketchy first impressions they had made. The newcomers
came on the scene with a cleaner slate.

Most of Jackie's charges rallied the night of the farewell party to pay
tribute to their polarizing leader at the Grosvenor Hotel. She planned to
head home a few weeks later to fulfill the goal of starting a women's ferry
service there. The decision was her own—the British hadn't asked her to
leave—but it was one of many reminders that nothing was certain for

long: not in the air, not in the war, and certainly not in the bumpy domain of the Anything To Anywhere service.

Whatever their tangled feelings about Jackie, most of the pilots were fond of her. Ann Wood, naturally, had organized the event for the woman she affectionately labeled the Blonde Bomber. Jackie announced that Helen Richey would take over as the American leader, keeping informal tabs on the others, although it was already clear that the title was mostly hollow, and Helen had no real duties to perform. The women were now all mixed up in the war together with everyone else in the ATA.

Jackie Cochran's final exit from England happened precipitously and not at all as she had planned. Despite her campaign from afar and General Arnold's promise that he would place her in charge of a women's ferrying service when it finally formed, Jackie was blindsided by scuttlebutt that someone else had beaten her to the job. Nancy Love, a ladylike twenty-eight-year-old with society roots, had run an aviation company with her husband until they both signed on to positions at U.S. Ferry Command. Nancy worked her way into an office job where she organized her own concept of a program for women to pilot aircraft from factories to air bases within the borders of the United States. On September 10, 1942, General Arnold made an announcement to the press: Nancy Love would head a new women's auxiliary of the Air Transport Command.

Woe be to anyone who stood between Jackie Cochran and her ambition. She boarded a plane immediately and made landfall the next day, hitting General Arnold's office with hurricane force. Five days later, a revised, awkward dual-leadership plan was announced. Nancy Love would run the ferry operation, and Jacqueline Cochran would recruit and train the pilots. The following year, these units would combine under the title of the Women Airforce Service Pilots, otherwise known as the WASP.

When the American flyers in Britain reached the end of their eighteen-month ATA contracts, they would face a decision. They could rejoin Jackie and serve in the WASP's more limited domestic service for women only, living in barracks within the security of the United States. Or they could stay within the freewheeling organization at the center of the action in Britain, the ATA. For most of these women, it was no contest. The more adventurous choice held more appeal.

But regardless of whether they might later want to join the WASP, they were alert to how much their own futures would ride on its success or failure. If the ferrying service ultimately integrated into the regular armed forces, which was by no means certain, the ATA pilots might someday join other women as military pilots in their home country. And if the WASP convinced the American people that women could excel in the air, it would also make all the difference in the private flying opportunities that emerged after the war. From thousands of miles away, the Atta-Girls saw their own careers at stake. They would keep a sharp eye on Jackie's progress and root hard for her to pull it off.

BEGINNER FLYING SCHOOL in Luton ran late the day of the farewell party, but the relatively new recruit Nancy Miller had resolved to attend. She already felt behind the curve, having arrived on the fifth ship at the beginning of August while others were already piloting Spitfires. Now she had missed the last bus to London and caught a train to town. Only twenty-three, Nancy wasn't a seasoned traveler. When she disembarked at St. Pancras terminus, she stumbled into a bewildering blackout, her first, that coincided with a visitation of London's signature dense and sooty fog. Creeping along toward the street, Nancy found that her flashlight was useless, the beam unable to penetrate the wall of grungy murk. She followed someone else's torch until it disappeared. Weirdly detached from any sense of place, "no shape or form to anything," she persevered.

"Scuse me, scuse me," Nancy pleaded again and again as she bumped into apparitions and tripped on curbs. Finally she simply stopped, an island in the fog, until a stranger offered to lead her to a bus.

When she got off, she asked a human shape, "Do you know where the Grosvenor Hotel is?"

"It's right here," answered a disembodied voice. Nancy felt her way through the unlit entrance just as the party broke up.

Nancy Miller served as the latest illustration that women pilots willing to risk their lives in wartime aircraft displayed a wide variety of personalities. She couldn't have been more different from the hard-partying first recruits, and it was easy for them to underestimate her at first. "She was young, and she was shy in social situations," said her niece, Margaret Miller. "She always thought of herself as a loner, and she behaved like a loner." Nancy presented as a classic girl next door, with round cheeks and a cheerful personality untainted by the cynicism or world-weary sophistication that marked some her colleagues. "She was plain," her niece said. Not in the sense of her appearance. "She was plainspoken, modest. She had a couple plain outfits she would wear over and over."

Relentlessly wholesome, Nancy regarded alcohol like poison as she already pined for the ice cream sodas, baseball games, and gentler pastimes of home. Her straight-and-narrow preferences came naturally. The daughter of a well-to-do Episcopal clergyman in Los Angeles, she was the only girl in a family with two boys. They considered her the "designated daughter" who would devote her life to caring for a mother incapacitated by multiple sclerosis.

Much like others in the ATA, Nancy found her calling when she flew with a barnstormer as a treat for her sixteenth birthday. The teenager was bored until the pilot struggled with a crooked landing. As her older brother froze with fright, Nancy felt a kick of exhilaration. "Suddenly I was grabbed by a wonderful feeling of motion and wonder at the plane's steep descent," she wrote later. "I let out a whoop of joy." Her father wasn't happy about it, but he signed a permission slip for her to take lessons. Nancy left college and became an instructor with the Civilian Pilot Training Program.

She didn't have enough flying hours to make Jackie Cochran's list in 1941, but by the summer of 1942, at the age of twenty-two, she had amassed 450. Her mother had died a few months before, freeing Nancy from her obligation to provide care. When a friend at the local airfield told her about the ATA accepting women, Nancy laughed in disbelief. "Quit kidding," she said. "Girls just don't do things like that."

Once Jackie gave her the all-clear, Nancy's fiancé forbade her to join. She ditched the guy and hopped a train to Montreal. "I wasn't ready to settle down," Nancy recalled later. "I enjoyed my flying too much."

On its return trip, the ship that had taken Nancy to England was hit by a torpedo and sank, a fact Nancy mentioned without comment or emotion in her journal. "She wasn't a particularly imaginative or introspective person," her niece commented. "I think that worked to her advantage. She never allowed herself to be afraid."

OTHERS WHO ARRIVED in the final August shipment wished they could set their emotions aside so easily. Most of them were greener than those who preceded them, and they encountered a rockier introduction to the work. The onset of cooler, wetter weather made their initial flying more precarious, and they were isolated from those who were already performing ferry duties. Roberta Sandoz, the twenty-four-year-old from the final ship, felt awkward and out of place among her peers, and she was initially overcome by fright. Although she was outspoken and independent, she had grown up in eastern Washington State, the most remote location of all the women. She felt insecure about her limited background, referring to herself a "backwoods gal" and "country bumpkin."

Roberta had earned a spotty living doing various jobs in the air. She developed a hacking cough by crop-dusting with a wet rag over her face, and one of her more novel gigs was the fake striptease she performed in an airshow. She climbed into the open cockpit, flew above the field, and started dropping articles of clothing over the side—a hat, a chiffon dress, spike-heeled shoes, gloves, and more. A stooge on the ground picked up each item and paraded it in front of the audience with lascivious glee. When Roberta landed, she emerged to applause, fully clothed.

"I was pretty young and wild and crazy," Roberta admitted later. She acknowledged that she got off to a clumsy start with Jackie Cochran after hearing about her and writing to her cold. Roberta had only 310 flying hours, fewer than most applicants, but Jackie agreed to meet in Fresno, California, near a farming company where Roberta worked. At five feet seven—tall for that era—Roberta slouched because she felt awkward about her height. She had never worn makeup except for lipstick, but went all-out for her introduction to the cosmetics mogul, dolling up her chestnut hair and painting around her eyes with garish results. "I must have looked like a floozy," Roberta said in hindsight. In response, Jackie delivered a stern lecture about how the job would entail more hardship than glamour. Roberta figured she'd missed her chance.

But after others washed out, she got tapped for the last group. The country bumpkin carried an old copy of *TIME* magazine on the four-day train trip to Montreal, hoping to pass herself off as a serious person. She planned to whip it out if she ever saw Jackie Cochran again.

Now that she was in Great Britain, she felt even more the parochial outsider. The first morning in a hotel, she was presented with a meal under a silver dome. When it was whipped off with a flourish, Roberta was aghast at a platter of pungent, dead-eyed, oily fish, her first encounter with kippers. She suffered from painful chilblains, her feet swollen and cracked from slogging through the cold in wet shoes. Her fiancé in the navy was killed in the Pacific. A few days after Jackie's party, just before her departure, Roberta crumbled when she turned up at the intimidating aviator's apartment for dinner.

"What the blankety-blank is wrong with you?" Jackie bellowed at the door, Roberta recalled, tidying up the obscenity after the fact.

"I'm homesick," Roberta whimpered. "I'm hungry. I haven't been warm since I got here, and I'm scared to death."

Roberta couldn't hold back tears, and Jackie transformed into a model mama. "Sweetheart, come on in," she said. She made Roberta the best food she'd eaten in weeks and tucked her into a warm bed. It was one of Jackie's last acts as a world-famous Flight Captain in the ATA.

MARY WEBB NICHOLSON of the final ship was better prepared for hardship. At thirty-seven, she had enough experience to have weathered some setbacks and had learned to cope.

The others knew her best as Jackie Cochran's secretary in New York, where she had begged for release from the job to fly for the ATA herself. But her list of credits also overflowed with prewar achievements as a stunt pilot. "She had a quiet tenacity about her," said a niece. Mary was the first woman in her home state of North Carolina to earn a pilot's license in 1929, followed by a commercial license in 1933. She made it to England with more than six hundred hours in her logbook.

She had earned this moment, having carried on through hard times in the 1930s. Mary escaped an abusive marriage, and she helped support her family when her father lost his job in the Depression. None of it diminished her determination. "She definitely had a quiet strength and a sense of faith that God is at work in the world," said another relative.

Nevertheless, the first month in the ATA shook her, despite her years of solid aviation experience, as the newcomers learned to navigate in deteriorating weather. "The training was difficult for her," said a niece, "mentally and physically difficult." After a few weeks, a medical officer placed her on a short sick leave, saying Mary suffered from "reactionary exhaustion." She tapped into her hard-won resilience and pressed on afterward with the dedication than had seen her through before.

The American women had all arrived in England by the fall of 1942, only to discover that their futures were unpredictable. It took mental toughness to fly for the ATA, and an ability to adapt. Now that Jackie Cochran was gone, it seemed possible that her advocacy and homey dinners might have been helpful after all. At least her fried chicken and over-the-top tenacity had rallied the spirits of the pilots when they were down. Helen Richey, the purported new leader, was busy flying, and Ann Wood, who provided the social glue, was about to be sent away to a new aerodrome as the Americans were transferred throughout the country. They would have to roll with uncertainty until they found their way.

CHAPTER 13

The Fabled Mischief of Ratcliffe Hall

September 23, 1942
Ratcliffe, Leicestershire

A nn Wood plodded along toward her first posting away from head-quarters on September 23, 1942, in a slow-moving Stinson 105, the number indicating the aircraft's top miles per hour. Now that she was accustomed to speedy fighters, the toylike Stinson was disconcerting. "Took off with all my fear," she told her diary. "It was so slow I felt I was stalling most of the time." Terrific rain showers reared up in her path. She circled around them to find the runway, par for the course at the rainy airfield of Ratcliffe, which was tucked next to a sleepy village of the same name. She was the first American woman assigned to the base, and she didn't know what to expect. Ann had no idea yet how much this assignment would change her, as a person and as an aviator.

In the fall of 1942, the twenty-four-year-old still identified as a hesitant flyer who followed the rules. She didn't push to fly the fastest, flashiest aircraft and didn't care who tried them out ahead of her. She always turned back if the weather looked touch and go. But the Ratcliffe Ferry Pool in the East Midlands was just the environment to turn a beginner into a seasoned pilot and a skeptic into a thorough Anglophile.

Ann's introduction to the aerodrome wasn't promising. A driver whisked her straight to a billet five miles away outside the industrial city of Leicester. Her hosts, a firefighter and his family, welcomed her to a rowhouse where a van would pick her up each day for the drive to the field. They served her an appropriate ration-book supper and took her to the cinema to see an American musical. "Nelson Eddy atrocious as usual," Ann noted dryly. They pointed out her tiny room, a bath upstairs, and an alarmingly chilly loo outside. "Honestly, I believe if there is an inconvenient or difficult way of doing something, the English will think of it," Ann wrote before bed.

Her first sight of the tiny village of Ratcliffe on the Wreake the next day made an endearing if low-key impression. A few redbrick cottages sat along a narrow, winding lane that hopped over the narrow River Wreake on little humpback bridges. A fourteenth-century church and a graveyard with timeworn headstones provided the only other points of interest. The surrounding lush rolling hills supported herds of sheep and cattle, the latter doing their bit to produce the goods for Stilton cheese.

It seemed she had landed in a backwater. But just up the road from the village, Ann soon discovered the sprawling estate of Sir Lindsay Everard, a beer magnate, Conservative member of Parliament, and bon vivant who also happened to be an early aviation enthusiast. In 1933, Sir Lindsay had built a private flying club, the Ratcliffe Aerodrome, a long grass field enhanced by a swank clubhouse, outdoor swimming pool, and brick hangar that boasted a ceiling made of polished oak. There he hosted festive air pageants for celebrities like Amy Johnson until the government requisitioned the property for use by the ATA. Sir Lindsay saw no reason to dial back the joie de vivre just because there was a war on. The posting retained the atmosphere of a select private club, where he treated the members to hospitality steeped in wealth and luxury. A favorite joke among the pilots originated with an American man who trilled before dinner with a practiced feminine shudder, "If they serve that 1916 vintage champagne again, I'll scream!" The whole setup was right up Ann's alley.

Often cranky about the time spent waiting versus flying when she was posted elsewhere, Ann quickly learned that this location in south central England supplied abundant work. The latest airplanes, from bombers to fighters, swarmed the field all day. "It was a pilot's heaven," said an American man, Gen Genovese, who served there just before Ann. "And though the work was a strain at times because there was so much of it to do, there wasn't a man among us who wasn't having the time of his life." While most of the pilots were male, the same went for a small international crew of women who shared the assignment. They could predict with accuracy when and where the next raids would occur over Europe, as four or five Ratcliffe pilots would deliver the appropriate aircraft to the appropriate base, then turn around to make three or four repeat deliveries the same day. Tuning into the radio late at night provided news of the outcome.

The busiest route led to Castle Bromwich, just east of Birmingham, where a Spitfire factory turned out legions of fighters while belching industrial smoke into the already misty air. The resulting smog made the area one of the most challenging for navigation. Ratcliffe pilots learned the trick of noting the location where white and gray clouds turned to brown, treating it like a checkpoint. When visibility allowed, they followed the Fosse Way, an ancient, arrow-straight Roman road that led north and south by the aerodrome. But Ann soon learned that they also got the job done by thumbing their noses at protocol, flying unacceptably low over rail routes or relying on instrument techniques they studied on their own. A cowboy sensibility took over, with pilots letting off steam by making maximum noise "buzzing" or "shooting up" the hangers and offices, flying in slow and low, then pushing hard on the throttle while directly over the target. The idea was "to rattle the windows of the building and scare the occupants half out of their wits," wrote Genovese. His favorite aircraft for buzzing was a two-engine Mosquito. "When you open the throttle on one of those babies you have enough stuff to send shivers down the spine of a buzz fan," he explained. He once earned a two-day suspension by shattering the commanding officer's window while an air vice marshal of the RAF sat by the officer's desk, stunned and pelted with broken glass. Confronted with the gap where the window had been, Genovese quipped, "You better get that fixed, Captain. You might catch cold."

Happily, the relative isolation and clubby environment at Ratcliffe fostered rapport that overrode rank. After a few weeks, Ann entered the inner sanctum when her billet switched to the main house at Ratcliffe Hall itself. Up a long gravel drive through evergreen trees, she discovered the perks of private rooms with hot and cold running water. Ann lucked into one upstairs in the Hall, while others lined up above the twenty-five-car garage. She joined an international consortium of pilots as they strolled about the stables, mingled in the many salons, played squash at the indoor court, danced to the radiogram in the ballroom, and listened to broadcasts while warmed by what was reputed to be the largest fireplace in England.

On Ann's first night at dinner, Sir Lindsay and Lady Ione Everard presided over the meal in a dark-paneled hall ringed with oils of hunting scenes. The butler, known as Smart, oversaw such a large team of maids and one youthful footman that one would hardly know there was a servant shortage. Once she settled in, Ann sometimes popped up to help serve and clear the table, which rattled the British diners.

But she got on famously with the dignified, silver-haired Sir Lindsay, age fifty-one. He regularly hosted distinguished guests who talked with her about the affairs of the day. Ann joined him in puttering in the garden, and once, she and Sir Lindsay explored the top-notch wine cellar on a sleepy afternoon and downed a bottle of one of the better champagnes. She met his high-ranking friends, the better to buttress her list of connections. The whole setup offered exactly the kind of sophisticated adventure that made her heart race.

ANN WAS POPULAR as ever at the tony ferry pool. She liked to dance, and she savored the cosmopolitan conversation. But she didn't stand out as a pilot, not at first. Her landings, she lamented, were "not something to dream about, but then perhaps they will come." Learning a new ship, she continued, "does take all I've got, and then I don't seem to catch on as quickly as some others to new types." She didn't fly her first Spitfire until October 6, when she completed a delivery out of Castle Bromwich.

Whatever she felt about her ability, her commanding officer was impressed. "A keen and competent pilot who has satisfactorily completed her training pool work in less than average time," he wrote in an evaluation in mid-October. "She is of good discipline, conscientious, and has the makings of a really good ferry pilot."

Perhaps recognizing her hesitancy, officials at Ratcliffe assigned her early on to piloting a reliable transport plane, the Fairchild, that shuttled groups of other pilots to their assignments. It suited her sociable nature. Gradually, in her desire to be useful, she pushed her limits, because little got done in the region if pilots held out for perfect weather. "It was definitely sticky," she wrote one day, "but I chanced it to see what I could do." Risk-taking didn't come naturally to Ann: "It really takes solid concentration to navigate unless you are a native, for if you let yourself lose a minute you are apt to be a goner."

Still, Ann took more chances. Once, she launched her Fairchild into foul weather that quickly blinded her and threw her off course. She stumbled across a railway line and decided to keep it in her sights. Every time she thought of turning back, she came across one clear patch or another that lured her on until the murk closed in again. Eventually, she made it to a base on the southern coast that had washed out for the day, rather proud of herself. Another day soon after that, with "visibility completely nil," Ann trembled as she landed a Hurricane nearly blind at an RAF base rather than turn back to where she'd started. And when she opened the hatch while flying another Hurricane, she panicked for a beat when her map blew away. She opted to forge ahead on memory, and even circled around along the way to do some sightseeing over Coventry amid a veritable forest of barrage balloons. By the time Ann made her first Spitfire delivery, she wrote, "Couldn't see a thing what with the haze and smoke, but kept going regardless." Toward the end of October, she had even loosened up enough to buzz an airfield. The prank gave her a naughty boost.

The raffish environment of Ratcliffe was having an effect. One idle day toward the end of October, one of the other Ratcliffe pilots—a "complete madman but he manages," Ann wrote—invited her to ride along as he ferried one of the RAF's enormous four-engine Stirling bombers. It was a Class 5 aircraft, but he let her fly it, despite her Class 2 status. "They are monsters of the sky," she concluded, "but handle beautifully and are extremely gentle in the air. I vaguely wondered if I would ever reach Class 5. There are times the size terrifies me." Then again, she decided that if she found herself on a desert island with a Stirling, she wouldn't hesitate to try it.

Dusk fell on the return trip of the taxi plane that day, and a deep bass rumble sounded up ahead. "Suddenly," Ann wrote, "the sky was black with flying Lancasters." There were nearly a hundred of them, heavy four-engine monsters of the sky like the Stirling, capable of carrying the largest bombs loads in the arsenal, clearly bound toward a mission of destruction. Perhaps the Stirling Ann had just flown would join the raid. The little taxi plane carrying the ATA personnel had to dodge in and out to avoid the oncoming rush of massive ships, like a lone cowboy on horseback encountering a stampede.

Watching the spectacle, "it made one think a bit," Ann mused. Just ten days before, in a mission that came to be known as Black Thursday, the American Eighth Air Force had lost sixty out of nearly three hundred heavy bombers in a bombing run over German ball bearing factories. Twenty percent of the men did not return. She knew that some of the Lancasters she saw grinding into the maw of battle that evening would not come back, taking the young lives carried on board.

A colleague pointed Ann toward another tableau unfolding below— twenty or thirty landed gentry on horseback, chasing after a skittering, harmless fox. It was a scene that recalled what felt like a distant era out of a Trollope novel, far removed from the mechanized menace of modern warfare. Ann disapproved. *Somehow it seems as though this energy could have been expended toward something more profitable*, she thought. Only later she considered that some of the hunters could be joining a dangerous raid the next night, or the next. In the coming months, Ann started to wish that she could afford riding clothes so she could join such diversions herself. Distraction was dear—who was she to judge?

WHEN SOME OF Ann's American colleagues joined her at Ratcliffe later in the fall, they added a casual note to the already irreverent atmosphere. Ann found herself picking up Winnie Pierce or Suzanne Ford on taxi runs, and they chased each other through the sky on tandem Spitfire deliveries. Virginia Farr, now cleared to fly two-engine bombers, made a valuable contribution to the pool's delivery record. She, Hazel Raines, and another American named Peggy Lennox entertained the after-dinner crowd with a salute to the Midlands set to the tune of "You Are My Sunshine":

> *Where is my sunshine?*
> *My only sunshine.*
> *The Met, he said it would be grand.*
> *The vis was measured in terms of inches,*
> *And the cloud base was touching the land . . .*

Others wound up crossways with the Hall's upper-class customs. Mary Zerbel Hooper was flustered by the servants' early-morning ritual of knocking on her bedroom door and opening it at the exact same moment. She waited in bed while they closed the windows, opened the blackout curtains, took shoes to be polished, and departed. A quarter hour later, a second knock heralded the return of the gleaming shoes. Only then would Mary rise, strip off her nightgown, and wash at a basin near the door, bare and shivering, because even at Ratcliffe Hall, precious coal would not be wasted to heat less-important rooms. But one morning, Smart, the butler, knocked while opening the door a third time, carrying a box of laundered blouses. Mary hit the floor, arms and legs flailing, clutching a tiny towel to cover as much of her body as she could. She felt her skin turn burning red.

In horrible fascination, she could not take her eyes from Smart. "With complete aplomb," Mary remembered, "he laid the box gingerly on the bed, looked me squarely in the eye, and said in a completely normal voice, 'Please don't throw away the box. Mrs. Smart will need it again.'" Each night at dinner, Mary cringed with embarrassment when the impeccable butler approached her place. As for Smart, "No visible sign of anything out of the ordinary showed itself."

As far as anyone could tell, the only American who ever got the better of Smart's composure was Opal Pearl Anderson. Opal was a divorced thirty-five-year-old, a former airport manager who became known as the "Chicago Foghorn" for her high-decibel profanity, even in the stuffiest settings. One night, Smart circled the dining hall to dish out a pudding made primarily of cornstarch, a soggy victim of ration rules. The guests mushed it around for a polite interval before quietly putting down their spoons, except for Opal. She took a hearty bite, slammed the table, and in her most unseemly voice bellowed, "Jesus Christ, what the hell is this stuff?"

At opposite heads of the table, Sir Lindsay and Lady Everard rendered their expressions completely blank. Smart followed suit, but in the rigid silence, he began to rapidly draw in his breath, like a runner winded at the end of a race. Finally, unable to contain himself, he let out a bark of laughter. From then on, he gave Opal a discreet signal when the noxious pudding reappeared.

ANN STILL KEPT up her London diversions on leave during the fall of 1942, often in the company of a new beau. She had met an officer named Avery Hand during the summer when American servicemen dropped in at White Waltham. He and Ann enjoyed a cocktail together, then dinner at Skindles, followed by a swim at the American Club at eleven P.M. "Army boys took me home in a Jeep," she wrote. "It was one of the glorious days one will remember in this land, for they come so rarely."

In the months after her move to Ratcliffe, she took the train to the city to meet Avery in clubs and hotel ballrooms like the fashionable one at the Savoy. Politicians and journalists gathered there, and bands played popular hits for swaying couples far from home. He met all the requirements for a suitable escort—he danced well and kept up an amusing patter. "Avery very easy—will do all the talking, which I like," Ann noted. He boasted the further advantage of serving in the Army Signal Corps, a communications branch that made him privy to gossip and secrets. "He has a weird job chasing around London at odd hours to deliver secret messages to the various Generals," she wrote. "He knows where they are at all times and is up on their social haunts—rather embarrassing at times, I gather."

Ann's talent for fitting in wherever she went also landed her smack in the liveliest circle at Ratcliffe. She organized parties, preferring to oversee the food and decorations rather than joining another "drunken brawl." Tall and self-assured, she made fast friends of the rakish guys at the base, including Johnnie Jordan, known as the "Crunchy Bar King" for his connection to a family cereal business. Johnnie's hotheaded flying had gotten him thrown out of the RAF, but in the ATA he provided a welcome sideshow, setting an insubordinate example by performing forbidden aerobatics whenever he got the chance. Ann followed his model on a more modest scale. She came to believe that tossing off a few 360-degree loops on the way to a delivery kept a pilot sharp.

Her growing self-assurance didn't keep her out of trouble, though. On November 9, 1942, after a nearly three-hour flight to the far coast of Cornwall, Ann squinted into the late-day sun as she approached a short airfield used for training pilots to land on aircraft carriers of the Royal Navy Fleet Air Arm. She came in too fast and ran off the end of the runway, then tried to stop on the soggy ground of a downward slope.

Like most crash landings, it all happened with shocking speed. The nose tipped forward, and the world turned head over heels. The Spit performed a somersault, still careening ahead, while Ann tumbled inside, powerless. When the plane slid to a stop fifty feet short of a ravine, Ann was dangling upside down from her shoulder straps. Gas spilled out and soaked the ground around her. She unfastened herself, dropped into the canopy, and crawled to safety through the tail.

Her only injury was the middle finger of her right hand, which had snapped backward. It remained absurdly bent for the rest of her life. The Accident Committee put the blame on Ann for landing when she couldn't properly see, and the medical officer kept her from flying for ten days.

Ann seemed to tell her diary everything, but her entry for the day said only, "Crashed at St. Merryn, spent night." As was her style, she just got on with it. "I merely chalked it up to the mishap department," she wrote later. Her first assignment after medical leave was a taxi run to collect Virginia Farr and Hazel Raines in bad weather. Ann carried it out without a tremor. "Wasn't the least bit concerned and enjoyed myself as much as ever," she concluded that night.

The Spitfire flip-flop didn't stop her from pulling off other capers. If anything, her lucky survival might have made her more nonchalant. When her irrepressible buddy Johnnie Jordan suggested that Ann fly in line with him and another pilot on a Spitfire delivery to Bristol, she knew there could be mischief afoot. She pushed the thought aside and agreed to bring up the rear.

At a cool three hundred miles per hour, Ann followed their lead, enjoying the wide-open day, until she saw the Severn Railway Bridge up ahead. The bridge was a well-known landmark that spanned the Severn River in Gloucester, a glorious, striking sight. Twenty-two columns, all less than 134 feet apart, supported the 100-foot-tall, 4,000-foot-long structure. Ann took in the sparkling vista with pleasure until she saw Johnnie swoop low over the water, keeping up a ripping speed. She looked on in amazement. *No—he wouldn't.*

But he did. Aiming dead ahead, Johnnie hurtled under the bridge between the supports. Seconds later, the second pilot followed suit.

Ann was tempted. Obviously, this was foolish, irresponsible, *reckless.* It was not how she behaved. But oh, so tempting.

The usually level-headed Ann Wood, the obedient student of the nuns at the Institut Notre Dame, the only pilot who made it to church every Sunday no matter where she found herself, took a bite of the apple. With a sneaky grin, she sucked in her breath, shoved her stick forward, and focused on the fast-approaching gap.

It looked impossible. Impossible, but not *impossible.* Ann threaded the needle to the other side and soared back up through the brilliant sky, light, light-headed, and free as an aerodynamic bird of prey. As Winnie Pierce would say: *What a life!*

Sometime later, Ann took a delivery on the same route on her own. The flight was routine, until there it was again, right in front of her—the bridge. The temptation was too great. Besides, she'd done it before. She lined up and brought the Spitfire down to skim just above the water, keeping up a wicked pace, on track for the narrow opening.

This is a little tight, she thought as the target came into range. Impossible. Maybe truly impossible. No one had told her about the variation between high and low tide on the Severn River. There was a thirty-foot difference, and this time the tide was high. Only seventy feet separated the bridge deck from the water. Too late to turn back. Ann's adrenaline spiked as she stayed the course and rocketed through.

When the story of her daring maneuver made the rounds, it ranked as one of the fabled hijinks among the renegades at Ratcliffe Aerodrome. And a newly confident Ann sealed her place in Sir Lindsay Everard's exclusive club.

CHAPTER 14

Her Heart Is Involved

October 24, 1942
Ratcliffe, Leicestershire

While Ann Wood savored her plum assignment through the fall, Winnabelle Pierce bounced among three airfields. High emotion and personal chaos followed wherever she went. In August 1942 the ATA had first transferred Winnie to Hamble, an all-woman ferry pool on the southern coast near Southampton, where proximity to the war excited her appetite for sensation. "The sirens are howling even as I write," she scrawled in her diary on her first evening there. "It is an eerie sound. Up go the balloons to the edge of the clouds, and everyone wonders if the planes will get through and drop their bombs."

Ack-ack guns defending the base from German sorties often interfered with deliveries at Hamble. And a disastrous British and Canadian raid on Dieppe that month, when more than three thousand troops died in an amphibious assault across the Channel in occupied France, meant that bullet-dinged Spitfires swamped the aerodrome. Winnie got a hobbled Spit whose gear stuck and pump broke shortly after takeoff, but once again, her skill kicked in and she managed to turn the defective plane back to land with the wind dangerously behind her. A few days later, the staff at Hamble took cover as Germans hit the airfield and antiaircraft gunners fought back. "Great excitement," Winnie concluded.

She liked keeping busy with multiple Spitfire deliveries each day. But she was glum that "the girls"—her sidekicks Louise Schuurman and Helen Richey—weren't posted with her at Hamble at first. Distance also stalled her ongoing campaign to seduce Captain Marc Hale, her commanding officer at White Waltham. "I have such a supreme feeling of being able to get everything I want, but what I want most—Marc—I am helpless about," she lamented.

Frustrated and melancholic, she lay awake late at night reading poetry like *The Rime of the Ancient Mariner*, suffused with guilt and suffering. Winnie was so fond of *Flight to Arras*, a wrenching new memoir by the French poet and aviator Antoine de Saint-Exupery, that she copied parts of it into in her diary. He had written this meditation on service, bravery, and mortality about a dangerous mission he flew in 1940. In 1944, he would disappear on another flight over the Mediterranean. "If I am alive, I shall do my thinking tonight," Winnie quoted from the book. "Night when words fade and things come alive . . ."

For transportation and kicks, she bought a motorcycle that she powered with bootleg gas. When Louise and Helen joined her at Hamble, Winnie drove fast with her friends on the back of the bike, sometimes as far as London, and rode home at night with no hands on the handlebars. Police stopped her for infractions like speeding and running a red light, but she "grinned" her way out of penalties.

However, when the women's ATA commander, Pauline Gower, spotted Winnie smashed at a pub, there were consequences. Gower summoned the unruly pilot the following morning to deliver a lecture on drinking. "English women don't, etcetera, etcetera," was Winnie's interpretation. She decided to "swear off for good, until my next birthday," which was coming up in three months. "It's the only way, as I won't risk going home."

Perhaps that vow finally won her a transfer back to White Waltham in mid-September for the coveted instruction on Class 3 two-engine aircraft, a month behind Virginia Farr. Starting on the lightest model, an Oxford trainer, she flew a few times with an instructor, practicing spinning and flying with one engine off. Moving right along to the larger two-engine bombers of Class 4, Winnie realized that the enormous Wellington gave her a workout. The long-range, medium-weight plane, known to pilots as the Wimpy, measured sixty-four feet long and seventeen feet high, with a wingspan of eighty-six feet. It had the kind of heft that led many to conclude it was too much to handle for the fairer sex. But the perfect putdown for that way of thinking came from Joan Hughes, a British instructor who stood only five feet two. "The idea is for the plane to lift *me*," she famously said, "not for *me* to lift the plane."

Winnie mastered the sluggish controls but considered the bomber a beast. After her first solo, she wrote, "God, what a huge thing. I really feel these ships are too big, but fly them I must." It was possible to see the massive wings flex in a strong wind, and it took more brute strength to operate a Wellington than smaller aircraft. In case of engine failure, the diminutive Winnie had to practice lowering the undercarriage manually by hand-pumping 250 strokes.

It didn't help that after two weeks on the water wagon, Winnie started flying through hangovers again. She had her excuses. She dreaded the onset of autumn weather, as more pilots were crashing and dying. The state of the war brought her down amid widespread concern that Stalingrad would soon fall to the Germans, who might then turn more attention back to attacking Great Britain. It was hard to envision when the Allies would make the pivot toward an effective offense and push for victory. And while American men were building up their numbers, they still awaited armaments before they could become a potent force.

On top of all that, news that her love interest, Captain Hale, now had a girlfriend sent Winnie into a tailspin. It wasn't long until she resumed her affair with alcohol, sharing a drink with Louise at noon on a day off to counteract a hangover from gin, scotch, brandy, and champagne the night before. "Each year without living with a man is time lost," Winnie groaned. "I miss their companionship."

A thoroughly modern woman willing to break the common rules of courtship, Winnie never felt shy about taking the lead if she set her sights on a conquest. So after a boozy lunch in Maidenhead in late September, Winnie jumped on her motorcycle and headed to London to give chase to a new prospect. This time it was Peter Beasley, the sociable fifty-seven-year-old former Lockheed executive advising General Eaker of the Eighth Air Force. Winnie had met Peter at Jackie Cochran's over the summer and, like everyone else, enjoyed his vivacious company. They rendezvoused for a drink at Claridge's, a sumptuous Victorian-era hotel where he had taken a room, and had a grand time. Winnie wrote, "He is so sweet and so much money and brains . . . I wonder!"

She stayed the night. The next day, she stepped up her game by getting her hair and nails done, then meeting Peter for shopping, although he did the buying. "Got me a lovely pair of flying boots and some ski socks," Winnie recorded. Only during wartime would such presents spark a romantic flame. Then she left for the train with more loot—a bar of chocolate and a bottle of scotch.

A week later, Winnie met Peter again in what she called "our room" at Claridge's. He left for work at one in the morning, and Helen Richey joined her friend for a night in the luxury hotel. Describing the tryst with Peter, Winnie told Helen, "I got very tight and can't remember much except that I had a good time."

"You should marry him," Helen advised.

Winnie thought for a moment and repeated, "I wonder . . ."

Only two days later, back with Peter in London again, Winnie told her diary that they engaged in "the usual talk of marriage." She didn't clarify who said what. Another two days after that, Peter told her, he would leave England for the United States, planning to return on a date to be determined. Winnie didn't know what his mission was, nor much else about his job except that it was important. He didn't explain, and she didn't ask.

THE FROTHY, SWASHBUCKLING culture at Ratcliffe should have appealed to Winnie Pierce when she followed Ann Wood there in mid-October, but once again she felt bereft at being away from her favorite familiar faces and vexed that she didn't know where Peter was three weeks after he'd gone away. Ann Wood paid a welcome visit to Winnie's billet several miles from the action at Ratcliffe Hall and got an earful about her hopes for Peter.

The relationship surprised Ann. She appreciated Peter Beasley as a well-connected friend, but the thirty-two-year age difference between

Winnie and the popular officer seemed insurmountable. Aside from his canny mind, Ann thought he appeared otherwise as an ordinary middle-aged man, five feet eight and slightly pudgy. Besides, Winnie's feverish serial romantic longings weren't Ann's style at all. Ann treated her own flirtation with Avery Hand, the signal corps officer, as one more entry in her busy social and professional calendar. They hit the dance floors when she could get to London, but she remained unbothered when their schedules didn't line up. He rarely merited a mention in her diary on other days. Winnie always ruminated on her latest beaus, sighing about them in her diary and planning futures with them in bed at night.

Before she left Winnie's mournful billet, Ann tried to spread some cheer by extending an invitation to a party celebrating the anniversary of the Ratcliffe Aerodrome on October 24. ATA characters from all over would be flying in.

Winnie turned up in top form that night, despite, or perhaps partly because of, some crushing news. Louise Schuurman's boyfriend, Ernest McGeehee, a pilot in the American Air Force, had been killed that day flying into a phalanx of barrage balloons over Manchester. Still, Winnie stayed true to form and cut a gay figure amid the Ratcliffe revels. As the party wound down, Ann Wood saw the tipsy pilot out to her motorbike and helped her start it up.

"Are you sure you're able to drive?" Ann asked. Winnie laughed and waved her off. "She was definitely happy and swerved around a bit," Ann remembered, "but I honestly didn't think too much about it, as she always acts a bit, and besides she has always returned from a party on her bike." Ann decided the event had turned more "drunk and dull" by then, so she tramped home to Ratcliffe Hall through moonlit meadows, alone, savoring the silence.

The next morning, when she returned from Sunday church, word had already swept through the Hall, piercing the fog of hangover headaches as the residents crept downstairs. Some RAF boys had found Winnie unconscious by a roundabout in the middle of the night. She had missed a turn and landed on some iron railings. No one knew her condition, only that she'd been taken to a hospital ten miles away.

Ann was supposed to board a plane for White Waltham, where Eleanor Roosevelt would visit the American women the next day, an event Ann wouldn't miss for the world. But with Jackie Cochran no longer looking out for the American women and Helen Richey nowhere nearby, Ann scrapped her plans so she could handle the emergency. Filled with apprehension, she borrowed a car and figured out how to drive on the left side of the road so she could track Winnie down at the hospital. Directed to a cold, bleak ward, Ann found a curtain drawn around the patient's cot. The scene was grim as patients on all sides wheezed and families stood in vigil. Ann steeled herself to pull back the fabric. When she did, she barely recognized Winnie's face, smashed and covered with blood. Nothing had been done since the police had brought her in at three in the morning. She was beginning to wake in a haze, with no memory of what had happened.

Ann swung into class-president mode. She tracked down nurses who told her that X-rays and a resulting prognosis wouldn't happen for several days. It was essential for now, they said, to retrieve Winnie's ration book, soap, and towels. Ann sped back to Ratcliffe, returning with the first man she could find in tow for added clout. "A man does make a difference," she reasoned. They located the home of the hospital's doctor and roused him to help, pointing out that Winnie was an officer. At this news, he agreed to transfer her to a semi-private ward, as was customary for patients of rank. Ann suppressed her irritation about this inequality even as she welcomed the favor. Otherwise, the doctor told her, there was nothing more to be done that day.

No one especially acknowledged how she was extending herself to care for Winnie, but in doing so, Ann once again had assumed a natural leadership role among the Americans. Her options exhausted, she caught a train to London. In St. Pancras Station, she heard a voice call out, "Hey Squirt." It was her beau Avery Hand, there to take her bag and steer her to a taxi. Someone looking after *her* for a change. Just before midnight, the couple pulled up at the Red Cross Club to find her a room for the night. They drank Coca-Colas and played records in the living room until it was time for him to go to work and her to sleep.

ANN, HAZEL, AND the other pilots who were focused on aviation careers—just about all of them—were charged up about the visit the next day from Eleanor Roosevelt. It was part of a publicity tour she was making through England to highlight the roles of women in the war effort. The pilots knew that the First Lady had long been an advocate for women aviators, from Amelia Earhart to Jackie Cochran. She had also used her voice to push for the women's ferry service in the U.S. Her photo op at the ATA field was intended as another nudge to advance the cause. As for the pilots, they wanted to see if she might shed some light on how the progress in the United States would affect their own opportunities to fly when and if they returned.

The busy women pilots of the ATA rarely thought about the politics surrounding women performing their work. For the most part, in Great Britain they found acceptance, even admiration, amid the overwhelming need for their skills in the war zone. "I never felt any animosity," Winnie once said. "We'd never heard of women's lib." But the appearance of Mrs. Roosevelt on October 26, 1942, reminded them that women flyers were still controversial in the United States, where the first twenty-eight women had just signed on to train for ferry duties amid public skepticism, and Jackie Cochran and Nancy Love were feeling out how far they could push their plans.

Debates over women in the British ATA simmered at a low boil by comparison. Pauline Gower had long since overcome the limitations that permitted women to fly only the lightest aircraft, and women no longer elicited surprise at RAF fields. "As the war went on and became very serious and people began to get tired," wrote British flyer Rosemary Rees, "it came down to men and women becoming just people. Any person who was capable of doing something did it. All those pretty little barriers that are put up in peacetime to make society more pleasant melt away in a big crisis, and life becomes a grim struggle of tired grey people all doing whatever it is they can do. Chivalry," she added, "was neither expected nor offered."

By this time in the fall of 1942, the British ace Lettice Curtis had been anointed the first woman to train on the heaviest four-engine Class 5 bombers, like the Avro Lancaster and the American Boeing B-17 Fortress. Mrs. Roosevelt was set to greet Lettice at White Waltham along with all the American women pilots who could make it there that day. The First Lady strolled the tarmac in front of the hangars, accompanied by

Clementine Churchill, the prime minister's wife, and trailed by journalists. They made conversation with clusters of women pilots who stood beneath fifteen models of the many aircraft they were cleared to fly.

The pilots looked as sharp as they could under the circumstances—it was raining up a storm. Women's uniforms in the ATA had stirred some minor disagreement from the beginning, when the service required skirts with tailored jackets at all times. It hadn't taken long for officials to recognize that climbing up and down wings and in and out of cockpits in skirts was downright indecent. Practicality soon won out, and slacks were cleared for flying, although one stuffy aerodrome, with unintended humor, posted this notice: "All women must remove their trousers before entering the mess."

The visit from Eleanor Roosevelt called for the full-dress uniform—that meant a skirt, jacket, black stockings, side caps, and any unruly hair secured above collars. Soon everyone was drenched and shivering, and the First Lady wasn't spared. Her luggage had been sent ahead, so she was obliged to tramp through the deluge without wellies or a raincoat, wearing an impractical feathered hat. She managed to exude warmth all around, especially when she singled out her society acquaintance Virginia Farr, praising her trim appearance in a dripping uniform. Hazel Raines laughed at the predicament. "After being so used to wearing my long-handles and slacks all the time," she commented, "it felt as though someone had left the back door open."

At tea afterward in the officer's mess, Hazel strode up to the president's wife and came right out with the question on all of their minds. When would women pilots be allowed to serve in the United States military? After a pregnant pause, the answer was vague but promising. Mrs. Roosevelt replied that she was pleased with the work the Americans were performing in the ATA and believed that their own country would soon find a need for their abilities.

Just as her car pulled away, the air raid siren sounded, and the sopping pilots piled into an underground shelter ankle-deep in water. For half an hour they sang to fend off misery and speculated whether the Germans were acting on inside information about Mrs. Roosevelt's presence. Bombs fell on a nearby airfield, possibly mistaken for White Waltham.

That night, many of the women saw Mrs. Roosevelt again at the Red Cross Club in London, where she made a statement by meeting two Black women Red Cross workers, part of a group arriving especially to support segregated Black troops. By now, it was becoming clear that the new American women's ferrying group that Mrs. Roosevelt had championed, destined to become the WASP, would not accept pilots who were Black, in alliance with policy of the U.S. Army Air Forces. While a few women of Asian, Native American, and Mexican American descent eventually served in the WASP, Jackie Cochran, reluctant to rock the boat, rejected Black applicants to her training program, including the pioneering Janet Harmon. No doubt the First Lady hoped her advocacy would lead to a change in the policy.

The American Atta-Girls received a flurry of publicity from the First Lady's visit. *LIFE* magazine ran a photograph, and newspapers across the United States printed stories. But the attention didn't necessarily benefit the cause of women flyers in the U.S., and it offered another hint that maintaining a women's flying service there might prove a rougher ride.

"What's going to happen when it's all over?" asked an article about the ATA women in the New York *Daily News*. Journalist Martha Martin asked:

> Will the girls be satisfied to go back meekly to civil life and take up where they left off as housewives, teachers, secretaries, and ladies of leisure? England fears that swarms of the girls . . . will be restless and dissatisfied when the war is over and they find themselves thrown out into a world to which they are not adjusted.
>
> They will want better pay, more consideration in a world that heretofore has been the exclusive province of men. They will want to make some use of the training they have acquired in the services. And they are likely to be aggressive about it.
>
> It is just possible that the men who have accepted the services of women in their desperation have started something they will have trouble finishing when the hostilities are over.

Sounded about right. When the American ATA women saw the coverage of their encounter with the First Lady, it put them on notice. It might take more than flying skill to pull off meaningful careers when it was time to go home.

WINNIE PIERCE HAD been driving hard to flourish on both tracks—the professional and the personal—when her motorbike accident knocked her out of commission and seemed to alter her ambitions. For three weeks, diagnosed with a concussion, she was held in the hospital, her face swollen, battered, and numb, her back aching, a vertebra chipped. She was ordered off flying for another month after her release. "Phooey," she wrote in her diary as soon as she could function.

Doctors ordered Winnie to lie still or she would experience headaches later in life. They predicted she would need surgery to restore feeling to her face if the problem didn't resolve when the swelling went down. Fortunately, things went her way. Ann, Louise, and other friends brought detective stories and other books. But Peter Beasley was AWOL. She wired and called his office without results—he should have returned to England by now.

Sprung from the hospital on November 16, Winnie chafed at orders to remain in bed for two weeks at her old billet in Maidenhead. When Peter made a surprise appearance two days later, they held hands on the couch like a couple of teenagers. Within days, she broke her curfew to go out to dinner with him. A week later, AWOL again, she took the train to the city to make the rounds at Claridge's, dinner parties, and the Gay Nineties Club, once again knocking back scotch and champagne with Peter. The scars on her face were receding, but her head and back still pained her.

The couple engaged in a stop-and-go tango on the subject of marriage. "My mind is in turmoil," Winnie wrote when he brought her flowers. "He made a remark about me having kids, etc., instead of going back to work in the States. I hope it's true."

But then Peter said he thought they should agree on a "courting contract," which he didn't quite define. Around Thanksgiving, marriage came up again. "I don't think you could put up with me," Peter insinuated, distancing the subject further. "I've been a bachelor a long time."

He softened the remark with a compliment: "You sure do know how to make love."

Peter's phone calls thrilled Winnie, but his reticence and unpredictable absences sent her spiraling and questioning her choices. On her twenty-sixth birthday on December 11, Winnie recalled how she stood by the bedside of her mother as she died when Winnie was seventeen. "I was headstrong, wild—and she wanted me to be a playwright. Now look at me—what have I become; what have I done; what will my future be? Is it too late to mold myself along much more desirable lines?" By the standards of the accepted 1940s playbook, if Winnie wanted to marry Peter, the prudent course would have been to withhold sexual favors until he put a ring on her finger. But Winnie could never resist the risky route, the wild and headstrong route, even if it led to a crash.

She vowed to walk away from him. But after an embassy party, they returned once again to the hotel and shared a quart of scotch. "I loved him a lot as a good-bye," she wrote afterward, "but I'm afraid I was weak in the end."

Winnie couldn't tell whether Peter's erratic behavior reflected lack of interest or something related to his work. Maybe it was both. The riddle kept her off balance, which for Winnie might have been part of the appeal. But even the thrill-seeking pilot would have been surprised had she learned the truth about her lover. She had no idea that Peter Beasley was not what he said he was—a deskbound logistics officer reporting to General Eaker—but was, in fact, a spy. He carried out clandestine missions for the United States throughout the theater of war when he told her he was engaged in mundane travel. He prowled the London hotspots for information from the mongrel cast of characters in the expat community. It seems possible he might have dabbled in picking up odd bits of information about the RAF from the pilots who ferried its aircraft. Or that his relationship with Jackie Cochran had been intended to keep an eye on her.

Ann Wood, sharp as she was, didn't catch on, either, even though he'd mentioned to her that he once thought the purpose of dinner parties was to pick the brains of other guests. She still joined Winnie, Peter, and their friends at nightclubs. "Winnie is his gal, and he seems to love it, although I think is a bit whacked by her manner at times," Ann observed. But she sensed Winnie's distress. "Her heart is involved."

FINALLY CLEARED BY doctors to fly on December 20, Winnie was sent back to school, as the ATA required after medical leave. "I found myself very scared and unable to calmly take everything in at first," she wrote. The uncharacteristic fear continued the next day when she soloed for half an hour. "I hope I get over it as I never used to be this way," she worried. Her air work improved, but her landings were bad. Fatigue slowed her reflexes.

The next night, she met Peter and their friends for drinks, dinner, and dancing. Once again, she felt Peter pulling away, cushioned by a merry holiday crowd a few days before Christmas. A British friend had died the day before, crashing after hitting low-hanging wires. Everyone performed the emotional multitasking that was familiar to people serving in the war. "Heard Stubbs was killed in Spit at Hawarden (burned)," was all Ann Wood put in her diary. The champagne flowed as the group checked out the scene at Hatchett's Hotel on Piccadilly, where the best band in London now played, according to the latest gossip.

"Peter was sweet, and the conversation kept away from the intimate," Winnie wrote about the night. "I was wrong to try to be mad at him and wrong to sleep with him." She stayed that night with her pals Helen and Louise at the Red Cross Club.

"He will never marry you," Helen said.

I love him, though, thought Winnie, but she didn't speak. She was about to be posted back to ferry duties at White Waltham, where she'd have to get a grip on her nerves.

CHAPTER 15

Stepping up to the Upper Class

November 21, 1942
Hamble, Hampshire

If Winnie stirred up constant turbulence with flamboyant behavior, Dorothy Furey Bragg attracted just as much notice while barely allowing a ripple to disturb her serene surface. When she transferred to the Hamble ferry pool in the south near the end of November 1942, Dorothy spent one day there and decided the place wasn't for her. The abundant charms of the little yachting village near the busy port of Southampton had turned this posting into one of the most coveted assignments in the ATA. The high-handed Dorothy took it in with a gimlet eye.

A first inspection didn't take her far, as there wasn't far to go. She strolled down the sloping High Street in the brisk salt air, barely glancing at the adorable shops. Gulls wheeled and cried overhead as she reached a marina filled with colorful small boats that bobbed on the Hamble River, the water in November the color of stone. *How dull*, she thought. A dozen inns with names like Ye Olde White Hart and the King & Queen reinforced a picture-postcard atmosphere that dated from the fourteenth century. Dorothy listened to laughter as she strolled by the Yacht Club and the Bugle, two creaky, ancient pubs where the pilots traded flying stories every night. She didn't join them.

The camaraderie extended to the billets, tidy cottages with flowered garden plots, where everyone shared bedrooms and homey meals. If they were honest with themselves, the flyers admitted that part of the appeal of Hamble was its proximity to the Channel and the larger war beyond. Living within easy range of Luftwaffe attacks added a dash of immediacy. The aviators had to move fast in their work, flying aircraft directly out of factories before they were hit.

Among the many enticements of the assignment was another unusual perk. The Hamble Aerodrome was served entirely by women pilots, thirty of them in 1942, right up to the commanding officer. No need to negotiate the usual sexual tensions or politics. No worries about making the right impression on men. This setup contributed to the easy air of the seaside posting. The ladies were free to focus on friendships and work.

This cozy, clubby, all-girl environment held no appeal for Dorothy, who vastly preferred the company of men over women. "She couldn't stand it at her billet, where there were a lot of women staying with a family," her son Adam Hewitt reflected many years later. Dorothy couldn't bear to share a bedroom and found the cooking gruesome. "She said it was so bad it made her sick. They served her this kind of warm, milky, sweet tea. It was absolutely godawful. She decamped to the Polygon Hotel in Southampton after one night, and she stayed there the rest of her service."

Not for her was a nightly slumber party in a quaint boating outpost. Dorothy didn't pal around with the other women, and she didn't do quaint. The chic scene at the premier hotel in Southampton was more the destiny she'd had in mind when she left New Orleans. She could afford the splurge thanks to a military discount on her room, her substantial ATA salary, and the fact that, unlike almost all of her colleagues, she didn't send anything to family back home.

DOROTHY HAD REACHED the level of Class 2 aircraft, taking on Hurricanes, Spitfires, and other fighters despite some odd evaluations during training. Most assessments of pilots kept to the basics—citing "average ability" and so on—but Dorothy's superiors felt compelled to grapple with her perplexing personality. "A complex character, difficult to assess fairly in writing," wrote Captain Marc Hale at White Waltham just before her posting to Hamble. "She is obviously a capable pilot and at times appears to be really keen, but in everything else but the actual flying from A to B she is completely undisciplined and in some ways sheerly indolent."

Whether it was the flying or the instructors that left her cold, it's impossible to know. "She never liked being told what to do by men, and she'd let them know she was done with them by acting totally bored," said her son. Her few encounters with the Accident Committee tipped both ways. A couple of times, she was blamed for taxiing without due care when she knocked into objects on the ground. But when the undercarriage of a Hurricane wouldn't go down for landing two weeks before her Hamble assignment, the committee blamed a jammed lever rather than Dorothy. The mishap could have ended in disaster, but she was fortunate to be dealing with a soft grass airfield and a plane with a low stall speed. Unruffled, she adjusted the flaps to reduce the Hurricane's momentum so it could touch down and slide on its belly. The plane sustained damage—pretty much unavoidable—but Dorothy did not. She remained a cool customer, on duty and off.

Like Dorothy, many women won the Hamble assignment once they learned to fly Spitfires, because a large factory for the fighter was based nearby, along with manufacturers for a wide array of other aircraft ranging up to Class 4 Halifax bombers. The area was a prime target for bombing early in the war, when Southampton harbor was nearly flattened. The frontline location still ensured that from time to time stray enemy aircraft machined-gunned the airfields and killed or injured staff. Protective balloon barrages popped up and down with frustrating frequency, so flyers had to hustle off the ground pronto whenever the way was clear.

Pilots needed greater skill than usual to negotiate the obstacle-filled skies and occasional encounters with the enemy. The American Edith Stearns spotted an unfamiliar plane coming up behind her on her first Hurricane delivery out of Hamble in the fall of 1942. She watched carefully in her rearview mirror until she spotted a swastika on the side. The weather was foul as usual, so she pulled up into the clouds, tapping some instrument training from prewar lessons to guide her. When she slipped back down a few minutes later, the German craft had disappeared. After landing, Edith learned that an air raid was on, and the sky surrounding the drome had filled with defensive ack-ack.

The women at Hamble racked up a splendid record thanks to steady leadership from the commanding officer, Margot Gore, who was good-humored and cautious. She adhered to the motto that ATA pilots were paid to be careful, not brave. The second-in-command, Rosemary Rees, liked to make the point that among famous last words in history, these stood out: "Oh hell, let's take a crack at it!"

In the sky, the women competed aggressively, but the mess and break room looked like they belonged in a genteel sorority house. Awaiting orders, the ladies sat on comfortable old sofas and dainty pink chairs requisitioned from the *Queen Mary*. They played bridge, performed calisthenics, cut out patterns for dresses on the floor, or shared tea with scones, shortbread, and jam. It was a true international mix—pilots from Poland, Chile, South America, Great Britain, and, over time, many from the United States. A mix of personalities, too. Roberta Sandoz, the self-described hick from Washington State, presented a sharp contrast to the seemingly worldly Dorothy Furey Bragg, while the gaiety of Winnie Pierce contrasted with the sensible work ethic of Nancy Miller.

The British contingent varied widely as well. Margot Gore, a flying instructor before the war, had worked as a secretary to pay for lessons, but her deputy, the daughter of a baronet, had been a ballet dancer. Some likened Dorothy Furey Bragg to another legendary beauty at Hamble, the British pilot Diana Barnato. Her father, Woolf Barnato, was a millionaire race car driver and heir to the De Beers diamond fortune who controlled the Bentley luxury motorcar company. Diana maintained a flat in London, where she kept up a splashy presence on the society pages. If Dorothy was born on a lower tier of society, Diana began at Class 4.

In the friendly environment at Hamble, the Americans and the British mixed more than at most other dromes. Some felt the sharp cultural contrast even as others came to find it amusing. The English operations officer Alison King wrote of her U.S. counterparts, "They said they exaggerated and we played down, they were exuberant and we were reserved, they worked hard and played hard, and we did a little less of both." Alison didn't mind. "The differences were certainly there, and thank Heaven for them—for they created an interest, each in the other's strangeness, which was most pleasant."

There were some men among the groundcrew who saw a group of women living and working together and labeled Hamble "the Lesbian Pool." No doubt there were a few lesbians who passed through Hamble, given the number of women posted there over the years, but no one called attention to it. There was one pilot, however, who later emerged quite publicly as a gender pioneer. Joy Ferguson, a trained engineer from Ireland who flew for the ATA at Hamble, worked postwar as a civil servant. Newspapers around the world covered the story in 1958 when Joy underwent gender reassignment surgery and became Jonathan. As a man in a government job, he enjoyed permission to wear trousers instead of a skirt—and won an immediate raise in pay.

DOROTHY FUREY BRAGG avoided all of it. Every evening after flying, she perched at the elegant Polygon Hotel bar in Southampton, enjoying a cocktail and the company of the stylish clientele. Packed before the war with well-to-do travelers awaiting passage on the White Star Line, the place now filled with high-level naval officers winding down from action at sea. "Oh, the Polygon!" Dorothy regaled her son. "I drank *buckets* of champagne there and danced every night." Pausing to consider how that sounded, she added, "Because you never knew if you were coming back."

Dorothy flexed her powers over the men at the bar, letting her remarkable appearance lure them to her side, then leaning in to their battle stories with a fixed, unblinking gaze that they found flattering and seductive. Or else she ignored them with a bracing indifference that worked wonders on ambitious suitors who were stung by the challenge.

Despite the occasional weekend with her husband, Richard Bragg, Dorothy had lost all interest in the marriage. While she had found him the most desirable man among the troops on the ocean voyage to England, she had since learned that there were layers of privilege in the United Kingdom, complex strata of wealth, nobility, and connections that opened portals to various worlds of glamour and comfort. She had once been impressed that her husband oversaw a crew of eight as the pilot of a four-engine Halifax bomber, but she now knew that in the RAF, bomber crews tended to come from working-class backgrounds, while fighter pilots, seen as the gallant chevaliers of the sky, skewed more aristocratic. The highest ranks of the services, those who commanded troops and plotted campaigns, were stocked with nobility.

One representative of this elevated realm descended into the Polygon bar one night. A dignified, somewhat older man, festooned with emblems of military distinction, he couldn't resist staring at Dorothy from a distant table. He was Lord David Field Beatty, the second Earl of Beatty, a lieutenant commander in the Royal Navy, the son of a renowned admiral from World War I, and a friend of leading politicians. A catch, if he hadn't already been married to another stunning American.

Dorothy understood her strength. Giving him the haughty treatment, she managed to communicate that she noticed his interest while maintaining a dazzling aloofness. The lady didn't have to say a word. The earl was a goner.

Desperate for a formal introduction, Lord Beatty contacted the commanding officer at Hamble to invite all the ladies from the air base to a ball at the Polygon Hotel. His men would also attend, but Dorothy was the only guest who mattered.

MOST OF THE pilots from Hamble attended the ball in December 1942 wearing lovely gowns pulled from their closets. Dorothy Furey Bragg once again deployed the one red dress she had brought from New Orleans and the cheap black velvet choker that passed for a necklace. Nevertheless, she entered the ballroom of the Polygon with the crystal confidence of a woman who felt her worth.

The other flyers, taking it in from the sidelines, grasped the true purpose of the ball and judged Dorothy accordingly. A few repaired to the ladies' room, where they helped her let her hair down and show more skin by loosening the neckline of her dress. The overall effect set off her black hair, her alabaster complexion, her startling blue eyes. Roberta Sandoz thought it was scandalous that her married colleague would make a play for a married lord. "She knew I didn't approve of her, but I helped her anyway," Roberta recalled. "I felt unsophisticated, whereas she was glamorous and worldly." Roberta stewed that Dorothy's brazen behavior damaged the standing of the Americans.

Dorothy couldn't have cared less. "She always did exactly what she wanted and didn't give a damn about what people thought," her son Adam pointed out. "The rules didn't apply to her."

Lord Beatty danced with Dorothy and no one else all night. "Oh, he was very romantic," Dorothy remembered. Imposing, with a long nose, dark hair, and sharp, prominent eyebrows, David Field Beatty was at his most charming—considerate, courteous, an enthusiastic conversationalist. Dorothy dazzled with her intellect and self-educated command of any topic. But mostly, she shone in her lifelong skill at captivating an admirer by the way her eyes bore into him. "She really turned her lights on and just focused on a man," said her son. "She could totally open him up."

David Beatty bloomed under the flattering attention. Even a lord was subject to trauma from the war, and he had recently suffered from his role in the disastrous August 1942 raid on Dieppe, the German-occupied port city across the Channel in France. The mission was poorly conceived, an attempt to show that Britain was playing offense to claw back territory, but otherwise without strategic merit. Dieppe was well defended by cliffs and artillery, and a German convoy overtook some of the landing craft before they even made it to the shore. The troops who got that far suffered heavy losses. More than half of those thrown into the debacle, mostly Canadians, were killed, wounded or captured, including 555 sailors. Commander Beatty had been in charge of transport and patrol boats. Although he couldn't be blamed for the overall bad planning, everyone involved was humbled by the humiliating defeat.

It had to sting all the more because David's father, Admiral David Richard Beatty, was widely renowned as a war hero. He had won his title as the first Earl of Beatty in 1919 in recognition for outstanding performance in World War I. His marriage to Ethel Field Tree, the only daughter of Marshall Field, the American department store magnate, supplied the Beatty family with a majestic fortune. Their son, Dorothy's admirer the second David Beatty, pursued his own less-distinguished naval career. He was otherwise handsomely fixed, as he'd inherited a million dollars from his mother's estate when she died in 1934. At his father's death before the war, the younger David ascended to the title and a place in the House of Lords. He also married another knockout American Dorothy—Dorothy Power Sands.

By 1942, at the age of thirty-seven, David Beatty was thirteen years older than Dorothy Furey Bragg, but on the dance floor at the ball, their romance caught fire. Everyone witnessed the connection, and many were shocked. Again, Dorothy didn't care what anybody thought. "For the upper classes," she said later, "it was like musical beds. They didn't"—necessarily—"break up their marriages, but they carried on affairs all the time." That model suited her fine. The upper classes were where Dorothy aspired to be. She had conquered Class 2 on her climb up the social ladder.

CHAPTER 16

Invitation from a Lady

December 19, 1942
Maidenhead, Berkshire

D orothy Furey Bragg acknowledged that piloting aircraft wasn't her highest ambition. Aside from fulfilling her goal of contributing to a worthy cause, the job for her was a means to a more personal end, an escape from home and a chance to frame another future in a land where no one knew her past. For just about everyone else, a career in the air *was* the end in itself. They endured long separations from their homes and families, suffered privations, and risked their lives day after day for a shot at the gold ring: lifetime work, somewhere, somehow, as an aviator. Maybe, when the war was over, they'd find a positions as flying instructors or performers in air shows, as some had done before. Or better, as pilots for commercial airlines or the U.S. military, if only their stellar achievements in Great Britain would prove the value of airborne women to the gatekeepers back home.

With commercial aviation on pause during the war, no one knew what opportunities would present themselves when hostilities ended. Nevertheless, the American Atta-Girls already meant business. By the end of 1942, most of them were flying a greater depth and variety of aircraft than just about anyone else—man or woman—anywhere else in the world.

Still, they pushed to fly more types, to stand out as pilots so accomplished that they would wing their way to the pot at end of the rainbow, pursuing their passion for decades to come.

Qualifying to fly a new class meant adding a whole new list of ships to their bulging logbooks, more convincing than any resume. Class 2 opened up possibilities to fly not only Spits and Hurricanes, but other fighters in the category: the new Typhoon, subject to frequent engine failure that led to catastrophic accidents; the American Mustang, a mixed blessing when first introduced that became a speedy favorite; and others with intimidating names like the Defiant, the Martinet, and the Vengeance. Once cleared for Class 3 and 4 twin-engines, the pilots tackled the Mosquito, which called for the virtuoso skills of a violin player to finesse the delicate throttles.

One of the nuttiest looking contraptions, the amphibious Walrus, had biplane wings with layers of other gizmos stacked on top, including the engine and propeller. "About three stories of hodgepodge sticking up there above you," according to Helen Richey. She felt like she should climb out and hang her laundry, but she flew the Walrus without any special instructions beyond the *Pilots Notes* that fall, because the women took on whatever new preposterous machine the ATA required. When the war ended and they completed such service, how could pilots so versatile be denied?

NO ONE RELISHED a foray in a new aircraft more than Hazel Jane Raines. She described her first encounter with a Hurricane fighter in whimsical prose to her mother. From fifty feet away, she wrote, she walked up to the ship slowly in the morning mist, as if to a skittish horse. "There she sat—to me the largest aeroplane I had ever seen."

"Good morning, Chum," Hazel said softly.

"She looked at me and made the most gosh-awful face and seemed to laugh out loud at the tune my knees were playing," Hazel maintained. "I fooled her, though, by getting in and showing her who was boss. After three weeks of circuits and bumps, we were the best of pals.

"Never shall I forget the first flight in this type of machine," she rhapsodized.

Back during the summer of 1942, Hazel had thrived in the warm, sunny weather. Virginia Farr shared her billet along the water with Hazel and bought a car so they could drive together to the aerodrome each day, sparing Hazel's weak heart and lungs from biking. Although she arrived in England six weeks later than her friend, Hazel so excelled at fighter training that the instructors told her she would soon skip ahead and graduate to two-engines as well. She assured her mother that the step up would enhance her opportunities for a long-term career. "This job I am doing now is the realization of a dream I've had since I first started flying," she wrote home. "A dream I had no idea would ever come true because it was too fantastic." Back when she thrilled the crowds at air shows throughout the south, Hazel never thought she would someday command such sophisticated ships.

Lacking the stamina to fly all day and carouse all night, she chose to sacrifice fun and keep rested for work. "You'll never have to worry about me taking too many cocktails," she reassured her mother. "I do join in and drink one and sometimes two just to be sociable, but that's as far as it goes." (The asthmatic Hazel did, however, ask her sister to send cartons of Camels.)

In the fall, when the weather began to chill, Hazel's health turned, too. She contracted influenza in September and was pulled from duty for ten days of medical leave. Before she could return to ferrying fighters, she had to go back to school to brush up her skills, further delaying her chance to fly two-engine planes. She dug deeper than usual to keep up her spirits and hold on to her often-expressed hope that the sky would remain her home as long as there was a place for her.

The ATA kept Hazel on Class 2 fighters for the time being, transferring her to Hamble and Ratcliffe as needed. To prevent further illness, she took shots and treatments with ultraviolet rays. She blew her budget on expensive fur-lined boots to stay warm in the air. ATA doctors ordered frequent sick leaves and rest breaks that broke up her flying.

Trapped in a cycle of illness, so close to achieving all she had ever wanted yet betrayed by her disobliging body, Hazel had to work at keeping up her lifelong posture of witty patter and relentless pluck. At Ratcliffe in the fall, she sang and vamped on the piano, accompanying the gang's satirical songs about flying, and her letters to her mother were perpetually cheery. But she was more candid with her sister. "I am slowly turning into a veritable old maid," she wrote, "whose life consists of an eight-hour work day, twelve hours sleep, and an occasional quiet evening at the movies."

Despite her setbacks, Hazel always flew with the panache honed during her flying circus days. Not a single accident marred her record, and she received rave reviews. Her commanding officer placed one in her file when she was recalled to White Waltham at the end of November so she could begin the long-awaited two-engine training. "A pilot of above average ability," he wrote, "safe and really keen on her job. Well-disciplined and undoubtedly is going to make a first-class ferry pilot."

Back in her original billet at Maidenhead, the Littlehales family cosseted Hazel. They sacrificed their own rations so that she could drink a daily glass of milk and eat meat three times a week. Olga Littlehales wrapped Hazel's pajamas in a hot water bottle after dinner every night to warm them in bed. By December 7, however, doctors pulled her from duty again, once more delaying her progress.

Hazel was ordered to recuperate through the end of the year at the Royal Canadian Hospital in Cliveden. It was one of the better options. Sick and injured ATA pilots lobbied for treatment at this deluxe institution, which was situated on the splendid estate of the wealthy Astor family, not far from Maidenhead. During both world wars, the Astors converted their covered tennis courts, bowling alley, and other buildings on the property to accommodate the hospital run by the Canadian Red Cross. Lady Astor herself was known to greet banged-up ATA pilots at reception with vivacious sympathy. "You young things!" she'd lament. "Whatever will you get up to next?" It was the perfect setting for a thorough rest, with a veranda where patients drowsed on balmy days. Hazel welcomed a line of visitors from the nearby base.

At the hospital, Hazel's story took another turn that offered the possibility of a different destiny. Three American pilots from White Waltham paid a visit to her bedside on December 19, when, like a shot out of a shell, as Hazel remember it, a petite, middle-aged woman burst into the room, carrying a basket of fruit.

"Where is that gal from Georgia?" she commanded. "I'm looking for the Georgia Cracker. I want to see some good old Southern blue blood."

Hazel sat up with a quick retort. "Here she is. So what?"

"I'm from Virginia, and I know all about us folks from the South," said the pushy intruder, who appeared from her simple civilian dress to be some sort of volunteer. "If you are from Georgia, I know I'm talking to a lady. But why would a Southern girl come off her dignity and do such an unladylike thing as fly?"

She had hit on the surest tack to goad the frustrated pilot. Hazel snapped, "The women of today are doing a man's job in a woman's world with unfaltering ability and finesse. If a woman of your integrity cannot see it in that light, she must be a very narrow-minded person."

The three visiting pilots stood at jumpy attention, growing more alarmed as Hazel piled on with her views about women, flying, and women flying. This sympathy visit, if that's what it was, had gone off the rails. When she came up for air, all five women—Hazel, the volunteer, and the three visitors—took a breath in the charged silence.

"Well," the volunteer finally said. "That's the first time in my life I have ever had anyone speak to me in such a frank manner." She looked down a long nose as if from a great height. "But, Georgia, I'm pleased to meet another rebel. I like you."

"I don't really care if you do or not," said Hazel. "I was just expressing my inner self."

Her colleagues flinched again, but before the volunteer beat a retreat, she said she would drop in again the next day.

"Say, what's your name?" Hazel called after her.

The volunteer turned. "Georgia, my name is Lady Astor."

"Well, I'm Mrs. Roosevelt," Hazel hurled toward the retreating figure. She assumed the whole thing was a joke.

The other pilots couldn't contain themselves. They had seen Lady Astor before, and knew that their friend had just thoroughly insulted her. Hazel shrugged. She had never hesitated to show disdain for people of supposed importance. She had hectored Eleanor Roosevelt about approving women pilots in the States and treated Jackie Cochran like any other aviator.

The next day, Lady Astor kept her word, stopping in to announce that she had already spoken to Hazel's doctor for permission. The lady would host the impertinent patient at Cliveden for a day.

★

THE FOLLOWING MORNING, Hazel dressed in her uniform with pants, not the skirt that was mandatory for off-duty occasions. The Astors sent a car, and Hazel passed through a gate to a one-mile approach toward the house. She was determined not to act impressed. In a letter to her mother, Hazel claimed she could already tell "the palatial mansion fairly reeks with a historical stench."

In fact, she found the setting stunning, as most visitors did. Cliveden House came into view as Hazel passed the Fountain of Love, a nineteenth-century extravagance of nymphs and cupids cavorting on an enormous clamshell. The home itself was shaped like a relatively simple box, but embellished with frothy Italianate details. It presided over sublime views of the Thames from atop a high wooded bluff. Long gardens extended from the house to overlook of the river, and important statuary stood guard among the topiary.

Inside, the décor and artwork took Hazel's breath away. Eighteenth-century gilded paneling in the dining room had been boxed up and delivered wholesale from a chateau in France. Tapestries lined the great hall, and Joshua Reynolds portraits of early residents stared out from the right side of a massive stone fireplace. "Truly great works of art," Hazel felt. But they couldn't compete with the showier portrait on the left, a John Singer Sargent painting that captured the dynamism of Lady Nancy Astor shortly before she married in 1906. Viewed from the side, the subject's pale bare shoulders emerged from a dress of gleaming white satin. Her hair floated above her head in a thick, lustrous, Gibson-girl cloud—her sister, Irene Gibson, as it happened, had been the model for the fashionable Gibson-girl look. But it was the face, turned boldly over Nancy Astor's shoulder, that commanded attention with its direct gaze, strong architectural jaw, and straight nose, like the image on a Roman coin.

The portrait summed up Nancy's forthright personality at a glance. Bold, confident, unconventional, unafraid to be herself. All qualities she surely recognized in Hazel, despite the pilot's humbler background. Nancy had emerged from well-off circumstances, but nothing to compare with the heights she reached upon her marriage to Waldorf Astor. She met him on an ocean liner to England, where she hoped to seek a better fortune after an early divorce. He was the son of William Waldorf Astor, considered the wealthiest man in the United Sates thanks to the family's early profits in real estate. In 1891, the elder Astor moved to England and raised his children as English. The country later rewarded him with the title of viscount in recognition of his clout and charitable works. When his son Waldorf married Nancy, William gave the couple Cliveden, along with a tiara that showcased a fifty-five-carat diamond for Nancy. She cared more for the house, because it positioned her as a prominent hostess of the era.

Her husband served as a member of the House of Commons, but when his father died, Waldorf ascended to the House of Lords. Nancy ran for his former position and won, becoming the first woman to be seated in Parliament. Already opinionated and acerbic, she championed her favorite issues with relish, especially women's rights and an opposition to alcohol. She wielded her wit with a vengeance, alternately scoring points and alienating her friends and foes. Nancy also made offhand anti-Semitic remarks, and in the 1930s, many of her friends, nicknamed "the Cliveden set," became known for supporting appeasement with Hitler. For that, she was vilified in the press. Once war became inevitable, she set about restoring her reputation by going all in for the British cause. Altogether, Nancy could be contradictory, forceful, befuddling. As a hostess, however, she was without peer, as Hazel would see.

On the occasion of her visit, Nancy and Waldorf, now both sixty-three years old, devoted themselves to paying close attention to Hazel and making her feel completely at home. Nancy teased their visitor as if they'd known each other all their lives, and Hazel gave as good as she got. It was easy to see what appealed to Nancy about Hazel, a woman intent on achieving her ambition, unafraid of rank and authority, who held her own in a rough-and-tumble conversation. In many ways she resembled a young Nancy Astor—beyond the fact that both of them barely cleared five feet tall. They were small but mighty.

The only mystery was why Hazel was being treated to Cliveden's famous hospitality. A middle-class woman who had paid for flying lessons by working in an office didn't meet the usual standard of the Cliveden guest list. The Astors entertained the most notable figures of the day. George Bernard Shaw was a favorite at their house parties. Others included people of consequence in eclectic fields: Winston Churchill, the adventurer T. E. Lawrence, Charlie Chaplin, President and Mrs. Roosevelt, the British aviatrix Amy Johnson, the American aviatrix Amelia Earhart, the novelist Edith Wharton, and whichever members of the royal family were in residence at any time at Windsor Castle, a few miles down the road.

Yet after tea on the day of Hazel's visit, Lady Astor summoned the young pilot to her study. "I've made arrangements with the hospital for you to be discharged to my care," Nancy announced. "You are to return tomorrow to stay for a week." The mystery deepened: Why would the humble Hazel be afforded this attention? Since the invitation extended through December 29, she would be included in such a personal occasion as the family's Christmas celebration.

On Christmas Eve, Lord Astor led Hazel around the estate and shared more of its fabled history. He also confided his view that the property as she saw it wouldn't last. The aristocracy would emerge from the war permanently diminished, he felt, as class distinctions blurred in the communal effort. Lavish estates like Cliveden would fade amid the double burden of upkeep and irrelevance. Thinking ahead, Waldorf had made arrangements that year to turn the property over to the National Trust, which would help preserve and maintain the site for posterity while allowing the family to remain.

Such changing social norms likely played a role in Lady Astor's fondness for Hazel, as the two surely recognized the qualities of humor and perseverance that they shared despite their vastly different circumstances. But Nancy had a further plan to bridge the class divide. As the house bustled with servants preparing stacks of presents and decorating a tree in the main hall, Nancy took Hazel aside once again in a private study. The real reason she'd been invited for Christmas, Nancy confided, was to introduce Hazel to the Astor's four eligible sons. The hope was that one of them would fall for her.

Hazel considered the opportunity for only a moment. "That's a good thought on your part," she said carefully, "but I don't think I'm interested or ready just yet to even contemplate falling in love with anyone— even an Astor—because I came over to do a job. A job that's just begun."

Lady Astor was disconcerted. "It's odd," she said, "to find a young girl these days who wouldn't jump at the chance to marry someone with money and a name."

Hazel didn't mention the fortune teller in Montreal who had predicted that Hazel would fund her flying by marrying just such a rich Englishman.

Now, faced with the possibility of exactly that, she saw that marriage, not even for vast wealth, wasn't an avenue she was willing to take.

She answered simply. "It's not what I'm looking for in life."

They had quite a talk about the merits of marriage in general and Lady Astor's sons in particular, but Hazel didn't budge before Nancy Astor gave up. "Although I was frank about the situation," Hazel wrote to her mother, no doubt meaning that she didn't mince words, "she seemed to like me all the more."

ASIDE FROM HAZEL'S Christmas, the holiday was a mixed bag for the American pilots. Ann Wood planned ahead, combing the shops for candy to give as presents to her buddies at Ratcliffe. She chose a flask for her beau Avery and a book for her friend Peter Beasley. "There was festive spirit about," she wrote. "One couldn't help but wonder at the plentitude of everything while remembering those in the captive countries or even thousands on this isle, particularly civilians, who have given up so much." She delivered two Spits on Christmas Eve before Virginia Farr joined Ann to wrap parcels in her room. "The skies were glorious and life was lovely," she wrote about the day. "I was feeling it in every limb."

Mary Zerbel Hooper had "a horrible Christmas," surrounded by gifts that had been sent for her missing husband. Out of sympathy, Nancy Miller, the minister's daughter from Los Angeles, invited Mary to her billet for turkey, even though Nancy was feeling low herself, far away from the candlelight Christmas service at her father's church. Both were sorry they had no flying that day to distract them from homesickness. After dinner, "we just sat in front of the fire and tried not to let our feelings get the better of us," Nancy wrote in her journal.

Winnabelle Pierce flew all day on Christmas Eve—she was back in the swing—afterward dashing into London to spend the night at Claridge's with Peter Beasley. On Christmas Day, they listened to the King's speech on the radio, then attended a party in Maidenhead, where other women "tried to make Peter," according to Winnie. She went off to bed alone. "Peter slept elsewhere," she wrote, "and must have had a good time, too."

Following Hazel's pivotal conversation with Lady Astor, the pilot returned to her billet in Maidenhead rather than remain for the rest of the holiday at Cliveden. She didn't want to marry a millionaire, and besides, she had long planned Christmas with the Littlehales. They had scrounged up a twenty-pound turkey, and she contributed some nuts and fruitcake her mother had sent from Georgia. Hazel also dispatched some parcels of food to Lady Astor, who likely didn't need them. Nevertheless, the lady sent an affectionate thank-you note and an invitation to visit during any future leaves. Three days after Christmas, doctors cleared a well-rested Hazel to fly again. It was settled. The sky would remain her home.

CHAPTER 17

Dicing with Death

January 1943
White Waltham Aerodrome, Berkshire, and Kirkbride Aerodrome, Cumbria

T he ATA pilots flew into the teeth of a bitter winter as 1943 began. On January 9, Hazel Raines thought she was flying into an ordinary cloud and planned to go around or over the top. Then something seemed off. The southern pilot realized she was enveloped in something she had never seen before—driving sleet and snow. She turned around and made it to the nearest airfield before ice on the wings could take the plane down. Things were a mess everywhere. Ann Wood returned to White Waltham for her shot at learning two-engine aircraft and found that the grass airfield had turned into a mud pit. Such conditions led to predictable results: more accidents, more injuries, more deaths. The American women had been lucky so far, but sometimes it seemed it was only a matter of time before one of them joined the casualty list.

News spread fast after each new disaster. The popular pilot Alan Colman of the Colman's Mustard family met his demise due to weather conditions on January 17. Ferrying a Hurricane on a route north toward Scotland, he intended to stop in at a grass aerodrome in Yorkshire, not realizing that snowmelt had left eighteen inches of water on the field. The

Hurricane tipped forward, catching its nose in the mud, and the plane cartwheeled to come to rest upside down, just as Ann Wood's Spitfire had done two months earlier. In these soupy conditions, however, Colman was trapped in a horrifying position, his head under the muddy water in the open cockpit. He slowly drowned in his straps while others stood by waiting for help to lift the plane. Word spread quickly through all the aerodromes. Bad weather also brought down two other pilots heading through the same corridor to Scotland that week. Both smacked into hills, one of them "burnt to cinders," another way no one wanted to go. The calamities felt like a drumbeat, growing closer to anyone who challenged the winter skies.

Even lesser accidents had the capacity to break a pilot's nerve. After a relatively minor mishap while trying to land a Hurricane crossways in forty-five-mile-per-hour wind gusts, the American Kay Van Doozer was so shaken that she wound up in sick bay, exhausted and anxious. She'd never had an accident before in twelve years of flying. Some pilots coped by compartmentalizing. Ann Wood noted Colman's fatal crash in her diary, but followed up by writing that she went off on "a gala hike—gloriously warm and feel like a million dollars." Others lived more consciously with the feeling of a sword hanging over their heads. At Hamble, many of the women quoted from a melodramatic poem that included the line, "dicing with death under leaden skies." They incorporated the language into their everyday talk, cheerfully asking, "What are you dicing with today?" or remarking, "I can't dice until eleven. My Mosquito has developed a snag."

If any American felt the pressure of impending doom, it was Helen Richey, who held the empty title of American leader after Jackie Cochran left. Ann Wood had mostly stepped into that role in an informal way, as she did when Winnie was injured in her motorcycle accident. Otherwise, Helen, the most experienced of the Americans, and the famous holder of air racing and endurance records, was the most prominent American pilot. The ATA looked upon her with the highest expectations and utmost respect for her valor, but she was nevertheless racking up a string of accident reports that shredded her reputation and her resolve. Helen was well aware that she was deemed responsible for accidents in June and July of 1942. In December she had to force land a Miles Master, but that time problems with a hydraulic pump got the blame. Yet on January 3, 1943, Helen failed to control the swing of a Wellington bomber on takeoff, and just as she became airborne, the mammoth ship tipped sideways. A wingtip struck a hangar and broke off. She managed to return the Welly to the field, "but her nerves were shot," thought her friend Winnie Pierce.

The veteran pilot was already despondent over the news that her mother had suffered a stroke in December. Helen wanted to go home to help, but the ATA, citing the dangers of travel, denied the request. Now, in the wake of a smash-up witnessed by everyone at the field, she brought down the wrath of the Accident Committee for once again violating the cardinal rule: Don't break the plane. Three mistakes resulting in three damaged aircraft were enough to draw the attention of the upper brass. To the shock of her colleagues, the ATA terminated Helen on January 20, 1943, less than a year into her service. She became the second highly renowned American aviatrix, after Jackie Cochran, to get the sack, the fifth American sacked for any reason, and the second terminated for hapless flying. This brought the number of American women down to twenty.

Ann Wood learned the news at a party at Claridge's with Helen, Winnie, Louise Schuurman, and Peter Beasley. Peter was all for fighting the decision. A few others had recorded three accidents without losing their jobs. "Or is it a question of nerve?" Ann wondered. She decided to investigate with the women's commanding officer and make the case for Helen, but Pauline Gower was evasive, and Ann made no headway. Peter Beasley, ever the fixer, looked into the matter with other officials, but he backed off when he learned what the chief medical officer had concluded about Helen's psychological state. She was under "considerable mental strain," said the doctor, due to anxiety over her mother, along with "the strain of ferrying in winter months in this country, superimposed upon a background of mental anxiety."

So Helen was out. She would return to the States at the end of March 1943 to enroll in Jackie Cochran's new training program for the U.S. women's ferry service. Jackie was making progress as the service grew, but even a famous pilot like Helen wasn't allowed to skip the instruction, and she would have to perform menial assignments like towing targets back and forth for live ammunition gunnery practice. Her friends were relieved that Jackie's program had given Helen a place to land, but after she'd sampled the smorgasbord of top planes in England, it was a comedown for the celebrated pilot.

Almost everyone had accidents at one time or another, but it was Helen's difficulty handling the stress that sealed her dismissal. For a service in the business of flying a vast variety of untried and dinged-up planes, jitters were considered worse than Winnie Pierce's carousing, worse than Dorothy's lukewarm enthusiasm, worse than Hazel's heart problems. The pilots who made the grade carried on regardless. Mary Zerbel Hooper flew with a clear head after her husband died. Winnie got right back in a Hurricane after her engine failed. Hazel strapped on her flying helmet after each illness. Given the pressure and exhaustion of the job, it took unnatural poise and concentration to never slip up.

Never. Because they were dicing with death.

FEW PILOTS WERE as strong, physically and mentally, as Virginia Farr. When the Rochester Chapter of the Junior League awarded the reluctant socialite an honorary membership in absentia in late 1942, her mother conveyed thanks on Virginia's behalf by noting, "Her amazing calm and sure faith is very comforting to us . . . We have heard from returning pilots in the Ferry Command that she is in great form." In the tradition of the family's philanthropy and public service, Virginia, her mother said, was "getting a long view of the war, and already thinking of the great task that will be necessary to rebuild the world when the war is over." Rocksteady in the air, Virginia's accident record remained clean, her evaluations stellar: "A sound, resourceful pilot with good judgment." "A good officer and a sound pilot. She is wisely cautious about the weather."

The somewhat brusque manner that was an impediment at the tea dances in her teenage years served Virginia well in a military setting where frivolity got in the way. Her British counterparts found it amusing when Virginia told them what happened to her while waiting for clear conditions at an RAF airfield, reading by the fire outside the mess hall. A group made up of air marshals and other dignitaries loaded with the gold signifiers of august rank created a flurry parading into the mess. Virginia glanced up briefly at the procession, which included an equally turned-out woman, apparently the guest of honor, who returned the scrutiny. Unbeknownst to the American, the lady was the Duchess of Gloucester, the wife of Prince Henry, the third son of the late King George V. On top of her many public engagements, she also served as air commandant of the Women's Auxiliary Air Force, which provided services on the ground to the RAF.

Sometime later, she and her entourage passed again on their way out. The duchess shot another look Virginia's way, clearly intrigued by the sight of a woman in flying boots and gold bars that signified rank of her own. The lady stopped to ask the men some questions. One of the air marshals directed his gaze at Virginia and beckoned with a finger. She looked behind her to see who they were summoning and concluded it had to be her.

Virginia didn't know the Duchess of Gloucester from a barmaid at the Gloucester Arms but later told friends, "I knew it was someone rather fancy." Now what? Virginia, who came from fancy herself, wasn't wearing a cap, so saluting was out. She wore pants, so she couldn't curtsy. She summoned her full five-feet-ten height, strode toward the duchess, and extended a hand to shake. "I'm Virginia Farr," she said, not standing on ceremony. "And who are you?"

In English society in peacetime, such an abrupt approach to someone so fancy would have been considered an affront. But Virginia pulled it off without an ounce of self-consciousness. When British ATA operations officer Alison King heard the story, she wrote, "How the Duchess must have enjoyed the freshness of it, the spontaneity." No evidence survives to judge whether that was true. But the British were learning that if they wanted these capable Americans to serve, spontaneity came with the package.

AS IS OFTEN the case in war, Virginia's merits on the job earned her one of the toughest, most arduous, and most dangerous assignments. On January 26, 1943, at the height of winter, she was posted to Kirkbride Aerodrome, better known by its nickname—the Salt Mines.

Isolated on the Solway Firth in the farthest northwest of England, locked in between the mountains of the Lake District to the south, the

Irish Sea to the west, the Cumberland Fells to the east, and Scottish peaks to the north, Kirkbride posed navigating nightmares for its mostly male pilots. In every direction, the Kirkbride contingent threaded low through twisty gaps in the landscape as clouds pressed down from the mountaintops, boxing the pilots in, especially on the notorious Dumfries Valley route to Prestwick. Flying too far into a narrowing valley could be a trap, leaving no room to turn back. Collisions with mountains caused many fatalities, including three the week of January 16, just before Virginia learned of her posting. Her colleagues believed Pauline Gower assigned Virginia and the experienced Canadian pilot Helen Harrison there to prove that women could handle the strain as well as men. Only the most hardened pilots drew the Kirkbride assignment.

The seaside skies around Kirkbride changed so abruptly that a weather report given before a pilot started her engine could be obsolete by the time she taxied to the runway. There was often no choice but to go over the top, in violation of the rules, hoping to find an opening to descend again. Had Kirkbride aviators not challenged the prohibition, some estimated, a third of the work would have gone undone. Friends in the RAF helped Virginia practice instrument flying on a simulator before she left for the post.

Adding to the woes of the Salt Mines, the base functioned as a repair depot, so she drew chits for more than her share of damaged planes. Virginia flew aircraft with wind whistling into the cockpit through bullet holes. Others had missing doors. Frequently, when a plane seemed that it wouldn't make it, she put down in a farmer's field and walked to the nearest house to report in. Also, "she came under fire from German planes, and she'd have to take evasive action and get out of there," said her niece, Cristy Rodiger.

But Virginia, now twenty-four, remained cool-headed and stalwart. She knew her prodigious skills were needed. "She would have done anything that was asked of her," said her niece. "She felt compassionate toward the men who were flying dangerous missions. She felt strongly that America should be in the war." As a result, her niece added, "She was never scared." It was the ideal temperament for an assignment that demanded mental toughness. Not that Virginia wasn't relieved when she learned she would be reassigned to safer skies when the weather warmed in April. She left the Salt Mines with her pristine accident record still intact.

The odd one out most of her life, Virginia Farr fit in like a trooper at a godforsaken place that called for courage and commitment. If the war effort needed unshakable pilots during winter in Kirkbride, they had picked the right woman.

CHAPTER 18

The Drumbeat of Fatality

March 2, 1943
Hamble, Hampshire

H azel Jane Raines had yet to make a misstep, either. When she
boarded a Spitfire Mark IX at the factory near Hamble on the
morning of March 2, 1943, there was no reason to think this job would be
different from any other, let alone that it would send her flying through
a roof in a bucolic village, creating a lifelong memory for two boys who
witnessed the crash. At twenty-six, Hazel had never had an accident in
her life. The weather looked fine, the aircraft was brand new. Theoreti-
cally, a test pilot would have taken it for a check flight to make sure it
functioned before handing it off to Hazel.

For once, before the crash, fate had been rolling Hazel's way. Since
her solid rest at Lady Astor's estate in December, Second Officer Raines
had managed to stay out of the medical pool. A posting on January 20,
1943, to the Hamble Aerodrome on the southern coast spared her some
of the worst winter cold. She was frustrated that her health had delayed
her advancement to two-engine bombers, the move that she thought
would do the most for her career. But Hazel had thoroughly mastered
the Spitfire and took pleasure putting the speedy, agile plane through its
paces. Her history performing stunts in air shows gave assurance and flair

to her flying as she dodged balloon barrages and whipped through serpentine valleys.

Hazel took it in stride that there was action at Hamble, the closest ATA base to the wider war. She learned to heed air raid warnings soon after her arrival when she delivered a Spit and descended from the cockpit to find no one to take her papers.

I suppose they're all out to tea, she thought.

Eventually she realized a raid was on and sat by the ship until the danger passed. A German plane had sprayed machine-gun fire across the field and killed three men. "What burns me up is they give us the best fighters built to fly but minus the ammunition," Hazel wrote to her family. "How I would like to take a shot at one of those so-and-sos!"

Her prewar fame as an aviatrix continued as American journalists followed her progress. "It's out of hoop skirts and into dungarees and denims for southern belles!" began an article in the February 1943 issue of *Mademoiselle* that featured Hazel's ATA service. "War has come to Dixieland, and these girls of the deep South are in it."

But Hazel's life, both before and during the war, bore little resemblance to the frothy prose. Known for wearing jodhpurs and boots in Georgia, her daily attire now consisted of layers of long underwear under trousers, sweaters, and a bulging flying suit. She lived quietly with a family a five-minute walk from the Hamble Aerodrome. On leave days, she returned to rest in Maidenhead with her old landlords the Littlehales rather than join the high life in London. She kept her mind on the job and the various aircraft that came her way. "The aeroplanes are so different in speed, handling, and navigation," she wrote to her mother in February. "In case of emergency, you don't have time to sit and debate with yourself what you will do—you must decide immediately and act accordingly."

WHETHER SHE HAD the prowess to follow her own advice under the worst possible conditions was put to the test on March 2, 1943. As usual, in her pocket she carried a silver dollar with the inscription IN GOD WE TRUST. On takeoff, she repeated the pledge—"In God We Trust." And she did—Hazel was philosophical about the risks of the work. But what saved her when her engine failed as she entered a wall of cloud and her

Spitfire spun to earth wasn't divine intervention. As a pilot with a thousand hours under her belt before she joined the ATA, her greatest advantage in this impossible situation was her experience in air shows across the American South. The loop the loops, the diving spins she'd executed to thrill the public, gave her a feel for how to recover at the last minute, when screaming crowds were certain she would crash.

Still, there were serious consequences. The thatched-roof house that she struck lost its second floor in an explosion of splintered furniture and beams. The precious Spitfire shattered in the neighbors' garden—a complete write-off. Luckily it didn't burst into flame. Before she hit, Hazel must have had the sense to switch off the ignition to prevent its spitting sparks. And although she managed before she fell unconscious to repeat the command she'd been taught to use if an aircraft fell into the wrong circumstance—"London! Guard that plane!"—blood poured from a wound above her right eye.

Hazel's injuries were so acute that for three months she lied to her mother in letters, pretending to be flying again when it was uncertain whether she ever would. Out of fear the story would make the papers in Georgia, she finally mentioned the accident nearly a month after it happened, describing "a funny experience" about her plane getting "tired" and refusing to run, resulting in "an interesting ride through a house." Supposedly, it all worked out perfectly. She claimed she suffered only "a bump on my head and two beautiful blue knees." The residents of the house she destroyed supposedly were delighted that it would be rebuilt by the government. They were swell, Hazel wrote, about cleaning her up in what was left of their home while she awaited an ambulance to the hospital.

In truth, Hazel, unconscious in the accident's aftermath, had no memory of it when she woke up in the Canadian hospital in Cliveden with battered knees and a concussion. It took thirteen stitches to close the four-inch gash on her forehead. Doctors shaved off her hair on one side, and Hazel made a joke of that, too. "I now look like a prisoner from Sing Sing," she eventually wrote to her mother.

In letters to her sister, Hazel stayed more on the mark. She admitted she was "darn lucky" to be alive. Worse, for a woman who lived to fly, the concussion had affected the vision in her right eye. Doctors released her from the hospital after two weeks but wouldn't clear her for duty unless she passed exams in three months' time. "It sure is a tough blow for me, but—I guess I can take it," Hazel wrote.

But what, exactly, had gone wrong? Losing lift in a whiteout had killed many a disoriented pilot, including one of those who crashed near Kirkbride during the deadly week in January. This was the kind of circumstance that decades later in 1999 would lead to the death of the pilot John F. Kennedy Jr., who lost equilibrium in haze and dove into the sea. Such crashes were common enough in the United Kingdom during the war that an initial investigation assumed that was all there was to it, despite Hazel's memory that the engine had failed before the cloud overtook her. "In difficult weather conditions she failed to maintain control and crashed into two cottages," read the immediate accident report.

But later, a fuller inquiry examined the aircraft itself and proposed that a loose screw in the primer pump for the gas line led to the initial sputtering of the engine and the subsequent full stop. The sudden clouds presented a double complication. Regardless, Hazel wasn't held responsible. Both weather and mechanical malfunction had conspired to bring her down. For the first accident in her career, it was a doozy.

UNFORTUNATELY, THE RISK of serious injury caught up with another American pilot that winter as well. Evelyn Hudson, at thirty-four, had brought a wealth of experience to her role in the war. An expert swimmer and former diving champion, she earned her pilot's license in 1931 in Hawaii, where she flew tourists on sightseeing trips. By 1935, based in Los Angeles, she set records for endurance and altitude—reaching an astounding eighteen thousand feet in a single-engine monoplane in 1939. By 1943, the ATA cleared her to fly the largest two-engine bombers, and ATA instructors considered her "well-disciplined" and "intelligent."

Like Hazel, Evelyn had never crashed before, but a bum Wellington bomber was her undoing when she wasn't even at the controls. On March 16, 1943, she and Dorothy Furey Bragg boarded the two-engine Welly to hitch a ride back to their home bases with the British officer Elizabeth May in the pilot's seat. Immediately on takeoff, the engine on the left wing failed. With the proper training, it was possible to fly a Wellington on just one engine, but the plane hadn't yet reached a speed that would support it. Following protocol, First Officer May crash-landed straight ahead, striking power lines at the end of the runway. She and Dorothy were slightly injured, but the impact flung Evelyn toward the fuselage. She later remembered thinking in a momentary flash about the unusual geodetic structure of the Wellington shell, a metal casing covered with linen, just before she hurtled through it and tumbled to the ground, crushing multiple vertebrae.

Five days later, Ann Wood once again took on the responsibility of looking after an American. She showed up at an understaffed hospital to lobby for transferring Evelyn to the better facility at Cliveden. Since Helen Richey's dismissal, no one had been placed specifically in charge of the American women, so Ann had established herself as an informal leader with the skills and temperament to handle an emergency, winning notice from higher-ups who might someday advance her career. She shouldered the task of getting headquarters buzzing about the case and finding a ride to move the patient. Evelyn, encased in a full-torso cast, suffered tremendous pain. "The agony of getting from one position to another was more than I could watch," Ann wrote in her diary. Doctors operated to move bone from Evelyn's shin to her back. She spent five months in a body cast before the ATA terminated her for disability and sent her home. Tapping into her renowned endurance, she regained her ability to walk but never piloted another plane. In 1944, she applied to return to the ATA, but it was no longer signing new pilots.

The number of American women in the organization continued to dwindle. Besides the four pilots who had left in 1942, including Jackie Cochran, and Helen Richey, who was fired in January 1943, there were two more who departed by the spring of that year. They were among three Americans who had traveled from the States to join on their own rather than travel with Jackie Cochran's group. Evelyn Hyam, ejected as "unlikely to become an efficient ferry pilot," quickly returned home determined to "become a good doctor or a poor flyer," as she put it. And Betty Lussier, eager to mix it up on the Continent, didn't stay long before joining the OSS, where she helped to recruit spies in Algeria, Italy, and France. Evelyn Hudson, released from her cast, would leave in August, and Hazel's future was in doubt. If she left, too, only nineteen of Jackie's original twenty-five would remain.

At least all the Americans so far had survived their close calls: Winnie Pierce's Hurricane engine failure on takeoff; Ann Wood's Spitfire somersault; Hazel Raine's blind, powerless Spitfire spin; Evelyn Hudson's ejection from the crashed Wellington. But the drumbeat of fatality felt ever closer. Too close. The English pilot Honor Salmon, who was based in Hamble and a good friend to many of the Americans, died on April 19, 1943, at the age of thirty when she encountered a cold front while ferrying an Oxford, a reliable two-engine trainer. A Spitfire on the same route turned back, but Honor persisted, plunged into the milky murk, and crashed into a hill near her home. Within hours, her name was erased from the assignment board at the aerodrome.

Ann Wood sounded resigned when she heard the news. "Poor weather is supposed—but when in doubt they always say this." She and the rest of the Americans had to wonder how long their cohort could carry on, cheating death in those perilous skies.

CHAPTER 19

Eyes Wide Open

May 22, 1943
Littleworth, Worcestershire

On an unremarkable day toward the end of May 1943, harsh winter conditions had given way to the solace of spring. A group of seven women aviators hoisted themselves into a fleet of Miles Master single-engine fighters to head north from an RAF base near Bristol, bound for a maintenance facility at Tern Hill in Shropshire. Skies were overcast in the west of England, but visibility looked acceptable below the clouds. All indications pointed to a routine ride if the aviators kept under a thousand feet and followed the railroad lines over the city of Birmingham.

Six of the flyers doubled up in three of the brand-new Miles Master trainers. Winnie Pierce and her pal Louise Schuurman shared one of the two-seaters, designed to accommodate both a student and an instructor. They knew the aircraft well from their Class 2 schooling, where the ship had served as an introduction to the high-performance qualities of other, sexier fighters. Piece of cake.

The American Mary Webb Nicholson flew alone in another ship, the better to stash all her gear. The trip marked a much-anticipated mile-stone for Jackie Cochran's former secretary. When Mary completed this delivery on May 23, 1943, she was scheduled to wind up at the Cosford

Aerodrome, an ATA base near Tern Hill, to begin her first posting at a ferry pool after completing Class 2 fighter training. In the rear seat and stowage compartment of the Miles Master II she had packed most everything she owned in England, including balls of yarn for the knitting that kept her grounded when she wasn't in the air.

Winnie Pierce, Louise Schuurman, and Virginia Farr had transferred into Cosford a month or so before. Winnie and Louise hated the location, a four-hour train ride from their regular romps in London. But Virginia was pleased at Cosford's distinction as one of two all-women ferry pools, where pilots took pride in keeping the standards as high or higher than they were when the base was an outfit for men.

The ATA women's matriarch, Pauline Gower, emphasized such merits when she pushed for equal status for women pilots. Unlike Jackie Cochran, who placed her quest for women's opportunities at the forefront of various public relations gambits, Pauline employed a persistent but low-key diplomacy. This soft-power approach, in combination with her connections in government, paid off with a momentous win for women the week before Mary's transfer. On May 18, 1943, Parliament approved equal pay for women pilots of the ATA, ending the policy that had allotted them 20 percent less than men. The change was a landmark in British employment equity when such protections for other occupations remained decades away. The perception that women pilots were performing the most traditional of men's work—and valiant, dangerous work at that—helped the Atta-Girls make that historic leap forward.

WHEN MARY REACHED Cosford, it seemed unlikely that she would be corralled into Winnie and Louise's fast and frenetic social set. Mary's background couldn't have differed more from theirs, and her reserved nature offered few hints of a daredevil within. Raised in a devout family in Greensboro, North Carolina, in a comfortable home with a long front porch, she had played the piano for services at the Quaker Church before she studied music at nearby Guilford College. She planned to finish her degree, but in 1925 when she was twenty, Mary, dark-haired with smiling eyes, met Harris Preston Pearson, a handsome doctor ten years her senior. They married and moved to his home in Portsmouth, Ohio. When the marriage turned sour, she devised an escape plan, taking courses in accounting and stenography to prepare for a future supporting herself. The goal of office work seemed to align with her careful personality until a bolt struck from the gods of happy accidents.

Try as one might, it's nearly impossible to draw a straight line from accounting and playing the church piano to stunt flying, but after she attended an air show, Mary was desperate to learn to fly. She struck a bargain with the nearest flying school: She could earn free lessons if she appeared in a show, making three parachute jumps from a biplane.

The school didn't offer Mary any guidance before the performance. A pilot took her up to 1,200 feet, where she edged out into the wind on the wing, bracing herself by clinging to the struts. Unlike later parachutes, the one she used in 1927 wasn't packed on her back. Instead, an assistant crept out on the wing behind her, clutching the loose cloud of fabric. Mary waited to pass over the show until she stepped off, hoping all the paraphernalia wouldn't get tangled with the plane. She made it. Two more leaps, and she was set for lessons. Mary may have been quiet, but she wasn't timid.

In 1928, she made another bold move for the time, filing for divorce on the grounds of neglect and cruelty. According to her petition, she claimed that her husband drank, quarreled, embarrassed her among friends and "otherwise abuses her." She insisted on restoring her maiden name.

Newly free, Mary returned to the family home in North Carolina only to face more troubles. Her parents had to take in boarders when her father lost his job at a bank, and Mary found work as a secretary. The soft-spoken aviator still managed to make noise as a barnstormer and performer of snap rolls and fancy loops at air shows, inspiring headlines like GIRL JUMPS OUT OF AIRPLANE. COME WATCH! An act of self-sacrificing heroism earned her more attention. While landing in Hickory, North Carolina, in 1936, Mary was startled when a woman driving a car full of children pulled onto the runway. To avoid hitting them, Mary put herself in danger by swerving and striking the ground with a wing. The children were saved at the price of a fractured skull and concussion for Mary, her first and only accident before the war.

Mary came to the notice of Jackie Cochran by becoming the governor for the southeast states of the Ninety-Nines, the organization of women pilots. Jackie had churned through her share of private secretaries, but she struck gold when she hired Mary in 1937. The famous aviatrix needed competence, not another diva in the room, and the unassuming Mary made a perfect match. She moved into an apartment two blocks from Jackie's, and the two flew around the country together in Jackie's powerful private plane. Mary also took over as the governor of the Ninety-Nines for New York and New Jersey before she joined the ATA.

By May of 1943, she had waited out a frustrating stretch of winter delays and moved ahead in her ATA training with the assurance earned through years of expert stunt piloting. "She was on cloud nine to be flying full-time," said her younger brother Frank. Mary took on Hurricanes and made her two first sorties in a Spitfire. "In Training Pool her work was excellent," said an evaluation, "and she has all along impressed her instructors as being a cautious pilot who is out to do the best ferrying job she can."

However much Winnie and her friend Louise might have regarded Cosford as a lonely outpost, Mary Webb Nicholson looked forward to the lack of distractions from work. "She wasn't there to party or to meet people," said her niece Mary Walton. "She was there to fly."

To begin her long-awaited service there, Mary joined the other six pilots on the gray day of May 23 at the Hullavington RAF base outside of Bristol. As they hustled into their Miles Masters to take off ahead of a front, no one noticed an oil leak in one of the engines. Winnie and Louise laughed as they lined up on the runway and took the lead. Mary loaded her luggage into every corner of her fuselage and followed.

ONE OF THE shocks of flying in that rushed and uncertain era was how suddenly the most freakish things could go wrong. The pilots in two of the Miles Masters that took off that afternoon turned back over concern about the overcast weather, but Winnie and Louise in tandem, and Mary Nicholson alone, pressed on. They had no trouble keeping well below the clouds. The Master was a quick aircraft. As befit an inexpensive plane used for training Spitfire and Hurricane pilots, it was more ungainly than they were in appearance and assembled in a more rudimentary fashion, constructed out of wood on a metal frame. Mary's logbook showed barely more than an hour practicing on the Master before that day, but at about fifty minutes into the two-hour trip, she was familiar enough to be cruising smoothly over farmland in Worcestershire at less than three hundred miles per hour.

Even for a pilot who flew modern wartime aircraft regularly, what happened next was bizarre. A sudden revving of the engine, a loud bang, and a complete loss of power. There was no way for Mary to know what had happened. Only later was it apparent that the oil leak and subsequent lack of lubrication had caused friction to develop in the mounting of the propeller. That propeller—the only one on the single-engine Master— seized up, broke loose, and sailed off in midflight. The part tumbled down to a vegetable field hundreds of feet below.

It would be hard for a pilot to tell that the prop was missing. A fast-spinning one wouldn't look much different from one that wasn't there at all. But as the nose dropped and the Master slowed down, Mary knew her power was gone. Revving the engine in the hope that it would pick up produced no effect. Time was short to get the plane on the ground.

Mary ran through the options. The city of Worcester, she knew, stretched out dead ahead. If she bailed out now with a parachute, a skill she certainly possessed, she might already be too low for safety. Besides, although a jump could offer a chance to save herself, she might lose the plane and endanger lives in the city.

She wouldn't risk harming civilians. But if she tried to glide to a forced landing, the flagging speed of the hobbled aircraft didn't give her many choices amid the terrain within range. Most farming fields in the vicinity were set apart with brick walls and strewn with obstacles like grazing cattle.

Mary chose the best alternative, a field outside the farming village of Littleworth. The pocket of open space was not especially long. Dotted with apple trees and hemmed in by houses and farm buildings, it wasn't ideal for landing an aircraft with the speed and thirty-nine-foot wing-span of the Master. But the little plot of farmland was all Mary had.

She'd been flying low with a tailwind before the crisis, so she harnessed the diminishing capabilities of the crippled Master, now nothing more than a very inefficient glider, to turn around, away from Worcester and into the wind. She needed that headwind to slow down enough for landing, but making the turn created drag that further limited the range where she could remain airborne.

Mary lowered the aircraft to fifty or sixty feet above a crossways road as she approached her target. She swooped across the country lane and eased down over some cottages beyond, the screaming sound of the large aircraft alarming their inhabitants. It was evident now how inadequate this landing strip would be.

She descended further, the narrow pathway to survival in her sights. A little boy running toward the plane momentarily caught her eye. She could see he was safe as she passed him by. A wingtip flicked the branches of an apple tree, slewing the plane to the right, but it didn't matter. The field was too short to bring the Master to a stop. It smacked headlong into a brick barn, bounced back into a ditch, and erupted in flame. The combustible wood of the fuselage fed the fire.

Moments later, the fuel tanks in the wings exploded. When boys ran from farmhouses with buckets of water, it was already too late. They saw a woman's head in a leather helmet dangling from a broken neck as the blaze overtook the scene. Mary Webb Nicholson was dead. After a fire brigade doused the inferno, the boys were surprised to see unusual cargo for a military plane—singed balls of knitting yarn scattered in the grass.

THE TELEGRAM FROM England set off waves of grief in Mary's family. The cremated remains of their oldest child and only daughter arrived soon after for burial in Greensboro. At the funeral, her father wept through the song "Danny Boy," the only time Mary's brothers and nieces ever saw him cry. Her niece Ann Smith, who was born two weeks before Mary's death, described an aftermath that persisted for generations. "In my lifetime I cannot recall my grandfather with a smile on his face," she said.

Mary's parents turned their home into a shrine, hanging a photograph of their daughter in a white prewar flying uniform over the fireplace and framed newspaper clippings along the wall. One of them reported on the time when she veered and crashed in Hickory, North Carolina, rather than risk hitting children on the runway. It was the same choice she made to avoid hurting civilians in Worcester. A local newspaper broke the news of her death with praise: "It is fitting to commend her courage. Hers was a tribute to womanhood. She asked no odds on a man's job. It wasn't feminine conquest. It was feminine fitness."

THROUGHOUT THEIR SERVICE, all the pilots worked to keep the same terrifying specter at bay—the knowledge that something as simple as an oil leak, a peculiar propeller mishap, a moment of inattention, or an unexpected conjuring of fog could bring about sudden, bolt-from-above death. The women counteracted such thoughts with drinking, knitting, love affairs, black humor, and willed obliviousness to the worst possibilities. All of these tactics were effective up to a point. But the death of Mary Webb Nicholson hit like a sucker punch—no one could get her defenses up fast enough. "I thought it might easily have been me," said Winnie Pierce. She was right—the chance had been one in four that she and Louise would be handed the chit for the defective plane that day.

Added to the jolt of this particular tragedy was every pilot's horror of fire. Some RAF fighter pilots carried a loaded pistol to shoot themselves at the first sign of flames. The British flyer Diana Barnato was haunted by the memory of her first day flying solo when a man at the airport, his face scarred by seared flesh, implored her not to fly. "I didn't mind the idea of being bumped off," Diana wrote, "but I didn't want to be maimed. A wounded man is a hero, but a disfigured woman is . . . nothing." The word was that Mary Nicholson died instantly, but the other women, never trusting the rumor mill, wondered whether this might have been a comforting fiction.

Nevertheless, most of the Americans faced her death squarely by attending the funeral in Maidenhead on May 29. They distracted themselves with complaints about the service, including the fact that Pauline Gower didn't attend. The highest officer present had to improvise the program after an embarrassing delay. Ann Wood made acerbic comments in her diary: "The service was simple and cold with many quotes from Mary Baker Eddy about strength, light, and sunshine, none of which would have helped me much." Afterward, Ann sunbathed on the roof of the Red Cross Club and declared, as she often did after other tragic events, that she "felt like a million dollars." In subsequent days, assuming a different sort of leadership role, she met with a Commander Fred Fish of Boston, "a staid, old-fashioned bachelor" who had attended Mary's funeral as a somewhat mysterious friend. Ann consoled him with meals at the Red Cross Club and bicycle rides through the city until she declared, "He has found his sea legs again after her going."

However much the others tried to distract themselves, the death led them to reflect. A few days after Mary's crash, Ann torqued violently on a botched landing of a two-engine bomber. She sorted it out, but the brief emergency made her speculate how she would behave in a fatal crash. "At first one wonders, then acts, and then a feeling of indifference and 'well, this is it' comes over me. [I] feel I wouldn't keep up the fighting spirit to the last." She felt more inclined to "give in and let it come."

THE OFFICIAL ACCIDENT report was cryptic as usual, emphasizing the oil leak and the fate of the plane. There was a war on, and little time to conduct a detailed inquiry. The pilot was found not responsible, for what it was worth. There were no notes on whether Mary had been able to deploy the flaps or the undercarriage to ease the landing. The lack of detail led Roberta Sandoz, who had shared Mary's ship to England the previous August, to visit the scene to walk the field and speak to neighbors. Roberta formed the opinion that Mary had possessed enough time and space to save herself and land the plane in that field. Mary was religious, Roberta knew, and she latched on to the theory that her friend had simply given up, closed her eyes, and prayed. "If she thought she was going to die," Roberta said, "you know, you search for an explanation. Well, maybe she had her eyes shut."

Roberta continued to assert this theory for years. It was a natural tendency—seeking reassurance that no predicament was hopeless, that a resourceful pilot could find a way. But it deeply upset members of Mary's family, who revered her skill.

Eight decades later, it was possible to assemble a fuller story based on the known parameters of the Miles Master and interviews with witnesses to the crash who were still alive. Put together, they demonstrate that Roberta's opinion was wrong—it had not been feasible for Mary to stop the plane before reaching the boundary of the field, and she was very much engaged in trying to pull off the forced landing to the end. A local boy named Eddie Collins, the child Mary saw just before impact, watched her rumble past at about twenty to twenty-five feet in the air within a thousand feet of the end of the field. A Miles Master would have needed nearly 1,800 feet at that point to safely come to a halt. "By the time he saw Miss Nicholson, I'm afraid her fate was already sealed," said Geoffrey Hudson, an aviation historian who lived in the area and arranged a memorial plaque on the site in 2019.

A number of children saw and heard Mary's final moments and vividly recalled the trauma throughout their lives. Murray Gill, who was thirteen at the time, was eating lunch in his family's farmhouse when he suddenly heard "a tremendous roaring noise just above the roof." Through a rattling window he saw the plane sweep overhead and just miss some farm buildings, then heard a thump at the far end of the field as it hit the ground. He remembered running with his father toward the crash with buckets of water as flames licked at the plane. They saw furrows in the wet ground where the fuselage had skidded before hitting the barn. When they were a hundred yards away from the aircraft, "it suddenly went up in a big explosion," Murray said. His father stopped him and turned him around. There was nothing they could do.

Eddie Collins, the closest to the crash, could see that Mary was fully alert and steering the plane as it came down. Eddie was a seven-year-old doing his business in an outhouse with the door wide open when he heard the plane approach. He ran out into the field, pulling his trousers up. By then the Master was so close that its wings bobbled only a dozen feet from where he stood. Catching sight of the child, the pilot turned her head and locked eyes with the last human being she would see on earth. "She looked out. She looked straight at me," said Eddie. "I will never, ever forget that face. She didn't look frightened at all, just straight-faced, traveling by."

He was shocked that the pilot was a woman, thinking maybe Germans had shot her down. And he was shocked again when he attended the unveiling of the plaque seventy-seven years later. He saw her in a photograph there, exactly as he remembered—her wide brow, firm-set mouth, and bright eyes. "She still had her hat on," he said, the same leather flying helmet he had seen that day.

In 1943, those eyes pinned him to the spot, but the moment couldn't hold. Mary turned forward again to focus on the fast-diminishing prospect ahead. The wing tip ticked the apple tree, tilting the plane toward the barn where Eddie's grandfather kept his pigs. "And the next thing, bang, into the wall she went." Eddie stopped looking after that. "I ran into the house, frightened to death."

There was no doubt. Mary Webb Nicholson went to her death with eyes wide open and a full awareness of her destiny.

CHAPTER 20

The Bomber Boys

May–June 1943
England, the Netherlands, Ireland, and Germany

Every night, the pilots of the Air Transport Auxiliary could hear the bombers they had delivered during the day heading out in force to inflict destruction on the enemy, risking heavy tolls on the aircraft and their crews. "Anything from twenty to thirty [ships] lost per night, which seems like a lot," Ann Wood recorded. The war was an ever-changing beast. Its latest incarnation devoured people on both sides—factory workers and civilians blown to bits in German-occupied territory and British and American men shot down inside the metal shells of the huge, lumbering Lancasters, Stirlings, Halifaxes, Wellingtons, Flying Fortresses, and other ripe targets for German fighters and exploding flak.

The German land army in North Africa surrendered in the early days of May 1943, setting the stage for an Allied invasion of Sicily that would begin in July. On the eastern front, German and Soviet troops slogged on, but for the most part in 1943, the Allies were still setting the stage for the eventual end game, a land war in the heart of Europe. Which meant that much of the fight was still in the air.

In January of 1943, Churchill and FDR had agreed to cooperate in escalating bomb attacks on German soil. The strategy called for a massive buildup of both strategic and area bombing, striking not only industrial facilities and military targets but workers and families in surrounding homes. The American Army Air Forces reached a critical mass and began to make a sizable contribution, mostly taking off from bases near Cambridge. Daylight raids by the United States got underway, more dangerous for the bombers than the night raids by the RAF but providing greater accuracy for strikes. The size and frequency of attacks gradually increased, and the tonnage of bombs they deployed more than doubled between January and May.

Crews on these planes commanded all the power of the fearsome bombs they carried while feeling powerless themselves. On every mission, they hunched inside the frigid, clattering metal bellies of the aircraft, tuning out the hair-raising noise—the rumble of the engine, the bursts of flak, the shrieking dive-bombs of German fighters, the deadly rattle of machine-gun fire—while knowing that at any moment the airmen could be blasted out of the sky. They knew their chances. Two thirds of them would die in combat or be taken prisoner. Only one in four would complete the required twenty-five missions.

These men, so many of them doomed, were the objects of sympathy for ATA flyers who cooled their heels at bomber bases between delivery jobs. The ferry pilots witnessed the silence at breakfast in the mess hall after a night of raids, the conspicuous empty seats, the lingering sensation of ghosts. More ATA pilots rushed through training to ferry bombers and feed the demand for replacements of the aircraft that were lost.

AT THE BEGINNING of March 1943, Dorothy Furey Bragg was cleared for Class 3 two-engine aircraft with a backhanded comment from her instructor—"should do well as long as she keeps her mind on the job at hand." Her conversion to Class 4 bombers would take place in June. Meanwhile, by the middle of May, her husband, the pilot Richard Bragg, had already led nine missions as the skipper of a four-engine heavy Halifax bomber. On the night of May 12, 1943, German antiaircraft fire shot fourteen holes in his aircraft, taking it out of service, so on May 13, he and his crew of seven boarded a brand-new Halifax on their tenth mission together. The airmen included gunners, a flight engineer, a radio operator, a bomb aimer, and a navigator. Bragg, at twenty-six, was the oldest. An apprentice copilot, only nineteen, was the youngest.

Bragg took off before midnight from an RAF base near York following a route over the Netherlands to Bochum, Germany, a center for manufacturing steel. His team was one of the first to reach the target, so there was little flak, and they turned around with relief. But at three in the morning, as Bragg followed the path of return over Friesland at nineteen thousand feet, a German fighter attacked—just three quick bursts of machine-gun fire. They hit the bomber near its tail, and fire flickered in the bomb bay.

Right away, the Halifax began to lose altitude. Bragg realized he could no longer control the plane and shouted an order for the crew to bail out. The bomb aimer, Sergeant Harry Gell, called back from a compartment under the nose of the ship, "Can you turn toward land? We're heading out to sea." It would be deadly to fall into the water in the middle of the night.

Gell briefly passed out from lack of oxygen, but when he came to, he saw land closer below. Bragg had succeeded in placing the plane over safe terrain for a parachute jump. The captain called out, "Hurry up! Get out! We're only at four thousand feet. We're in a steep dive."

Gell opened his escape hatch and jumped first. The next thing he remembered was that all the noise had stopped, as if a switch had been thrown, and he was lying in a pasture with three curious black-and-white cows staring him down. He was taken prisoner the next day.

In the sky, the Halifax could no longer withstand the scorching speed of the fall. The aircraft broke apart, at least three separate pieces shooting to the ground like trails of fireworks. The local police saw some burning parts hit a farm near the Dutch coastal town of Harlingen. Six bodies were found there the next morning, and another some distance away.

In Bochum, the target of the bombing raid, 394 houses were destroyed and 302 inhabitants were killed that night. The RAF lost 29 of 442 aircraft, and 131 crewmembers died, including Richard Bragg, Dorothy Furey's husband of less than a year. He was buried beneath a cross by strangers, residents of Wijnaldum in the Netherlands, the village where he fell.

★

DOROTHY FUREY BRAGG later confided to close family that she was sad when Bragg was killed, but the couple had never been devoted—she had seen her husband only a few times during the previous year. "I didn't even know how to contact his parents," she said. "I assume the RAF did." She impressed her colleagues with an ability to tamp down grief and carry on. But Dorothy still haunted the bar at the Polygon Hotel, and men still lined up to take their chances with the remote beauty. Lord Beatty held his place in the queue, more eager than ever to continue their affair, and she obliged him. She didn't seek comfort in friendships with other women, rarely joining the American flyers at the Red Cross Club in London, always staying at the Savoy on leave and visiting nightclubs on the arm of one escort or another.

However limited her affections were for her husband, Dorothy had liked and trusted him, according to her family, no small thing for a woman traumatized in her teenage years by the ghastly death of her father, the alcoholism of her mother, the sexual molestation by a priest, and the sexual assault by her boss. She never spoke about those events, and she rarely spoke about the death of Richard Bragg. "She may have felt she made a mistake, but that's the sort of thing you can't talk about with anyone, not then anyway," said her son.

Bragg's death added a new layer to Dorothy's emotional scar tissue, a thick, rigid residue of suppressed pain that held attachments at bay. Secure in her ability to exercise control over men with her astonishing looks and intricate mind, she never wanted for company, but she also maintained a façade that was distant and bored, whatever the war threw at her.

DOROTHY WAS THE second American woman, after Mary Zerbel Hooper, to lose a bomber pilot husband. By the spring of 1943, enough time had lapsed since Wes Hooper disappeared for Mary to conclude that he was dead, although she didn't acknowledge it to others. It felt disloyal.

Bomber crews presented risky prospects for love affairs, but they crossed paths often enough with the ferry pilots that many women ignored the odds and gave their hearts anyway. Ann Wood had always been clever about managing an active social life without placing herself in such a vulnerable position. She enjoyed the company of men, but she kept it light and disdained the entanglements of commitment—there was too much else on her agenda. She was more concerned with securing an aviation career than a husband.

The love interests she chose held established positions within the safety of England. They often came with connections to the elite military and diplomatic circles that Ann appreciated for their in-crowd conversation. Her relationship with her long-running boyfriend Avery Hand, the Army Signal Corps officer who delivered messages to officials around London, was fun but never exclusive. Avery was a chum, a reliable escort, a relief from work. They did the town up right—danced at the Landsdowne, a private members club that admitted women as well as men; drank cocktails in Mayfair hotels; and took in British plays and American movies, like *Pride of the Yankees* with Gary Cooper in the Lou Gehrig role. They laughed as they navigated the crowds around Piccadilly Circus with stop-and-go signals as the only sources of light.

Sometimes at the Red Cross Club they ran into Jackson Kelly, a Pan Am executive from Philadelphia who was based in London to help ferry aircraft and military supplies. He started to ask Ann out, too, and he knew an effective pitch. He was friends with the exiled King Peter of Yugoslavia and invited Ann to meet him at Jack's apartment. "I am all agog," she wrote in her diary. "Guess I'm just a royalty seeker, but I love it." They chatted late into the night about American culture—the king was a fan—and the current state of Europe. Ann was always up for such inside dope—"these little things that the average newspaper reader never knows about the war."

The London Red Cross Club had become an epicenter for American networking, so Ann visited as much as she could. She was well aware that the high-powered people whose company she most enjoyed were also the ones who might help her land on her feet after the war. Ann cultivated the woman who ran the club, Margaret Biddle, the wife of Anthony Biddle Jr., the ambassador to various governments in exile in London, including Hungary, Greece, Czechoslovakia, the Netherlands, Norway, Poland, and Yugoslavia. Mrs. Biddle, for her part, added popular innovations like a three-piece band and a waffle-making machine, which King Peter's fiancée often operated on volunteer shifts. Ambassador Biddle called Ann "Woodie" and once asked her to set up a back-channel meeting with a Polish leader whose daughter flew for the ATA. "Little does he know that's right up my alley," Ann chuckled as she banked the favor.

There were other heady habitués, as well. Ann shared meaty chats about politics with John Daly, a foreign correspondent for CBS and colleague of Edward R. Murrow, keeping in mind that she had once thought of working in journalism, too. Jack Kelly of Pan Am drifted away from Ann when he started seeing Kathy Harriman, the daughter of the wealthy diplomat Averell Harriman. But sometimes Peter Beasley invited Ann and other friends to the country headquarters of the U.S. Army Eighth Air Force in High Wycombe. They golfed, played tennis, and dined in luxury with General Ira C. Eaker, Peter's boss who commanded the Eighth Air Force. Ann also stayed in touch with another man she had met the first time she had dinner at Jackie Cochran's, Tony Satterthwaite, a diplomat in charge of civil aviation at the American embassy in London. Ann figured he would be a good person to know in peacetime when commercial airlines started hiring again. Ann spoke to him often over cocktails about helping her to find work related to private air travel or the government regulation of same.

When Avery wasn't around, Ann viewed it as her patriotic duty to entertain lonely American guys, visitors to the club or friends of friends eager for a few hours of frivolity with an agreeable girl, no passion and no expectations. A typical example was a twenty-one-year-old Fortress pilot who'd flown six missions over the Continent. "Apparently loves telling you all about it, so I listened enthralled," she noted in one of her dry asides. She also stepped up to amuse a nice southern boy on a macabre assignment. The fuse had blown on a five-hundred-pound bomb at his aerodrome, killing nineteen men. "It was one of those strange accidents of war time that takes lives the public never learns about," Ann commented. Her date had the job of picking up the pieces and delivering the bodies to a cemetery, but when his truck broke down, he took a detour to London while awaiting repairs. He needed diversion, Ann wrote, "and was relieved to know that I furnished same without the usual demands of a drunken stupor."

THE TENOR OF Ann's war relationships shifted in May 1943, but not before a diversion of her own: She got a job to Northern Ireland the first week of the month and took advantage by traveling south by train to catch a glimpse of peacetime in the neutral Republic of Ireland. Ann took in some sightseeing in Dublin, caught a play at the Abbey Theater, and stocked up on fruit and candy in a city not at war. "Surely peace is a healthy, sane, and natural state and one that all should be able to enjoy," she concluded. On her return, she found a letter from Bill Brown of Cleveland, referred by a friend. He was recently assigned as a bomber wing navigator at Alconbury, one of the cluster of American airfields near Cambridge.

The first time Ann met Bill, he sent a jeep to pick her up when she delivered a Hurricane to a base near his. He gave her a tour of the Boeing B-17 Flying Fortress heavy four-engine bomber that he would soon be guiding over Europe as the navigator for his unit. Daytime raids—the most dangerous but effective. A twenty-seven-year-old graduate of Yale law school, Bill had enlisted at the outbreak of the war. He was particularly tall, which appealed to the five-feet-ten Ann, and shy in a good way, because his speech, once he committed to it, was all substance. They clicked immediately.

A week later, Ann drew another job that allowed her to stop in for a few hours. This time, bedlam had overtaken the base, which was teeming with high-ranking officers because the bomber group's first raid was heading out that day. Bill was excited, eager to serve, which Ann admired. They shared a sturdy, nothing-fancy meal at the mess, and Ann took off again before he did, "eying the Fortress-laden sky and wondering how many would return." Her feelings were mixed—excited to see history in the making but wondering if it was worth the price.

The next day she got tangled in her own dangerous situation after receiving a chit for a battered old Lysander, a nearly obsolete reconnaissance aircraft, to be returned from Northern Ireland. After five minutes of flight, the ropy plane practically shook to bits. The starboard mag, necessary for firing the spark plugs, was cutting out, so she had to force land at a small airfield to avoid a trickier attempt in populated Belfast. Ann made it back to Ratcliffe the next evening in time for a party where she spilled red wine on her favorite yellow suit. Smart, the butler, put in overtime working out the stains, knowing that Ann planned to wear it for dinner with Bill on her next leave.

As luck and the need for more bombing aircraft would have it, Ann was assigned on May 18 to train for Class 4 bombers at White Waltham. She chose to stay at the Red Cross Club in London and catch a train to work each day in Maidenhead, the better to fill her downtime. Bill joined her on a three-day leave near the end of the month. He bowled over the generally brisk and unsentimental Ann, who described this new suitor in her diary with none of her usual sardonic prose. He "impressed [her] no end" by reserving dinner at three different restaurants and asking her to choose. She wrote that she indulged in an uncharacteristic three drinks before they swanned over to the Dorchester for "a lovely dinner, glorious dancing (which he loves, thankfully, and does it to perfection)."

The next day he brought two carnations for her hair and pleased her with his personality—"so much savoir-faire"—and his ambitious plans for the future. Bill hoped that law would serve as a gateway to government in Washington—just Ann's sort of thing. For now, he was keen to do his bit for democracy. The patriot in Ann approved. So far, he'd shown his mettle on one of the three raids he'd joined, removing a bullet from the leg of his co-navigator. Bill played it down, but he was awarded the Distinguished Flying Cross medal for the incident. After lunch and an Errol Flynn movie, he reported back to Alconbury while Ann shopped to find him new flying goggles. "He is as grand as I ever thought he might be," she wrote. She had never written about Avery this way.

Things were moving fast, but that was how it worked during the war. Bill called the next night to let her know he'd made it through another mission, number four. Ann joked in her diary that it was nice to be informed that he was "still to be counted among those present." He wrote regular letters, too. "He can really wield a pen with that underlying reserve, which I like," she told her diary.

They booked a daytrip on June 7 to the historic waterfront town of Ipswich in Suffolk. The couple talked as they strolled around streets full of other visiting Yanks. The more Ann learned about Bill, the more highly she thought of him. He admitted he had toyed with the ideas of the America First movement in the thirties, hoping it would help avoid war. But once his country joined the Allies, he felt so guilty about his previous views that he signed up and "volunteered for everything." He felt he

The adventure began with a telegram to leading women pilots from the world-famous aviatrix Jacqueline Cochran. PHOTO COURTESY OF THE STATE ARCHIVES OF FLORIDA

The first eight British women pilots joined the Air Transport Auxiliary in January 1940, flying open-air training aircraft in freezing conditions.
HULTON DEUTSCH/ CONTRIBUTOR, VIA GETTY IMAGES

By the time American women arrived in 1942, women flew a full range of bombers and fighters. Virginia Farr, Louise Schuurman, and Helen Richey joined a photo op with the ATA's women's leader, Pauline Gower; the American leader, Jackie Cochran; and the British pilots Pamela Duncan, D. Williams, Zita Irwin, and Audrey Sale Barker.
KEYSTONE-FRANCE VIA GETTY IMAGES

Despite hard times and an eighth-grade education, Dorothy Furey sought to reinvent herself in Britain.
IMAGE VIA FAMILY OF DOROTHY FUREY

She dazzled the millionaire Lord David Beatty with her beauty and self-taught intellect.
IMAGE VIA FAMILY OF DOROTHY FUREY

Before the war, the fun-loving Winnabelle Pierce embraced excitement and danger. VIA MICHAEL BEASLEY COLLECTION

Left: Wearing the ATA uniform didn't constrain her wild behavior.
Right: Her lover, the mysterious Colonel Peter Beasley. VIA MICHAEL BEASLEY COLLECTION

The celebrated stunt pilot Helen Richey in 1935, signing autographs at the airport in Pittsburgh.
COURTESY OF SAN DIEGO AIR & SPACE MUSEUM/THE PITTSBURGH POST–GAZETTE

Left: Helen on the flying circuit with Jackie Cochran in 1940.
PHOTOQUEST VIA GETTY IMAGES
Right: The ATA promoted Helen quickly but blamed her for accidents under stress.
PHOTOQUEST/CONTRIBUTOR
VIA GETTY IMAGES

A member of the family of the Western Union fortune, Virginia Farr was expected to behave like a debutante. Escaping to Britain allowed her to live as she pleased.

Shown here with Louise Schuurman, Virginia quickly advanced to the most advanced aircraft and challenging assignments.

Raised by a hat-and-gloves mother, in 1940 Hazel Jane Raines performed in jodhpurs for the thrilling Georgia Air Races and Show.
IMAGE VIA FAMILY OF HAZEL RAINES

Hazel's skill with death-defying stunts was essential in the war when faulty aircraft failed her.
IMAGE VIA FAMILY OF HAZEL RAINES

SENIORS

Ann W. Wood, B. A.

Melrose Academy

Philadelphia, Pa.

Kappa Chi
Sodality 1, 2, 3, 4
Secretary of Sodality 2
Treasurer of Student Government 2
Secretary of Student Government 3
President of Student Government 4
Glee Club 1, 2, 3, 4
Choir 1, 2, 3, 4

Dramatics 2, 3, 4
Shakespearean Play 2, 3, 4
Staff of Magazine 1, 2, 3, 4
Le Cercle Jeanne d'Arc 1, 2, 3, 4
Alice Meynell Club 3, 4
El Club Castellano 1, 2, 3
Athletic Association 1, 2, 3, 4
Physics Club 2
Junior Prom Committee
Senior Ball Committee

Words simply are inadequate to describe Ann.
But this we can say, her place in our hearts
must forever remain unfilled.

Top: President of her college class, Ann Wood was a high achiever set on launching a diplomatic or aviation career.
VIA ANN WOOD–KELLY ARCHIVE, D'YOUVILLE UNIVERSITY LIBRARY
Left: She cultivated connections high and low.
IMAGE VIA FAMILY OF ANN WOOD

Ann prepared to take off in a Spitfire.
SMITHSONIAN NATIONAL AIR AND SPACE MUSEUM (NASM 9A16154)

Above: Mary Zerbel was the youngest woman flight instructor in the United States. This is one of her later certifications.

Left: Her wedding to Wes Hooper captivated newspapers around the world. Jackie Cochran congratulated the couple. COURTESY OF THE SAN DIEGO AIR & SPACE MUSEUM

Mary persevered in the face of tragedy.
© CROWN COPYRIGHT IWM

Left: Nancy Miller transferred to Scotland to master a wider variety of aircraft, like this Swordfish torpedo bomber. IMAGE VIA NANCY MILLER

Below: The former crop duster Roberta Sandoz planned a route with Mary Zerbel Hooper and Kay Van Doozer. © CROWN COPYRIGHT IWM

Mary Webb Nicholson was an accomplished stunt pilot before the war. COURTESY OF GREENSBORO HISTORY MUSEUM

Left: She encountered disaster in 1943 when a propeller flew off her plane.
Right: Her parents kept this prewar photo of Mary on their mantel.
IMAGES VIA FAMILY OF MARY WEBB NICHOLSON

Above: In a downpour, First Lady Eleanor Roosevelt inspected American pilots, including, from left, Opal Pearl Anderson, Hazel Jane Raines, unidentified, and Ann Wood, with the women's commander, Pauline Gower. VIA MAIDENHEAD HERITAGE CENTRE

Left: Roberta Sandoz, Kay Van Doozer, the Polish pilot Jadwiga Pilsudska, and Mary Zerbel Hooper in the spring of 1943.

© CROWN COPYRIGHT IWM

Many ATA pilots were killed or injured. Evelyn Hudson was hospitalized for five months in a body cast. VIA RAF MUSEUM ENTERPRISES LTD

Jane Plant was pulled to safety from the burning shell of a Hudson bomber.
VIA MAIDENHEAD HERITAGE CENTRE

A Stirling bomber towered above the British pilot Joan Hughes. For those who thought women were too weak to fly such aircraft, Joan had this retort: "The idea is for the plane to lift me, not for me to lift the plane." HULTON ARCHIVE/STRINGER VIA GETTY IMAGES

Louise Schuurman with a Spitfire. When the war ended, she took a mission to Holland to search for Jewish relatives who had been in hiding. POPPERFOTO/CONTRIBUTOR VIA GETTY IMAGES

Dorothy Furey scaled the heights of society, little caring what scandal ensued. IMAGE COURTESY OF DMG MEDIA/ DAILY MAIL

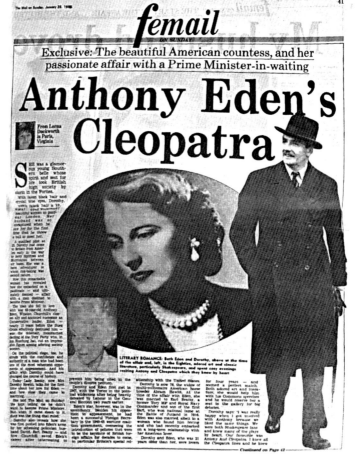

The Mail on Sunday, January 28, 1996

femail
ON SUNDAY

Exclusive: The beautiful American countess, and her passionate affair with a Prime Minister-in-waiting

Anthony Eden's Cleopatra

From Lorna Duckworth in Paris Virginia

Left: When no airline would hire Nancy Miller after the war, she blazed a new trail in helicopters. IMAGE COURTESY OF THE TWU LIBRARIES WOMAN'S COLLECTION, TEXAS WOMAN'S UNIVERSITY, DENTON, TX

Below: Some of the pilots reunited at the ranch of Winnie Pierce Beasley in 1979. Left to right: Ann Wood-Kelly; Nancy Miller Livingston; Roberta Sandoz Leveaux; Virginia Farr (standing); her partner, Vivien Jeffery; Opal Anderson; Peggy Lennox Drown; and Winnie. VIA MICHAEL BEASLEY COLLECTION

could afford to do it. He had no commitments back home, he told her. It was tougher on guys who were married with families.

Most of all, she was overjoyed to hear a man state that he admired her hard-won independence. "The majority to date find it most annoying," she said. She didn't go so far as to commit a particular word to paper in her diary, but her language about Bill Brown was so different from what it was about anyone else, so full of genuine appreciation and affection, that it seemed the free-and-easy Ann Wood, who was never swayed by sentimentality, was falling in love. And with that most endangered species of the war, an airman on a bomber crew.

BILL BROWN SERVED as a human cog in the machine of the most ambitious bombing offensive of the war to date, the Battle of the Ruhr. It kept both the RAF and U.S. Bomber Command fully engaged that June, targeting steel and armament factories in the heavy industrial cities in the vicinity of Germany's Ruhr River. Hamburg, Essen, Cologne, and Kiel were on the regular itinerary. Bill flew on the perilous daylight raids, his twenty-eighth birthday on June 11 passing with little notice. With the ATA busier than ever, Ann performed multiple daily deliveries, including her first Wellington bomber and her first American Mustang fighter, a swift-flying treat.

On June 17, she noticed that Bill hadn't called in several days, as he usually did when he'd returned from a mission. Ann shook it off by going to a goofy American movie and laughing herself silly, all the more amused that the English audience sat in uncomprehending silence.

The next day, she grew more concerned. She sent a telegram that went unanswered. It was the only discordant note in an otherwise happy time—Ann had received word that she was entitled to a trip home on leave. She could get the clearance to board a ship any day. "I am in a complete fever about going home," she wrote, but in a different kind of fever about Bill. Was he injured, killed, missing in action? Too busy to call? Or had he cooled on Ann and wasn't bothering to break the news?

She phoned Peter Beasley, her most influential friend, who invited her for tennis on June 23 at his country headquarters. Peter appeared not to know Bill's whereabouts and promised to look into the matter. When she returned two days later, he still had no word on Bill, but she learned what everyone else was talking about—a raid gone horribly wrong over Kiel on June 13, the day Bill's regular phone calls ceased.

The assignment that day called for seventy-six American B-17 Fortresses to assault the heavily reinforced concrete yards that serviced U-boats in the German port city. Fighter aircraft didn't possess the range at that point in the war to ride shotgun on such long-distance missions, so bombing groups were subject to heavy attacks with only the gunners on the Fortresses themselves to defend the ships. The June 13 mission would engage in an experiment, trying out a new formation devised by Brigadier General Nathan B. Forrest, the great-grandson of a Confederate general. Instead of flying the planes stacked like boxes at different altitudes, the plan called for a flat arrangement, wingtip to wingtip, which the general was convinced would allow more coordination of defensive fire. General Forrest was so committed to the plan that he flew in the lead plane himself as an observer. It also happened that the German propaganda radio broadcaster Lord Haw-Haw had been taunting the general to join a mission himself. Bill's bomber group took off with Forrest on Sunday morning, around the time Ann Wood walked to church.

The Germans were more than ready. Before the American B-17s could reach Kiel, Messerschmitt and Focke-Wulf fighters already swarmed like gnats in what would become one of the most savage engagements of World War II. "For the next fifteen minutes, I was in a state of absolute and incredulous shock," said one of the American pilots, William Lindley, who witnessed flak shells and machine-gun fire bringing down Fortress after Fortress. The flak was frightening, he said, but the fighters were something else. They "would put the fear of god into anyone. To see them head-on from the twelve o'clock position with their wings flaring and smoking . . . awesome . . . particularly when one realized they were firing directly at you." Some pilots flew with their heads ducked below the instrument panels.

The first hit was the lead aircraft carrying General Forrest. Flak knocked out its fourth engine, and then three German fighters simultaneously homed in on the nose and raked the Fortress with fire from one end to the other. A gunner watching from another plane, Arlie Arneson, "could not believe that anyone could possibly be alive in there." The other bombers in the new flat formation couldn't shoot back against such a frontal assault without hitting other U.S. aircraft flying at the same level—a disastrous situation. They saw Forrest's aircraft slow down, bank sharply right, and plummet as more fighters overran the skies with devastating results.

Many who survived the Battle of Kiel described what unfolded next as pure hell. "There were B-17s out of control doing unbelievable aerobatics, exploding, on fire, going straight down in near-vertical dives, shedding parachutes," said Arneson. "One was hit so hard that the complete ball-turret fell free."

A tail-gunner, Earl Underwood, glanced down and saw a nearby B-17 breaking in two. The front half—radio room, wings, engines, cockpit, and nose—fell intact. But Underwood was riveted by the sight of a German fighter chasing the tail as it floated on while the gunner inside still fired at the enemy plane, unaware that the rest of his aircraft was gone.

Of the seventy-six American ships, twenty-two were lost and even more damaged. Virtually all were shot through with bullet holes. It was no wonder that in the chaos casualty counts were all over the map, the greatest percentage listed as missing in action for lack of more accurate information. Initial reports showed only 3 dead, 20 wounded, and 213 missing. The ultimate count would be more like 158 killed, 22 wounded, and 61 taken prisoner. The aircrew of the lead plane carrying General Forrest was unaccounted for, as far as Peter Beasley knew. Three months later, the general's body washed up on the German island of Rügen in the Baltic Sea. He was the first U.S. general to die in the war in Europe. After that one test run at Kiel, the new Forrest aircraft formation was cast aside.

Peter told Ann some of what had transpired, including the loss of the general's Fortress. The ground shifted under her again. Officially, Bill's fate remained a mystery. But Ann had fallen for a man on a bomber crew and knew the odds. She couldn't fend off a feeling. First Lieutenant Willard "Bill" Brown—as grand as she ever thought he might be—had been navigating that lead plane.

CHAPTER 21

The Shock of the Familiar

Summer 1943
The United States

T wo eggs at breakfast, streetlights at night. The shock of the familiar was disorienting and delightful for a fraction of the American women who returned home for leave in the summer of 1943. The Allies had developed better defenses against U-boats by then, so a summer lull made it safer to travel. Passenger ships like the *Queen Mary* and the *Aquitania*, converted for carrying troops, offered more gracious accommodations than the women had endured on their trips to England the year before.

This time, though, they shared ships to New York with German prisoners of war. The men stayed on the same corridor with a wire grill across the door. As the women passed by, they heard the captives say, "Those are girl?" Some were shocked at the sight of the New York skyline. They had been under the impression that much of the city had been destroyed by Axis attacks.

Before the departure in mid-July, Ann Wood devoted every free moment and all of her contacts to searching for word about Bill Brown. She finally got some when Peter sent her a copy of *Stars & Stripes* that confirmed what she suspected. Her guy had been the wing navigator in charge of guiding the attack for the entire bombing group while traveling on board the general's vanquished Flying Fortress. She chose to regard this as hopeful news. There was the slimmest chance she would someday receive word that Bill had parachuted into enemy hands and remained among the living as a prisoner. Better than the alternative, if less likely.

The others who chose to take a break in the United States in the summer of 1943 included the two women who had lost their husbands, Mary Zerbel Hooper and Dorothy Furey Bragg, as well as Virginia Farr, Grace Stevenson, and Roberta Sandoz, who won an early leave to visit her parents two days after marrying a dashing British cavalry officer. The American press, reminded of these exceptional women by their presence stateside, churned out stories about the unconventional lives they were living. The *New York Herald Tribune* wrote a glowing feature under the headline 17 AMERICANS SERVE IN A.T.A., WHERE WOMEN MUST BE TOUGH. Pauline Gower was quoted as saying that an ATA pilot "doesn't have to be particularly strong physically, but she must have absolutely steady nerves." True enough. The subhead better reflected the story's emphasis on the drama of it all: GIRLS TAKEN TO BRITAIN BY JACQUELINE COCHRAN FLY 121 TYPES OF PLANES, SLEEP WHEREVER THEY LAND, FIND ROMANCE AND TRAGEDY. Also true.

A VERY DIFFERENT drama was playing out for one aviator who made the journey. Hazel Jane Raines waited three months for clearance to fly again following the concussion she received in March when her ill-fated Spitfire blasted through the thatched-roof house. She spent the interim puttering in the garden at her billet in Hamble and pondering whether to re-up when her ATA contract ran out in October. From Fort Worth, Texas, Jackie Cochran wrote to tell the injured flyer that she and her colleagues would be welcome in Jackie's Women's Flying Training Detachment, soon to merge into the Women's Airforce Service Pilots, or the WASP. The offer sounded less than appealing. Jackie admitted that she was struggling to get permission for her recruits to fly anything beyond light trainers. Besides, she wrote, "It isn't very nice to live out in the middle of the country so far removed from the real activity of the war."

Hazel figured that remaining in England, where women flew the full range of aircraft, would offer better options for her future. She vented to her mother about her home country, "If they would only realize that 'it can be done' by a woman in the States the same as they are doing over here!"

Three months after the crash, she still looked like an accident victim, with a prominent gash on her forehead and half a head of shaved-off hair sprouting back like new grass. But on June 4 she won approval to return to flying. It never occurred to her to shun the cockpit, despite the nightmare of the accident. At least the injury provided a reverse benefit. Doctors advised her against wearing a tight helmet on her head for six months, so she was finally referred for training on twin-engine bombers, where a helmet wouldn't be necessary in closed cockpits.

Second Officer Raines proved that she hadn't lost any of her skill. She aced the lessons in a couple of weeks and returned to ferrying Class 3 twins exclusively while her instructor recommended a swift promotion to Class 4s. "It was good getting back on the job," she wrote.

An ophthalmologist took a closer look at her eyes on the tenth of July. His record noted the laceration of her scalp and a "fairly marked post-concussion syndrome," which she already knew. But there was more. "She now complains of occasional mistiness of vision in the right eye and difficulty judging distances," the doctor reported. The diagnosis was exophoria, a frequent side effect of concussions in which an outward-wandering eye can lead to double vision. Within two weeks, the Air Transport Auxiliary made an unsparing decision: Hazel Jane Raines was terminated.

She was the sixth of Jackie's women to get the boot, which after the death of Mary Webb Nicholson left eighteen still in Britain. Despite the many obstacles presented by Hazel's marginal health, she had won highest marks throughout her service and never dinged a plane through any fault of her own. But now, without recourse, she was out.

One of the most talented and proficient of the American pilots, Hazel packed up and left, tucking photographs of her days with Lady Astor at Cliveden into her luggage. The Montreal fortune teller's prediction of a prosperous English marriage and thriving career had missed the mark. By the first week of August, the twenty-seven-year-old pilot was already home, still wearing her heavy wool uniform with sturdy black British stockings and flat-heeled shoes in the sweltering sun of Macon, Georgia. Hazel had always been proud of that uniform.

That summer, she moved back in with her mother and fielded inquiries from the press with practiced cheer. Hazel didn't admit she'd been sacked; she said she was deciding when to return. In the meantime, she told the *Macon Telegraph*, "I want a Coca-Cola and a hot dog and a good American shampoo and permanent wave. Then I want some fried chicken. And then I want to rest. The rest is what I'm home for." She delivered speeches about her war experiences to churches, civic groups, and a national meeting of the Ninety-Nines. Often, she quoted from the poem "High Flight," which was popular with her ATA colleagues. Written by a Canadian Air Force pilot who was later killed in a Spitfire crash, it began:

> *Oh! I have slipped the surly bonds of earth*
> *And danced the skies on laughter-silvered wings . . .*

The poem concluded on the spiritual vision that Hazel experienced so many times herself:

> *I've trod*
> *The high untrespassed sanctity of space,*
> *Put out my hand, and touched the face of God.*

The aviator who felt the sky was her home couldn't bear the thought of remaining earthbound. Within three months, she signed up for the WASP at Avenger Field in dusty Sweetwater, Texas, 120 miles southeast of Lubbock. By many measures, the ferry service had become a success, well on its way toward employing more than a thousand women. Jackie Cochran and Nancy Love were still often at odds but remained in charge of the corps. Yet it was an adjustment for Hazel. The whole setup couldn't have been more different from her posts in England. When she flew for the freewheeling ATA, men and women were treated as equals, and no one cared much what they did on their own time or interfered in their flying decisions. The women in the WASP, on the other hand, operated under strict controls and a cloud of public doubt about their abilities. Local residents were known to keep their children indoors for fear that inept women pilots would crash.

Although the WASP wasn't officially part of the armed services, the women slept six to a barracks and marched everywhere in military formation. "This is certainly a rigid life and schedule," Hazel wrote home. Every Saturday the pilots scrubbed their quarters for inspection and got slapped with demerits for any imperfections that confined the residents to the post for the weekend. It was hard to imagine Dorothy Furey, Winnie Pierce, or the unruly denizens of Ratcliffe Hall in such a setting. But Hazel remained willing to do what it took to stay in the air and serve her country.

THE OTHER AMERICANS landed in New York in a more festive mood. Mary Zerbel Hooper, Grace Stevenson, and Ann Wood made straight for a soda fountain to launch their month-long leave, each ordering a chocolate soda and a fresh lemonade. From there, they scattered by train and plane to visit family around the country. When she arrived in Michigan, Mary once again attracted the attention of reporters as she had before the war, this time as a pretty young wife willing to tackle dangerous work despite the disappearance of her husband. Reporters couldn't help themselves—they once again focused on her appearance. One dispelled the notion that a woman pilot had to be "an Amazon type." He swooned, "She looked like a charming doll, which would make Mrs. Hooper draw her dark brows together in a frown . . . For she wears her head set solidly on her shoulders and though enjoying the excitement that comes from flying, to her, the ferry job is serious business." He added, "by the way she doesn't smoke," like an entry in a latter-day dating profile.

Her local paper quoted Mary saying she still believed Wes was alive, possibly in Norway: "I have hopes that someday I'll see him again." Outside of interviews, she harbored no such expectation, but she quickly realized that her family and friends all did. Mary had been ignoring the likely reality that Wes wasn't coming back by keeping busy at work. Now the subject overwhelmed her as she had to shatter the illusion for everyone who broached the subject. "Too many questions," she wrote. When she flew to California to see Wes's parents, they were the only people she couldn't look in the eye to state what she knew with all her reason: Their son, her husband, was dead. "Too many questions again." When her leave ended, she described her feelings as "extreme lack of desire to live—let down after telling all at home." Which, she added, wasn't the same as actively wishing to end her life, but not minding if it happened.

ROBERTA SANDOZ HAD a more celebratory reason for taking her leave—to see her family in Washington State after a marriage that would shift her life far from the upbringing she was now permitted to visit. Oddly, the parochial pilot had come to feel more at home in England than she had growing up. This journey home would allow the "backwoods gal" to come to terms with the dislocation she had often felt as a child. It would also give her space to reflect on the adjustment she would make as a new bride in an international setting that had broadened her horizons beyond what any woman in the 1940s could expect.

Roberta had mixed feelings about visiting her mother and stepfather. As their only child, she had felt isolated living in the wilds of the Columbia River Basin, much of which would soon be engulfed by the Grand Coulee Dam, where her stepfather worked as a construction engineer. Roberta had no friends within shouting distance, so she occupied herself with a dreamy inner life. Her mother worried that her tomboy daughter was odd. "I wasn't much for dolls," Roberta wrote later, "but I was fascinated with the sky." She would lie in her wagon watching migrating geese, studying the patterns of their flying formations. Roberta rode a horse to a one-room schoolhouse and loved to perform daredevil tricks, like swinging on a rope off the edge of a high cliff. Her mother disapproved.

"Mom kept trying to hammer out of solid granite a little lady," Roberta said, "and it just wasn't my speed." It was her stepfather who encouraged the girl, letting her ride with a barnstormer when she was ten. The soaring ride over her house and the upper reaches of the Columbia River opened Roberta up to wider possibilities. "It changes your perspective of the world once you see it from the air," she said. "This was the sensation that interested me: a wonderful feeling of expansion." That year, she got a ten-volume encyclopedia for Christmas.

A scholarship took her to Whitman College in Walla Walla, where she studied psychology and sociology. When she graduated in 1939, she took a job as far away as she could, as a social worker in a San Francisco settlement house for immigrants. It wasn't long before she signed up for a night school course in aeronautics. Years later her heart still thumped at the memory of the second plane ride of her life. "I caught it like measles," she exclaimed. "Oh! It was so exciting!" She abandoned social work to dust crops and fly a farmer to the distant reaches of his California holdings.

ADJUSTMENT TO LIFE in the ATA was almost enough to make Roberta miss her hometown of Chewelah, Washington. Her insecurity and relative lack of experience made for an anxious beginning, and British customs, not to mention the horrifying breakfast kippers, baffled her. But in the months since, Roberta had sorted herself out. "I was frightened at first," she said. She knew she was flying over her head. "But I listened to the other pilots and finally copied their courage and good form."

ATA instructors praised her common sense, sound judgment, and "pleasing personality." She was even granted the uncommon accolade that she had "reached a good average standard"—a step up from the usual high praise of "average."

Like others at her home base of Hamble, Roberta had some run-ins with the enemy. Once, she was the passenger on a flight taking pilots to distant pools that got mixed up in a German air raid on Reading. She saw puffs of smoke below from antiaircraft fire, and bullet holes pierced the wings. Another time, alone, she stumbled too close to a Luftwaffe bombing run over Bournemouth, realizing what was happening only when she saw explosions on the ground. She followed the training for evasive action, changing her speed and route and flying low. But nothing shook her so much as the death of Mary Nicholson, her friend and shipmate from the final group to cross the Atlantic. It was just like Roberta to visit the scene, trying to make sense of the accident.

Sorrow couldn't linger for long during the war. A couple of weeks after Mary's funeral, Roberta found herself on a date with a high-ranking American officer at the Shepherd's Tavern pub on a market street in Mayfair, a quick walk from the Red Cross Club. Roberta loved to dance, but not so much at the posh places where her more cosmopolitan colleagues made the scene. Shepherd's was more Roberta's speed—fancy for a pub but still casual, a wood-paneled hideaway with beamed ceilings and wood floors. The place brimmed with British and American officers in their uniforms rather than evening clothes. It was Roberta's kind of crowd, unpretentious and friendly.

While she sat between dances with her date, another man, a cheeky British officer a few ranks lower, brazenly crashed the table. Lieutenant Peter Leveaux looked like something out of a Gilbert and Sullivan operetta in the showy regalia of the King's Royal Hussars, a cavalry unit that served in the Middle East. "Peter was a knockout," Roberta later declared. "I fell for his spurs and his uniform."

Her own uniform, with the gold U.S.A. flash on the shoulder, gave him an opening to launch a conversation. "I know America well," he said.

Later she learned this meant that he had once attended a camp in upstate New York for one season, but that was all he needed to plant a flag. Eight weeks later, they were married. She was twenty-five, and he was twenty-two. "He was a guy who played with the truth a little bit," said their son Mark. "He was a bit of a womanizer, but very loving, with a hilarious sense of humor. He was maybe a little pushy, but she fell in love with him because I think she liked a rascal."

Even more, her son said, Roberta "really fell in love with the family." Soon after they met, Peter took her to meet the whole extended clan at his parents' apartment complex, Oakwood Court, in the Holland Park area of Kensington. Several branches of Leveaux lived in the prestigious redbrick Edwardian block with rows of bay windows, wrought-iron balconies, and coffered ceilings. It was a Hollywood vision of prosperous urban English comfort.

Despite her insecurities about her own background, Roberta stood up to the family scrutiny. One distant aunt objected that the pilot arrived wearing a uniform . . . with trousers! The rest were tickled by the singular American and her daring occupation. Her military service helped overcome the mild disdain that many well-to-do Brits felt for Americans.

It was an easy fit. An absence of snobbery came naturally to the Leveaux relations. Situated higher than middle class but not aristocratic, the family hobnobbed with a crowd that included musicians, dancers, and theater people who could have walked out of a Noel Coward play, about as far from Walla Walla as Roberta thought possible. Peter's father had been the co-owner of the Alhambra Theatre on Leicester Square, a palatial space that presented live musical revues. Peter's grandmother on his father's side was Jewish, so tolerance came naturally to the otherwise Anglican group. Peter himself attended an elite school, where he earned distinction as the gregarious guy who cheered up every party.

The family was happy to invite a bold and unusual woman into their midst, amused that her mother had failed to make a little lady out of her. It was no wonder she jumped into the precipitous marriage. She'd long been a girl willing to swing from a cliff. Roberta, a child of isolation, fell into this foreign embrace.

The bride and groom wore their mutually smashing uniforms to the wedding on August 7, 1943, at St. Barnabas Church, a Tudor Gothic-style edifice girded with buttresses, located around the corner from the Leveaux apartments. "Seems to me a bit hasty," Roberta's fellow pilot and maid of honor, Emily Chapin, wrote in a letter to her family. Roberta, Emily continued, "insists it isn't war hysteria (but what else?). Anyhow, what I or anybody else thinks doesn't seem to worry her."

The opinions of others had never figured heavily in Roberta's choices. The event set another marker on her route to leave the Columbia River Basin and its one-room schoolhouse behind. Roberta concluded she was right to distance herself from her origins and vault into another realm with another family, despite the separation from her own. Now a well-respected pilot with a handsome husband in a faraway land, the once-lonely backwoods gal felt she had found her place at last.

The couple skipped a honeymoon so that she could use her leave to pay her parents a bittersweet visit in late August, likely for the last time in years, before Roberta returned to work. Her mother was stricken by this news, but the journey provided more evidence that the article in the *New York Herald Tribune* had gotten the story right: The American women in the ATA were tough, and they were no strangers to romance and tragedy.

CHAPTER 22

A Parachute of Faith

September 1943
Greenland
———

T he ladies had proven their worth to the extent that they were sent
back from leave by air, tasked as copilots on B-25 Mitchell bombers
from Montreal to Scotland. This was likely the first time that women
were permitted to ferry aircraft across the Atlantic, aside from the one
exception made for Jackie Cochran in 1941. No publicity this time, just a
long, cold flight to deliver the two-engine Mitchells, manufactured in
North America, into the hands of the RAF. It raised the pilots' hopes that
U.S. military might consider trusting their services someday.

If anyone made the trip with a renewed sense of purpose, it was Ann
Wood. After weeks of tension over the fate of Bill Brown, she received
definitive news in August. Over the summer, the bodies of his crewmates,
one by one, had washed up on the shores of the Baltic Sea as the death
tally mounted from the disastrous June 13 mission to Kiel. Eventually,
Ann learned that everyone on board General Forrest's Flying Fortress was
considered killed in action—everyone except one. Bill Brown was now
a prisoner of war at Stalag 3 in Zagon, Germany.

Ann didn't know how he survived. But she sprang into action, deci-
phering the rules for sending letters and parcels through the Red Cross

to keep up the spirits of captives. She established regular contact with Bill's mother in Cleveland and dispatched cards, letters, books, and cigarettes to the prison camp. The relief at the news, combined with the opportunity to take some action, kicked her into high gear. She wrote, "I feel like I could tear down houses."

Still, she didn't learn details beyond the fact that Bill had somehow broken a rib. Only Bill himself knew what happened the day of the raid. Ann's theory was correct that he had flown as the wing navigator on General Forrest's lead aircraft. The general positioned himself to observe the overall operation from the nose, where Bill performed his calculations. It certainly appeared that the Germans were waiting for them. After antiaircraft fire took out one of the four engines of the Fortress, it pressed on in the lead. But when machine-gun bullets from three Messerschmitt fighters gutted the fuselage and the bomber began to dive, the crew bailed out at twenty-three thousand feet. Bill passed out in the thin atmosphere.

When he came to, the rest of his crewmates were opening their parachutes, swinging like the clappers of ringing bells over land. But a strong wind soon swept them out to sea. As they disappeared over the horizon, Bill waited to reach a lower altitude before activating his chute. He hit water in a narrow shipping channel of Kiel Bay.

Two hours later, a German boat picked him up and sent him for interrogation at a prison camp outside Frankfurt. His captors followed the Geneva Convention and "treated me with the dignity afforded an officer," he later reported. "They respected that it was my duty not to reveal any information." Soon he was transferred to an American compound at Stalag 3, run by the Luftwaffe. Ann would do what she could to lighten his days there.

ANN HAD HER own duties to perform. At Dorval Field in Montreal, she and each of the other women returning from leave got a quick tutorial on operating the Mitchell bomber. As copilots, they would sit shoulder to shoulder with the captains to handle cockpit checks, monitor fuel consumption, and raise and lower the flaps and landing gear. With a wingspan of sixty-eight feet and a range of less than 1,400 miles, the Mitchell would hopscotch across the Atlantic, making refueling stops along such stepping stones as Newfoundland, Labrador, Greenland, and Iceland. The route traced close to the Arctic Circle and passed through some of the nastiest weather on the planet, so the RAF Ferry Command crammed as many flights as it could into the summer months.

No one had thought about accommodating women on such long segments, where male pilots routinely relieved themselves in tubes behind a curtain in the frigid cabin. To accomplish the same necessary function, the women had to strip off their flight suits, pants, and underwear while still winding up unpleasantly damp.

Only Dorothy Furey Bragg refused to cooperate. When she realized what the setup was, she announced to the navigator and pilot, "I am *not* peeing in a bottle."

"There's nothing else we can do," said the pilot, not without sympathy.

"We're going to radio Reykjavik and tell them we're coming down," Dorothy declared. No such stop was authorized, but Dorothy spoke with a high-handed conviction that was not to be crossed.

The radio operator in Reykjavik wouldn't budge. "Don't you know there's a war on? We've never had a woman on this base in the whole war."

Dorothy employed her most imperial tone. "Well, I'm coming in. You'll just have to clear out the bathroom."

And so it came to pass that Dorothy Furey Bragg made history at the base, even keeping men waiting outside while she combed her hair and applied her lipstick in her own improvised powder room.

Ann Wood encountered a more perilous dilemma. At a stop in Labrador, the ground crew couldn't repair a leak in one of the B-25's fuel tanks. Ann and her three crewmates—a pilot, navigator, and wireless operator—concluded they could fly on by making regular stops to keep the fuel level within safety limits. The decision didn't look so wise as they approached Greenland. The clouds and fog turned impenetrable along a craggy coastline leading toward the notoriously hazardous airfield at an American base called Bluie West One. The crew played for time by circling around to wait for an opening, but the delay only used up more fuel. When Ann determined that the level had dropped to the bare minimum to make it back to Labrador, the pilots decided to reverse course. Ten minutes into that plan, Greenland radioed to say that a fighter plane, flown by a pilot who presumably knew the area by heart, was heading out to guide the bomber in—Plan C. But after waiting for another fifteen minutes, the Mitchell got word that the fighter wouldn't turn up after all. Would they kindly now return to Labrador?

Ann knew they'd never make it with the remaining fuel. She glanced out at peaked icebergs reaching toward the low ceiling in every direction. The only way to reach the Greenland base was to traverse a long narrow fjord, now thoroughly socked in. She ordered the radio operator to tell the base: "If you can't send another escort, you will have to send a boat, because we're going to have to ditch in the sea."

More confusion ensued until another fighter approached and Ann heard an absurdly reassuring American twang over the radio: "Tuck your wing behind daddy's, and everything will be fine and dandy."

The Mitchell followed the trail of the fighter down to two thousand feet and into an opening in the jagged terrain. Through twenty miles of winding fjord, Ann and the pilot squinted into the mist to follow the twisty path of their homespun guide. Cliffs jutted out on either side, and blind-alley canyons branched off in between. Up ahead, they saw a final dead end backed by tall mountains that prevented any escape. It was the airfield of the base.

Once on terra firma, Ann discovered that Mary Zerbel Hooper and Grace Stevenson had made it in hours before. With no chance of anyone flying out anytime soon, the men of Bluie West One, wildly excited, scrambled to impress their first female guests in eighteen months. "What a stir," Ann wrote. "The boys acted as if they'd seen an apparition." This being an American base, the food was copious, and the ladies were led through cheering crowds from mess hall to mess hall, each one decorated for the occasion with ad-hoc centerpieces made out of beer cans and old Christmas ornaments. Wherever they went, they were hailed like the stars of a Bob Hope USO show without having to sing, dance, or prance in skimpy costumes. Simply existing, in all their female splendor, was enough.

The three women sacked out on comfortable beds in the hospital, where chivalrous patients guarded the door to the bathroom. The next day at the American base, officers provided Mary, Ann, and Grace with the best entertainment available, cruising through the fjord in a Chris-Craft motorboat and shooting off the tops off icebergs with rifles. It was as if the presence of the women had plunged the base into an undeclared holiday. Dinner became a gala party, and later the ladies were honored guests at the screening of a middling movie. Every head swiveled as they entered the makeshift theater until enthusiasm built and the entire audience rose for a standing, cheering ovation. Whenever a woman appeared on screen, it brought down the house again.

Ann noticed that all those men "marooned without women—bright lights and all that" might have grumbled a bit but were intent on getting the job done and getting home. "The good fellowship and high moral purpose were magnificent to see."

AT TAKEOFF THE following morning, Mary's pilot groused that someone at the base, it wasn't clear who, had finagled to delay their departure to keep her on the premises. Mary had to turn aside and suppress a guilty smile. She could guess the most likely suspect. In the PX the day before, she had run into Jack Ford, an old friend from flight school in Los Angeles. Back then, Jack, Mary, and Wes had called themselves "friendly enemies" because the broad-shouldered Jack had played football for a rival university when he wasn't working as a stunt man in the movies. He made her laugh when he joked, "I'm not good at riding a horse, but I'm really good at falling off one."

Now Jack was flying a bomber to Scotland to lead missions over Europe. Held up by the weather, as Mary was, he delighted in seeing a familiar face, especially a pretty one. The meeting lit a spark. Mary arranged to meet Jack in London when they made it to the UK. While Mary's plane headed straight for Prestwick, Jack ungallantly said he would stop in Iceland "to check on the reputation . . . of the local blond talent."

Mary's ship took off into spectacular clear skies over icebergs that glowed aquamarine as if lit from below, but the crew had a hard time from there on. The marginal heating went completely bust on the Mitchell, and a gas leak developed short of Scotland. The crew joked that Mary's twenty-pound box of candy from the PX would come in handy in a lifeboat if they ditched. Then the overcast skies that had plagued them in Greenland smothered the visibility, and the mood turned grimmer. The crew circled Prestwick at four thousand feet, unable to venture lower until a small, bright circle appeared in the clouds. The pilot dive-bombed through it and straightened out barely in time to land. Just off the runway, the crew got a glimpse of what they'd narrowly escaped: the crashed and burned carcass of a B-24 Liberator. Despite the long journey, Mary felt fully awake. She always said she never experienced fear in such circumstances. "There's a difference between being afraid and being hyperalert."

MARY AND ANN returned directly to White Waltham to train on two-engine Class 4 bombers like the Wellington and win first officer status. When they made it back to their luxury billet at Ratcliffe Hall in October, they racked up a new range of such ships in their logbooks—Mosquitos, Blenheims, Whitleys, and Hudsons—all increasingly in demand as the bombing aspect of the war continued to escalate.

During the summer of 1943, a break in the weather had allowed both the RAF and the U.S. Eighth Air Force to set new records for tonnage dropped, mostly over Germany. The destruction—and horror—peaked as well. Among the most hellacious episodes of the war occurred in Hamburg on the clear, hot night of July 27 through early the next morning. Following a daytime raid by the Americans, the RAF sent seven hundred bombers armed with half high explosive and half incendiary bombs. The fires they set off, combined with air that was dry as tinder, formed an enormous cyclone of fire. Winds in excess of a hundred miles an hour whipped the flames into a man-made firestorm of unprecedented scale. Terrified citizens, running for their lives, caught fire and were sucked up high above the streets, lit up like torches. Others suffocated in air raid shelters as the inferno consumed the oxygen in the air. Charred and desiccated corpses, many unrecognizable, filled the city. It was estimated that forty-five thousand bodies were recovered and another ten thousand buried in rubble or turned to ash. During a ten-day period, more civilians were killed by the Hamburg bombing than Great Britain had lost to German bombs in the entire war until that time.

The Allies sustained heavy aircraft losses in such raids—eighty-six in that shocking Hamburg conflagration, for example. But the combination of British and American industrial might provided a stream of new and replacement aircraft that were tipping the scales of the air war. The cross-Atlantic Allies produced 151,000 new aircraft combined in 1943, more than double the year before and triple the German output. By the fall, the British and American air forces also capitalized on rudimentary radar and better fighter escorts to carry out more overwhelming missions. The end of November marked the largest force sent to Berlin to date. All ATA leaves were canceled for six weeks as the ferry service issued an emergency order to move the backlog of new and damaged planes.

BY EARLY NOVEMBER, six weeks had passed since the end of Mary's summer leave, and she had heard nothing from Jack Ford. With too-familiar dread, she called his station adjutant to see if her old friendly enemy was killed or missing in action. Jack, she learned, had begun flying combat over Europe as the captain of a B-24 Liberator nicknamed the *Hell-Bent Angel*. So far, he was fine. A few weeks later, he finally called Mary to schedule their date. She took advantage of a grounding due to persistent fog to spend one night in London. Mary and Jack dined and danced in civilian clothes at Hatchett's. Then he walked her back to the Red Cross Club, ignoring the sirens of an air raid. In the morning, he joined her in a taxi to the station so she could return to Ratcliffe in time to fly. Faced with her departure, they found it tough going saying their goodbyes. Jack jumped on the train and rode with her all the way to her stop in Leicester. Then he turned around and returned to London in time to catch another line back to his own base in Scotland. At that point in the war, he would be required to complete twenty-five missions, and they didn't know yet that more would be added later.

From that day on, there was not one evening when the phone at Ratcliffe failed to ring for Mary as Jack reported on returning safely from the day's work and made sure the same applied to her. Surrounded by colleagues who kept their defenses up against becoming too close, it was a comfort to know there was one person out there who openly cared. On only the third phone call, Mary thought Jack's voice sounded strained until he worked his way around to the point: Would she marry him? They had seen each other only twice since before the war. Mary demurred but didn't rule out the possibility.

She and Ann Wood had become good friends during their time at Ratcliffe. They often attended church together—Ann for the religious service, and Mary because she loved the music. But Ann, never one to allow sentiment to rule her choices, couldn't believe her widowed friend was harboring feelings for another pilot—another *bomber* pilot with a target on his back, a pilot like Wes, like Dorothy Furey Bragg's husband, like Bill. "Mary is in a dither," Ann wrote to her mother. "I try to suggest that she be less obvious, but it's no good."

Ann didn't allow her own heart to show on her sleeve, although she was thrilled when one of Bill's rare letters from prison made it through to her. She hinted to her mother that he wrote with affection, but kept the details to herself. Day to day, Ann mostly got on with it, her acerbic wit intact, flying with ever greater confidence, fewer nerves, and if anything even less sentiment than before. The war had made her stronger and harder. She gave up sharing her thoughts in a diary and asked her mother to save Ann's letters as a record instead. The ATA doctor told her that "obviously" she smoked and drank too much.

But Mary, clear-eyed in her own way, still believed in romance. Amid all the savagery of the air war, she toyed again with falling in love, pushing away the obvious downside. "Sometimes in life," she liked to say, "you have to be like a spider. You spin yourself a parachute of faith and fling yourself on the wind."

CHAPTER 23

Grounded

December 1943–February 1944
Hamble, Hampshire, and Ratcliffe, Leicestershire

Each American ATA pilot had a decision to make. Their contracts ran out after eighteen months. To stay or to go? For just about everyone, it was no contest. Two decided that come March 1944, they would head off to join the WASP—Emily Chapin, who had been the maid of honor at Roberta Sandoz's wedding, and Myrtle Allen, who'd been out on sick leave. The other sixteen who remained by the end of 1943 re-upped for more. Whatever the dangers and discomforts, they were having the time of their lives, and they didn't want it to end until the war did or the job was done, whichever came last.

Dorothy Furey Bragg was among the first to renew her contract. It was an example of the contradictions in her personality that she remained committed to the work while receiving evaluations that criticized her seeming lack of interest. "She would do much better if she looked upon flying not only as a job of work but an interesting one," an instructor grumbled in October 1943. "She proved a difficult pupil as she is inclined to be self-willed and showed a bored attitude to the whole affair." Such was the fallout from her blasé temperament. By that time, she'd been held to blame for three out of five minor accidents, mostly due to sloppy taxiing on the ground.

But in December 1943, Dorothy encountered a new difficulty as she began to suffer spells of dizziness and nausea, which led to vomiting. Her weight fell below one hundred pounds. Doctors believed she'd contracted food poisoning. One day in December 1943, Dorothy was landing a fighter at her Hamble base. Something seemed off as she guided the aircraft to touch down on the grass airfield and prepared to hit the brakes. Suddenly she realized she hadn't touched down at all—she was still twenty feet in the air, her depth perception gone haywire. Dorothy gunned the engine and circled back to bring the plane down once she regained her perspective.

The ATA grounded her, issuing a medical leave on December 29, 1943, to await a resolution of this alarming condition. Eventually, she was diagnosed with Meniere's disease, a disorder caused by fluid buildup in the ear. It tended to trigger dizziness and vertigo, provoking a sensation that the world was moving or spinning. Serious vertigo induced the sort of vomiting Dorothy had been experiencing. In any form, Meniere's made it impossible to safely fly a plane and could end Dorothy's career if it didn't abate.

Weeks passed with her flying future in question. During this break, the former Dorothy Furey of New Orleans began to live the life of an English lady of leisure, or at least a lady in waiting—waiting for Lord Beatty to divorce. The current Mrs. Beatty was supposedly filing papers without demonstrating much progress. Meanwhile David Beatty returned from duty in the Mediterranean and took up a post at the Admiralty in London, where he and Dorothy maintained separate residences to keep up appearances. David paid for her to move to a suite at the posh Grosvenor House hotel across from Hyde Park in Mayfair, on the same street as his own apartment. They also spent a few country weekends with others of his social station, inviting gossip and scandal. Dorothy didn't see what the fuss was about. "I don't think she really cared or thought much about what the other aristocrats thought," said her son. "And anyway, adultery and having mistresses was entirely accepted." For Dorothy, the greatest danger in taking on the customs of the titled set turned out to be learning to ride a horse, which was de rigueur. She fell off a mount and received a mild concussion, adding another complication to her medical woes.

Many weekends she and David slipped away from the city to his country estate, Brooksby Hall, a sixteenth-century manor house in Leicestershire, only five miles from Ratcliffe. The main house was given over to a wartime convalescent home for injured naval officers, so the couple slummed it in a well-appointed four-bedroom cottage nestled on the grounds. They sometimes invited Ann Wood to stay the night as a sort of chaperone, popping over on a new motorcycle. The trio strolled around the thirty acres of gardens and an ornamental lake, but mostly Ann enjoyed sharp-tongued conversation with her unfiltered hostess. "Dorothy always amuses me," Ann wrote. "She is good-natured and frank, and one can say anything to her and get away with it."

For intimate dinners, the butler positioned a small table next to the fireplace in the living room. David dazzled in a vivid blue evening tux with natty slippers to match, embroidered with a golden coronet and a "B" on the front. He was a generous host, eager to please his fiancée as much as his guests. They drank Veuve Clicquot 1929 to accompany menus David had devised especially to gratify Americans—chicken that was perfectly fried, cauliflower made with real flavor for a change, and genuine lemon meringue pie—divine nostalgia. It helped that his mother had come from Chicago and his current wife from Virginia, informing his culinary choices. David made a solid impression on Ann, sharing what he knew about war, within the bounds of discretion, and conversing with animation. Pacing the floor as he spoke and magnifying his thoughts with avid expressions and gestures, "he commands your attention not only by what he says but the way he says it," wrote Ann.

Dorothy tossed off wicked remarks about the ATA gossip Ann dished out over dinner and brandy. For example, there was a brouhaha over at Ratcliffe Hall involving Opal Anderson, the American known for her colorful language. She had returned from leave hopping mad that the *New York Herald Tribune* article identified her as a "former strip-tease artist," without citing any source. While Opal, thirty-eight, often shocked the British and Americans alike with her sizzling vocabulary, she had in fact conducted as respectable a career as anyone. She'd been a stay-at-home wife and mother until her husband divorced her with the claim that she no longer cooked for him once she took up flying. After that, she managed a small airport in Illinois, hosting and performing in its air shows. She had a nine-year-old son back home and was considered so good-hearted that Lady Everard tried for a time to convince Opal to adopt the illegitimate baby of a housemaid at the hall, a relatively common occurrence.

Dorothy took more interest in such doings than she might have had she not been keeping a low profile. The isolation wore on her, and the constant togetherness with her lover tested her capacity for boredom. Still, she appeared entirely at home among the trappings of luxury. At dinner, she presided with elegance, wearing a favored a gift from David, a diamond brooch set in a delicate floral design, like an Easter bouquet. Dorothy didn't have a title, not yet, but she had become a woman with jewels.

ROBERTA SANDOZ LEVEAUX was gung ho for her new contract at the end of her eighteen-month stretch, despite a grueling schedule. There were times when she flew a Hurricane north to Scotland, returned to Hamble on the night train, and then repeated the drill the next morning. "It got so you could sleep anyplace," she said. "Many times I would wake up with my head in someone's lap, having no idea who they were. And when no seats were available, I went to sleep in the aisle with my head on a parachute." She'd awaken to find that an anonymous fellow passenger, grateful for her service, had covered her with a blanket. Once, she had the pleasure of stretching out in a baggage car.

On leave days she stayed with her new husband, Peter, at the Leveaux family apartments in Kensington. The girl from the rural west found it eye-opening to enter the daily flow of London residents patiently going about their lives, as opposed to the hard-partying expats who packed the clubs like there was no tomorrow. She developed an appreciation for the fortitude and formal manners of "mend-and-make-do" England. "It helped everything a lot, that British courtesy," she said. The city gave her a newfound cosmopolitan perspective, and back at Hamble she counted among her friends many non-American flyers.

At work, Roberta felt she was finally getting the hang of it. On her trip back from leave, a U.S. Army Air Forces sergeant at one of the stops took pity on her and gave her an oversized heavy sheepskin jacket, so she finally felt warm on the job. In rough flying situations, she tapped into the early lessons she had taken in the San Francisco area, where her instructor would cut the engine randomly so Roberta would develop confidence that she had the skill to get a disabled plane back on the ground. She realized she could handle any aircraft that appeared on a chit. Roberta even ferried a German Junkers 88, a fast two-engine bomber that an escaped RAF prisoner had found unattended and commandeered to fly himself home. But there would always be crazy mishaps to put a pilot in her place.

In December 1943, Roberta made a momentary error of judgment while taking off in a Spitfire. Impatient at running late, she waited until well into the takeoff run to close the hatch over her head. When it proved too stiff to budge, she gave a mighty yank and caught her fingers as the hatch slammed shut. She could neither open it nor pull her fingers out. "This left me with my left hand, knees, chin, and prayer to gain enough altitude to work on the problem," Roberta said. She fell back on her old training, which had taught her that she could recover a plane from just about any position. Roberta gained altitude and let the Spit flop around in the sky while she used her left hand to extricate the right. Then she regained control and returned to base. A member of the ground crew reprimanded her for bleeding all over the brand-new cockpit as he cut off her glove.

Roberta received a bigger fright on another trip soon afterward. To achieve takeoff speed in a Spitfire, it was always necessary to over-rev the engine, redlining it for about a minute. Longer than that, and the engine could blow up or catch fire before the pilot brought the revolutions back below the line. On February 9, 1944, at an aerodrome north of Hamble, Roberta took control of a brand-new Spitfire IX reconnaissance aircraft. Painted baby blue for camouflage against the sky, it felt light as a feather without armor plate or guns. Once she got the ship into the air, though, the revs remained stuck on high. Roberta watched the temperature gauge redline and realized that her only option to avoid going up in flames was to turn off the engine, search for a spot to put down, and glide. On a wing and a prayer, she cut the power. "Never stretch a glide," she remembered her first instructor warning her. "If you think you might not clear something, dive at it until the last minute." She plunged down hard to keep up speed toward an airfield under construction, hopped a pile of gravel, and landed solidly on the other side without damaging the plane.

The Accident Committee found that a defect in the propeller mechanism was to blame, an unnerving reminder of the crash that killed her friend Mary Webb Nicholson. Roberta was rightfully shaken. Her husband had been worrying about her flying to begin with. The close call prompted her to reveal a secret she had planned to keep from her superiors: She was two months pregnant. Roberta knew that pregnant women were forbidden to fly. That alarming flight would be her last of the war.

Without delay, two days later, on February 11, 1944, Roberta Sandoz was terminated. The original twenty-five American women were depleted by spring to thirteen. Those remaining were all seasoned and cocksure, but anything could happen, even an unexpected baby.

Roberta moved into her husband's apartment building in London, where she began to nurse a lifelong resentment that he hadn't taken precautions to prevent the end of her flying career. "I have a message to the women here," she said, speaking about it sixty-two years later. "When the love of your heart says, 'trust me, just trust me,' pay no attention. I became pregnant before I planned to." Roberta was crushed that the highlight of her life, piloting the world's finest aircraft in the world's greatest war, had come to an end.

CHAPTER 24

Flying Under a Lucky Star

Winter, 1944
Ratcliffe, Leicestershire

I n many ways, the Atta-Girls lived outside of time; certainly outside the rules that otherwise would have governed women's lives in the 1940s. Because they were brave—beyond brave—and possessed a rare skill needed to help save democracy, these women could perform the work they loved while garnering admiration, respect, and a thick scrapbook of wild, unforgettable experiences. Occasionally one of the women landed at some unfamiliar base and encountered men who expressed surprise at her gender or questioned her abilities when she hopped down from the cockpit of a thundering aircraft they didn't know how to fly. But then those men usually nodded, shrugged, and stepped aside to let the woman get on with her work. Sometimes the guys would toss in an invitation to meet up later at the mess hall or pub.

In their jobs, the Atta-Girls behaved during the war the way the most empowered women would behave in the twenty-first century, working toward careers that they were increasingly confident they would win based on their merits. And they foreshadowed the women of the future in their private lives as well. The pilots loved whomever they loved, however they wanted to love them. They pursued men, women, people they chose to marry, or people they didn't. They committed shameless adultery. They kept multiple lovers on the line. Sometimes they spent a crazy night or two with somebody new before both took off again, possibly to die. They conducted themselves privately the way they flew their Spitfires, with a bracing sensation of velocity and control.

By the winter of 1944, the Americans were coming up on two years in the United Kingdom. Enough time had passed so that their early social and sexual exploits of free and easy liaisons—often fueled by alcohol—had evolved into some serious relationships, like Dorothy's affair or Roberta's marriage. A few pilots allowed those ties to interfere with the goal of flying. Most did not. Some, like Roberta, found that private choices led to unexpected consequences. But this being the 1940s, when traditional marriage and homemaking were the default option for most women, deeper relationships couldn't help but pose questions about which norms to follow and which to defy. The right choice—a relationship that didn't interfere with flying—could sustain a career enhanced by companionship, comfort, and support. But as Roberta had learned, the wrong choice could kill the career. Commitment was fine. The trick was choosing a commitment that didn't limit the pilot's aerial ambitions, unless she wanted it to.

ON NEW YEAR'S Day 1944, Mary Zerbel Hooper's enthusiastic new boyfriend, Jack Ford, borrowed an Oxford two-engine trainer from his commanding officer to fly Mary home from a three-day holiday at Jack's base. She had logged more experience than he had with the Oxford, but he took the controls. In the copilot's seat, Mary felt lighthearted for the first time in a long time, soaring over the swoon-worthy view of the Scottish Highlands on a day that promised fresh beginnings. Jack sensed that the moment was right to advance his cause. When the altimeter hit five thousand feet, he slipped his fraternity ring onto Mary's finger and shouted over the engine noise to renew his request. "Would you marry me?" This time, Mary said yes.

When Mary had been back in Michigan on leave the previous summer, she gave a newspaper a conventional quote. What she wanted in life, she said, was to serve in the war and then make a traditional marriage. "This war is a job for all of us, and I want to be right in the thick of things until it's over," she said, but then added, "The flying life is okay for a girl in times like these, but after the war my greatest ambition is to settle down and raise a good old-fashioned American family." The engagement to Jack set that plan in motion.

All smiles, Mary spilled the news to Ann Wood as soon as she returned to Ratcliffe Hall. Ann couldn't hide that she was appalled. Seeing the look on her face, Mary said, "I hope for your approval and advice, but I know you won't give it." She understood that her second wedding wouldn't inspire the same unfiltered joy as her first, a union of fresh-faced, hopeful kids still innocent about the price of war.

That ill-fated marriage weighed on Mary's new plans. She had to break the news of a remarriage to Wes's parents, who refused to believe what she had now accepted, that the depths of the North Sea had become their son's grave. Ann Wood's objection, however, had nothing to do with whether there was any hope for Wes. Brisk and practical in matters of the heart as in everything else, Ann considered it folly for Mary to once again join her future to a bomber pilot with dismal odds of survival.

"I can't see the marriage angle myself," Ann wrote to her mother. "He has only just begun his ops, and if Mary is going to sweat it out through those, waiting it out each night to hear . . ." Ann left the conclusion unwritten. "All I can say is that she must like to worry."

Ann's view of the wedding was so negative that she refused to serve as her friend's bridesmaid. Jack telephoned Ann to try to enlist her as an ally. "I don't want Mary to have to take a jolt twice," he assured her.

She argued for him to postpone until he completed his required bombing runs, prompting Mary to scoff at her friend. "You are too sensible to understand."

PERHAPS ANN REGRETTED that she hadn't been more sensible with Bill Brown. In one of his long-delayed letters from the prison camp, he asked her to send a photograph of herself to "lend some credence to the license I have taken in referring to 'my girl.'" Otherwise, between sentences blacked out by censors, she gathered that he wanted her to send him an English dictionary and some biographies. From what she could tell, few of the letters she had written to him made it through. It was a patchy sort of communication that left their future together ill-defined.

The blowback from his capture had altered Ann's social life. Once, she couldn't devour enough of the action in London, but the city no longer held the same magic for her, as Bill's captivity left her limbo. "I am a misfit *par excellence* and realize it more and more into each visitation," she wrote her mother. "I feel like a round peg in a square hole and am often at a complete loss to know what to do." During her leave, Ann sometimes remained in Ratcliffe, organizing flights to Scotland to pick up booze for the nonstop parties, where she worked the bar while hugging the sidelines. Her old beau Avery Hand had replaced her with a new love interest. She mostly kept company with other couples, dining with Dorothy Furey Bragg and Lord Beatty or playing tennis with Winnie's beau, Peter Beasley. She also took to tagging along with Louise Schuurman, who had been reassigned to Ratcliffe while she conducted an affair with a high-ranking American colonel. He sent a plane each leave day to bring Louise to his headquarters, a sixteenth-century Tudor manor in Cambridgeshire with gardens for sunning and other luxe amenities. Although he was twice Louise's age and had a wife and daughters back home, Ann suspended judgment about the illicit romance and accepted the hospitality. Louise, Ann rationalized, "is very continental in her outlook along these lines." As pilots around Ann paired up, she had tied herself to a phantom.

ON A THREE-DAY leave at Ratcliffe Hall beginning February 19, 1944, Jack Ford and Mary Zerbel Hooper lay in front of a flickering fire. Jack had returned from a bombing raid on the shipyards of Kiel, where Junkers and Messerschmitts dove out of the sun from three o'clock to decimate the American formation. He saw one of the Liberators explode in flame. Another staggered, lost speed, and fell behind, tongues of fire spreading across the wing as parachutes sprouted underneath. Jack had persisted through heavy flak. "Bombs away!"

Alone with Mary, Jack abandoned all the caution he'd discussed with Ann Wood. He blurted out, "Let's get married tomorrow if we can, honey."

Embracing the challenge, Mary ran to the little Ratcliffe on the Wreake church before breakfast in the morning and petitioned the parson: "If we can get the license, can we get married this afternoon?" She and Jack both reached their commanding officers for written permission, and Sir Lindsay Everard himself drove the couple to the bishop's office in Leicester for a license. Mary had already picked out a pretty white wedding gown at a local shop, which offered to finish alterations and attach a veil to a wax-flower headpiece by noon. The couple got lucky again at the local florist. Flowers couldn't be transported in bulk by trains during the war, but the shop had a single bouquet of lilies of the valley and rare white Scottish heather in stock. Sir Lindsay whisked the couple to a local wine shop for a celebratory glass of champagne, "sparkling and bubbling almost as much as Jack and Mary were."

Following a quick stop at the aerodrome to invite whomever was present, they changed out of their heavy uniforms, overcoats, and woolen underwear into wedding finery. This would be only the third time that Jack had seen his bride in a dress. She would come to regret the choice when they arrived at the church to find that the parson had forgotten to light the fire. Ann stuck to her guns and declined again to serve as Mary's bridesmaid. But she did agree to attend and pitched in to find a best man for Jack, pouncing when Louise Schuurman's colonel happened in for a one-night visit.

The entire Ratcliffe ferry pool and nearly every resident of the tiny village showed up for the five o'clock ceremony at St. Botolph's, an Anglican stone church surrounded by tilting gravestones dating from the fourteenth century. Sir Lindsay, decked out in his RAF commodore's uniform, escorted Mary down the aisle, and the colonel passed the ring to Jack while the bride and groom shivered with cold and nerves. The parson broke the tension when his gurgling stomach sounded off and echoed from the vaulted ceiling, prompting peals of laughter.

Sir Lindsay and Lady Everard hosted a packed a reception at the hall, having somehow managed to obtain a roast goose and a dessert thrown together from chocolate-covered graham crackers. A woman pilot from New Zealand contributed a fruitcake, a late-arriving Christmas present that had circled the world and arrived in the post a day earlier. Ann served as underbutler to the ever-smart Smart at dinner, as the staff was caught short. Sir Lindsay served a venerable 1902 port, and "miracle of miracles," Mary wrote, "Ann had been able to talk some wine merchant out of a whole case of champagne." All accomplished on one day of a three-day pass. There were other advantages to the midwinter celebration. Lady Everard said to Mary afterward, "I'm so glad that you got married, because otherwise I would never have found the moths in my mink."

Granted a one-week compassionate leave, the newlyweds dashed to the cliff-lined coast of Cornwall for a quick escape from war duties. When they moved on to London, though, the atmosphere was oppressive. Hitler's reprisal blitz in response to Allied bombings of Berlin pounded the capital with bombs, while sirens, ack-ack batteries, flares, fighters, and search-lights convulsed the night. Also known as the Baby Blitz, this assault killed 1,556 British citizens between January and May 1944, mostly in London and other cities. Jack returned to base in late February to join the Eighth Air Force in the biggest escalation yet—6,200 sorties in one week, 248 Allied aircraft lost. As predicted, Mary sweated through until his call each evening.

So far Jack had remained charmed. He called in safe after the "Bloody Monday" Berlin raid on March 5, when sixty-nine American bombers were lost. One by one, the other crews in his original squadron were torn asunder. Eventually, his was the only one still intact. They moved on from the damaged bomber *Hell-Bent Angel* to the *Sky Queen*, the *Bucket of Bolts*, and eventually the *Yankee Gal*. Jack had gotten each of those wrecks back to base, except once, when he crashed into the English Channel, popped open a life raft, and waited for rescue. One of the crew was bleeding from serious injuries, but when Jack reached into a pocket of the raft for its first aid kit, he found only a piece of paper that said OUT OF STOCK.

At the other end of each call, Mary heard it all—"the terror, anger, and fight," as she described the ordeal. In her own work, she was particu-larly pleased to deliver her first new-model P-51 Mustang, a long-range American fighter that finally, in 1944, had the capability to escort bombers like Jack's all the way to Berlin, shooting down enemy fighters and improving his chances for safety.

Mary Zerbel Hooper Ford's new husband had always been a scrappy, happy-go-lucky guy, but the stress showed in the wedding photos, where the former football player and stunt man looked anxious and gaunt. The couple planned to take new pictures when their service was over. But the way they saw it, he had won the girl of his dreams, and she had won her boy. They had pulled off a perfectly executed wartime wedding in less than a day. Maybe they could survive as the couple that flew under a lucky star.

CHAPTER 25

Her Future at Stake

March–May 1944
Cosford Aerodrome, Shropshire

L ove was in the air at the Cosford Aerodrome, too. One of the two all-woman pools in the ATA, Cosford, the outpost in rural Shropshire near the border with Wales, offered few diversions beyond the West Midlands scenery. Of the five Americans transferred there in the spring of 1943, only two remained by the spring of 1944. Mary Webb Nicholson had been killed on her way to the assignment; Evelyn Hudson was terminated after her back injury; and Louise Schuurman had transferred to Ratcliffe the previous fall. That left Winnie Pierce and Virginia Farr, much to the frustration of Winnie. She still harbored resentment toward one of the only pilots to best her flying record. Plus, she lamented the dearth of nightlife in Shropshire.

Virginia, though, cared little about living in a social vacuum and thrived under the heavy workload at Cosford. The airfield served as a repair and maintenance hub, where many assignments involved ferrying bombers damaged by missing parts or gaping holes. "They were shot up in all kinds of ways," Virginia's niece Cristy explained. Engine failures led to many forced landings. Virginia never lost her cool and continued to fly without damaging a single aircraft.

For a lesbian in Britain in 1944, the geographic isolation of Cosford had the advantage of providing some cover for sexual relationships. Joining the ATA had given Virginia distance from the hothouse of her family's wealth and visibility, but it also landed her in a country with draconian laws against same-sex liaisons. Sexual activity between consenting men provided grounds for imprisonment. No one was safe, regardless of stature. Oscar Wilde famously was sentenced to two years' hard labor in 1895, and Nancy Astor's eldest son from her first marriage was jailed for four months in 1931. Women felt less threatened, as they weren't made part of the "gross indecency" statutes. Nevertheless, they could be arrested under such vague pretenses as "public nuisance" or "undermining public morality." So far, Virginia Farr had pursued relationships discreetly, but far from London in Cosford, she was less likely to stir up harmful gossip. Colleagues like Winnie Pierce mentioned in their diaries that Virginia had casual affairs, but unlike her friends who confided their blow-by-blow romantic adventures in diaries and letters, Virginia was mum.

In Cosford, however, she found a soulmate. Vivien Jeffery, age thirty-three, was an Englishwoman who had grown up middle class as the daughter of a bank manager near Leicester. At twenty-five, Virginia was large, powerfully built, and blunt-spoken, "not a frilly person," according to her niece, while Vivien was fine-boned and petite. Although Vivien had been certified to fly on a Piper Cub in 1939, she worked on the ground as the operations manager at Cosford, serving as the right hand to Marion Wilberforce, the commanding officer who had been one of the first eight women to join the ATA. Each morning, Vivien woke up earlier than anyone else to match the list of aircraft to be moved that day with the available pilots. Then the real work began, retooling the plan when weather, accidents, and breakdowns scuttled the whole arrangement. Virginia's stellar evaluations only improved as she pitched in wherever needed to help Vivien run the base.

What lent romance to their attachment was Vivien's enchantment with America, especially mythic tales of adventure in the American West. For years, the dainty, responsible operations officer had lapped up every popular novel by Zane Grey, who set stories of bravery and romance amid the majestic grandeur of the Western landscape. His characters in novels like *Riders of the Purple Sage* were often greenhorns stirred to heroism by encounters with the red rock cliffs, deeply shadowed canyons, and sparkling silver creeks of the landscape. Vivien dreamed of living there herself among rugged Americans.

Vivien's fantasies synced with Virginia's idealized memories of childhood summers at the family ranch in California, where she felt most at home living a pioneer life—herding cattle, riding horses, and exploring the vast, scenic splendor of the property overlooking the Pacific Ocean. It had offered a physical outlet for an active girl far from the fuss of Eastern society. The two women fantasized about moving there from soggy Shropshire someday, a fitting follow-up to their adventurous wartime service.

They also felt a bond over tragedy. Virginia's younger brother had died from an illness at the age of sixteen. In May of 1944, Vivien's brother Philip, thirty-two, a major in the infantry, was killed while fighting in Italy. He was buried in the military cemetery at Cassino. The shared sorrows only deepened the women's desire for a more idyllic future.

NO DISCUSSION OF romance in the ATA could leave out Winnabelle Pierce, arguably the group's most outrageous and vivacious flirt. She was miserable at Cosford, stuck for a year at the remote all-woman pool with her archrival. Winnie zipped eight miles by motorcycle every day between the base and a small pub where she kept a room, the liveliest billet she could find. But distance didn't lessen her spite. In her journal, she made note of Virginia's and Vivien's arrangements: "They take a house together," she wrote, "and all is ducky."

It seemed possible that Commander Pauline Gower had tucked Winnie away to keep her out of trouble, but boredom led her to take risks. She took to flying in all weather, as she wrote, "just to get away from the rancid competitive atmosphere of a bunch of women crowded together in one room on a rainy day—all hating the sight of the other fellows." Only instincts and luck kept the reckless pilot from harm. With a front moving in fast one day, she escaped Cosford's sleepy waiting room by taking a Beaufighter, a slow, weighty, old-school two-engine fighter, to Prestwick, Scotland, landing in a sixty-mile-per-hour gale. Then, determined not to be stranded god-knows-where for the night, she took off into the same tearing wind to start the run back in a Spitfire.

By then the front had cornered her in earnest. It was too windy and rough to land along the way, so Winnie carried on, following the coast for guidance, trying to stay below the clouds without hitting the hills, feeling as if the wind would rip the fighter apart. She prayed when the gauge told her the fuel would last only fifteen more minutes. Winnie spotted her home aerodrome just in time and turned to land. "A two-hour flight has taken over three in the battle of the elements," she wrote later, unrepentant about her decision to fly.

Adding to Winnie's isolation, she and her closest friend, Louise Schuurman, fell out with a vengeance when Louise transferred to Ratcliffe and embarked on her romance with the married American colonel. He was Murray Clarke Woodbury, soon to be promoted to general, the commander of the 66th fighter wing. Winnie was so offended that she wrote searing critiques in her journal about "Louise promiscuously moving from affair to affair, blind to her folly," adding for good measure, "She has gone sex-mad and to the dogs, though her work is still okay."

While the general led the fighter wing over Germany by day, Louise relaxed in the landscaped gardens of his headquarters. Eventually, though, she took her privileges too far and learned the limits of her power. She created a scene at a party at Ratcliffe by dancing enthusiastically, in a dress that showed off her impressive figure, with Frankie Francis, the commanding officer of the aerodrome. She didn't bother to hide the fact that she spent the night with him, and word circulated that the general was displeased. From then on, Francis starting ducking when he saw Louise. Their affair went no further, and she returned to Woodbury after her very public exhibition. None of this overcrowded melodrama endeared Louise to her former friend Winnie, stuck out in Shropshire, now an advocate for monogamy.

FOR WINNIE, SUFFERING through a year at Cosford, it felt like a lifeline to civilization when Peter Beasley made a rare visit. He set off on more of his secretive travels in the spring of 1944, and her frustration simmered. Unbeknownst to her, his work involved interrogating Germans captured in liberated territory for insight into their strategies. He'd already carried out this work in North Africa and Italy. As usual, she wasn't sure where he was and heard nothing from him while he was away. She arranged to take her entire two-week summer leave at one shot in May when he was expected to return. Winnie checked into Claridge's on the appointed day and waited by the phone, cradling a cocker spaniel she had adopted and named Peter the Great.

A week passed, and she began to worry whether she would have to cover the hotel bill herself. Just as her leave wound down, Peter appeared, regaling Winnie and her friends with amusing but innocuous stories of encounters in Italy and Jerusalem. His next assignment, he said, would be to oversee modifications of operational aircraft, which he thought he could do more effectively from the States. When he and Winnie were alone, he spoke the words she'd been waiting to hear. "Let's go home and get married."

She struggled with the decision, conflicted. It presented a stark choice: marriage or career. Winnie had been angling to marry Peter Beasley since they'd met, but now, with his decision to leave, it would mean giving up her position in the ATA. The woman who before the war disdained lovers who were "the marrying kind," who relished the absence of "ties and obligations," now was torn. She weighed those views against a growing desire for safety and security, a break from the routine dangers of the work. "Her whole future is at stake," she wrote, using third person in her journal, "and death may be in the next cockpit. So after two and a half years of ferrying every type of plane and no accidents, she decides marriage is the answer." Besides, she added, she had "always wanted what Peter has to offer." She would follow Roberta Sandoz as the second pilot to leave the service for domestic life.

Winnie elaborated on her decision in an interview with a reporter in London. Out of uniform, wearing a canary-yellow sweater and powder-blue skirt in the lobby of Claridge's, she insisted she would always fly for pleasure, "but you get tired of being a professional flyer. The first year was lots of fun, but lately it has been just hard work." She also admitted that the death of Mary Webb Nicholson had frightened her, especially considering that Winnie could have been handed the chit for the Miles Master that turned into a death trap for Mary. "When I came over here, I was young and carefree and had no love interest," Winnie told the journalist. "But now I'm going to get married. I have everything to look forward to, and I want to live."

The resourceful pilot took her final flight for the ATA at the age of twenty-seven in the second week of May 1944. She delivered her last British aircraft, a Hawker Typhoon, a long-range fighter, a plane of the future. However impulsive and devil-may-care Winnie's behavior might have been during her tenure, there was no denying that she flew to the end without a scratch on a single aircraft or on herself. Just a shattered motorcycle and a concussion on her own time, during one of many nights of heavy drinking. In daylight, on the other hand, she had racked up 1,500 flying hours on a full range of aircraft types. Perhaps most important for Winnie, "it was one glorious adventure," she said later. Ann Wood wrote that she considered Winnie "one of the best," and even Pauline Gower, who had so often upbraided Winnie for her ceaseless carousing, composed a farewell note saying how much she would be missed.

Peter suggested they move to New Mexico, buy a ranch, have children, and raise some dogs. New Mexico had never been on Winnie's radar, but she was all in. As was often the case with Peter, it wasn't clear exactly why or when this would happen. There were bureaucratic hoops in order for Winnie to obtain an exit permit, so she stayed on at the London hotel after her resignation. To move things along, she asked Jackie Cochran to write a cable claiming Winnie was needed in the WASP, even though she didn't plan to join.

This was not the couple's only spin on the truth, or at least not Peter's. He remained a man of contradictions and secrets, even to his fiancée. Despite his rather vague duties in England and his frequent, incommunicado absences, it never seemed to occur to her that Peter might not have been what he appeared to be or that his stated plans might have been yet another cover. The fact that New Mexico was an unlikely location for overseeing aircraft modifications failed to set off any alarm bells. During their engagement, Winnie still considered Peter a high-level air force aide, now a colonel, nothing more. In diaries, postwar journals, and stories shared with friends, none of the American women mentioned the possibility that the middle-aged former aircraft manufacturing executive, the man who seemed to know everyone as he traversed the furthest reaches of the combat zone, had in fact been engaged in espionage. Or that quietly putting down roots as a married man in New Mexico might not have been the actual plan. His son, Michael Beasley, said after the war, "She mistakenly did believe, at first, that they would settle down in New Mexico." Whatever Winnie believed, there would be more twists to the story in the year to come.

Peter had always amused the women of the ATA with his hints of inside knowledge. He told them before Winnie resigned that he didn't expect the war to end soon, but he advised them to keep an eye out for opportunities when it finally did. There wouldn't be enough employment for all the pilots who served, and men in the U.S. military would have a leg up over women who flew for a British ferry operation.

The women didn't need top secret information to sense that something big was coming in the spring of 1944. Everyone serving in the United Kingdom could feel it, a bass note sounding like the deep throb of a Spitfire engine beneath the surface of everyday duties. Leaves were cancelled, and ferry pilots routinely delivered four aircraft a day. Ambitious pilots like Ann Wood started pushing for assignments to fly to the Continent if new fronts opened there. They knew that a vast expansion of the field of battle could be weeks or even days away. It would change the direction of the fight and mark the beginning of the middle, possibly clearing a path to the end.

CHAPTER 26

The World-Shaking Day

June 6, 1944
Hamble, Hampshire

O n June 6, 1944, Nancy Miller awoke to a steady roar in her ears. She turned on the light in her bedroom, saw the time, and groaned. Only five A.M. She shook her head to rattle her brain awake. She identified the sound, even louder now that she was conscious—a terrific flight of B-17 Fortresses, rolling overhead. Nancy wondered if that was how it would sound on D-Day. Then she fell back into a doze.

At five thirty, the noise disturbed her again. When she caught a bus at eight thirty to the Hamble Aerodrome, the closet ferry pool to the English Channel, the roar still hadn't let up, growling overhead through low, dirty clouds. Some Fortresses flew low under the weather, a stirring and intimidating sight. Others buzzed above the impenetrable curtain of gray, hour after hour, setting off reverberations along the southern coast with a force Nancy had never felt before. The yacht harbor, once filled with gaily colored pleasure boats, echoed with a different sound, the chugging of small military craft putting out to sea.

An eerie anxiety pulsed at the all-woman field, only twenty-eight miles from France. The broadcast system passed along a report that the Germans were claiming the invasion had begun. The pilots already knew.

"Everyone was filled with the awe and wonder of it," wrote Alison King, the Hamble operations officer. The night before, she and her colleagues had seen landing craft loaded with the small figures of men sailing off from a newly constructed jetty. "We looked at each other, but did not say a word; there was nothing to say; it was obvious the bubble of tension which had been growing had burst. This was it."

Before night fell on June 6, there would be a heavy reckoning. Many would perish. The outcome would set the destiny for millions around the globe. The pilots at Hamble waited and held their breath.

Nancy, one of the youngest American officers at twenty-four, had observed the buildup for several weeks. She flew eighteen new types of aircraft in a single month, including torpedo planes, air-sea rescue amphibians, and the sleekest new fighters, the Typhoon and the Corsair, used by American marines. She'd been forbidden to fly over restricted routes. On June 4, she saw a ground crew painting white and black stripes—invasion markings for easy identification—on the wings and fuselages of American P-47 Thunderbolts, the go-to American fighter-bomber for ground attacks. The next day, a familiar aerodrome was jammed with more invasion-striped DC-3 troop transports. At bases throughout the south, the airfields were coated with heavy-gauge wire reinforcements over the mud to handle the higher volume of takeoffs and landings.

A few days before D-Day, Nancy and other Hamble women flew Spitfires to a hastily constructed aerodrome for Polish pilots assigned to attack railways in France. The men slept and ate in flimsy tents, everything slick with mud. She watched them make skidding takeoffs with five-hundred-pound bombs dangling from the fuselages, nerve-rackingly close to the pitted runway.

"Something was going to pop soon," Nancy figured.

Alison King noted that the Solent shipping lane that flowed by Hamble "had a lot more ships in it—that it was filled—was jammed." Roads near the coast were suddenly gridlocked with convoys of armored trucks, amphibious duck boats, and tanks. "A new type of fighting man appeared in the woods around Hamble," noted the British pilot Rosemary Rees. "Very tough, hardened-looking soldiers, from the Desert War, with smeared faces, and vegetation draped on their tin hats." They would bring the war to the ground in Northern Europe. Air power had taken the lead until June 6, 1944, when 160,000 Allied soldiers and paratroopers and 7,000 seagoing vessels entered the fight in a single day.

It was possible for the ATA pilots to divine pieces of the D-Day strategy from the goings-on they observed. In the days leading up to the invasion, the Eighth Air Force had pounded the Pas-de-Calais area in an effort to convince the Germans that the assault would take place there. Elsewhere, attacks focused on railroad hubs, bridges, airfields, and coastal fortifications. The goal was to weaken German defenses and prevent reinforcements from reaching the real objective along the Normandy beaches. The Polish Spitfire squadron that took Nancy Miller's delivery, for example, played a role in the Allies dropping a total of seventy-one thousand bombs on the French rail system. On the day itself, those B-17s passing over Hamble before dawn joined an unprecedented fleet of aircraft—more than ten thousand in all—including heavy bombers dropping thousands of tons of bombs on the French coastline in the hours before the infantry landed. Meanwhile, fighters preyed on their Luftwaffe counterparts, picking them off like arcade targets to prevent them from reaching the beachhead and attacking exposed Allied troops.

The women at the aerodrome hung on every scrap of information, knowing it would be days before the they would learn the outcome of the landing and the terrible cost of achieving it. In fact, it took seven weeks for the infantry to break out from the beaches and begin the long, deadly grind toward Berlin. But right off the bat, the women witnessed how the combined efforts of the American and British airmen had won command of the sky. They had effectively isolated the invasion zone and cut off its supply lines, a strategy that would become more damaging to the enemy as the days progressed.

The Hamble airfield had been designated as a "prang patch," where aircraft in trouble could return to land. But the base was strangely quiet. The crash crew and "blood tub"—as the ambulance was known—sat mostly idle that first day. Nancy Miller saw only one injured Spitfire wobble in, a surprising sign of how much pre-invasion sorties had crippled Luftwaffe air defenses. The pilot of that Spit said he marveled at how little fighter opposition he had seen. Nancy craved a part in the action herself. Everyone at Hamble on D-Day "had romantic but vain thoughts that there would be spectacular, life-saving jobs to squadrons," she wrote. "We had done our work previously, although we didn't know it at the time."

ANN WOOD, WHO placed the highest priority on being in the know, couldn't let the invasion pass without seeking her own observation post on history. "I am ubiquitous," she wrote to her mother. She swooped in when a man at her airfield offered his chit for a flight south on what turned out to be the day before the invasion. After arranging to tack on a few days' leave, Ann bid farewell. "I'm off to D-Day!" she quipped. "You can pick me up in Paris."

Billeting with colleagues in Hamble, Ann saw the activity pick up that night, the invasion confirmed the next morning. "I was glad I was on leave," she wrote. "One didn't feel as though one could go on in the same old way that day." Proximity to the action thrilled her. She was beside herself just to see the lone Spitfire pilot bring in his shot-up ship, and she strained her neck counting the black specks of Fortresses winging to France.

By midday, she decided she'd seen all the available local news and called a friend who ran a nearby rest home for aircrew suffering with post-traumatic stress disorder. Together, the women drove throughout the Southampton area ogling colossal convoys of men and materiel waiting to go aboard barges. Red Cross workers known as Doughnut Dollies doled out the last coffee and snacks the troops would see before battle. (Possibly the last in their lives—ten thousand Allied troops were killed, wounded, or missing in action that day.) Ann was amazed that the men could sleep, read, shave, cut each other's hair—"that in the face of momentous happenings [they] can do the commonplace."

She felt guilty to arrive at the Red Cross home, a lavish country house intended to provide rest and recreation for air crews injured in body and mind. On this of all days, it was uncanny to enter a space designed to do everything possible to help the residents forget the war. They wore an assortment of donated sweaters and trousers to avoid the reminder of uniforms. Some men were antsy to return to their squadrons; some were sorry to miss D-Day. Others were glad to be out of it altogether. Ann felt a mixture of all three. The gala dinner made her feel guilty, and so did seeing her friend chatter with all the boys without ever appearing bored, a skill Ann knew she did not possess. After dinner, she escaped to listen to the news, then sat outside to watch the aircraft still streaming toward the front. She counted the holes in the formations on their return.

The next day Ann played badminton with one of the guests, a bombardier, hospitalized for four months with flak injuries after twenty missions. She joined some Red Cross volunteers to buy cases of local strawberries and drive up and down the convoys, dispensing the fruit. Then she returned to Ratcliffe ready to work. Sitting on the sidelines of the world-shaking day didn't sit well with a woman of action.

CHAPTER 27

Good Girl

Summer 1944
Prestwick, Scotland

T ime had stopped for a day. When work resumed for the ferry pilots,
it was impossible to continue as before. Everyone felt the whiplash
of the abrupt turn and what it could mean. An end to the war? It now
seemed possible, somewhere down the line. The women felt relief, of
course, and anticipation. But they also felt a tug they couldn't admit aloud.
Along with the end to all the horror would come an end to this golden
period in their lives. Where else could they find the gleeful engagement,
the autonomy they had enjoyed while flying anything to anywhere?
Anywhere. They were resourceful, or they wouldn't have made it this far.
Some of the women turned their attention to another form of navigation—
one that would extend their glide should the ATA engine fail—into
postwar life, normal life, wherever or whatever that would be.

The finish wouldn't happen anytime soon. It took seven weeks during
the summer of 1944 for the invasion force to advance only through
Normandy. But while the attention of the world focused on the long drive
to take back territory, the air war reached new intensity. Carpet bombing
cleared the way for the army, and fighters supported ground troops even as

the air forces continued their ongoing bombardment of Germany. The number of RAF sorties ballooned from less than twenty thousand during the first three months of 1944 to more than fifty thousand in the last three.

THREE OF THE best-known American pilots stayed on in England for a time despite leaving the service, including Roberta Sandoz Leveaux. She volunteered for ground work at the ATA during the summer while awaiting the birth of a son in September. When her husband was assigned to teach at the military college at Sandhurst, they moved to quarters in the stable of a nearby manor house. It was so cold that sometimes she slept in her cherished sheepskin flying coat. Ever resourceful, Roberta bought a dozen day-old chicks to provide eggs for the family, but it turned out that only one was a hen and the rest were cockerels, an embarrassing mistake for a self-described country bumpkin.

Winnie Pierce, following her resignation in May, remained as visible as ever in London as she waited for an exit permit. While Peter disappeared on another mission, she volunteered to work the waffle bar at the Red Cross Club and ran up another colossal bill at Claridge's. Her fiancé had left her only enough cash to cover a few weeks, and Winnie had never saved a penny from her ATA salary. Ann Wood came to the rescue with a two-hundred-dollar loan, quite a sum for that time.

The other prominent American who left the ATA without leaving England was Dorothy Furey Bragg. The service finally terminated her contract after D-Day in June 1944 due to her continuing problems with vertigo. The twenty-six-year-old widow had advanced to large two-engine bombers and reached the rank of first officer before her illness. She had been blamed for five accidents, a fairly high count, though none were particularly serious. Her last evaluation marked a step up from earlier ones that critiqued her blasé attitude. "A capable pilot whose discipline whilst on ferrying duties has improved," the record stated with frosty economy.

Dorothy was fine with moving on. "I enjoyed my time in the ATA," she wrote later, "but I was not impassioned by flying, which I think most of the other young women were."

She was well on her way to the next objective. A large portrait in oil, with Dorothy in full uniform, now graced a place of honor above the mantle in David Beatty's London flat. Her friends Winnie and Ann found it impressive—the eyes were especially fine. But Dorothy hadn't hit it off with the fashionable painter, James Proudfoot, "which would probably happen with any man asking her to sit still," her son conceded later. Dorothy herself never warmed to the forbidding likeness. She said, "He made me look like a hardened bitch."

Still unflappable, she remained in London despite the latest scourge of the war, the V-1 flying bomb, otherwise known as the buzz bomb or doodlebug. Germany launched this new unmanned weapon just after D-Day. Shaped like a cigar, powered by a jet engine, the buzz bomb puttered along, sounding like a small plane, until the engine timed out near its intended target. A true weapon of terror, it left people on the ground crouched in suspense when the abrupt silence indicated a coming explosion. More than ten thousand V-1s were launched over the summer of 1944, mostly aimed toward London, where six thousand people died from the strikes before the Allies would overrun the launch sites in October.

Dorothy felt secure in her second-floor suite in the Grosvenor House, with enough floors above to provide protection from collapse. To avoid flying glass from the force of blasts, she stayed away from the windows and threw herself on the floor when she heard a doodlebug approach. Ann Wood promised her mother that she took all sensible precautions at the sound of immediate danger by hopping into one of the slit trenches dug by the Home Guard or sprawling on the ground. This didn't sound particularly reassuring.

Nancy Miller happened to be in London the first night the buzz bombs descended, a few days after D-Day. The alert went out as she was climbing into bed at the Red Cross Club. Five minutes later she leaped out and ran downstairs for shelter when she heard a roar directly overhead. All night long, she couldn't sleep—as much from the terrific firing of the defensive ack-ack as from the assaults of V-1s themselves. Later, when she learned how they worked, she understood what was happening at the sound of one approaching, "getting closer and louder until your eyes almost pop out trying to see it. Your ears sort of stretch, trying to place the location." When she heard an explosion strike nearby, it felt "like a vicious earthquake—sudden, jarring, violent." Several hundred passed overhead every night. It was impossible to rest.

WITH THE VARIOUS departures, only ten of Jackie Cochran's original stalwarts remained in the ATA by summer. They included Virginia Farr and Louise Schuurman from the first group to sail in the spring of 1942; Suzanne Ford and Grace Stevenson from the second; Ann Wood from the third; Edith Stearns, Peggy Lennox, and Mary Zerbel Ford from the fourth; and Opal Anderson and Nancy Miller from the fifth. One American who joined on her own and also stuck it out was Jane Plant, who was only twenty years old when she joined in 1943. She persisted even though she survived a spectacular crash in the summer after D-Day when she force-landed a Hudson bomber with an engine on fire. Her instructor, Ben Warne, jumped out and sprinted away, but when he turned around, he saw that the fuselage was burning with Jane still trapped inside. Ben dashed back to find that she was caught in the window, her hips a tight squeeze to clear the opening. He managed to pull her out through the billowing smoke. From then on, Ben joked, he would measure the hips of women pilots.

The holdouts by mid-1944 were serious aviators, most with eyes on postwar careers. But with the air war still escalating rather than waning, they were committed to seeing the mission through. The remaining pilots represented a range of ages—from twenty-one to forty-four—and their experience before the war varied from a few hundred hours flying to more than a thousand. Neither factor was a sure indicator of which women had made it this far. "It might have started as a lark for many," wrote Nancy Miller, "but the work soon told." Their personalities ranged from fun-loving to sober-minded, reckless to cautious, but what they all shared by now was a steadiness of purpose and iron self-assurance. Pauline Gower had gotten it right when she told a newspaper that physical strength didn't count for as much as steady nerves.

After D-Day, Opal Anderson went so far as to contact the Russian air force, knowing that it allowed women to fly in combat, but she got no reply. Others lobbied hard to begin ferrying aircraft to recaptured territory on the Continent. Only RAF pilots performed those duties, but everyone knew the ATA would step up soon.

Nancy Miller, who demonstrated some of the steadiest nerves among the Americans, went to one of the greatest lengths to catch a continental assignment. She applied for transfer to Prestwick, Scotland, thinking its large stock of heavy two-engine bombers, with their relatively short range, would be in demand for runs within Europe. She also shared the view of colleagues who believed that two-engines were most similar to the passenger planes that might—fingers crossed—serve in private aviation after the war.

NANCY HAD STAYED under the radar of other Americans most of this time. One of the youngest of the Atta-Girls, she never joined the rambunctious social set. She kept to herself, quietly befriending like-minded British and other international flyers. But as the war progressed, Nancy emerged as one of the most hardworking and ambitious in the American group.

It was no wonder others had overlooked her until now. The quiet loner had arrived on the next-to-last ship in 1942 and dug into her training without calling attention to herself. She was one of the least inclined to drama of all the recruits, performing without much self-reflection or emotion, and certainly without fear. Her more worldly colleagues didn't take notice of the clean-living daughter of a clergyman with a sensible wardrobe and teetotaling social life who eschewed the clubs in London. When she chalked up her first Hurricane solo, some pals spent their mad money at a pub trying to find a hard drink Nancy would like. She took one sip of each, grimaced, and passed it on for others to finish.

Assigned to the women's base at Hamble, Nancy took her duties seriously. "Can never be given too much work," said one of her first evaluations, setting a pattern for all that followed. This being the ATA, however, even Nancy engaged in a little mischief. Once as she sped along in a Spitfire at two thousand feet, a pilot in an American Mustang had pulled alongside. He made hand signals, indicating that he was up for a practice dogfight. Nancy shook him off twice, but when he persisted, she found a more effective way to knock him off balance. She pulled off her goggles and helmet, shook out her long hair, and blew him a kiss.

Over time, she began to feel her oats and buck a few guidelines. On her first flight in a P-51 Mustang, Nancy was so tickled to be flying "one of the finest American machines in the world" that she explored its capacity for low-altitude attacks, hopping over trees and telegraph wires at only fifty feet. As a finale, before she landed, she buzzed the airfield at three hundred miles per hour, only ten feet above the surface. She chose to see this not as showing off so much as testing the capabilities of the aircraft.

Nancy was too focused on flying to go on the hunt for a boyfriend. A lonely American serviceman in a railway station once spotted the U.S.A. patch on her uniform and asked, "U.S.A.? What does that mean, lady?"

Nancy put on a herky-jerky accent: "Union South Africa."

His face dropped. "Wrong country," he sighed. "Wrong girl."

AT HAMBLE, NANCY'S flying was spot-on. No accidents, no mistakes, no crazy exploits defying protocol in the wrong conditions. Hamble was an ideal posting for good girls, with its emphasis on safety, on holding back when circumstances weren't right. Nancy was as good as a girl could get.

Prestwick was another story. It usually dawned on pilots soon after they transferred in: If you wanted to fly the hot stuff, if you wanted to make a vital contribution to deliveries, you had to fly above the clouds or use forbidden instruments. To thrive and survive at Prestwick, it was better to be bad. Nancy would have to choose whether to fly in opposition to her most essential qualities.

Conditions at Prestwick set a high degree of difficulty. Ocean winds swept the station, where RAF aircraft mingled with the largest American models landing from transatlantic deliveries. Rain could pour down in torrents, and to the north, the vivid green Scottish Highlands rose to forbidding heights. If aircraft failure forced a landing, it would be impossible to survive. ATA pilots from the south often brought planes as far as the aerodrome so that hard-core members of the Prestwick pool could relay them into the more menacing north.

When Nancy arrived in July 1944, the men at the drome, less accustomed to women in the cockpits, radiated skepticism. Few other women had served there aside from Suzanne Ford, the New York socialite who modeled herself as one of the guys, transporting cases of beer to high altitudes to chill them for grateful drinkers. Later, the American Peggy Lennox added her own note of aplomb. She had been an instructor before the war who appeared as a glamour-girl flyer in an ad for Camel cigarettes. "Don't let those eyes and that smile fool you," it said. "When this young lady starts talking airplanes, brother, you'd listen." They did. But the commanding officer took one look at straitlaced Nancy and assigned her to stodgy little aircraft. After two months of single-minded work, as more women joined the pool and proved their worth, she won an equal share of the more difficult jobs, like the Warwick, a 42,500-pound big brother to the Wellington bomber.

Nancy faced a Scottish challenge soon enough when she entered one of those "bowl of milk" cloudbanks in a Spitfire. Before she hit it, she had seen an opening in an overcast sky "like the Devil waving his hand to come on through." She took the dare, but the break disappeared in an instant. As visibility hit zero, she realized that she was already involuntarily tipping left in a spooky abyss.

Thank God for that instrument panel—proof that the Spit was headed down. The artificial horizon showed that she had slid into a sixty-degree bank, perilously close to the point when the aircraft would lose its lift.

Until that information registered, Nancy's meager instrument knowledge hadn't kicked in. Fortunately, she had taken some rudimentary instruction in California—possibly just enough, she had worried, to get herself in trouble by flying beyond her skill. Now she was startled into action. Like it or not, she was flying on instruments. Trusting the information on the panel alone and refusing to look outside, she wrote later, "was one of the hardest things I ever had to do."

She brought the wing up to a thirty-degree bank and stopped the descent at only four hundred feet off the ground. Then she climbed to six hundred feet and tried to remember what the compass reading had told her when the whole mess started. Guessing her previous flight path, she executed what she thought was a 180-degree turn. She emerged from the solid cloud into a still soupy sky, found an airport, and made it down.

The turnaround, she wrote, was "basic instrument flying, and a basic fight for survival. Amen!"

The pilot had learned the first lesson of flying in Scottish conditions. Unless she wanted to hold out for fine weather in the waiting room day after day, the well-behaved Nancy Miller would have to take a turn to the dark side.

BY THE TIME Nancy joined the Prestwick pool, so many ATA pilots had died in the war that many who remained objected to the policy forbidding instrument flying and openly defied it. Nancy approached some RAF guys at the field who allowed her to use their Link Trainer flight simulator to learn the basics. She practiced staying level and making turns using only the information she could glean from the instrument panel, including airspeed, altitude, direction, and artificial horizon. Then she performed some real-world landings in real-world planes.

Her covert lessons came to the rescue on August 16, 1944, when Nancy won an assignment that would enhance her resume for a possible postwar career. It was her first job ferrying a DC-3 Douglas, an aircraft that American airlines used to carry passengers. In the military, where it was known as the Dakota, it served as a troop transport. The size required that a flight engineer accompany Nancy to perform tasks the pilot couldn't reach, like operating the landing gear. Heading south along the coast, they climbed to a thousand feet, cruising under some clouds. The engineer flipped on the radio and tuned into a swing dancing program playing "Twelfth Street Rag."

She noticed more clouds forming on the right and just a few patches underneath. Shortly, as so often happened, the ground disappeared.

Nancy changed course and tried to drop beneath the threat, but it was already solid to the ground. She climbed above, seeking to break into the clear, but the weather still had her in its grip. There was nothing to see but the instruments.

The pilot made sure to head out to sea, away from the mountains. When she saw a hole near her destination, she shot down through to four hundred feet, then two hundred feet. Even there, mist still obscured most of her view of the aerodrome. She nearly collided with a taxi plane trying its own approach.

When she caught sight of a red beacon that marked the beginning of the runway, Nancy realized she was off to the right. A firm turn brought the Dakota nicely into line, and she came down smoothly.

"The training," she said later, "saved my life." From then on, Nancy Miller, the innocent loner, would employ whatever dark arts she needed to keep testing herself in new machines. If she had to play the bad girl, if only in the sky, so be it.

CHAPTER 28

Eager for the Air

September 1944
The United States

The obligations of war had a way of upending expectations. And so it was after Winnie Pierce left London behind and sailed home on the *Queen Mary* on July 17, 1944. She was as eager as ever for her next escapade. But when she reached New York, Peter wasn't there, and no date was set for her marriage. Peter had been reassigned to the U.S. Strategic Bombing Survey, a quasi-civilian organization tasked with evaluating the impact of bombing against Germany. The survey was also used sometimes as a cover for employees of the OSS, the precursor to the CIA. Winnie took refuge in her stepfather's house in Des Moines to wait. She had sought relief from the rigors of the ATA, but this quiet interlude wasn't what she had in mind. Boredom was anathema to Winnabelle Pierce.

Mary Zerbel Ford also uprooted herself for love. In August 1944, her husband, Jack, reached the end of his required missions as a bomber pilot, one of the few in his squadron still standing. In September, Mary resigned from the ATA so they could sail home together and fulfill her desire to create an all-American family. Nine of her colleagues now remained. Mary left with a clean record and a long list of aircraft in her logbook, from Class 1 to Class 4. The twenty-four-year-old pilot felt proud of her achievement and not a little relieved. She "had some very close calls," Mary wrote in a postwar journal, "and at times doubted that the airplane was here to stay."

However, as she prepared to board the ship in Liverpool, the situation took a turn—Jack dropped the news that he had volunteered for another round of risky flights. It seemed he couldn't resist the adrenaline of combat. Mary understood the impulse—she, too, had thrived on danger. But now she was departing alone, without career or husband. At home in Michigan, she'd have to wait out the rest of his service strained by the all-too-familiar tension of wondering whether she would emerge from the war as a two-time widow. Later, she would often say that she was comforted by observing animals. "We can learn a lot from dogs and cats," she mused, "because for them there is no tomorrow and there is no yesterday. There is only now." Now, however, without her own work to distract her, she waited in a vacuum.

Both Mary and Winnie had left their ATA careers for men, only to learn that those men were still ensnared in the war.

NANCY MILLER HADN'T taken a home leave in the two years she'd been in Britain. She jumped at a chance for a break in September 1944, landing at New York Harbor on the seventeenth. The visit would give Nancy a sense of the opportunities that might be available to a woman pilot if the day came when the ATA ceased to be. First, however, she walked the streets of the Manhattan by herself, overwhelmed by the sensory shock of life in the United States.

Accustomed to the sacrifices and shortages in Britain, she was dazzled by the sheer bounty of her home country. The lights! Thousands of them in Times Square, flashing and winking from newsreels, movie marquees, cafes, shop windows, and the blazing headlights of late-model automobiles. "It would be a magical and unbelievable sight to any five-year-old child of Britain who had never known anything but blackouts," she thought. And the noise—not doodlebugs but nearly as disconcerting—the blare of horns, the sheer rumbling horsepower of the engines that powered the speeding cars. The water—*hot* water! Nancy prepared to take a bath in her hotel when she noticed a shower attachment. She'd encountered few showers in Britain and little hot water to operate one. She settled into the steaming luxury, wracked with guilt at the waste.

Then there was the food. Fresh vegetables and fruit, meat for days, and double servings of ice cream at every meal. Nancy came across her first automat—anything she wanted on the spot for the price of a dime or a nickel at the press of a button. She joined the throng of contented customers.

The next day she caught a commercial flight home to Los Angeles, paid for by the ATA. The entire extended family greeted her and whisked her off to more plenty. Steaks, sweet potatoes, salad with Thousand Island dressing, white flour rolls, bacon, eggs, and rich, creamy butter. Divine. Nancy spent most of her money on ice cream. "What a joy!" she wrote. "No cabbage, no brussels sprouts, no Irish potatoes, no beets."

The family urged her to shop for new clothes, which were subjected to some rationing in the States, but nothing like the British limitations. Nancy resisted—she rarely wore civvies in Britain and preferred to travel light. Instead, she sent parcels to all her friends in the ATA—socks, dehydrated soups, nail polish, compacts, lipstick. For herself, she bought more woollies, heavy socks, fur-lined shoes, and gloves.

After a few days of rest, she turned her attention to the state of aviation in the United States and what it might mean for her future. Nancy visited an old friend from flying school, Dot Avery, who hadn't piled up enough hours to join the ATA but joined the WASP instead. The two met at March Field, a vast training base in the desert east of Los Angeles. The flying conditions there were starkly different from the foggy confusion of Great Britain. Nancy tagged along for a quick hop on a Vultee BT-13, a basic single-engine trainer. She took charge of the navigation, such as it was, and had to laugh. It was child's play, miles and miles of open desert landscape with straight, well-delineated roads, illuminated by endless sun. Her arms tanned brown for the first time in two years.

That evening, she lounged in a wooden barracks with Dot's colleagues, comparing their experiences, WASP versus ATA. Most of the WASP flew only single-engine aircraft, but some, like Dot, had trained on two-engines like the B-37 Ventura bomber. A few handled four-engines. The women might be assigned ferrying or test pilot duties, but often the drill involved towing targets behind the aircraft—back and forth, back and forth—so ground and air gunners could practice their aim. The job was doubly unpleasant—tedious but also dangerous, since it often involved live ammunition. It held no appeal for Nancy, but she did envy the WASP for receiving above-board training on instruments. They also amassed impressive miles in their logbooks due to distances between the bases in the United States that far exceeded those in the United Kingdom. On the other hand, Dot's friends couldn't believe the array of aircraft Nancy had enjoyed the opportunity to fly. The WASP tended to specialize in limited models once they passed through training.

Officially, the WASP were considered civilians, as ATA flyers were, but without the same benefits and standards of equality. Nancy found it shocking that the WASP weren't provided with insurance, whereas the ATA supplied compensation for injury or death. The more Nancy's hosts described their situation, the more she realized the level of discrimination the WASP put up with. If a commanding officer opposed the idea of women flying, he stuck them with bum assignments—little planes and target towing. Jackie Cochran called this work "aerial dishwashing," necessary but menial jobs. Nevertheless, the pilots often suffered the wrath of hostile men. Some women experienced sabotage—rags or sugar in gas tanks, or tires slashed. One pilot, Betty Davis, died in a crash when sugar was discovered in the tank. If that weren't bad enough, when a woman was killed, the others had to take up a collection to ship the body home.

By contrast, the ATA was practically a feminist utopia. Aside from the random biased remark, treatment was essentially equal. "The women are mixed with men so much that they are taken for granted," Nancy explained to the WASP flyers she met.

Little did they know their days were numbered. During Nancy's leave, word came through that the WASP would be disbanded after only two years, a victim of American attitudes toward women in military cockpits. Since the birth of the service in late in 1942, the public and media had squabbled over whether the women should be flying at all. Unlike the ATA, where women pilots were gradually accepted—and occasionally revered—the WASP program only festered in growing controversy over time. It reached a head in June 1944 when Congress considered a bill that would allow the organization to become part of the army.

The idea was intended as an act of basic fairness, but it set off a backlash. Groups rallied against the bill, asserting that women would steal the few jobs available in an unsettled postwar economy. Media coverage, once mixed, turned vehemently against the women. "The fact remains that they are not as suitable for ferrying work as men," said *American Aviation* magazine, against all evidence to the contrary. Jackie Cochran urged her charges to keep quiet and concentrate on their jobs, lest they feed the dispute, but she came in for potshots that implied her sex appeal had won the military over in the first place. The *Washington Times-Herald* mocked General Hap Arnold for gazing into the eyes of the "shapely pilot." And the *New York Times* lamented that experienced and deserving men "may soon be cleaning windshields and servicing planes for 'glamorous women flyers who have had only thirty-five hours of flying time.'"

The bill went down to defeat, and on October 1, General Arnold announced that the Women Airforce Service Pilots would be shut down entirely on December 20, 1944, with the war still rolling on and the need still great. Around 1,100 women had served. Thirty-eight had died. Soon the pilots would be out of work in a society that disparaged their skills.

The ugly demise of the WASP boded ill for any American woman seeking to stay employed in the air. For ATA pilots observing from afar, this was the worst possible outcome. Jobs as U.S. military pilots would be off the table, and the image of women pilots, once widely admired, had now sunk lower than before the war. The ATA women, even with their vast and varied cockpit experience, realized they would encounter severe headwinds when they returned home. Nancy Miller absorbed this troubling firsthand look and recognized that her path to a career as an aviator would be narrower than she thought. Ann Wood began to consider seeking postwar work in England, where she had built a solid reputation and a long list of friends. Others thought they might have to take a step back to their prewar jobs as flying instructors for beginners. Nancy spent the rest of her leave clipping pictures from aeronautic magazines of every aircraft she had flown in the ATA and pasting them in a scrapbook. Something to remind her of the golden opportunity she had enjoyed. She knew it would take even more drive than she expected to keep herself aloft.

Nancy caught a last glorious sight of American opulence on her journey back to Scotland as her plane landed in New York on a starlit night. "All the jewels of the city's lights glittered splendidly," she wrote. "You could tell that the air was crisp." It was the first time she'd seen any city at night-time from the air. "When I return," she vowed, "I want to fly at night between two skies of brilliant diamonds."

WHILE NANCY WAS away, a new German weapon, the V-2 flying bomb, had become the latest reminder that people in Great Britain didn't enjoy the same sense of safety that Americans did. The V-2 was a guided rocket-powered missile that exploded on impact without the buzzy warning of the V-1. The new threat would kill an estimated 2,754 people in London through March 1945. One hundred and sixty died in a single strike at a Woolworth's store in New Cross.

Back in the land of cabbage and chilly bathtubs, Nancy felt worlds away from the casual extravagance of the United States. It bothered her that Americans weren't following the news of the war in detail, that they griped about sacrifices. When it was over, she thought, the atmosphere would be different, but there would always be "a slight breach between those at home and those who were overseas."

Nancy realized her conscience had pricked her. All the relative afflu-ence, all the comforts and luxuries of the United States—she had eaten it up, there was no denying. But they couldn't compete with the sense of purpose she felt in her role ferrying aircraft, helping to win the war in the best way she knew how. "I wasn't fighting an actual war," she wrote, "but I was doing a darn sight more in Britain than most of the fancy dressed gals swaggering down the street [in the United States]. There was nothing at home for me to do equal to that work." She could live without ice cream. She lived for the job.

Nancy Miller liked to quote the Latin motto of the ATA: *Aetheris Avidi*. "Eager for the Air." After her return to the aerodrome in Prest-wick, trussed up again in her long johns and flying suit, she felt the meaning more than ever.

CHAPTER 29

C'Est la Vie

November 1944
Brussels and Paris

The pilots who joined the ferry service were always eager for more. More time in the air. More participation in the wider war. More opportunity to pack in every possible experience before the big finale and the uncertainty that lay beyond.

By the fall of 1944, they were itching to fly to the Continent and do their part for the Allied advance, or at least score bragging rights by witnessing the long-awaited scene. Interest peaked when American troops liberated Paris on August 25, 1944, after four years of German occupation. Then things moved fast: British troops freed Brussels in the early days of September. The Air Transport Auxiliary got the call to begin transporting aircraft toward the front lines that month, and the most ambitious pilots were hell-bent on snagging the jobs.

This time, the ATA's policy of equality fell short. Only men were authorized to cross the Channel. The official reasoning went that facilities to house women on the other side were scarce, and it would have been possible to drift off course and wind up over areas that remained in German hands. But in the showboating tradition of the ATA, rules didn't stop a few women from conniving to be among the earliest to touch down on recaptured terrain.

The honor of being the first man to make a continental delivery fell to the first Frenchman to join the ATA, Maurice Harlé. On September 6, taking a Spitfire to one of the bases closest to the front line south of Dieppe, he gaped down at the former launch sites of German flying bombs. They'd been reduced to craters of crumbled red earth. In Rouen, he spotted the legendary cathedral. It was still standing, but everything around it was smashed flat. Every bridge within sight had been destroyed, dropped into the water. Other male ATA aviators soon ferried to more bases in France and Belgium, situated among pockets of German resistance.

For women, it would take a potent combination of high-level connections and flying bona fides, not to mention epic chutzpah, to get around the restrictions, which was why Diana Barnato, the captivating British ace and daughter of the Bentley motorcar tycoon, became the first woman to make a continental run. She had an inside angle—her new husband, Derek Walker, was the wing commander of an RAF fighter squadron. They had married in May 1944, exactly two years after her first fiancé died in a crash on a reckless off-duty trip to visit Diana. A hardened veteran of aerial combat, Derek had served with distinction in Greece, Crete, and the African desert before he was put in charge of a Typhoon wing in England. Diana found him swashbuckling, jaunty, "a leader of men." "Many of my admirers had, by then, been killed in the war," she wrote in her memoir, "so I thought I should hook him quick, in case one or the other of us got bumped off."

She and Derek shared a high tolerance for risky, unauthorized capers, which made them an ideal team to prove that women could fly to liberated territory as well as men. Diana fumed over the ban on women pilots in Europe, so Derek hatched a plan. Two Spitfires fitted for photoreconnaissance work were needed to scout German positions near Brussels. He arranged to fly one of them, and his boss signed a letter certifying that one First Officer D. B. Walker would fly the other. They would make the trip during Diana's five-day leave, so it wouldn't be considered an official ATA job.

The scheme worked. On October 2, they took off for Brussel's Evere aerodrome, flying in formation with Diana's left wing tucked under

Derek's right. "I wanted to sing, throw the aircraft around in celebration of my freedom from my English bonds," Diana wrote. Once over Belgium, she witnessed massive bomb damage, but Brussels seemed to be in a gala mood when they arrived. The streets were full of crowds, strangers kissing strangers, still celebrating liberation despite the distant rumble of guns. Over the next couple days, Diana made dicey so-called flight tests with the Spit, heading fifteen miles east to the line where German forces had dug in. "Nobody took a potshot at me," she recalled.

After three days, the couple was scheduled to return the two aircraft along with reconnaissance photos the RAF had taken, but a great fog descended. On the sixth day, Diana's leave ran out, stranding her in Brussels when she was scheduled for duty. She and Derek decided to take off and to turn around if the visibility remained poor. His Spitfire was outfitted with a working radio and instruments, while Diana's was not, so he proposed that they head home the way they had come in finer weather, with Diana trailing his lead.

Once airborne, a yellowish muck closed in around them. Diana assumed Derek would circle back, but he plunged on. She had no choice but to follow. It was impossible to read a map and keep sight of him at the same time, and so it wasn't long before she had no idea where she was. When even thicker clumps of cloud amassed, Derek vanished into one. Diana scanned the sky, but no matter where she looked, her husband wasn't there. She was on her own in the soup.

Where in heaven am I? she cast about. Was she over Belgium or France? If she turned back toward Brussels, she risked overflying and cruising into enemy territory.

Diana wound up over some coastline pocked with craters. She decided to push out over the sea and climb above the clouds to four thousand feet. If luck was with her, she would spot Dungeness, England, in seven and a half minutes. But at the appointed time, she peered through a gap in the weather and saw only water. Where *was* she? Possibly over the North Sea, she realized, with nothing ahead of her but open water stretching to the Arctic. Or possibly flying crossways west through the center of the English Channel, toward the Atlantic Ocean.

She glanced at the fuel gauge. If she continued on either route, she would run out of petrol and crash into one sea or another. She tamped down a spiraling sense of alarm and tried to think logically. Guessing she was over the Channel, she headed toward what she guessed was due north and dropped under the clouds to two hundred feet, straining for any hint of her location.

Eventually, a glimmer of light flickered ahead. There was a storage tank for gas, one she recognized, near an aerodrome at Tangmere. With enormous relief, she turned in the direction of the base until she sighted runway lights gleaming and green flares firing above. Just her luck, Diana thought. The field must have been lit to guide a squadron in from a raid, and she would have to wait her turn as the fuel depleted. Soon she decided she had no choice but to head in. The landing was perfect, as often happened when adrenaline took the lead.

Diana stopped in front of the watch office and jumped down from the cockpit, knees trembling like rubber bands. Derek ran out to greet her, his face deathly white. "How on earth did you get here?" he sputtered, looking half out of his mind. He had found the way because his radio informed him that this aerodrome was the only one in the entire south of England that was open. Bearings and course instructions had guided him home. That Diana found it on her own seemed beyond possibility. On a prayer that she was somewhere in the vicinity, he had ordered the enormous display of lights.

Derek did not sleep that night. But Diana slept well, convinced that while her husband had a radio, "The Fellow Up Top" had assigned a guardian angel as her navigator.

NEWS OF DIANA Barnato Walker's near disaster made the rounds. It didn't provide the best case for women to take on continental routes, although she could hardly be blamed for the weather. The ATA took another three months to approve women's trips in January 1945. In the meantime, the intrepid Ann Wood cut the line and made a jaunt to Paris on November 2, 1944. Unable to wheedle an assignment to fly there herself, she hopped a ride with friendly American air force pilots. As usual, she wanted to place herself at the center of whatever was happening in the world, to feel the dizzying force of history and secure a bond with the people making it. She also plotted a reunion in Paris, the first in three years, with her older sister, Jane, a go-getter in the tradition of the women in the Wood family.

The two sisters shouted with joy when Ann appeared at Jane's desk in the American embassy. Jane served as the secretary to Sheldon Chapin, the *charge d'affaires* who served as temporary ambassador to France. On September 9, they had arrived from Algiers in the wake of the Paris liberation to set up shop in the original embassy building on the Place de la Concorde. The flag flew overhead, but a coal shortage made for a frosty interior.

The sisters talked into the night in Jane's even chillier hotel room up the Champs-Élysées. By day, Ann embarked on a full Parisian experience, surprised that the charms of the city hadn't dimmed as she might have expected. She got her hair done, "with an added Parisian twist, for it looked lovely, but I can't tell why or how." They drank coupes of champagne and took meals at the posh Hôtel de Crillon, where many diplomats enjoyed cuisine made from typical U.S. Army ingredients but "prepared with French cooks, which really takes it out of this world." A friend of Jane's staying at the hotel allowed the sisters to use his bath on Saturday evening, when the Crillon provided hot water. They also attended a cocktail party at her boss's residence, an elaborately mirrored home with a blessed "suggestion of heat, which is a colossal luxury." The electricity went out, so they mingled by candlelight with international journalists, including Helen Kirkpatrick, who had covered the invasion of Normandy for the *Chicago Daily News*.

Friends of friends treated the sisters to evenings at a diplomatic club that served divine filet mignon and fruit tarts. The bill was stupendous—the equivalent of more than three hundred dollars for one night of dining and dancing. Ann suspected the hosts didn't mind because they were flush from black market profiteering. She sympathized with the British who had denied themselves so much during the war, thinking that all the French were destitute. C'est la vie.

Shortly after Ann's return, the ATA announced that anyone flying to Europe without explicit permission from the chief, Gerard d'Erlanger, would be fired. Once again, the ubiquitous Ann Wood had hit the timing on the nose.

★

ECONOMICS WERE OFTEN front of mind for Ann. She sent a portion of her ATA salary to her mother and put aside more in hopes of buying her a house. With the war advancing, Ann began to worry that within a year or so she would face a stark choice about how to survive. She and Jane knew they had to support themselves, war or no war. Ann preferred to remain self-sufficient by finding a good job. But she also knew that the safest alternative for a woman in the 1940s was to secure a husband.

Winnie Pierce, Mary Zerbel, Roberta Sandoz, and Dorothy Furey had all decided to marry for love, but there was no denying that marriage was also the low-risk strategy for a comfortable future. With the exception of Dorothy, who planned to settle into aristocratic grandeur, most of the pilots hoped that matrimony wouldn't prevent them from flying as well. Ann Wood was clear-eyed about the practical advantages of lining up a man to support her, but she resisted the very idea. Work remained her priority—that is, if there was work to be had. Yet she knew that flying positions would be scarce, and she dreaded the claustrophobia of typing in some office.

As 1944 wound to a hopeful close, her mother's letters brought up the subject of marriage with escalating frequency. They argued that "the only life" for a woman was one with a husband and children, lest she suffer a lonely old age. After visiting Jane in Paris, Ann, now twenty-six years old, sent a tart response. "I continue to be unusually happy in my present state so am unperturbed. But would like to see Jane hitched to a grand guy who would care for her."

Ann's mother buttressed her case by sending an article filled with gauzy sentiments about children representing the future. "If that is to spur me on, you have failed, little one," Ann replied. "I fear your grandmother tendencies are frustrated again. I agree it is tough on you, but then you have some tough children—a bit on the independent side—and it was not our doing but yours."

Bill Brown would have seemed an obvious solution. During their lightning romance before he was shot down and taken prisoner, his fine qualities appealed to Ann. The navigator was brave, patriotic, intelligent, ambitious, and respectful of her career. Even his tall stature matched well with her rangy frame, which intimidated other suitors. Ann's mother sent parcels and letters to Bill in prison, and she often pressed for details from his letters to Ann. But as the months dragged on—a year and a half since his capture—Ann and Bill's correspondence, subject to censorship, settled into harmless musings that didn't convey much passion. Purple prose had never been their style anyway. The couple had barely embarked on their love affair when he was captured, and it was hard to tell how things would stand after a long separation. This presented yet another question mark about the future that would remain unresolved until the fighting stopped and the stars decreed where everyone would land.

CHAPTER 30

Spinning Into a New Reality

New Year's, 1945
Ratcliffe, Leicestershire, and Prestwick, Scotland

The rapid progress made by Allied armies in the fall of 1944 had buoyed hopes for a quick resolution to the bloodshed as the year turned toward 1945. But on December 16, 1944, Germany launched a surprise counterattack, crushing Allied optimism and leading to one of the ugliest and deadliest battles of the war. German Panzer divisions poured across the front that extended from southern Belgium to Luxembourg in hopes of splitting the Allies and reaching the port of Antwerp to cut off their supplies. The Germans penetrated seventy miles into the Ardennes Forest, so far that the recaptured territory appeared like a bulge on the map, granting the battle its nickname: the Battle of the Bulge. The Allied boys fought for their lives, wielding rifles, small arms, grenades, mortars, and bazookas to hold off German tanks in the snow.

The fighting dragged on in subzero temperatures as weary troops on both sides suffered heavy casualties. Superior Anglo-American air power wasn't much help. Filthy weather that reached all the way to Britain prevented air support that could break the stalemate.

The ATA declared a super emergency, cancelling leaves so aircraft could be rushed to the front when the weather allowed. At the least sign of a manageable sky, pilots had to be ready to scramble and clear the backlog, but their frustration built as dense fog and clouds prevented action for a week. Finally, on December 23, medium bombers and fighters were able to set upon the German tanks, while heavy bombers set a record for tonnage dropped, hitting rail hubs and other infrastructure behind the German lines. On the next day, Christmas Eve, one of the largest air operations in history launched even greater explosive power. Some 2,046 bombers released more than five thousand tons of bombs, while 853 fighters made sorties and 160 airborne troop carriers dropped supplies. Another huge operation followed on Christmas Day. The combination broke the German momentum, but it would still take all of January to recapture the lost ground.

The Luftwaffe had another surprise in store on New Year's Day when its fighters hit Allied airfields in Holland, Belgium, and France. They put 450 fighters out of action, including aircraft like the low-flying Typhoon that provided support to ground troops. ATA pilots would have to play catch-up though January to replace the losses and feed the need for new aircraft as winter weather continued to sabotage the effort.

EVEN THE LIVELY crowd at Ratcliffe Hall felt the pinch in their holiday celebrations. Ann Wood washed out due to weather from December 19 to 29 while remaining within fifteen minutes of the aerodrome so she could move fighters on short notice. She bartered perfume from her jaunt to Paris to supply the Ratcliffe Christmas party with wine, and she distributed gifts of lipsticks from Jackie Cochran to all her friends. She gave Dorothy Furey a more lavish present—Worth perfume, her favorite. In return, Dorothy gave Ann a silk scarf in RAF blue from the Jaeger shop in London.

By December 30, however, Ann was hard at work ferrying priority fighters to the southern coast. When the return taxi aircraft broke down, she and five colleagues piled onto a packed train, napping on their parachutes in the corridor. The next day, she flew in a daze and packed it in for the night by eight thirty, most unlike her on New Year's Eve. Back in the air following the German new year's raid on the European airfields, she hoped the need would be so acute that she would be waved on to the front. But even though Ann was clearly one of the top pilots at Ratcliffe, seven men, less eager (and perhaps less qualified) than Ann, had gotten the assignment to go all the way. "I am green with envy and must organize something soon," she stewed. She invited her commanding officer and his wife for cocktails in her room, serving little appetizers made from fancy jars of chicken livers and smoked turkey that arrived in a Christmas parcel from home. Ann would push until she got her way.

A HOLIDAY WITHOUT festivity suited Nancy Miller. It kept her rested for the air. Stranded in Bristol on New Year's Eve, Nancy sought shelter at a Red Cross lounge as the minutes ticked down to midnight in a tired world. She nodded off over a book while two other stranded travelers, a doctor and an engineer, carried on an intrusive conversation. At ten minutes to midnight, Nancy woke up. The three strangers shook hands, mumbled a hasty "happy new year," and shuffled off to their beds. "A very quiet evening," she recalled. "A very lonely one compared to what we might have had in the United States. But a much more comfortable one than the front-line boys were having."

The introverted Nancy took a different approach from Ann to rising in the service. Too shy to lobby for herself, she appreciated that the added winter deliveries gave her more opportunities to keep her head down and let her flying to speak for itself. Had Ann Wood been assigned to the worldwide crossroad for people and aircraft at Prestwick, she likely would have taken advantage of the nexus to make useful contacts and petition for flights to Belgium. Nancy seized the chance to expand her repertoire as a versatile aviator. Over the holidays she operated her first B-25 Mitchell bomber with a flight engineer who whined about taking what he called a "nursing trip" with a woman pilot.

"What have I done to deserve this?" he moaned.

Nancy answered, "Probably a lot."

From there, she moved to her first Albemarle, a British twin-engine with a tricycle undercarriage designed for towing gliders. She followed up with a Wildcat, a U.S. carrier fighter that was tricky on takeoff but flew with the lightest touch. After that, the larger Hellcat, which she had to put down at the wrong airfield when the wind proved too strong at her destination. Despite that hiccup, she enjoyed one of those dream landings that pilots aspire to, so smooth that she couldn't be sure when she made contact.

Her first flight on a Dominie Rapide, used by British airlines as a passenger plane, took a bizarre turn. The Dominie was a plywood biplane, slow and reliable. Otherwise, Nancy might not have taken off during a lull between snowstorms. She bucked around in forty-mile-per-hour winds for an hour before she saw a second squall approach. Ahead of her, the two fronts appeared to be converging. She made for the closest field and executed a tight U-turn to line up as fast as she could. From four hundred feet up, she could see snow begin to fall on the far end of the runway. Nancy raced to beat it, feeling "amused but not frightened."

The pilot realized she might have made the wrong decision when the snow rushed toward her, "just as if a window shade was being drawn about every fifty feet." The Dominie touched down, still in the clear, and plowed right into the blizzard. Nancy couldn't see a thing. She turned into the wind and stopped, keeping the engine running to hold the aircraft steady.

Half an hour later, she could see just far enough to make out a fire engine pulling within feet of her starboard wingtip. A fireman climbed into the plane. "We saw you roll into the storm," he said, "and we've been wandering around ever since trying to find you."

EACH TIME NANCY expanded her repertoire, each time she let instruments guide her to dice with death in skies that kept more timid pilots on the ground, her confidence grew. She was so engaged by all things aviation that in her downtime she even wrote a technical article about the Spitfire for the American *Air Facts* magazine. During the winter of 1945, it seemed there was no delivery she couldn't pull off.

This thinking led to a perilous episode when she was handed a "particularly ornery" Wellington bomber to fly north. Strong crosswinds didn't dissuade her, although something else was clearly amiss. Nancy expected some trouble on takeoff, but it was worse than she expected. As the nose began to rise, the Wellington suddenly jerked to the right. Nancy slammed back the port throttle and brought the aircraft back down, but when she applied the brakes, they had little effect. She groaned and prayed as she ran off the runway, finally stopping only ten feet from a worker's hut. A quick look at the brake gauge showed that the pressure was well below the minimum.

This was the moment when a cautious pilot would taxi back to the ground crew and wash her hands of a faulty aircraft. But Nancy was loath to give up. She blamed the snafu on the crosswind and decided to try again. Starting slowly, she worked the throttles carefully to compensate for the wind. It was only when she passed the point of no return that she glanced at the instruments and saw that the engine rpms were well below standard. It was no wonder the crosswind had deflected her before—there wasn't enough engine power to counteract it. She slammed on the left rudder as hard as she could just as the Wimpy took off, but it still turned about thirty degrees right toward a clutch of houses.

Nancy fought to straighten out without success as the bomber's swing grew worse. Just when it seemed hopeless, the Wellington shook violently and slithered onto course. It wasn't due to anything Nancy had done. She was simply lucky that the engine had picked up on its own. Nancy flew on to finish the job. But she would always remember the houses that lay in her path on that second takeoff. "Those houses are very vivid indeed."

The incident humbled her. Reviewing it in her mind, Nancy knew she should have walked away from the damaged Wellington. Its ragged condition was the immediate culprit for the near-accident, but in a broader sense, the twenty-five-year-old blamed her own hubris. "I think I'm an average pilot, maybe a little above average," Nancy said later. "I was not a natural pilot." She had to remind herself not to overestimate her skill. Too much confidence could make a pilot cocky to the point of danger.

LOOKING BACK AFTER the war, the Allied victory over Germany appeared inevitable by the beginning of 1945. But at the time, in January of that year, the terrible price of the Battle of the Bulge and the surprise nature of the attack left Allied leaders discouraged that the carnage would end any time soon. Even though their forces dominated in the air, and ground troops pushed forward again, nineteen thousand Americans had been killed in the battle. The powers on high decided that it would take even more carnage to bring the war to a timely close.

They were unaware how much Germany's ability to keep up the fight had deteriorated. Shortages of coal, gas, and food left the Reich helpless to defend itself from armies to the east and west. Manufacturing of German weapons, aircraft, and anything else of use ground down to a meager output as supply chains crumbled. Luftwaffe fighters sat idle for lack of gasoline, ceding the skies to the Anglo-American air squadrons. Allied leaders didn't yet realize the extent of the enemy's weakness. What they did know was that Hitler was unwilling to capitulate. They decided that it was time to abandon their repugnance for terror bombing and direct the Allies' superior air power to crushing the will of the German people—by targeting civilians.

The U.S. Eighth Air Force sent 1,500 heavy bombers and 948 fighters over Berlin on February 3, 1945, aiming for the central city rather than military targets. In the chaos, it was impossible to compile a casualty count, but it is known that 120,000 homes were obliterated. Ten days later, the objective was the beautiful city of Dresden, its ornate architecture utterly destroyed by fires from incendiary bombs. At least 35,000 of the city's people were killed. Aerial attacks continued to escalate through the winter, one city followed by the next, then back to Berlin.

Many officials maintained that there were legitimate military targets in those cities, and there were—railroad marshalling yards in Dresden, for example. But the pilots knew that innocents were also perishing in the onslaught. Having no say in the matter, the aircrews flew their daily routes like bus drivers through smoke-heavy skies, many still shot down by antiaircraft guns on the ground.

The pace was relentless. The RAF dropped more bomb tonnage in late March 1945 than during any other week of the war. The month overall set a record for the volume of bombs striking Germany. Meanwhile Allied ground troops chased the enemy into Western Germany in February 1945 and crossed the Rhine in March, while Russia closed in from the east. In April, waves of individual German units started to surrender.

ACTION IN THE ATA didn't let up as rumors flowed about an end to the war, but one date would pass and then another without news. The job would remain as dangerous as ever until hostilities ceased. During that period, Nancy swung too close to the harbor of Greenock, Scotland, where battleships and troop transports docked. Black puffs of heavy ack-ack fire popped to her left—friendly fire. "They were not shooting *at* me," she wrote, "just—ah—limiting my curiosity."

Diana Barnato, topping her perilous flight home from Brussels, wound up in another outrageous life-threatening situation just as everyone was sure the fighting was over. The pilot felt a powerful bang in the cockpit of a well-worn Typhoon she was ferrying to an airfield in Gloucestershire. Her map blew away, and tiny bits of metal blasted her face and body. Diana assumed the engine had blown up, so she cast about for a suitable field to make a forced landing.

A quick glance down revealed a more surreal scenario. She saw the ground zipping by beneath her feet. The underside of the fighter had blown off completely. Diana's uniform flapped around her arms and legs in the wind, and her teeth chattered with the cold while she figured out what to do. First, she made a smart move. She climbed up high to test what her stalling speed would be without the normal airflow around the fighter. The minimum was now 230 miles per hour, nearly three times as fast as usual and well above safe landing speed. Next, she made a few fast passes over the drome, hoping a crash wagon crew would notice her predicament and prepare to help, but no one moved a muscle. "They all probably thought I was some lunatic doing a beat-up," she decided. She lowered the undercarriage, hoping it would stay put and provide some protection from the stones and earth that kicked up as she hit the field.

Diana touched down at just under 230 miles per hour and lightly tapped the brakes, afraid to do more in case she flipped over. The Typhoon needed every inch of runway, but eventually it stopped. The pilot opened the hood to look outside. The fuselage was torn and jagged, with loose shards of metal still billowing into the air. A gasping duty airman approached. "Why," he asked with a startled expression, "are you bringing us only half an aeroplane?"

Like many ATA pilots who owed their lives to a combination of talent and luck over the last few years, Diana believed that her guardian angel was working overtime again, even this late in the war. It was April 30, 1945, the same day Hitler committed suicide in his underground bunker as Red Army troops pierced the heart of Berlin. The world was about to spin into a new reality.

CHAPTER 31

What Now?

VE Day, May 8, 1945
Ratcliffe, Leicestershire; Brussels; and Paris

Spontaneous jubilation broke out across the United Kingdom on Monday, May 7, as word spread that Germany had surrendered unconditionally. The next day was declared a national holiday, Victory in Europe Day. Strangers embraced on the streets and kissed goodbye to nearly six years of suffering. It was almost too much to process.

The afternoon of the seventh, Ann Wood delivered a Hurricane and a Mustang. When she landed at the Ratcliffe Aerodrome, the boys on the ground told her that the war in Europe was over. "Had quite a funny feeling," she wrote in a letter. Of course she was "pleased," but her emotions registered as "inadequate" rather than purely joyful.

It was a common reaction. Even as crowds danced in public squares and lit up the night with bonfires and fireworks, many felt exhaustion, physical and emotional, after all they had endured. Those who had lost their lives would not be returning because something as intangible as a treaty had been signed. Troops who served in Europe might be redirected to the Pacific, where the war with Japan still raged. But civilians who had survived German attacks would revert to a routine of security they could barely recall, a transformation of such magnitude that it was breathtaking, almost bewildering.

Ann Wood returned to Ratcliffe Hall the night before the holiday to find the staff dithering over whether to let the champagne flow. Smart the butler informed her that Sir Lindsay wasn't sure the news was final. Shortly afterward, Smart rushed to her room—pop the corks! The celebration was on.

Ann contributed one of two bottles she had been saving to share with Bill Brown upon his release and return to England. The plan had changed after a letter arrived from Bill that morning. He broke the news that he had escaped from Stalag 3 in the confusion of the final weeks and made his way to the American lines on April 29. Now he was in Paris, all in one piece, and under the vague impression that Ann might be back in Maine. It seemed possible that he would be sent home directly from France. Their reunion appeared as uncertain as everything else.

Ann and her Ratcliffe friends passed the holiday listening to Winston Churchill's speech and playing croquet. That night, she joined a crowd for fireworks and a bonfire in the village, where Hitler was burned in effigy. "So that was my VE Day," she wrote, rather flatly. Her mind was already racing ahead.

Lurking on the margins of the festivities was the question on everyone's minds: What now? The ATA would continue to function, redistributing aircraft scattered throughout the former theater of war and transporting cargo and personnel for the Allied occupying forces in taxi planes. But ATA pilots knew their jobs would not continue indefinitely. Soon enough they would have to find work and meaning elsewhere.

Many men left to return to former careers or take on essential work rebuilding the country. Some women were leaving as well, including Opal Anderson, whose contract had run out in April. The rambunctious flyer rejoined her nine-year-old son in Chicago after three years overseas. Her most dangerous incident had occurred a few days after the funeral of Mary Webb Nicholson, when a mournful Opal found herself flying vacantly out to sea. Another pilot pulled alongside to redirect her back to base. Otherwise, she was as dependable as British rain. Grace Stevenson, who had force-landed many a defective aircraft, departed in May. She planned to return to flying instruction at the school in Oklahoma where she worked before the war.

Ann Wood was hard-core. She planned to stay as long as the service would let her.

It still galled her that she hadn't reached the goal of flying to Europe while the war was still active. She had engaged her commanding officer, Thomas Whitehurst (nicknamed "Doc" because of his prewar medical career), in the campaign, and he had done his best. Three days before VE Day, he arranged for Ann and five other Ratcliffe women in his command to deliver aircraft to Nijmegen, Holland, near the German border. "We fairly went mad," Ann wrote, but weather scuttled the attempt.

But four days after VE Day, on Saturday, May 12, Doc Whitehurst delivered the goods with a ferry job for three women—Ann, the veteran British flyer Joan Hughes, and Pat Beverly, an English pilot who had emerged in recent months as Ann's closest friend. The aircraft were low-speed, single-engine Auster observation planes—Ann called them "puddle jumpers"—but they would do the trick. At three o'clock in the afternoon the ladies left Ratcliffe for a refueling stop on the southeast coast. By three thirty they were gaining height over the white cliffs of Dover, preparing to cross the Channel on a pristine day. As the French coastline came into sight, Ann wrote, "my tummy felt as though an electric mixer had gotten loose inside and was churning for all it was worth." Passing the harbor at Calais, a complete ruin, they turned east toward their destination at Brussels. From above, she could see colossal flags flapping everywhere. She wondered where they'd come from—they looked so new.

The pilots emerged dripping wet from their steamy cockpits at five thirty and made their way into town. The Hotel de Ville stood proud, undamaged, and yellow trams still trundled through streets where customers packed the cafes. At a hotel, the women met Doc, who had followed them in a taxi plane. They cooked up a plan to fly it to Paris the next day. Ann's sister Jane scrounged hotel rooms for them in the overflowing city.

Their arrival midday Sunday coincided with a maddening missed connection. Bill Brown had shipped out for home a few days before. The vast bureaucracy that still governed his fate had placed him, once again, out of Ann's reach.

Since Bill's letters from prison had been censored, Ann still didn't know the full extent of his experience after he parachuted out of his crashing Flying Fortress, the only survivor from his crew. Life at Stalag 3 wasn't as tedious as she assumed. It was the scene of what became known as the Great Escape, when seventy-six British prisoners dug their way out on the night of March 24, 1944. A search rounded up all but three. Fifty were executed.

Bill didn't let this stop his own escape attempts. Once he jumped from a moving train and turned his jacket inside out to pose as a German civilian, even joining a group that was searching for him. He was caught later floating down the Danube in a stolen boat. His final escape succeeded, when he found his way to American forces in the final days of the war.

Despite the disappointment at missing him, Ann, Jane, and Pat turned the overnight visit into a fine frolic. They drove up the Champs-Élysées in a borrowed car and circled the Arc de Triomphe to take in the victory lights. They screamed with mirth as they fantasized about the future of the Family Wood. Jane would work in Paris, and Ann would find something in London. They would buy a cottage outside one city or the other to keep their mother and siblings nearby. The sisters formed a mock agreement to adopt Ann's friend Pat into the family as well. Everything was settled in theory by Monday, when the ATA contingent had to wing back to England.

ANN HAD BEEN cultivating her ATA superiors to include her among those allowed to linger through the fall. She brought her administrative prowess to the fore by volunteering to help build the ATA benevolent fund for the families of the lost. And she maintained that those who needed the income, as she did, should stay on. Nationality, she argued, shouldn't be a factor. By this time, she considered herself to be a citizen of the world. Pauline Gower promised to look out for Ann, and so did Doc, her commanding officer. There were those who felt women should be the first to leave the ATA, but Doc counted eight women among his twelve best pilots. They jokingly referred to themselves as Doc's Harem. A mixed international group from England, Poland, and South Africa, they became Ann's dearest friends.

By now even the intimidating Lettice Curtis had come around about the merits of American colleagues like Ann. "To me the American girls seemed enormously self-sufficient and practical," Lettice wrote after the war. "They appeared to know exactly what they wanted and went all out for it."

By the formal end of hostilities, Ann had evolved. She'd arrived in 1942 as a twenty-four-year-old with sophisticated manners and a polished wardrobe, but uncertain flying skills. Now she had come into her own—a pilot who owned the air. Caught up in her work and female camaraderie, she had come to appreciate the country ambiance of the Ratcliffe airfield more than the clubs of London. The harem teased her about her weather-worn face, begging her to soften her appearance with moisturizer. She showed up in pants and boots at a gathering in Hamble where everyone else wore frocks. Her girdles stretched out before she replaced them, and her freckles burst out like a map of stars. "I look like a country cousin in London, but am undaunted at my robustness," she wrote to her mother.

Ann's favorite flying circuit that spring was ferrying battle-worn Mosquitos, no longer needed at the front, to storage depots at the very northern tip of Scotland. Her most intimate sidekick and confidante, Pat Beverly, usually made the same delivery. Like Ann, Pat was nearly six feet tall, and she had flaming red hair, so they made a dynamic impression wherever they went. She amused Ann no end with droll side talk like "my dear, it's madly dangerous." The friends hummed along in tandem over some of Scotland's highest peaks, frosted like sponge cakes with snow. Ann felt "infinitesimal amid such grandeur." On the way back, they set down for the night at Oban, a picturesque fishing village on the Firth of Lorn, where they took a bracing morning plunge in the sea.

At the peak of her piloting, surrounded by like-minded friends, Ann gloried in the work, cast already in a glow of nostalgia. "I will be really sorry when I have to stop flying the world's loveliest airplanes and living the world's easiest life," Ann reflected. Slowly coming to terms with the knowledge that the splendid ATA interlude couldn't last, she realized it was necessary to air out her original power suits and slip back into another role at which she excelled—the well-connected mover and shaker, the girl from Maine whom everyone assumed was on top of the social ladder.

LONG BEFORE VE Day, Ann was already scouring her book of contacts in search of a substantial postwar position in aviation. But what would that be? She chewed through the possibilities and found most of them wanting. Teaching at a flying school held no appeal, even on the outside chance that a woman would be hired. Overseeing repetitive circuits and bumps would be a grind, she knew, and "one is likely to be pigeon-holed forever."

She ruled out secretarial posts entirely. "I have a horror of working behind a desk," she wrote. Barnstorming and performing in air shows drew another thumbs-down. Showmanship had never been her style. Other possibilities in the field—from commercial airline pilot to executive—were unheard of for a woman. Even with wartime experience under her belt, such jobs would be less available now, considering that she would be competing with the decommissioned air force pilots who would flood the labor market. The bum's rush given to women who served in the WASP indicated that her prospects in the United States were poor. Great Britain might offer more opportunity.

By the spring of 1945, Ann had the inside track on an ideal alternative: a diplomatic post related to aviation. It offered the perfect fit for her strengths, from people skills to expertise in the air. Even better, it was based in England, which she had come to love. She knew just the person who could help her land the job.

Ann had met Livingston Lord Satterthwaite, known less grandly as Tony, the first time Jackie Cochran invited her to dinner in 1942. Tony served as the civil air attaché for the State Department to the United Kingdom, Ireland, and various European governments in exile. After the war, as civilian aviation rebounded, he would negotiate the rights to own and operate international air routes. Naturally, Ann had befriended him. She knew he was seeking an assistant—not a secretary—who could manage diplomatic duties and also fly him wherever he needed to go. Ann was all over this opportunity.

Likewise, she was Tony's only choice for the job. Ann wrote to her mother to set in motion moving the family to London when the appointment would begin. All the paperwork was set by VE Day. The only obstacle remaining was a rubber stamp from State Department headquarters, understandably mired in red tape during the worldwide commotion. Jane's boss in Paris was now in charge of personnel there, so Ann figured that if she was called to Washington for an interview, all the better. It would also give her a chance to see Bill. Tony hinted at a small hiccup—the gender of the applicant. "It's difficult to consider, primarily the female angle," Tony told Ann. "But I'm confident it will come through in time."

A delay suited her fine. Ann's logbook showed its busiest month ever in May 1945, and that was just as she wanted it. After three years of drinking in all that this British adventure had to offer, Ann Wood couldn't bear the thought that the excitement would end, and she could become mundane. She would work through the summer and fall while she sought a place to land.

CHAPTER 32

"The Spitfire Brought Me Home"

June 1945
Aston Down Aerodrome, Gloucestershire

D espite the European ceasefire, a job ferrying RAF aircraft was still as demanding and dangerous as ever. At the end of May 1945, the British pilot Betty Keith-Jopp was the talk of the ATA after she tried to fly a Barracuda torpedo bomber from Prestwick to the craggy north. On the way, Betty encountered heavy cloud over the Firth of Forth. She turned back but made the classic mistake of tipping too far to the side in the milky sky. The relatively inexperienced pilot lost her lift and couldn't recover.

She saw the water only a second before she hit it. The Barracuda sank straight to the bottom of the sea with Betty inside. She recalled, "I can remember more or less accepting it," just the way Ann Wood once thought she would react if death seemed inevitable.

After a moment of calm, Betty's survival instinct kicked in. She pulled the red lever to release the canopy over her head, allowing the water to engulf her. Only then she realized she had forgotten to unfasten her straps. Somehow, she managed to hit the release mechanism. It seemed to take forever to disentangle herself, but eventually she kicked her way to the surface.

By then her situation seemed nearly as hopeless. Betty was a poor swimmer. The water was cold, freezing cold, and the waves were strong. She couldn't get her bearings in the dense fog. Betty shouted into the void. What a futile situation.

In a twist of extraordinary luck, it happened that a fishing trawler was passing nearby. The captain heard what he thought was a barking seal. Out of curiosity, he made his way toward the sound and spotted the pilot flailing in the sea. "Hold on, Laddie!" he called out. She was taken to an RAF station and placed in a chamber used to treat hypothermia. The Accident Committee held her to blame for the crash, but in the following weeks Betty persevered and flew four more Barracudas out of Prestwick.

WORD WAS OUT that the Air Transport Auxiliary would cease to exist on November 30, 1945. After years performing the most exciting job the Atta-Girls could imagine, it was coming down to the finish for those who wanted to secure the next step.

One American still in the United Kingdom was on the verge of achieving exactly what she set out to do. Granted, Dorothy Furey Bragg's goals steered clear of aviation. She'd put the gothic family horror of her childhood in New Orleans far behind her. Now she was closing in on the marriage that would elevate her once marginal standard of living to the heights.

Dorothy was a woman who had made her way out of the United States with no money, no formal education, one acceptable party dress, and not a single piece of jewelry to her name. Now she draped herself in furs and genuine diamonds and pearls as the future wife of a wealthy earl. Unfortunately, Lord David Beatty's current wife was still dragging out the divorce. But one year after Dorothy, still only twenty-six, stopped flying for the ATA, she remained on course to breach the aristocracy.

On weekends away from her London flat, she now presided over a country estate called Astrop Park near Oxford. David purchased it in the spring of 1945 as a step up from Brooksby Hall. The new seven-hundred-acre property included two farms, a lovely park with towering trees, and a 1740 limestone house with two wings added in 1805 by the prominent Regency architect Sir John Soane. The imposing size allowed for ten spacious bedrooms and seven bathrooms, a far cry from the wood-frame house Dorothy had known as a child. A colossal drawing room designed to lure the toast of society opened onto a terrace overlooking a lake. The original designer of the park was Lancelot "Capability" Brown, a celebrity landscaper of the eighteenth century who also created settings for other prominent houses, including Blenheim Palace and Highclere Castle. He set pleasing stages for country entertainment with clusters of trees broken up by wide swaths of lawn.

The easily bored and chilly Dorothy "was kind of chuffed that she was going to be a countess and all, see all the right people," according to later conversations with her son. With the backing of wealth and position, Dorothy's status rose. Word spread that she was the heiress to a banana fortune. Sir Lindsay Everard invited her to Ratcliffe Hall as a guest rather than a paid billetee like the other pilots. In June, Dorothy turned heads at the Derby Stakes amid a crush of dressy spectators that included the King, the Queen, and Princess Elizabeth. The betting was dull, as all the favorites won. David Beatty's fiancée was the dark horse.

The reorganization of postwar civilian life provided an opportune moment for a dazzling American with a murky background to win acceptance in the upper class. No one in England knew the true story of her past, and she was already developing a reputation as a storied and cultured beauty. "One of the most beautiful women in postwar London," the *Daily Mail*'s Sunday edition noted years later, also praising her ability to quote at length from Shakespeare.

"How did she out-aristocrat the aristocrats?" her son asked rhetorically. "She could hold her own with anyone." Reflecting on her extraordinary rise, her son recalled the story of how as a flying instructor in New Orleans before the war, Dorothy had closed her eyes and cut the engine to test the competence of her students, refusing to watch until they made it to the ground. She was that certain she had taught them well. "That takes considerable chutzpah," he said. "I think she brought the same self-confidence into British society." Dorothy Furey Bragg never looked down.

AT THE END of May, Nancy Miller transferred to Aston Down, a ferry pool in the heart of the Cotswolds, because it was one of three bases designated for trips to the Continent. Nancy moved people, supplies, and planes to and from Belgium and Holland to tidy up the inventory. She always carried her own Boy Scout canteen full of fresh water to avoid the local beer and champagne. Nancy emerged from three years of war still an incorrigible square.

The Aston Down pool closed on June 30 and transferred its remaining pilots to the headquarters at White Waltham. Work was drying up. Nancy decided she would resign in July, her mission accomplished, her future uncertain, aside from a determination to keep flying, wherever she could find work.

Several other American women chose to leave at the end of June. They included the veteran pilot Edith Stearns, forty-two, a Powder Puff champion back in 1929 who planned to teach. She was one of the best pilots at Hamble, often assigned to the toughest emergency jobs in bad weather due to her knowledge of instrument navigation.

Louise Schuurman resigned on the last day of June as well. Known for her joie de vivre, Louise revealed a more serious side at the end. She requested a last ferry mission to Holland so she could track down her Jewish relatives who remained in hiding during the German occupation. She found them, "desperately in need of everything," Louise told a reporter. The family had endured famine in the last months of the war, surviving on tulip bulbs roasted over fires they built from scavenged wood. RAF food deliveries had only recently helped to alleviate the misery.

Virginia Farr also said goodbye to the ATA on June 30, her plans still in limbo as she stayed on temporarily in England. She knew that she wanted to build a life together with her English partner Vivien Jeffery. The couple considered settling in the United States, where they might conduct their lives more openly, away from the dictates of the British legal system. They spoke about moving West to bask in the Zane Grey vistas that Virginia had loved and Vivien had long dreamed of visiting, close but not too close to Virginia's society relations.

BY STAYING INTO July, Nancy Miller squeezed in a few last moments flying the era's most exciting aircraft. Her last introduction to a new type of plane was the delivery of a Hawker Tempest, a fast single-engine fighter similar to the Typhoon. Even at this late date, she had to adapt to a tricky, unfamiliar touchdown that called for a hard jerk of the stick into her belly to lower the tail and keep the aircraft from bouncing. But the flight itself was swift, smooth, and spectacular. On an exhilarating clear day, Nancy hit three hundred miles per hour over the heart of London—no barrage balloons now to slow her down. Hyde Park, Parliament, St. Paul's Cathedral, all still standing—Nancy checked off glimpses of them as she whipped past. She followed the Thames east, toward the morning sun. "The river made a shining spectacle," she wrote. "It's no wonder that German bombers were able to bomb London so well."

On her last taxi job, Nancy had to wait for the passengers, so she took her Fairchild up for a little showboating. First some 180-degree spot landings—cutting off the power, executing a turn, and landing at a specific target on the runway—and then a 360 as a finale. For once, she didn't care that she was wasting petrol, but she felt perturbed that her performance felt a little rough. It would be something to work on when she made it home.

Her last delivery on July 7 was a problematic old Mosquito on its way to retirement with throttles that wouldn't fully open. It had just enough power to stagger into the sky. Nancy had never let fear intrude on the job, and her final assignment was no different. By this time, operating a Mosquito felt as natural as a riding a bike, even if the Mossie was wonky. Besides, her mind was elsewhere. While she was conducting her flight check, she watched a test pilot take off in a new-model aircraft, putting it through its paces. The ship was a de Havilland Hornet, the latest generation of fighter, "just off the secret list," Nancy noted. "I nearly cricked my neck watching him going straight up. My neck gave out before it rolled out level!" This latest wonder was marvelous and fast, Nancy thought. She wished she could fly one. Alas, it was too late.

DESPITE ALL THE chances she took, Nancy was never once at fault for breaking a plane. Waiting for passage on a ship home, she bunked at the Red Cross Club in London and filled the days writing a chronicle of her time in the United Kingdom to present to her father. "I loved all the flying, the freedom, doing what I liked to do," Nancy wrote. "It was wild and woolly at times. I was a lucky person in my career. I smile. I have absolutely no regrets."

Free from the pressures to deliver aircraft six days a week, she reflected on her fleeting encounters with the pilots who took her deliveries into battle. In the last month of the war, she had attended a farewell party at her old Hamble base. A quiet, smooth-shaven fellow with friendly eyes approached. He recognized Nancy as the pilot who had delivered a Spitfire to the muddy airfield of his beleaguered Polish squadron a few days before D-Day, when tensions were high.

"I took the Spit you brought in," he told her in an accent she recognized. "It was a nice ship. I had good success with it, shot up many railway cars, bombed them, bombed stations and other things." One day over Germany, the ack-ack got him.

I must make France, he told himself. The Spitfire crossed the border just before it crashed. The pilot wasn't badly hurt. He looked at Nancy with tenderness. "The Spitfire brought me home."

CHAPTER 33

On Top of the World

Summer–Fall 1945
Nuremberg, Germany, and Ratcliffe, Leicestershire

A nn Wood couldn't resist taking the last months to tear up the skies with the fearless command she had gradually acquired over three-plus years. With the official shutdown of the Air Transport Auxiliary still set for November 30, 1945, she decided to enjoy the finale to the hilt.

Ann loved to fly in part because it took her where she wanted to be, showed her what she wanted to see. Vaulting over the Scottish Highlands that last summer in the ATA, she savored vistas that the earthbound would never know. Trips to Europe fed another fascination, landing her where history was being made. Ann appreciated that all this had been granted to her because she possessed the ability and the means to fly.

Flying to Europe that summer put her right at the center of world events. In June, an assignment to Ghent with her dear friend Pat Beverly took them on a tour of the Continent, as was common for ATA flights then. Officials traveling around the recaptured territories often button-holed pilots to divert passengers or goods to other destinations. A group of RAF guys in Belgium arranged for Ann and Pat to move on to Nuremberg, Germany.

After Sunday morning mass in Ghent, they winged over Brussels, Maastricht, the Rhine, and Frankfurt toward a conquered city that lay in ruins. The scenery along the way was "indescribably lovely," Ann recorded in a letter, "but no town has missed the Allied might. The destruction is unbelievable—whole cities utterly and completely devastated." She saw miles and miles of barbed-wire enclosures full of what looked from the air like tiny specks—prisoners, she discerned, from the German army.

In Nuremberg, an American GI gave Ann and Pat a tour in an open-air Opel. "To see German people about whom I had read so much seemed somehow unreal," Ann wrote. "Frankly I hardly knew how to act or where to look when they smiled and greeted you." She was surprised how clean and well-dressed the children appeared. Their living conditions had to be unspeakable. "There is literally not a house standing, and they couldn't get in the cellars for the rubble piled high."

The two women toured the Zeppelinfeld, an arena the size of twelve soccer fields that once held two hundred thousand people for stage-managed rallies that glorified the Nazi Party. Ann had seen the photographs—zombielike Hitler youth marching in formation, the Führer haranguing rapt crowds from a terrace designed to look like an enormous altar, 150 searchlights pointing skyward—"a cathedral of light." The awe-inspiring spectacle had fed Hitler's rise to power. In recent weeks, American troops had blown up the giant swastika that once loomed over the pageantry. Displaced persons from Poland, Russia, Belgium, and France now filled the space with their bewilderment and despair.

Elsewhere, Ann saw German soldiers who had been released from captivity—"a grim sight trudging to some spot in Germany they once knew as home," she commented. They looked "filthy, unkempt, and [they] walk with a dejection that makes me wonder what they will turn to next." By nightfall, she and Pat made it back to Brussels, tired and pensive from the jarring tableau. They had come face-to-face with the logical conclusion of the work they had performed—the defeat of an enemy, the destruction of a society in defense of another. It was overwhelming to see what they had wrought.

★

NOW IT WAS coming down to the finish for the Atta-Girls who wanted to secure the next step. Ann Wood persisted in the job, of course, along with Suzanne Ford and Peggy Lennox, who served in Prestwick. Jane Plant, who joined on her own after Jackie's group, held on, too, into October.

Nearly all of the women dreamed of remaining pilots when their terms ended, but few were optimistic. Ann had always seemed among the most likely to succeed. She had a fine career option on the hook *and* a possible future with Bill Brown, who took her ambition seriously. She thought she could secure her family's future, too, supporting her mother and providing a home for her siblings. But as the summer of 1945 played out, none of this was certain. Ann couldn't be sure whether the State Department would hire her for the London aviation job, whether Bill loved her (or really, after all this time, whether she loved him), and whether her mother would go along with any of the plans. She faced the same collision of work and family forces that shaped women's choices in any era.

"I am in a complete quandary," Ann admitted to her mother as she tried to game all the variables. She could spend half her savings for a round-trip flight to the United States, where she might lobby for the State Department position and suss out where things stood with Bill. She could find a cottage for the family in England over the summer or wait until other elements fell into place. Or she could just keep doing the job she loved and hope the rest sorted itself out by November. Flying an airplane was so much simpler.

While Ann's priority was to find substantive work, her mother continued to post letters extolling the advantages of marriage. Ann tried to check any expectations. "A thousand times, I thank God that you were generous enough to let us be different," she replied. A perfect marriage, she continued, could offer a most perfect life, but she doubted she could find one that worked the way she wanted. She was willing to keep Bill on hold, even though he sent a gold bracelet and a card signed with love.

Tony Satterthwaite kept assuring Ann that the job as first assistant air attaché at the American embassy would soon fall her way. She flew him to Paris for a weekend to emphasize the benefits of her flying capability. But in July, he conveyed a discouraging report. A State Department factotum had written enigmatically that Ann's "employment at the moment was impractical."

Tony urged patience, but the news spurred Ann to form a backup plan. The suffering she had witnessed in Germany impressed upon her that relief efforts weren't reaching enough people left starving, homeless, and displaced by the war. She recruited Pat Beverly to join her at the United Nations Relief and Rehabilitation Administration in London, where an overwhelmed staff was scrambling to provide necessities throughout Europe and the Middle East. The two towering women in uniform charmed their way past a receptive official, who within minutes whisked them upstairs to explain the idea to the men in charge.

"Your agency is failing miserably," Ann told them bluntly. She blamed their reliance on charity from the military to move their supplies. As an alternative, she proposed that the agency use its own planes and pilots—ideally, she and Pat would fill the role. They could make deliveries in decommissioned warplanes, which Ann's RAF and ATA connections could arrange. The officials agreed on the spot that there was a great need for exactly what she suggested. At the agency's request, she submitted a written proposal. Ever resourceful, she now had two irons in the fire.

Japan surrendered in mid-August, and peace descended throughout the world. The pilots enjoyed their last clear days of summer flying without the pressures of wartime urgency. Tired of group living after three years at Ratcliffe, Ann and Pat moved into a billet at a farmhouse, where the food was plentiful and the weather glorious. "I often feel guilty that I seem to be enjoying myself so much," she wrote to her mother. "But hope you will soon be joining me somehow—somewhere."

THE UN OFFICIALS called Ann and Pat back in at the end of August. The agency was inclined to adopt their plan, but as for Ann and Pat carrying it out, nothing was said. Absorbing the cruel news, Ann consoled herself that Plan A was still in play. That very day, Tony invited her for drinks at his home to meet the State Department's head of aviation, who was visiting London. She flashed all her charm, turned on the high beams, but Tony's boss acted only vaguely aware of her application.

Days later, she got the word that Tony's boss wasn't on board, with an exasperating explanation. Her chief claim to the job, Ann was told, was "that I can do all that Tony can do plus doing some bits better, which would be flying." The chief wondered why the office needed an assistant more suited to the job than her boss and suggested "a report-minded person" for the assistant role. A dreaded desk job, in other words, best performed by someone without Ann's excess qualifications.

Ann was distraught. She went to the American embassy to appeal to her friend Ambassador Biddle. She had once helped him out by arranging a meeting with a Polish leader he couldn't reach on his own, but he declined to see her. All her assumptions about her worth in the postwar landscape seemed to be coming to naught. Her mother advised that Ann should finish her service and come home. The hypercompetent pilot for once felt inadequate. The frustration was making her frantic.

There was also the complication that Bill was moving forward with his life. In September, the army assigned him to Washington for six months to work as a lawyer. It was a dream assignment for him, but Ann knew that Washington wife was not the role for her. The added pressure to return and give up on the adventure she envisioned for herself only made her more determined to follow her own course. "I suppose if I were a get-your-man type of female I wouldn't harbor the idea of remaining here a minute longer than necessary but would be dashing home and swing the situation," she thought. The last thing she wanted was to be saved by a man. She would let the situation drift with Bill and keep pressing to go her own way.

WITH TIME RUNNING out, Ann managed to fulfill a last wartime wish that had seemed out of reach. The ATA had stopped training pilots on four-engine aircraft, the biggest birds in the arsenal, before Ann got a shot at one. But in the fall of 1945, Doc Whitehurst, her ever-loyal commanding officer, found himself with the task of delivering some hulking four-engine Short Sunderlands, ungainly craft with four 1,200-horsepower engines. The Sunderland was a flying boat, an enormous metal tub that took off and landed on water, resting on its waterproof hull rather than on pontoons. At thirty-two feet high and eighty-five feet long, with a wingspan of one hundred and twelve feet, it was one of the largest aircraft Ann had ever seen, the largest in the RAF fleet earlier in the war, and still one of the largest at the end. Equipped with bombs, machine-gun turrets, mines, and depth charges, the military craft had destroyed U-boats in the Atlantic and conducted surveillance in the Mediterranean. It was considered a Class 6 aircraft, off-limits to women because there were no quarters for them at sea.

The Sunderland was nothing like any aircraft Ann had flown. For two days, she took the unusual ship through circuits and bumps at the RAF flying-boat base at Beaumaris, on the northwest coast of Wales. With satisfaction, she got a feel for how to rock the Sunderland as it reached takeoff speed to break the suction between the water and the hull. Then she and Doc flew together to its final destination at Wig Bay, a shoreline base in Scotland with an end-of-the-world quality.

Now that the war was well and fully over, the surplus Sunderland would be beached among idle rows of its fellow ships or towed out into the Irish Sea and scuttled. A sorry fate for a warrior still capable of serving. On the way to its resting place, Doc took over while Ann crawled up into the top gunner's turret. She felt the rumble of the engines and spun around to scan the water in every direction, going out on top of the world. In the privacy of this vantage point, she pulled out another letter from her mother. It had arrived just before the flight, urging Ann again toward marriage and home. Ann knew more than ever—she couldn't settle for that life.

From here on, Ann would be flying into poor visibility. She wasn't afraid. It was something she knew how to do.

THE LAST TAXI plane arrived at the last remaining ATA aerodrome on the last day of November in 1945. Gray weather had washed out most of the month, but on this rare bright afternoon, Ann Wood lingered at the wide grass airfield at White Waltham to watch a few men disembark and turn in their parachutes. Diana Barnato Walker dawdled, too, even though her husband, Wing Commander Derek Walker, had died in a senseless crash of a P-51 Mustang two weeks earlier. He'd been on his way to meet a contact about a job as a test pilot when fog obscured the ground and something went wrong with the oil gauge. The cause of the failure no longer mattered, decided Diana, who was still in shock.

The reminder that death still stalked anyone willing to operate 1940s aircraft put the final precious hours of flying into relief for the few remaining aviators on the clock. Danger had always infused the job with dread but also a perverse exhilaration, an addictive adrenaline bump that made each moment in the air burn brighter. In an hour, the most demanding and fulfilling work the pilots had ever known would be extinguished.

The sunset glowed on the horizon as a small group of stragglers circled the flagpole near the aerodrome gate, like patrons at a pub hanging on until closing time. They brought down the blue-and-yellow ATA flag for the last time. Then they said their goodbyes and made their separate ways to the train station. Lettice Curtis, unsure what she would do next, described the mood as melancholy. "Already the days filled with flying were assuming a dream-like quality—it was almost as if they had never been."

Two days later, Ann Wood quietly boarded the SS *Queen Elizabeth* for passage home on a peaceful sea.

CHAPTER 34

The Look

The Postwar Years

The ATA had thrown a splashier sendoff on September 29, 1945. Twelve thousand spectators thronged an airshow at White Waltham to see all the aircraft that captured their imaginations during the war. Spitfires, Lancasters, Tempests, Meteors, and more showed off their stuff like the runway models they were. The pageant raised money for the benevolent fund that would aid the widows and orphans of the fallen. Lord Beaverbrook, who had jump-started the ATA when he was minister of aircraft production, spoke eloquently about the courage of the "Ancient and Tattered Airmen."

There had been 1,246 pilots and flight engineers who flew for the organization, including 168 women. They delivered 309,000 aircraft of 147 types. Those who gave their lives included 173 aircrew, 17 of them women, including Mary Webb Nicholson of North Carolina. Lord Beaverbrook's warm farewell praised the men of the organization, but never mentioned the women. The era when women pilots would fall out of mind had already begun.

★

ONLY THE MOST tenacious would endure. Fortunately, the Atta-Girls were no strangers to tenacity. It was a struggle to find their footing once the egalitarian workplace of the Air Transport Authority ceased to exist, but some of them managed. Most went on to careers, often distinctive ones. Several even found a way to fly for a living.

The postwar fates of Jackie Cochran's recruits were as varied as the women themselves. The stories of those who were featured most prominently in these pages appear below, roughly in the order in which they departed from the ATA.

Jacqueline Cochran remained in the thick of it as the world turned from war to peace. Her husband, Floyd Odlum, bought *Liberty*, a magazine that featured celebrity contributors, so she could become a correspondent and travel the world. Ann Wood, who once schooled Jackie on her vocabulary, assumed she used a ghostwriter. Yet Jackie made it to the Philippines for the Japanese surrender. She met Madame Chiang Kai-shek in China and the pope in Rome. She hopped from Japan to the Buchenwald concentration camp in Germany.

It didn't take long before Jackie resumed her campaign to remain the world's greatest woman aviator. She took second place in the 1946 cross-country Bendix race in a P-51 Mustang as the only woman among men. The advancement of jet engines enticed her to run up the score on her many air records. After Jacqueline Auriol, the wife of the president of France, flew a British Vampire to break one of Jackie's old speed marks in 1952, Jackie got her hands on an F-86 Sabre jet. Her friend Chuck Yeager, the first man to break the sound barrier, coached her for six hours before she exceeded Mach 1 herself.

In England, Diana Barnato Walker heard the news that Jackie was once again the world's fastest woman. Diana borrowed the latest Lightning model jet from the RAF and pushed the afterburners to Mach 1.65. Jackie soon snatched the record back.

She also ran unsuccessfully for Congress and launched a program with NASA in the 1960s to prove that women could qualify as astronauts. Thirteen passed the medical tests before NASA barred them from missions.

All the while, Jackie racked up more speed and altitude records. In 1964, at age fifty-eight, she hit Mach 2 in a Lockheed F-104G Starfighter.

The woman who reapplied her lipstick after every race proved the worth of her gender by her own example, but her conflicted feelings about women in general continued to mar her record as an advocate for others. At the end of the world war, she argued against integrating women into the armed services, cutting off access for the pilots she'd championed in the WASP. And in the 1970s, she testified before Congress that it would be "unnatural" for women to fly in combat.

Jackie Cochran always wanted to be the *top* woman at whatever she did, and she often was, thanks to the extraordinary drive that powered her mythic, unlikely life. She died in 1980 of heart failure, sitting up in a wheelchair, because she refused to face death lying down.

Pauline Gower, the ATA's fearless women's leader, served on the board of the British Overseas Airways Corporation, the precursor to British Airways. She died in 1947 at the age of thirty-six after giving birth to twins.

Next to Jackie Cochran, **Helen Richey** had been the most renowned of the American women for her racing and endurance feats. Following her dismissal from the ATA after a string of accidents, Helen put a good face on joining the WASP. "It isn't as exciting as England, but I love it," she told a reporter. Yet when the U.S. dismantled the service in 1944, Helen couldn't find consistent work as a pilot. She refused to take secretarial jobs. On January 7, 1947, her body was found in her one-room New York City apartment, dead at thirty-seven from an overdose of sleeping pills.

Mary Webb Nicholson left behind a multigenerational legacy when she died in the crash of a defective Miles Master on an ATA delivery in 1943. By the next century, three generations of Nicholsons, inspired by Mary's heroism, had launched careers as commercial airline pilots. They included her brother, her nephew, her niece, and a grandniece.

After all this time, Mary is often on their minds. Some made a pilgrimage in the 1970s to the field of apple trees where she crashed. "I wonder sometimes if Aunt Mary is up there laughing and getting a kick out of seeing me and my brother," said her niece Lauren Scott, a pilot for Allegiant Air. "Does she know what she started?"

Hazel Jane Raines was serious when she resolved in 1942 that the sky was her home. She persevered to reclaim that place after the head injury she sustained in England ended her service there. In her new position in the WASP, Hazel received instrument training and operated a heavy two-engine B-26 Marauder bomber. She often took it through the numbing task of target towing, which provided plenty of hours for her logbook, if not much in the way of her favorite aerobatic thrills.

When the WASP folded in 1944, Hazel once again turned her back on her mother's plea to assume the role of a proper southern lady. Hazel never married, and as far as her family members knew, the woman who rejected the idea that she wed an Astor never engaged in a romantic relationship, at least not one that she told them about. Instead, she continued to pursue her aviation dreams. A plan to start a business selling aircraft supplies didn't pan out. Neither did renting cars to travelers at airports, a novel idea at the time. Unable to find meaningful work in the United States, Hazel learned Portuguese in order to teach at a ground school in Brazil. On her return, she made entertaining speeches at events for women pilots, but she was barely able to cobble together a living.

She found career security in 1949 when she joined the U.S. Air Force Reserve and successfully applied to be placed on active duty. Hazel worked her way up through desk jobs until she was named the women's air force advisor for the Third Air Force in England, traveling throughout Europe from a base near her old airfield in Maidenhead. While she excelled in the work, she was never assigned to fly.

Hazel had always bluffed her way through medical exams so she could continue to work despite her fragile health. "The extra beat in my heart," as she referred to the troublesome rhythm of her ticker, finally caught up with her in 1956. She died of a heart attack in London at the age of forty.

Roberta Sandoz Leveaux ended her ATA adventure when she became pregnant at the height of the war, but her immersion in the homeland of her British husband continued through 1951, when they emigrated to the United States. "It was not a marriage made in heaven," she said, "but we wanted to keep our family intact." They moved three children around the country every time he changed jobs in sales—cars, then class rings, then real estate. Once the youngsters were grown, Roberta circled back to social work, her field before she followed her heart to fly. She earned a master's degree in psychology in 1970 and worked with traumatized children in an Arizona mental health clinic.

It never occurred to Roberta that she had been a pioneer in aviation until a friend invited her to a WASP convention in the 1970s. Entering the hall in her old ATA uniform, she was startled. Women approached her for autographs. One after another told her, "Without those girls with the ATA, the WASP wouldn't have been able to do what we did." She was moved after all those years at "how wonderful it was to be considered valuable and useful for things other than housewifery and motherhood."

Roberta died at the age of ninety-five in 2013, but not before she flew again. When she retired in the 1980s, she and a friend constructed their own Ultralight aircraft, a real seat-of-the-pants, thirty-five-horsepower traveling toy. They flew over mountains to the San Pedro Valley, navigating by landmarks in the terrain, just as she had in the war. She felt like one of the migrating geese she used admire when she was a rebellious child with fantasies of joining them in the sky.

The irrepressible **Winnabelle Pierce** led an exuberant postwar life. When she returned to the United States in the spring of 1944 to marry Peter Beasley, everyone assumed they had tied the knot. She let them assume. Peter resumed his evasive maneuvers, even after a son was born in 1945, the first of four. Another son, Michael, said, "She just called herself Mrs. Beasley and got away with it."

Winnie found a rambling old adobe house on a twelve-acre ranch outside Santa Fe. Over the next several years, the secretive Peter was usually off somewhere on his inscrutable work. Every once in a while, he visited Winnie, and nine months later another a baby appeared. Peter finally married her in 1948, but the pattern never changed.

Practically a single mother, Winnie made the most of the role. She developed a persona as an outrageous local character, a one-woman carnival, the most flamboyant resident of Santa Fe. She was also the city's most visible supporter of art, theater, and the opera, where she served on the board. Riding a motorcycle like the one she'd crashed in England, she zipped out five nights a week to cultural events and parties, making entrances in sequined bodystockings with jewels on the crotch, or fringed miniskirts with outlandish matching boas and wigs.

Winnie divorced Peter Beasley in 1956, a year before his death. At a reading of the will, she discovered the existence of four children from other marriages in addition to her own. Peter left no assets beyond his veteran's benefits.

The former first officer of the ATA flew only occasionally while raising her family, but after divorcing Peter, she joined the local Civil Air Patrol. She searched for lost airplanes and took aerial photographs of archaeological sites for the Museum of New Mexico, all while cultivating the madcap personality that won her attention during the war. When she died in 1997 at eighty, an obituary eulogized her as "a living treasure . . . equal parts bon vivant and ne'er do well."

Peter Beasley merits his own follow-up as a major presence in the lives of the American women flyers. For years, he remained a mystery to his wife and sons as well as everyone else. They wondered at his seemingly unfettered access to the nuclear weapons laboratory in Los Alamos, less than thirty miles from Winnie's ranch. His children eventually learned the truth that he had been a spy, although they doubted Winnie did before she died.

His most notable mission dropped him into Germany in the final weeks of the war to track down German rocket scientists who led him to caves full of documents. Days before Russian troops took over the area for occupation, the U.S. whisked the scientists out of Germany along with blueprints for V-1 and V-2 rockets as well as future secret weapons. The cache contributed to the United States' development of atomic weapons, missiles, and the space program.

Dorothy Furey Bragg Beatty Hewitt Miller ultimately made four marriages, each serving her needs at the time, and had one affair that rattled the British government. Poised and desired through the decades, Dorothy held the seductive center of a lifelong drama.

She and Lord David Beatty wed on February 1, 1946. Almost immediately, she decided she'd made a mistake. Her husband, she concluded, "was a neurotic, insecure, social-climbing snob." And also a bit of a bore. Still, the countess did her duty. She produced an heir, another David, later that year.

Every Friday night, a selection of London toffs descended on the country manor of Astrop Park, expecting her to entertain them. They included Kathleen "Kick" Kennedy, the daughter of the former American ambassador, and Rita Hayworth with her husband Prince Aly Khan. Another frequent guest was Anthony Eden, the forty-nine-year-old protégé of Winston Churchill who was expected to become a Tory prime minister himself one day. Separated from his wife but still married, Eden's illicit combustion with Dorothy crackled through a three-year affair that began in 1947. Dorothy's son by a later marriage said she and Eden mourned a stillborn child.

Dorothy thought Lord Beatty encouraged the affair to enhance his own position. "It was thoroughly and completely condoned," she claimed. But when David threatened to name Eden in a divorce proceeding in 1950, Churchill intervened and told the politician to end the affair. Eden went on to become prime minister in 1955.

David Beatty and Dorothy divorced in 1950, but the next year, she married a third husband, American Abram S. Hewitt, sixteen years her senior. He was a member of the Cooper Hewitt family that made a fortune in steel and held sway in New York politics and philanthropy. The couple moved to a farm in Virginia where Abram could breed horses. Dorothy had four more children, all boys.

In her eighties and widowed, she married a fourth time, to Kent Miller, a jovial horse trainer twenty-two years her junior. Dorothy scuba-dived and traveled to countries ranging from Uzbekistan to Indonesia, while Kent handled the luggage. She believed until the end of her life in 2006 that rules did not apply to her. According to her son, she chose not to fly herself, but on commercial flights, she still acted like she was in charge. She always stood to stride to the exit while the plane was still taxiing, however many times she was told to sit.

Dorothy's power over men never flagged. Shortly before her last marriage, an old flame called her out of the blue. It was the fiancé from New Orleans back in 1941, the one whose car she stole to escape her past and drive to Montreal to join the ATA. She had swiped that car nearly sixty years ago without remorse, and yet the retired doctor still wanted her back. Dorothy listened impatiently and spurned him again. His life sounded too, too utterly dull.

Mary Zerbel Hooper Ford's husband, Jack, made it home from the war, and together they formed a business that transported surplus U.S. military aircraft to private companies and governments around the world. They delivered P-51 Mustangs across the United States for the U.S. Air Force; B-25 Mitchell bombers to the Chinese; and B-17 Flying Fortresses to the French.

Calling themselves "The Flying Fords," they lived a life of over-the-top adventure and risk, taking on dicey aircraft in dodgy circumstances. The two of them once came under machine-gun fire while transporting a flying boat to Brazil. In Bangkok they picked up a C-46 transport plane that failed on takeoff because half the sparkplugs were missing. The pilots discovered that someone had filled the gaps with twigs and cigarette butts.

The Fords made such a charismatic couple that Universal Studios dramatized their story in a 1958 movie, *The Lady Takes a Flyer*, starring Lana Turner and Jeff Chandler. Mary laughed at the Hollywood spin: "They had Lana Turner walk out of a blazing crash without a speck of dirt on her."

Real life was melodramatic enough for the Fords. Jack was charming with the ladies, "and he didn't say no very often," said their daughter

Pam, who was born in 1946. Long separations and Jack's infidelity led the couple to divorce in 1955.

Four years later, Jack took off from the Pacific atoll of Wake Island in a twin-engine Beechcraft he had equipped with portable gas tanks for a long haul to Japan. When he switched on the radio at five thousand feet, it sparked. The plane exploded in a brilliant fireball. A few flaming fragments fell into the sea.

Mary decided she was done with flying. She worked as a clerk for the air force and later earned a degree at the age of forty-eight to become a school librarian. When she died at ninety-two in 2012, the obituary consisted of three sentences in the hometown paper of Pocatello, Idaho. There was no hint of the early celebrity of the girl who had once inspired coverage for her youthful flying. Nothing about her milestone wedding in England, nor the career that inspired a Hollywood film. But Mary Zerbel Hooper Ford had succeeded in her youthful goal of playing the heroine in an exciting, glamorous, romantic life, whatever anyone else remembered.

The flyers who continued into 1945 were a dogged bunch. **Peggy Lennox,** who served in Prestwick, joined the air racing circuit, taking the Bertram Trophy for winning an all-female race from Montreal to Miami. Her Prestwick colleague, the socialite **Suzanne Ford,** took over her family's large homeopathic medicine company. **Opal Anderson,** the Chicago Foghorn, worked as a forewoman at a plant for the defense contractor General Dynamics and flew for fun (and a little profit) until the age of seventy. She dusted crops and performed stunts in her own biplane.

Louise Schuurman found instructing work and married a highly decorated flying ace, who, unlike her former lover General Woodbury, was her own age. She met a calamitous end on her forty-second birthday in 1962. Flying a light Ercoupe monoplane, she struck power lines and then hit a shed at the Galveston airport, dying instantly.

Virginia Farr and her partner Vivien Jeffery fulfilled their fantasy of living in the American West. Virginia's relatives helped them take over a portion of the family's ranch in Templeton, California, near San Simeon. She embraced the relative isolation in a place all the family visited and loved. "She did her own thing, and we all respected it," said her cousin Harper Sibley III.

Virginia and Vivien called their property the V2 Ranch, where they raised Hereford beef cattle, Welsh Corgi dogs, and Siberian huskies. The setting was idyllic, worthy of a Zane Grey novel, with Pacific breezes and huge views of distant mountains, rolling hills, and pastures shaded with oaks. The women settled into strenuous work. A neighbor remembered them building a fence through a patch of poison oak. "Those girls would take on jobs that guys wouldn't do," he said. Virginia and Vivien ran the V2 for forty years.

In 1988, while boarding a plane on vacation in Fiji, Virginia had a heart attack and died at sixty-nine. She had requested a Viking funeral. Her body was placed on a boat, lit on fire, and set afloat. Virginia Farr left life the way she'd lived it, following her own course.

Despite **Nancy Miller**'s singular focus on flying, the aviation industry did not open the gates for her when she returned to Los Angeles. She took the only work she could get, spewing pesticides at a top speed of 125 miles per hour while crop-dusting in Oregon's Willamette River Valley. Her duties also included janitorial work, bookkeeping, instructing, and flying in air shows. All of these were jobs performed by women before they proved themselves in the war.

Nancy kept striving for more. In 1947, she earned a seaplane rating and became only the second woman in the United States certified to fly commercial helicopters, placing herself again on the cutting edge of aviation. Nancy flew helicopters for shows and photo shoots. She fought wildfires and delivered Santa Claus to pressing public appearances.

Looking back in 2024, she said, "I wasn't going to let marriage interfere with flying." But in 1956, in her midthirties, she took the plunge with Arlo Livingston, her boss at the crop-dusting company. The two moved to Alaska and launched the state's first fleet of commercial helicopters, living in a trailer while they cleared trees for a landing pad and hangar. The business boomed along with the Alaskan economy. Nancy transported mountain climbers, including Sir Edmund Hillary, to remote peaks. She took tourists on holiday trips and oil executives and construction workers to the Trans-Alaska Pipeline. Operating a helicopter in the cold was doubly dangerous, said her niece, "but that was the kind of thing she was inured to."

Nancy was designated Whirly-Girl Number Four, the fourth woman in the world to receive commercial certification, by the Whirly-Girls organization of women helicopter pilots. She collected shelves full of other citations for the trails she blazed. Her hearing damaged by aircraft engines, she retired in 1978. After her husband died, she remarried—to her former fiancé from 1942 who had tried to stop her from joining the ATA.

Nancy Miller outlasted all her peers as the last living pilot of the Air Transport Auxiliary. At the age of 104, as this book was being completed, she still remembered the most hair-raising experiences yet still insisted she had never once been afraid. "No!" she protested. "I was busy. I had a job to do."

Clipped of her ATA wings, **Ann Wood** provided a test for whether a decommissioned pilot with everything on her side could land on solid ground. Although she'd joined in 1942 as an inexperienced, even timid flyer, she had by the finish developed into one of the most accomplished pilots in the ATA, having flown seventy-seven different types of aircraft. The British government awarded her the King George Medal for Courage in the Cause of Freedom in recognition of her extraordinary service. Yet it took Ann time to find her bearings when the ATA job ended in November 1945.

She eventually jumped through enough hoops in 1946 to win the title of first assistant civil air attaché at the American embassy in London. She didn't last there long. The job called for her to fly herself in a Spitfire to aircraft manufacturers throughout the United Kingdom, reporting on their conversion to postwar aviation. It was fun, but Ann was treated like a volunteer, paid a pittance to cover her expenses pending budget approval from the State Department. When it denied the request, she was out. By then, she had let the relationship with Bill Brown slip away. In London, Ann crossed paths again with an old suitor, Jack Kelly, who had enticed her to his apartment in 1942 by arranging a get-together with the king of Yugoslavia. Jack worked at Pan American Airways as the regional director for the United Kingdom and Europe. They married in 1949 and had a son.

Ann weathered some painful losses that illustrated how treacherous flying remained, even during peacetime. Two close colleagues from the ATA died in airplane crashes, including Ann's most cherished friend, Pat Beverly, the copilot on a chartered passenger plane that failed on takeoff in 1949.

By 1952, Ann's career was dormant, her marriage rocky, her best friend gone. Despondent and isolated, ready to admit failure, she phoned the one person among all her connections willing to marshal the resources to turn Ann's course around.

"I'll fly over from Paris," said her strongest ally. "Meet me at the airport in London." Ann anxiously paced the waiting room until she spotted the gleaming blond curls, bright lipstick, and tailored attire of Jacqueline Cochran. The relief was immense.

"Don't make a move now," Jackie advised after hearing the whole story. "I'll be home in ten hours and discuss all this with Floyd. We'll get back to you."

With Jackie Cochran's help, Ann separated from her husband and set herself up in Boston. She took a job as director of publicity at Northeast Airlines, where Jackie sat on the board of directors. It was Ann's first step in a four-decade corporate career in aviation that led to Pan Am, where she served as the first woman vice president for a major airline, in charge of public relations and government affairs. Ann was still living ahead of her time.

Until she died at the age of eighty-seven in 2006, Ann flew a Piper Arrow, often with her son, Christopher, who also learned to fly. They ran into sleet on one of their final trips. "Look sharp!" she admonished him. Peering through the windscreen, she called to mind the unshakable Ann Wood from the war years—focused, with not a hint of nerves, relishing the challenge. Tenacious. Her fellow pilots would have recognized the look. They had all worn it at one time or another. If anyone could make it through in the face of trouble, it was an ATA girl.

EPILOGUE

August 1979
Tesuque, New Mexico

The American Atta-Girls were an independent lot. It never occurred to them to reunite after the war until 1979. Eight of the pilots who were still around spent a rowdy weekend in the sun at Winnie Pierce Beasley's ranch in New Mexico. Still animated with that old sparkle, they looked pretty much the same except for some gray hair and glasses. Winnie set aside her rivalry with Virginia Farr to fit her in, along with her partner, Vivien Jeffery, who made the ninth guest. Others from the west included the former Nancy Miller, Opal Anderson, and Roberta Sandoz. Suzanne Ford came from New York and Peggy Lennox from Florida. Ann Wood flew in from Massachusetts with a treasure trove of photos. Winnie set off fits of laughter by reading passages from her unfiltered diaries. They sounded like excerpts from *Fear of Flying*.

The women all agreed: Flying in a war in a faraway land was the best thing they ever did.

Roberta Sandoz Leveaux had come up with the idea for a reunion after she'd found herself hailed as a trailblazer at the WASP convention a couple years before. "I came home with the feeling that we had undervalued ourselves," she told the others in New Mexico. "It was time we got together and gave ourselves some recognition."

Most of them stuck to the old story—when they answered the call to serve in 1942, they did it for themselves and for the free world. They gave no thought to advancing the status of women. But thirty-seven years later, it was clear that, however inadvertently, they had opened doors, even if some of them shut again.

"We were unique," Roberta said. "We were aware of our options when most women were not."

In crossing the sea to England all those years ago, the young pilots were transported into a dream of the future. Afterward, the world struggled to catch up. The first woman to pilot a plane for a major U.S. passenger carrier was Bonnie Tiburzi at American Airlines in 1973. It wasn't until 1993—a half a century after the American Atta-Girls—that Jeannie Flynn flew the first fighter in the U.S. Air Force. Around the same time, Eileen M. Collins blasted off as the first woman space shuttle pilot. No woman served as the CEO of a major American airline until Joanna Geraghty took over JetBlue in 2024. And forget about equal pay. Women everywhere still struggle for what the ATA women won.

The Atta-Girls scored firsts that led the way. The first American women to fly the biggest, fastest, scariest aircraft. The first to fly them in a war zone. The first to be accorded that all-important equal pay. Their other milestones were harder to quantify, but just as real. They were brave enough to live as if they already possessed the rights that women would fight to win over the next eighty years. In the air, they threw out the rulebook when their lives depended on it, and they didn't pay a price—ferry flying wasn't a job for good girls. Their personal choices were their own. And they didn't retreat into conformity when the job was done.

Roberta said it out loud at the reunion, although all of them knew. "We were the thin edge of the wedge."

The thin edge of the wedge.

The Atta-Girls strove for the sky and all it represented—freedom, adventure, challenge, pleasure, respect, purpose. Danger, too. The list stretched to the horizon. For three and a half years, in the crucible of a world war, they got it all. They did it for themselves. But they left a gift for anyone who shared the ATA creed. *Aetheris Avidi.* Eager for the air.

ACKNOWLEDGMENTS

This book started with my mother, Barbara Aikman. I told her I wanted to write about someone who deserved to be remembered. Her short-term memory was beginning to fade then, three years before her death, but she answered without hesitation. "The American women who flew in England during the war." All these years later, she remembered seeing something—perhaps a newsreel or magazine article—about them when she was a child. "I thought they were so noble and glamourous," she continued. "I wished I could do what they did."

Like most Americans, I had never heard of these women. I doubted their existence at first. But as I found traces, my gratitude grew that my mother understood how grand and remarkable their stories were. I dove into what documents had been preserved, but soon realized that I would also have to rely on the few remaining people who had kept alive the tales of the American Atta-Girls.

As I completed the manuscript, one of the pilots, Nancy Miller, remained the last living member of the Air Transport Auxiliary at 105 years of age. She was kind enough to meet me and describe her experiences serving in Great Britain as if they had played out yesterday. Nancy's niece Margaret Miller helped me sort through more details.

I'm also immensely grateful to the families of all the other pilots. They passed along the stories told by their mothers, aunts, and cousins and climbed into attics to pull out diaries, letters, photos, and keepsakes that no one outside their circle had seen before. Dorothy Furey, for example, had told her son Adam Hewitt delicious anecdotes about her life, and he was pleased to pass them along. Other family members were equally forthcoming, including Dorothy's last husband, Kent Miller; Michael Beasley, the son of Winnabelle Pierce; Regina T. Hawkins, the niece of Hazel Jane Raines; Christopher Wood Kelly, the son of Ann Wood; Pam Ford, the daughter of Mary Zerbel; Mark Leveaux, the son of Roberta Sandoz; and Mary Walton, Lauren Scott, and Ann Smith, nieces of Mary Webb Nicholson. A special nod to Lauren, a pilot herself, for treating me to a flying lesson in a Cessna Skyhawk.

Virginia Farr left few written records, so many of her relatives did their best to fill in the blanks, including Cristy Rodiger, Harper Sibley III, Nancy Kennedy, and Hiram Sibley, as well as neighbors who befriended Virginia after the war, Tim Barlogio and Tom St. John. Ebets Judson, an authority on the upper-class society of Rochester, NY, and Elizabeth Stefanik of Virginia's alma mater, Chatham Hall, also weighed in. In an unexpected windfall, Evan Berardi, the owner of a house where Suzanne Ford once lived, managed to dig out papers he found there.

At the beginning of my research, many public archives were closed for visitors due to Covid, so a number of librarians and archivists went the extra mile to provide me with digital information. Since few of the pilots had been deemed famous enough for their records to be digitized, these archivists created some original versions for me: Corynthia Dorgan and Kimberly Johnson at Texas Woman's University in Denton, Texas; and Jill Church, Mark Bialkowski, and Katherine Hammer at D'Youville University in Buffalo. Others who won my eternal gratitude include the staff at the Hoover Institution at Stanford University and Debbie Seracini and Katrina Escador of the San Diego Air & Space Museum. Marjorie Searl, the retired research curator of the Memorial Art Gallery of the University of Rochester provided me with information on Virginia Farr's family, as did Andrea Reithmayr of the special collections at the University of Rochester Library. For general background about the war, I must thank Paul Friedman of the New York Public Library and Alex M. Spencer of the National Air and Space Museum.

Once Covid restrictions lifted to allow travel to England, I gained access to essential information, including personnel and accident records, with the assistance of Gary Haines at the RAF Museum London. The private historian Terry Mace shared his collection of ATA personnel files to flesh out those that were missing. Jane Rosen of the Imperial War Museums provided more material.

My visit to the charming Maidenhead Heritage Centre and ATA Museum in Maidenhead, Berkshire, proved invaluable. I'm indebted to its chairman, Richard Poad, for guiding me through the archives and White Waltham airfield, sharing his deep knowledge of the Air

Transport Auxiliary, and checking the manuscript for mistakes. I trust he will overlook my ignominious crash in the Centre's Spitfire flight simulator, which I highly recommend to visitors.

I am indebted to John Webster, the secretary of the ATA Association; his wife, Maria; and the local historian Ian Underdown for showing me the Hamble airfield and surrounding area. Erika Steward arranged for me to ramble through the former Astor estate at Cliveden. Andrew Yell, Paul Walters, and Helen Grant of Ratcliffe College led me around the Ratcliffe village and aerodrome. John Besford, a relation of Roberta Sandoz's English husband, gave me family background and arranged for Richard Kossow to show me the apartment building where the couple lived during the war. The filmmaker Harvey Lilley supplied footage of interviews with some of the pilots.

Capturing all the excitement and occasional terror of flying in the unreliable aircraft of the era meant that I had to understand how they worked and how they were flown under all conditions. For this I relied on a kitchen cabinet of aviation experts. Geoffrey Hudson, an enthusiast of World War II aircraft, was so knowledgeable and generous with his time that it felt like we were running a historic aviation detective agency. We reconstructed the crashes and close calls central to the story by piecing together cryptic punch-card records, eyewitness reports, and technical information about the aircraft.

Local residents and witnesses to the Hazel Raines crash included Laurence McGowan, an authority on the history of Collingbourne Kingston; Andrea Palmer, a member of the family whose home was destroyed; and Olive Bishop, who lived in town at the time. For the Mary Webb Nicholson crash, I relied on the knowledge of local residents of Littleworth, especially Kelvin Gill and John Waizeneker; and the now-grown children who saw the crash, Eddie Collins and Murray Gill.

Others who provided insight into flying warplanes during the era included Steve Williams and Gerard Crutchley of the Spitfire Society and the vintage aircraft pilots Howard Cook, Ronald C. Bunch, and Dave Unwin.

The team at Bloomsbury couldn't have been more supportive, beginning with my brilliant editor, Grace McNamee. Her clarity and thoughtful understanding guided me in streamlining the many strands of the

Atta-Girls' lives. Others included the talented art department, as well as Katherine Kiger, Suzanne Keller, Kenli Manning, and Morgan Jones. Joy Harris is my canny agent and so much more—insightful critic, no-nonsense ally, and loyal friend. Too many friends to mention kept me going, but I will make an exception in thanking Glenn Kessler of the *Washington Post*.

It's a shame that my late father, John Aikman, was no longer alive during this project, yet he had left for me a certain familiarity with the subject. He rarely spoke about his accomplishments as an air force navigator during the war, but he became a licensed pilot later and shared his love and knowledge of aviation. My other great regret is that my mother did not live to see the book to completion. The subject still fired her imagination, and her faith in my ability to pull it off sustained me throughout. My sister, Nancy Martin, provided her own good-humored encouragement.

Unlike the pilots in the story, I never felt that I was lost or undertaking this challenging journey alone. For this, I thank the love and support (and sharp-eyed editing) of Bob Spitz.

BIBLIOGRAPHY

The following archives and publications provided diaries, letters, journals, and memorabilia from some of the pilots:

Personnel records of Air Transport Auxiliary Pilots: the Archive of the RAF Museum, London.

Records of Air Transport Auxiliary accidents: the Archive of the Maidenhead Heritage Centre, Maidenhead, UK, and the RAF Museum, London.

Dorothy Furey memorabilia: the collection of her son, Adam Hewitt.

Nancy Miller postwar recollections: Nancy Miller Livingston Stratford, *Contact! Britain! An American Woman Ferry Pilot's Life During WWII*, California: self-published, 2010.

Mary Webb Nicholson memorabilia: the collections of her nieces, Lauren Scott and Mary Walton.

Winnabelle Pierce diaries, postwar journal, and memorabilia: the collection of her son, Michael Beasley.

Hazel Jane Raines's letters were published in a book by her niece Regina T. Hawkins, *Hazel Jane Raines: Pioneer Lady of Flight*. Macon, GA: Mercer University Press, 1996.

Helen Richey memorabilia: Helen Richey Personal Papers, San Diego Air & Space Museum Library & Archives.

Roberta Sandoz journals, memorabilia, and oral histories: Roberta Boyd Sandoz Leveaux Papers, Hoover Institution Libraries & Archives, as well as the collection of her son, Mark Leveaux, as noted.

Ann Wood diaries from May 11, 1942, to June 28, 1943: Ann Wood-Kelly Papers, Hoover Institution Library & Archives.

Ann Wood letters from September 19, 1943, through May 13, 1945: Ann Wood-Kelly Papers, Texas Woman's University Archive.

Ann Wood letters from June 6, 1945, to November 1, 1945: Ann Wood-Kelly Archive, D'Youville University Library.

Mary Zerbel journals, logbook, and memorabilia: Mary Ford Personal Papers, San Diego Air & Space Museum Library & Archives.

―――

Ayers, Billie Pittman, and Beth Dees. *Superwoman Jacqueline Cochran: Family Memories About the Famous Pilot, Patriot, Wife and Businesswoman.* Bloomington, IN: 1stBooks, 2001.

Baker, David. *The Aerial War: 1939-1945: The Role of Aviation in World War II.* London: Arcturus, 2020.

Beasley, Norman, "The Capture of the German Rocket Secrets." In *Military Intelligence: Its Heroes and Legends,* compiled by Diane L. Hamm, 73–86. Honolulu, HI: University Press of the Pacific, 2001. Reprinted by permission of the *American Legion Magazine,* 1963.

Beasley, Winnabelle Pierce. Postwar journal. Collection of her son, Michael Beasley, undated.

Bristol, Helen Harrison. "Flying When the Living Was Easy," *Airforce,* Summer 1982. Mary Zerbel Ford Archive. San Diego Air & Space Museum Library & Archives.

Brown, Willard. 95th Bomb Group (H) Association, Oral History Project, 2000.

Chapin, Emily. Letters. Hoover Institution, Stanford University.

Cheesman, E. C. *Brief Glory: The Story of the Air Transport Auxiliary.* Croydon, UK: CPI Group, 2008. First published 1946 by Harborough.

Cochran, Jacqueline. *The Stars at Noon.* Boston: Little, Brown, 1954.

Cochran, Jacqueline, and Maryann Bucknum Brinley. *Jackie Cochran: The Autobiography of the Greatest Woman Pilot in Aviation History.* New York: Bantam Books, 1987.

Curtis, Lettice. *The Forgotten Pilots: A Story of the Air Transport Auxiliary, 1939–45.* 4th ed. Cheltenham, UK: Westward Digital, 1998. First published 1971.

Deighton, Len. *Fighter: The True Story of the Battle of Britain*. London: Jonathan Cape, 1977.

Douglas, Deborah G. *United States Women in Aviation, 1940–1985*. Washington, D.C.: Smithsonian Institution Press, 1990.

Du Cros, Rosemary. *ATA Girl: Memoirs of a Wartime Ferry Pilot*. London: Frederick Muller, 1983.

Dziadyk, William. *S.S. Nerissa, the Final Crossing*. Privately published, 2019.

Ellis, John. *The World War II Databook: The Essential Facts and Figures for All the Combatants*. London: Aurum, 1993.

Ellis, Mary. *A Spitfire Girl*. Yorkshire, UK: Pen & Sword Books, 2016.

Ford, Mary Zerbel. Journal. Mary Ford Personal Papers. San Diego Air & Space Museum Library & Archives.

Ford, Mary Zerbel. *Untitled Biography of the Flying Fords*. San Diego Air & Space Museum Library & Archives.

Genovese, J. Gen. *We Flew Without Guns*. Philadelphia: The John C. Winston Company, 1945.

Glancey, Jonathan. *Spitfire: The Biography*. London: Atlantic Books, 2020.

Hamilton, Joan E. "Roberta Sandoz Leveaux." Manuscript based on interviews by Joan E. Hamilton, May 2005, with excerpts from *Our Service in England* by Roberta Sandoz Leveaux. Collection of Mark Leveaux.

Hawkins, Regina T. *Hazel Jane Raines: Pioneer Lady of Flight: A Biography in Letters*. Macon, GA: Mercer University Press, 1996.

Hudson, Paul Stephen. "Hazel Jane Raines." In *Georgia Women: Their Lives and Times*, edited by Ann Short Chirhart and Kathleen Ann Clark, vol. 2, 260–280. Athens, GA: University of Georgia Press, 2014.

Irons, Roy. *Hitler's Terror Weapons: The Price of Vengeance*. New York: HarperCollins, 2003.

King, Alison. *Golden Wings: The Story of Some of the Women Ferry Pilots of the Air Transport Auxiliary*. London: C. Arthur Pearson, 1956.

Landdeck, Katherine Sharp. *The Women with Silver Wings*. New York: Crown, 2020.

Leveaux, Roberta Sandoz. Manuscript based on interviews by Joan E. Hamilton, May 2005, 1. Collection of Mark Leveaux.

Leveaux, Roberta Sandoz. Interview by Rebecca Wright, March 25, 2000. NASA Johnson Space Center Oral History Project, Houston, TX.

Leveaux, Roberta Sandoz. Journal. Collection of Mark Leveaux.

Leveaux, Roberta Sandoz. Oral history, September 7, 2006. Flying Heritage Museum. Collection of Mark Leveaux.

Magee, John Gillespie. Jr., "High Flight." 1941.

Malcolm, Ian M. *Shipping Company Losses of the Second World War*. Cheltenham, UK: History Press, 2013.

Middlebrook, M., and C. Everitt. *The Bomber Command War Diaries: An Operational Reference Book, 1939–1945*. London: Viking, 1985.

Miller, Donald L. *Masters of the Air: America's Bomber Boys Who Fought the Air War Against Nazi Germany*. New York: Simon & Schuster, 2006.

Mundy, Liza. *Code Girls: The Untold Story of the American Women Code Breakers of World War II*. New York: Hachette Books, 2017.

O'Brien, Keith. *Fly Girls: How Five Daring Women Defied All Odds and Made Aviation History*. New York: Mariner Books, 2018.

Moggridge, Jackie. *Spitfire Girl: My Life in the Sky*. London: Head of Zeus, 1957.

Overy, Richard J. *The Air War: 1939–1945*. New York: Stein and Day, 1981.

Pierce, Winnabelle. Diary. Collection of Mark Beasley.

Reese, John, "Lady in the Sky," *Frontline*, 2-5-1980.

Rich, Doris L. *Jackie Cochran: Pilot in the Fast Lane*. Gainesville, FL: University Press of Florida, 2007.

Robertson, Terrence. *Dieppe: The Shame and the Glory*. Boston: Little, Brown, 1962.

Roosevelt, Eleanor. Diary. Eleanor Roosevelt Papers Project. Washington, D.C: George Washington University, Columbian College of Arts & Sciences.

Stratford, Nancy Miller Livingston. *Contact! Britain!: A Woman Ferry Pilot's Story During WWII in England*. California: privately published, 2010.

Turner, Walter R., "Mary Webb Nicholson: Blazing Sky Trails," *Carolina Comments*, 7-2007, North Carolina State Documents Collection.

Walker, Diana Barnato. *Spreading My Wings*. London: Patrick Stephens, 1994.

Whittell, Giles. *Spitfire Women of World War II*. London: HarperPress, 2007.

Wood, Ann. Diary. Texas Woman's University, Denton, TX.

Wood, Ann. Letters. Hoover Institution, Stanford University.

Wood-Kelly, Ann. Oral history, interview by Dawn Letson, June 20, 1997. Women Airforce Service Pilots Official Archive, Texas Woman's University Library, Denton, TX.

NOTES

Full citations, including publishers of books and archives of documents, appear in the bibliography.

PROLOGUE

xi **The Spitfire had just rolled:** Many sources reconstruct this incident: Hazel Raines, letters to her mother, 3-28-1943, 4-23-1943; Hazel Raines, letter to her sister, 4-3-1943. They appear in Regina T. Hawkins, *Hazel Jane Raines: Pioneer Lady of Flight*, 71, 73, 78, 79; "Macon Girl in Crack-up While Flying in England," *Macon Telegraph*, 6-20-1943; Accident report punch card, RAF Museum Cosford (courtesy of Geoffrey Hudson), 3-2-1943; ATA accident report, Maidenhead Heritage Centre, 3-2-1943; Hazel Raines personnel file, RAF Museum London, 9-6-1943.

Commentary from aviation experts on Spitfire Mark IX flying characteristics and the actions pilots take in an emergency include author interviews with Steve Williams, vice chairman of the Eastern Region of the Spitfire Society; Richard Poad, chairman of the Maidenhead Heritage Centre; and Geoffrey Hudson, a private aviation historian.

x **Nearly one in seven died:** Of the 1,250 pilots who flew for the Air Transport Auxiliary, 173 were killed, atamuseum.org.

x **"Mother, if you could know":** Hazel Jane Raines, letter to her mother, quoted in Mary M. Holtzclaw, "Macon Girl Ferries War Planes," *Atlanta Journal*, 7-5-1942.

x **The engine made a quick series:** Accident Report, 3-2-1943, RAF Museum Cosford, courtesy of Geoffrey Hudson.

x *There's not much time:* Hazel Raines quoted in "Macon Girl in Crack-up While Flying in England."

x *Too low to parachute:* Hazel Jane Raines, letter to her mother, 3-28-1943. Hawkins, *Hazel Jane Raines*, 70.

xi **wallowing in a bowl of milk:** Nancy Miller Livingston Stratford, *Contact! Britain! An American Woman Ferry Pilot's Life During WWII*, iii.

xi **I've had it . . . rose in the windscreen to meet the plane:** Hazel Jane Raines, letter to her sister Martha, 4-3-1943. Hawkins, *Hazel Jane Raines*, 73. Hazel told her sister a more alarming version of the accident than she wrote in letters to her mother: "Of course I didn't tell her what actually happened for fear she would worry unduly."

xi **Two little boys:** In addition to the sources above, accounts of what happened in the village include www.collingbournekingston.org.uk/history/spitfire-crash, undated; author interviews with local residents Laurence McGowen, Andrea Palmer, and Olive Bishop.

xii **"digging the dead man out"**: "Macon Girl in Crack-up While Flying in England."

xii **"London! Guard that plane!"**: Ibid.

xii LOCAL GIRL AIR INSTRUCTOR: "Local Girl Air Instructor Desires to Be U.S. Bomber Pilot Despite Male Snickers," *Fort Lauderdale Times*, 8-11-1941.

xiii **More than 1,700 British aircraft**: David Baker, *The Aerial War 1939-1945*, 123.

xiii **70,000 British civilians killed**: UK Parliament, "The Fallen: Military Strength and Deaths in Combat," undated, https://www.parliament.uk/business/publications /research/olympic-britain/crime-and-defence/the-fallen/.

xiii **another 70,000 aircrew dead**: Records are inexact. These figures appear in "Fact File: The RAF 1918 to Present," https://www.bbc.co.uk/history/ww2peopleswar /timeline/factfiles/nonflash/a6649248.shtml.

xiii **at least 20,000 aircraft destroyed**: This is an estimate, because RAF records are incomplete. *The World War II Databook: The Essential Facts and Figures for All the Combatants*, 259.

CHAPTER 1: THE NORTH ATLANTIC PASSAGE

1 **Sleep in your clothes**: Author interview with Adam Hewitt, Dorothy Furey's son. He is the source for other stories from her early life.

1 **The Germans would sink some 720**: Uboat.net, "Ship Losses by Month," undated, https://uboat.net/allies/merchants/losses_year.html.

1 **Dorothy had heard**: "Dorothy Furey Bragg Beatty Hewitt," US ATA Veterans website, ATA Archive, Maidenhead Heritage Centre, https://atamuseum.org/us -ata-veterans/ (site discontinued).

2 **the fate of eleven male flyers**: William Dziadyk, *S.S. Nerissa, the Final Crossing*, 195.

2 **"Someday," she vowed**: Author interview with Adam Hewitt.

3 **a priest got his hands**: Ibid., and author interview with Kent Miller.

3 **"Gothic dysfunction"**: Ibid.

3 **Dorothy projected a look of wariness**: Author interview with Adam Hewitt.

4 **She wrote an ardent editorial**: Ibid.

4 **"I felt this would be"**: "Dorothy Furey Bragg Beatty Hewitt," US ATA Veterans, ATA Archive, https://atamuseum.org/us-ata-veterans/ (site discontinued).

4 **"I didn't envision flying combat"**: Ibid.

4 **well under a thousand women**: Kelli Gant, "Women Involved in Aviation," undated, www.ninety-nines.org/women-in-aviation-article.htm.

4 **weighing only 110 pounds**: Author interview with Kent Miller.

4 **an editor sexually assaulted her**: Ibid.

5 **"Is that your car?"**: "Dorothy Furey Bragg Beatty Hewitt," US ATA Veterans website, ATA Archive, https://atamuseum.org/us-ata-veterans/ (site discontinued).

5 **"Dorothy needed the money":** Author interview with Kent Miller.

5 **"You passed":** Author interview with Adam Hewitt.

6 **"I had the confidence":** Ibid.

6 **Only in sleep:** Ibid.

6 **"snappy little Studebaker":** Ibid. In her own narrative, Dorothy claimed she owned the car, but Adam Hewitt, in an author interview, said she later admitted many times that she "borrowed" it from her fiancé.

6 **"I'll pay you back for it someday":** Ibid.

7 **"My goodness," she added, "the gadgets!":** Stratford, *Contact! Britain!*, 13.

7 **"the yellow peril":** Emily Chapin, letter, 7-7-1942.

7 **"My stage fright was tremendous":** Stratford, *Contact! Britain!*, 14.

7 **"perfectly dreadful noise":** E. C. Cheesman, *Brief Glory: The Story of the Air Transport Auxiliary*, 14.

7 **He made it known:** Roberta Sandoz, journal, *Our Service in England*, May 2005, courtesy of Mark Leveaux.

7 **Ultimately, he rejected:** Ibid. Also Hawkins, *Hazel Jane Raines*, 18.

8 **"When I got to England":** Giles Whittell, *Spitfire Women of World War II*, 143.

8 **"was extremely feminine":** Winnabelle Pierce, Journal, written after the war but undated, courtesy of Michael Beasley.

8 **"One thing remains":** Author interview with Adam Hewitt.

9 **"There wasn't anybody":** Whittell, *Spitfire Women*, 14.

9 **But she also made space:** Ibid.

CHAPTER 2: A COBRA IN A HURRICANE

10 **"Confidential," it began:** Multiple sources, including Stratford, *Contact! Britain!*, 10–11.

11 **Jackie's triumph capped a decade:** Keith O'Brien, *Fly Girls: How Five Daring Women Defied All Odds and Made Aviation History*, xiv.

11 **In 1937, Jackie set the world's unlimited speed record:** Katherine Sharp Landdeck, *the Women with Silver Wings*, 58.

11 **One of the highlights of her trophy collection:** Whittell, *Spitfire Women*, 140.

12 **Race may have played a role:** Information on racial segregation in the U.S. military and the exclusion of Black women from the WASP appears in Landdeck, *The Women with Silver Wings*, 129–133. Notable among other multiple sources on Willa Brown and Janet Harmon, later Janet Harmon-Bragg, is Federal Aviation Administration, "Black Aviation Pioneers Outfly Prejudice," undated, https://www.faa.gov/sites/faa.gov/files/about/history/pioneers/Black_Aviation_Pioneers.pdf.

13 **"We were full of apprehension":** This quotation and other descriptions of the voyage appear in Winnabelle Pierce, Diary, 3-5-1942 and 3-6-1942.

13 **On bracing but clear days at sea:** Winnabelle Pierce, Diary, 3-12-1942.

13 **"What a sight!":** Winnabelle Pierce, Diary, 3-3-1942.

13 **It was one of five:** Ian M. Malcolm, *Shipping Company Losses of the Second World War*, 120.

13 **"It's not bad":** Winnabelle Pierce, Diary, 3-4-1942.

14 **"She had ten stitches without anesthesia":** Winnabelle Pierce, Diary, 3-12-1942.

14 **"has any guts":** Winnabelle Pierce, Diary, 3-7-1942.

14 **"We were a remarkable group":** Anne Hillerman, "WW II women pilots: Mavericks of the Sky," *New Mexican*, Santa Fe, 8-26-1979.

14 **Back when women made up:** Landdeck, *The Women with Silver Wings*, 17.

14 **a refueling line from an airborne:** Landdeck, *The Women with Silver Wings*, 18. Helen Richey's partner in the endurance record was Frances Marsalis.

14 **Helen crawled out:** "Airwomen near Endurance Mark," *New York Times*, 12-28-1933.

15 **Photos captured excited children:** Undated photos, Helen Richey Personal Papers, San Diego Air & Space Museum Library & Archives, San Diego, CA.

15 **They even helped her buy:** "First Woman to Fly Mails," *The Evening Bulletin*, Philadelphia, 7-22-1935.

15 **"Yes, she's a girl":** W. B. Courtney, "Ladybird," *Colliers*, 3-30-1935. Cited in Landdeck, *Women with Silver Wings*.

15 **"My getting this job":** "First Woman to Fly Mails."

15 **Male pilots objected:** Landdeck, *Women with Silver Wings*, 19.

15 **but Helen preferred to keep her head down:** Helen Richey told the press, "I don't want to be drawn into any controversy, because I left Central Airlines in a very friendly spirit." "Feminists Stirred Over Woman Flier," *New York Times*, 11-8-1935.

15 **"Helen was reluctant to leave":** Winnabelle Pierce, Journal, 3-4.

16 **Winnie described herself:** Winnabelle Pierce, Journal, 5.

16 **At a time when only 4 percent:** Liza Mundy, *Code Girls: The Untold Story of the American Women Code Breakers of World War II*, 23.

16 **"Conservative Middle-Western families":** Winnabelle Pierce, Journal, 6.

16 **Stories about air races:** "Only Feminine Flying Instructor in Southwest Joins City Airport." *Journal-Tribune*, Blackwell, OK, 9-16-1940.

16 **she baffled prospective employers:** E. B. Butler, United Airlines, "Letter to Winnabelle Pierce," 3-18-1939. Collection of Michael Beasley. In answer to Winnabelle's application for a job combining secretarial work and flying, Mr. Butler answered, "I am still confused about the type of work you are seeking." In addressing qualities that would be valuable in a secretary, he said: "Too much beauty interferes with efficiency."

16 **she used an inheritance:** Don Downie, "Winnabelle and her Flying Sidecar," draft article, undated, courtesy of Michael Beasley.

16 **"I get an aesthetic pleasure from flying":** "Only Feminine Flying Instructor in Southwest Joins City Airport."

16 **"Flying is about the last activity":** "Winnie Pierce to Join Flying Club," *Des Moines Register*, 8-27-1939, courtesy of Michael Beasley.

17   **On a flight to Texas in 1940:** "Only Feminine Flying Instructor in Southwest Joins City Airport."

17   **In August 1941, she got both:** "Girl Flyer in War Role," *Des Moines Tribune,* 3-30-1942.

17   **She made a sale to Argentina:** Anne Hillerman, "WW II women pilots: Mavericks of the Sky," 8-26-1979.

17   **On her twenty-fifth birthday:** Winnabelle Pierce, Letter to herself, 12-11-1941, collection of Michael Beasley.

18   **"I am convinced that Bill is the man for me":** Winnabelle Pierce, Diary, 3-15-1942.

18   **"I wonder if Mac is right":** Winnabelle Pierce, Diary, 3-19-1942.

18   **"She saw a chance to meet someone new":** Winnabelle Pierce, Journal, 4.

CHAPTER 3: FLY ANYWHERE, ANYTIME

19   **"We expect them to get":** Winnabelle Pierce, Diary, 3-21-1942. Her diary provided many descriptions of the journey for this chapter.

19   **those boys seemed impossibly young:** Winnabelle Pierce, Diary, 3-19-1942.

20   **She had told the others:** Winnabelle Pierce, Journal, 5.

20   **At twenty-four, he was tall:** Author interview with Adam Hewitt.

20   **"I just wanted to be married":** Ibid.

20   **had emerged as the misfit:** Ann Wood, letter to her mother, 7-25-1942. She said of Virginia, "I gather she has been the outcast of first group." Winnabelle Pierce, Journal, also criticizes Virginia Farr for not fitting in, 8.

20   **Her photo had been a fixture:** "Georgiana Farr Sibley, Daughter of Mr. and Mrs. Harper Sibley of Rochester, Becomes Bride of Rev. Charles Leslie Glenn of Jersey City," *Democrat and Chronicle,* Rochester, NY, 4-23-1930, shows a photograph of Virginia as a flower girl to her cousin the bride. The wedding was "thronged with a brilliant assemblage of society," and a full choir of boy sopranos performed the wedding march from *Lohengrin.* Virginia is named as a bridesmaid in another article by Wanda A. Smith, "Jane Harper Sibley Becomes Bride of New Yorker at Colorful St. Paul Ceremony," *Democrat and Chronicle,* Rochester, NY, 6-12-1938. The groom was Gordon Auchincloss II.

20   **As a bona fide American aristocrat:** Descriptions of Virginia's early life are drawn from author interviews with Nancy Kennedy, a second-generation cousin; Hiram Sibley, a second-generation cousin; Harper Sibley III, a third-generation cousin; and Cristy Rodiger, a third-generation cousin. Further information on the family and local society was provided by Ebets Judson, a friend of the family; Marjorie Searl, research curator at the Memorial Art Gallery of the University of Rochester; and Andrea Reithmayr, archivist of the special collections at the University of Rochester Library.

21   **Later she attended the exclusive:** Chatham Hall yearbook, 1936, 14. Courtesy of Chatham Hall, Chatham, VA.

21   **"She was a large person":** Author interview with Cristy Rodiger.

22   **Photos on the society pages:** "Society," *Democrat and Chronicle*, Rochester, NY, 7-15-1934; "Ann Osborne Makes Debut at Dance," *Democrat and Chronicle*, Rochester, NY, 9-9-1934.

22   **In 1934, when she was sixteen:** "From Coat and Suit to Cap and Gown," *Democrat and Chronicle*, Rochester, NY, 9-9-1934.

22   **At a Junior Assembly dinner:** "Youth is Served—Royally—at Third of Junior Assemblies," *Democrat and Chronicle*, Rochester, NY, 9-13-1935.

22   **"It must have grated on her":** Author interview with Harper Sibley III.

22   **Virginia's manners:** Author interviews with Harper Sibley III, Nancy Kennedy, and Cristy Rodiger.

22   **"She had something of a heavy personality":** Author interview with Harper Sibley III.

23   **"She must have hated it":** Author interview with Nancy Kennedy.

23   **It gradually became clear:** Her later relationships make it clear that Virginia was attracted to women, including her partnership with Vivien Jeffery.

23   **"Difficulties are things":** Chatham Hall yearbook, 1936, 14, Courtesy of Chatham Hall, Chatham, VA.

23   FLY YOURSELF ANYWHERE ANYTIME: George Morton, "Woman disproves belief that there wasn't any 'future in flying for women,'" *Los Angeles Times*, 10-25-1980.

23   **"My family was dead set":** Ibid.

23   **"flying socialite":** G. J. Dunkleberg, "Airports and Airpilots," *Democrat and Chronicle*, Rochester, NY, 7-10-1939; Jack Burgan, "Let's All Fly Like the Birdies Fly," *Democrat and Chronicle*, Rochester, NY, 2-21-1937.

24   **"She believes there is":** "Blue Book Miss Up in the Air, Would Teach Girls to Fly," *Democrat and Chronicle*, Rochester, NY, 11-23-1936.

24   **"More and more women":** Ibid.

24   **The local paper wrote:** "Let's All Fly Like the Birdies Fly."

24   **Hoping the notion would pass:** "Virginia Farr Flies Again After Return from Europe," *Democrat and Chronicle*, Rochester, NY, 8-4-1939.

24   **"There was competition":** Anne Hillerman, "WW II women pilots: Mavericks of the sky," *New Mexican*, Santa Fe, 8-26-1979.

24   **In February 1941:** *Junior League Magazine*, cited in Jane C. Fales, "Party Line," *Democrat and Chronicle*, Rochester, NY, 2-13-1941.

25   **Then in May:** "Learning to Fly," *LIFE*, 5-5-1941, 56.

25   **"filthy," as Virginia called it:** This account is from Hillerman, "WW II women pilots: Mavericks of the sky."

25   **"She gassed up":** Ibid.

25   **She'd packed pants:** Ann Wood, Diary, 12-13-1943.

25   **The extroverted Winnie Pierce:** Winnabelle Pierce, Journal, 8.

26   **"A tall, heavy-boned mannish girl":** Winnabelle Pierce, Journal, 2–3.

26   **Many of the passengers stayed up:** Descriptions of Liverpool harbor from Winnabelle Pierce, Diary, 3-22-1942, and Ann Wood, Diary, 5-25-1942.

26   **"Much of the city is gone":** Winnabelle Pierce, Diary, 3-23-1942.

CHAPTER 4: A FOREIGN LEGION OF THE AIR

28 the spectacle of five rowdy ladies: Three sources describe the Liverpool arrival in detail: Winnabelle Pierce Beasley, Journal, 8; Winnabelle Pierce, Diary, 3-23-1942; and King, *Golden Wings*, 56–58.

28 "So overjoyed was everyone": Winnabelle Pierce Beasley, Journal, 8.

28 "what carefree loose women": Ibid., 9.

28 The cultural disconnect continued: King, *Golden Wings*, 57–58.

28 "British reserve! American bewilderment!": Ibid., 57.

28 "They had come with much experience": Ibid., 56.

28 "when they finally docked": Ibid., 57.

29 The streets looked bleak and grimy: Ann Wood, Diary, 5-25-1942.

29 "a ghastly marble-pillared, high-ceilinged cold edifice": Winnabelle Pierce, Diary, 3-23-1942.

29 "In peacetime a dull, dirty factory city": Winnabelle Pierce Beasley, Journal, 9.

29 "We saw bombed-out areas": Stratford, *Contact! Britain!*, 17.

29 Bombing had killed more than 4,000: "Spirit of the Blitz," www.liverpoolmu-seums.org.uk/whatson/merseyside-maritime-museum/exhibition/spirit-of-blitzLiverpoolMuseum.org.

30 "Never in the field of human conflict": "War Situation," Hansard, 5th Series, Vol. 364, August 20, 1940, www.parliament.uk/about/living-heritage/trans formingsociety/private-lives/yourcountry/collections/churchillexhibition/churchill-the-orator/human-conflict/.

31 "God, but it's swell to be here in England": Winnabelle Pierce, Diary, 3-25-1942. This is also the source for what occurred that day and the next in London and Maidenhead, 3-24-1942 through 3-26-1942.

32 "What a thrill it will be": Winnabelle Pierce, Diary, 3-26-1942.

32 Hollywood had given them a picture: King, *Golden Wings*, 58.

32 "the walk past the windows filled with silent male faces": Ibid.

32 "ill-mannered Americans": Whittell, *Spitfire Women*, 14.

32 "To get flying experience": Winnabelle Pierce Beasley, Journal, 10.

32 the others were "furious": Ibid.

32 "Dubious, resentful Britishers": Winnabelle Pierce Beasley, Journal, 9.

32 "I often wonder if the ATA will ever get over their first impression": Winnabelle Pierce Beasley, undated draft of letter of apology, addressed to "Sir," her private papers, collection of her son, Michael Beasley.

33 They included Stewart Keith-Jopp: Cheesman, *Brief Glory*, 13. This book, published in 1946, is also the source for much of the early history of the ATA.

33 "that his Majesty's Government, even in its extremity": Cheesman, *Brief Glory*, 16.

33 "making do and patching elbows": Author interview with Richard Poad, chairman of the Maidenhead Heritage Centre.

33 **unable to account for this loss of property:** These anecdotes about ATA improvisation appear in Cheesman, *Brief Glory*, 26–28.

34 **As France was falling:** Ibid., 31.

34 **"It shows the straits into which our Country had fallen":** Ibid., 32.

34 **The United Kingdom produced 131,549 aircraft:** Ibid., 252

34 **The ATA grew, ultimately deploying:** "Anything to Anywhere—A true story of courage, skill and sacrifice," Air Transport Auxiliary, undated, www.atamuseum .org.

34 **Among those who served:** ATA Personnel records, RAF Museum, aided by a search of museum files by Terry Mace, who keeps a private archive.

35 **"decadent and unnatural women":** "The Women of the Battle of Britain," www.history.co.uk/article/the-women-of-the-battle-of-britain.

35 **"The trouble is that so many of them insist":** Lettice Curtis, *The Forgotten Pilots*, 12.

35 **The women completed 2,000:** Cheesman, *Brief Glory*, 73.

35 **medical exams in the nude:** Whittell, *Spitfire Women*, 16.

36 **"too, too swank":** Winnabelle Pierce, Diary, 3-27-1942.

36 **"She had a loud way of speaking":** Roberta Sandoz speaking in *Spitfire Women* documentary, director Harvey Lilley, Atlantic Productions, London, BBC Four, 2010.

36 **"She messed about and gave us hell":** Winnabelle Pierce, Diary, 3-31-1942.

37 **The others thought she made a fool of herself:** Winnabelle Pierce, Diary, 4-4-1942, 4-5-1942.

37 **"Most of them resented our presence":** Stratford, *Contact! Britain!*, 32.

CHAPTER 5: THE CONCRETE

38 **"The weather got terrible in a rush":** Winnabelle Pierce, Diary, 4-11-1942.

39 **"Flew today!":** Ibid.

39 **Winnie found the city grim:** Ibid. 4-9-1942.

39 **There were bomb shelters everywhere:** This and other descriptions of her stay in Luton: Winnabelle Pierce, Diary, 4-8-1942 to 4-10-1942.

39 **The ATA paid women:** Hawkins, *Hazel Jane Raines*, 17.

39 **Winnie couldn't find shampoo:** Winnabelle Pierce, Diary, 4-23-1942 and 4-24-1942.

40 **ATA pilots could fly as many as 147:** "Anything to Anywhere—A true story of courage, skill and sacrifice," Air Transport Auxiliary, undated, www.atamuseum.org.

41 **"Was scared stiff.":** Winnabelle Pierce, Diary, 4-13-1942.

41 **"oh it was wonderful":** Ibid.

41 **Jackie Cochran lost even more:** Winnabelle Pierce, Diary, 4-18-1942 and 4-22-1942.

41 **"She put up a big fuss":** Winnabelle Pierce, Diary, 4-30-1942.

41 **Dorothy Furey got lost:** Winnabelle Pierce, Diary, 4-17-1942.

41 **But once she got so lost:** Winnabelle Pierce Beasley, Journal, 11.

41 **A strong wind so unnerved Louise:** Winnabelle Pierce, Diary, 4-17-1942.

42 **Winnie speculated about marrying:** Winnabelle Pierce, Diary, numerous mentions, 4-1942.

42 **"God, my nerves":** Winnabelle Pierce, Diary, 4-30-1942.

42 **"Perhaps I shall live through it":** Ibid.

42 **"Usually deaths":** Winnabelle Pierce, Diary, 4-21-1942.

43 **The Americans were well aware:** Richard Poad, "Thrills and Spills: Stories of the ATA," 10-21-2020. This lecture at the Maidenhead Heritage Centre told the story of the crash.

43 **Seventy-nine pilots had died in the service:** "ATA Casualties by Date," www .raf-lichfield.co.uk/ATA%20Casualties.htm.

43 **The first woman to die:** Curtis, *The Forgotten Pilots: A Story of the Air Transport Auxiliary, 1939–45,* 61.

45 **Others who idolized her:** "A fellow pilot in the ATA," "Amy," *The Woman Engineer,* 3-1941, 85.

45 **"frozen and frightened":** Amy Johnson, "A Day's Work in the ATA," *The Woman Engineer,* 3-1941, 90.

45 **Amy had said she would:** Whittell, *Spitfire Women,* 49.

45 **"I rammed open the throttles":** Jackie Moggridge, *Spitfire Girl: My Life in the Sky,* 98. Moggridge's maiden name was Jackie Sorour.

45 **"the clouds stretched to all horizons":** Ibid.

45 **"The clouds embraced me":** Moggridge, *Spitfire Girl,* 99.

46 **WE PAY YOU TO BE SAFE, NOT BRAVE:** Whittell, *Spitfire Women,* 209.

48 **Headquarters issued one of the most urgent priorities:** Accounts of the mission to Malta include King, *On Golden Wings,* 101-108; Curtis, *The Forgotten Pilots,* 129-133; Whittell, *Spitfire Women,* 189-191; and Charles Debono, "Glorious 10th of May, 1942: the Battle of Malta day," *Times Malta,* 5-14-2022.

47 **"It was very bad indeed":** King, *On Golden Wings,* 104.

47 **"There can be few things more frightening":** Curtis, *The Forgotten Pilots,* 131.

48 **"dull and sticky":** Winnabelle Pierce, Diary, 4-16-1942.

48 **"I am glad I have no desire":** Winnabelle Pierce, Diary, 4-16-1942.

48 **"Funny how *not* having a man":** Winnabelle Pierce, Diary, 4-5-1942.

48 **She would no longer serve as a pilot:** Winnabelle Pierce, Diary, 5-2-1942. Pierce wrote: "Cochran has been kicked out because of ill health." Also, on 5-6-1942: "Cochran has been washed out because her sinus is so bad she can't fly open ships."

48 **Lettice Curtis looked at them as if they had a bad smell:** Whittell, *Spitfire Women,* 90.

48 **"was altogether too high-powered for the ATA":** Curtis, *The Forgotten Pilots,* 143.

CHAPTER 6: LEFTOVER PARTS

49 **"Horrors!":** Winnabelle Pierce, Diary, 5-12-1942.

49 **her sheer number of flying hours—one thousand:** Hazel Jane Raines personnel file, RAF Museum, London.

50 **"What's the matter, Miss Raines"**: Hazel Jane Raines, Journal; Hawkins, *Hazel Jane Raines*, 12.

50 **"But is that the ship we are sailing on?"**: Ibid.

50 **She had her answer**: While Hazel refers to the ship in her journal as the *Tetina*, it is called the *Tetela* in shipping records and in a note on stationery from the captain in Hawkins, *Hazel Jane Raines*, 17.

50 **"my too-tight girdle"**: Hazel Raines, Journal, Hawkins, *Hazel Jane Raines*, 12.

50 **At twenty-five, she was often fatigued**: Hazel's health is a frequent subject in her letters and in narrative sections of Hawkins, *Hazel Jane Raines*, including 215.

51 **Her flying went against everything**: This and other family observations come from author interview with Regina Hawkins.

51 **"She started disappearing in the afternoon"**: Ibid.

51 **Hazel became the first woman in Georgia**: Paul Steven Hudson, "Hazel Jane Raines," chapter in *Georgia Women: Their Lives and Times*, 260.

51 **A highlight of her act**: Untitled article, *The Cordele Dispatch*, 4-19-1940. In Hawkins, *Hazel Jane Raines*, 2.

52 **To perform a loop, for example, Hazel would first dive**: Patty Wagstaff, "Loop: How Airshow Pilots Turn Sport into Art," 2-1-2017.

52 **she never felt so close to God**: Letter to Bessie Raines, quoted in "Macon Girl Ferries War Planes."

52 **"She could get music out of anything,"** Hawkins, *Hazel Jane Raines*, 214.

53 **the "pretty Macon aviatrix"**: Associated Press, "Shotgun Greets Pretty Aviatrix Forced to Alight Near Toccoa," *Atlanta Constitution*, 10-24-1938.

53 **"clear blue eyes"**: "Local Girl Air Instructor Desires to Be U.S. Bomber Pilot Despite Male Snickers," *Fort Lauderdale Times*, 8-11-1941.

53 **when crosswinds blew several pilots off course**: "Shotgun Greets Pretty Aviatrix."

53 **She gets plenty of kidding**: Virginia Roach, "Lauderdale Prop Wash," *Fort Lauderdale News*, 8-26-1941.

53 **"Male snickers"**: "Local Girl Air Instructor."

53 **"as English women are doing at present"**: Ibid.

53 **"Me, a two-bit Flight Instructor"**: Hazel Raines, Journal, Hawkins, *Hazel Jane Raines*, 7.

53 **her only dress suit "was fast growing too small"**: Ibid.

54 **Hazel found Jackie to be "a grand person"**: Hazel Raines, Journal, Hawkins, *Hazel Jane Raines*, 7.

54 **"300 Lbs Baggage Allowed STOP"**: Ibid.

54 **"It is a wonderful thing to have a daughter"**: "Macon Girl Ferries War Planes," Hawkins, *Hazel Jane Raines*, 22.

54 **"It would surely help"**: Hazel Raines, letter to her mother, 3-18-1943, Hawkins, *Hazel Jane Raines*, 7-8.

55 **"I think I must have been made out of 'leftovers'"**: Hazel Raines, letter to "Mother and All", 3-25-1942, Hawkins, *Hazel Jane Raines*, 8.

55   "The rest of the girls": Ibid.

55   "fear of being disgraced with an old maid sister" Hazel Raines, letter to her mother, 4-1-1942, Hawkins, *Hazel Jane Raines*, 10.

55   "still carrying on with that true American spirit": Hazel Raines, Journal, Hawkins, *Hazel Jane Raines*, 15.

55   The band of thirty pilots who had started the ATA: Cheesman, *Brief Glory*, 94.

56   One ATA instructor was killed: Curtis, *The Forgotten Pilots*, 147. The pilot who was killed was John Erickson, an American.

56   "sure 'nuff stuff": Hazel Raines, letter to her mother, 6-19-1942, Hawkins, *Hazel Jane Raines*, 25.

56   "would be not only qualified but capable": Hazel Raines, letter to her mother, 6-20-1942, Hawkins, *Hazel Jane Raines*, 27.

56   "I never intend to grow up": Ibid.

56   "I am so tired all I can do": Hazel Raines, letter to her mother, 6-6-1942, Hawkins, *Hazel Jane Raines*, 22.

56   "It almost killed me at first": Ibid.

56   "In God We Trust": "Macon Girl Ferries War Planes."

CHAPTER 7: THE IMPOSSIBLE TURN

58   "a heap of scrap": Winnabelle Pierce, Diary, 6-24-1942.

58   "It took ten minutes": Winnabelle Pierce, Diary, 6-23-1942.

58   Richey flubbed it: Helen Richey personnel record, 6-21-1942, RAF Museum.

58   "It was a horrible way of bumping and skidding": Stratford, *Contact! Britain!*, 42.

58   "It was an entirely different feeling": Ibid.

59   "The excitement of stepping into a fighter": Winnabelle Pierce Beasley, Journal, 11.

59   feeling cocky and cheating: Winnabelle Pierce, Diary, 7-2-1942.

59   She declared the trip "swell": Winnabelle Pierce, Diary, 7-4-1942.

59   But no sooner had Winnie launched the plane: Multiple sources describe the engine failure episode: Winnabelle Pierce, Diary, 7-11-1942; Winnabelle Pierce Beasley, Journal, 13; ATA Accident Report, 7-11-1942, ATA Museum, Maidenhead, UK; author interview, Geoffrey Hudson, aviation historian. Various sources explain engine failure on takeoff and impossible turns, including "Engine Failure on Takeoff— What If?," *Vector*, 1998, Issue 3, https://www.aviation.govt.nz/assets/publications /vector/Vector_1998_Issue-3_May.pdf.; and Jorgo, "The Impossible Turn—Tips To Survive Engine Failure on Takeoff," *Pro Aviation Tips*, 1-23-2021, https://proaviationtips .com/efato.

61   "Angels were with me today": Winnabelle Pierce, Diary, 7-11-1942.

61   "and all that rot about 'good show'": Winnabelle Pierce, Diary, 7-12-1942.

62   "Lord but I was lucky": Winnabelle Pierce, Diary, 7-11-1942.

62   "to celebrate my escape": Ibid.

62   "binge," "buzzed," "plastered": Winnabelle Pierce, Diary, 6-25-1942 to 8-10-1942.

62 she tumbled off her bike: Winnabelle Pierce, Diary, 6-28-1942.

62 "Heigh-ho, must get over this yen for drink": Winnabelle Pierce, Diary, 6-23-1942.

62 Her commanding officer at White Waltham warned her: Winnabelle Pierce, Diary, 7-5-1942.

62 a bloodshot eye and a cigarette burn: Ibid.

62 "tight as a tick": Winnabelle Pierce, Diary, 8-12-1942.

63 "I wish I could have remembered": Winnabelle Pierce, Diary, 8-2-1942.

63 "There was this inexplicable pressure": Mary Ellis, A Spitfire Girl, 6.

63 "Because one never knew: Author interview with Adam Hewitt.

CHAPTER 8: THE WHOLE GLORIOUS FEAST

65 only one in three aircraft made it to within five miles: Richard J. Overy, The Air War: 1939–1945, 110.

65 Almost half of all bombs: Baker, The Aerial War, 136.

65 The year 1942 saw a ramping up in the manufacture: Overy, The Air War, 150.

66 "[I] am vaguely lost most of the time": Ann Wood, Diary, 6-10-1942.

66 "She absolutely lapped it up": Author interview with Christopher Wood Kelly.

67 Ann was twelve: This and other details from Ann Wood's childhood, ibid.

67 "She spent the rest of her life flying": Ibid.

67 The well-traveled coed studied: Ann Wood, Diary, 2-10-1944.

68 Classmates elected her president: "1938 D'Youvillian," D'Youville college yearbook, 1938.

68 "our genial, all-round and born leader": Nigel Fountain, "Ann Wood-Kelly: US Woman Pilot at the Heart of Britain's War Effort," Guardian, 6-18-2006.

68 WOMAN HIGHEST RANKING STUDENT IN AVIATION CLASS: Special to the Bangor Daily News, 9-25-1940, 13.

68 "My mother was very pleased": Whittell, Spitfire Women, 140.

68 Forty-one British bombers were lost: Baker, The Aerial War, 143.

68 "Terrible thing": Winnabelle Pierce, Diary, 6-1-1942.

68 "Somehow these jaunts to London fill me utter glee": Ann Wood, Diary, 5-31-1942.

69 Canterbury Cathedral survived: "75-year anniversary of Baedeker Blitz on Canterbury when city was showered with bombs," Kent Online, 6-1-2017, https://www.kentonline.co.uk/canterbury/news/the-day-bombs-fell-like-126561/.

69 "I managed to lose myself just cruising around": Ann Wood, Diary, 6-9-1942.

69 "People are getting the gate every day": Ann Wood, Diary, 7-5-1942.

70 "bad airmanship": Dorothy Furey personnel file, Accident Report, RAF Museum, 6-24-1942.

70 "Lots of fun jazzing about": Ann Wood, Diary, 6-27-1942.

70 "Putting in at new aerodromes is [the] best part": Ann Wood, Diary, 7-7-1942.

70 "I have terrific desire": Ann Wood, Diary, 11-27-1942.

70 *Mrs. Miniver* was "splendid": Ann Wood, Diary, 6-15-1942.

70 "My every footstep resonated far and wide": Ann Wood, Diary, 6-7-1942.

71 "Invitations to dinner consist merely": Ann Wood, Diary, 8-26-1942.

71 "Such a tremendous thrill to see": Ann Wood, Diary, 6-22-1942.

72 "What was it like?": Ann Wood, Diary, 5-31-1942.

72 "Damage is ghastly, entirely flattened": Ann Wood, Diary, 6-19-1942.

72 "Not such a bad apple": Ann Wood, Diary, 6-5-1942.

72 "Always wonder if I'm being a bit of a sissy": Ann Wood, Diary, 7-3-1942.

CHAPTER 9: BEHIND THE FAÇADE

73 felt conspicuous: Ann Wood, Diary, 7-4-1942.

74 "I was much infatuated": Ibid.

74 "Ann, can you be here at the Statler": Ann Wood quoted in Jacqueline Cochran and Maryann Bucknum Brinley, *Jackie Cochran: The Autobiography of the Greatest Woman Pilot in Aviation History*, 186.

74 "Annie, you went to college": Whittell, *Spitfire Women*, 155.

75 "would fling those words about": Ann Wood, *Comments at the Jacqueline Cochran Memorial*, 9-18-1980. Collection of Michael Beasley.

75 Even the famous name wasn't real: I used many sources to piece together Jackie Cochran's story. The most authoritative in reconciling the many versions is Landdeck, *The Women with Silver Wings*, 52–58. When sources disagreed, I relied on Landdeck's scrupulous research. Other sources included Jacqueline Cochran, *The Stars at Noon*; Cochran and Brinley, *Jackie Cochran*; Doris L. Rich, *Jackie Cochran: Pilot in the Fast Lane*; and Billie Pittman Ayers and Beth Dees, *Superwoman Jacqueline Cochran: Family Memories About the Famous Pilot, Patriot, Wife and Businesswoman*.

75 "I was the youngest and a regular little ragamuffin": Cochran and Brinley, *Jackie Cochran*, 13.

75 "I'm going to be rich": Cochran and Brinley, *Jackie Cochran*, 35.

76 "I passed through the School of Hard Knocks": Cochran and Brinley, *Jackie Cochran*, 27.

76 The father of her child, Robert Cochran: Landdeck, *The Women with Silver Wings*, 53.

76 "I was no fool even then": Cochran and Brinley, *Jackie Cochran*, 30.

76 The flames spread to his clothing: Landdeck, *The Women with Silver Wings*, 53.

77 "Are you really a beautician?": Cochran and Brinley, *Jackie Cochran*, 57.

76 "I've been thinking about leaving Antoine's": Ibid.

78 "She was a woman who wanted to make something happen": Ann Wood quoted in Cochran and Brinley, *Jackie Cochran*, 185.

79 "Some speed": Ann Wood, Diary, 6-6-1942.

80 Jackie "had the face of a dog": Author interview with Adam Hewitt.

80 "She wanted to cause a riot": Ann Wood-Kelly interviewed by Dawn Letson, Women Airforce Service Pilots Official Archive, 6-20-1997.

80 **"She felt inferior":** Ann Wood quoted in Cochran and Brinley, *Jackie Cochran*, 190.

80 **"If he wants you to strip, strip":** Ann Wood quoted in Cochran and Brinley, *Jackie Cochran*, 186.

80 **"I gathered that this American set-up":** Ann Wood, Diary, 7-20-1942.

CHAPTER 10: THE LEGENDARY SPITFIRE

81 **Hazel Raines's first day of ferrying:** This description of Hazel's first ferry flight appears in Hazel Raines, letter to her mother, 11-5-1942, Hawkins, *Hazel Jane Raines*, 45.

82 *my goodness, another woman*: Ibid.

82 **"It was quite an odd scene":** Ibid.

83 **"I gather she has been the outcast":** Ann Wood, Diary, 7-25-1942.

83 **"You would think at our age":** Ann Wood, Diary, 8-5-1942.

83 **"The atmosphere is really hysterical":** Ann Wood, Diary, 8-13-1942.

83 **"More American girls began to arrive":** Winnabelle Pierce Beasley, Journal, 15.

84 **Jackie Cochran had learned that she couldn't invite:** Ann Wood, Diary, 7-27-1942.

84 **"was slow and pedantic":** Winnabelle Pierce Beasley, Journal, 6.

84 **"To hell with Farr":** Winnabelle Pierce, Diary, 7-20-1942.

84 **"Gosh, it felt like someone had kicked me in the rear":** Freydis Sharland, quoted in Inge Oosterhoff, "Beauties and Their Bombers: Meet the 'Top Gun' Heroines of WW2," *Messy Nessy*, 8-10-2020, https://www.messynessychic.com/2015/07/28/beauties-and-their-bombers-meet-the-top-gun-heroines-of-ww2/.

85 **"felt exhilarated by the eager":** Moggridge, *Spitfire Girl*, 103.

85 **the Spit "was altogether more feminine":** Curtis, *The Forgotten Pilots*, 103.

85 **it was Helen Richey who called the Spitfire:** Ernie Pyle, "Roving Reporter," *Pittsburgh Press*, 10-21-1942.

86 **The Spitfire Mark IX, probably the most common model:** For many details about the design and history of the Spitfire, I am indebted to Jonathan Glancey, *Spitfire: The Biography*, 80th Anniversary Edition. (London: Atlantic Books, 2006). Specifications of the Mark IX appear on page 244.

86 **"raining revenge from the wings":** Glancey, *Spitfire: The Biography*, 4.

87 **She ran off the end:** Helen Richey, personnel file, 7-21-1942, RAF Museum Archive; ATA Accident Committee Report, Maidenhead Heritage Centre Archive, 7-21-1942.

87 **"Where was your judgment?":** Winnabelle Pierce Beasley, Journal, 15.

87 **"Why didn't you go around again":** Ibid.

87 **"Bad airmanship":** Helen Richey, personnel file, RAF Museum Archive, 7-21-1942.

87 **"Had two myself—a Mark V and a Mark IX":** Winnabelle Pierce, Diary, 7-31-1942.

87 **she buzzed her billet:** Winnabelle Pierce, Diary, 8-6-1942.

88   **"Error of judgment on the part of the pilot"**: Louise Schuurman, personnel file, RAF Museum Archive, 7-31-1942; ATA Accident Committee Report, Maidenhead Heritage Centre Archive, 7-31-1942.

88   **"flying anything and everything"**: Deborah G. Douglas, *United States Women in Aviation, 1940–1985*, 13.

88   **"An above average pilot"**: Virginia Farr, personnel file, RAF Museum Archive, 8-17-1942.

88   **"were, for the most part, happy to take the ATA as it was"**: Curtis, *The Forgotten Pilots*, 143.

89   **"Farr is doing Class 3 and 4"**: Winnabelle Pierce, Diary, 8-17-1942.

89   **When the engine failed in the air**: Helen Harrison, personnel file, 6-25-1942, RAF Museum Archive.

89   **The first Hurricane encounter**: The full description of this flight appears in Helen Harrison Bristol, "Flying When the Living Was Easy," *Airforce*, Summer 1982, 42, from the archive of Mary Zerbel Ford at the San Diego Air and Space Museum.

89   **"a real greaser"**: Helen Harrison Bristol, "Flying When the Living Was Easy," *Airforce*, Summer 1982, 42.

90   **"To say I was mortified"**: Ibid.

90   **"Miss Harrison, I would think"**: Ibid.

90   **"Endeavored to make flaps-up landing"**: Helen Harrison, personnel file, 9-3-1942, RAF Museum Archive.

CHAPTER 11: PLAYING CHICKEN WITH A VIOLENT END

91   **The shy, insecure daughter**: Author interview with Pam Ford.

91   **"What irony then"**: Mary Zerbel Ford Personal Papers, unnumbered, San Diego Air & Space Museum Library & Archives.

92   **"both enriched and tore apart my life"**: Ibid.

92   **"Look at *me*!"**: Ibid.

92   **"She wanted to excel"**: Author interview with Pam Ford.

92   **"Angel Seeks Wings"**: "Aviation Test Passed by 30," *Los Angeles Times*, 4-10-1940.

92   **"These Women!"**: "These Women! What will They Get Into Next?" *San Bernardino County Sun*, 7-15-1941.

92   **"slim, but not too slim"**: E. D. Ball, "Girl Pilots from U.S. Ferry Planes for Royal Air Force," Associated Press, 4-16-1943.

92   **"One short venture above the earth"**: Mary Zerbel, "Pilot's License Treasured Possession of First Girl to Complete C.A.A. Course," *Extension Division News*, 5-24-1940.

92   **"were more likely to go to pieces in an emergency"**: Ibid.

92   **Her greatest ambition**: Ibid.

92   **"They won't let us fly in the States"**: "Women Go to U.K. for Ferry Duties," *Montreal Gazette*, 6-10-1942.

93 his wife "is just as good a pilot as he is": "Came 4000 Miles to Marry Here," *London Evening Standard*, 8-17-1942.

94 Mary omitted "obey" from her vows: "U.S. Girl Among ...," *The Pictoral*, 8-18-1942, Partial headline from clipping in Mary Zerbel Ford Personal Papers, San Diego Air & Space Museum Library & Archives.

94 MARRIED LIFE IS SUPER COLOSSAL: Telegram to Raymond Zerbel, 8-23-1942, Mary Zerbel Ford Personal Papers, San Diego Air & Space Museum Library & Archives.

94 These were among the first: Imperial War Museums, "American Airmen in Britain During the Second World War," undated, www.iwm.org.uk/history/american -airmen-in-britain-during-the-second-world-war.

94 "Flying is quite gay now as we jazz over": Ann Wood, Diary, 8-18-1942.

94 "but felt guilty about the petrol": Ann Wood, Diary, 8-16-1942.

94 "Amused myself watching Sue go to town": Ann Wood, Diary, 8-15-1942.

94 "It will forever be a mystery to me": Ann Wood, Diary, 9-8-1942.

95 "Faulty airmanship on the part of the pilot": ATA Accident Committee Report, Maidenhead Heritage Centre Archive, 7-21-1942.

95 "unlikely to become an efficient ferry pilot": Una Goodman, personnel file, 7-21-1942, RAF Museum Archive.

96 "It's a great life if you don't weaken": Ann Wood, Diary, 8-13-1942.

96 "It takes just such a thing to pull us up": Ann Wood, Diary, 7-30-1942.

96 "persisted too far into hilly country": ATA Accident Committee Report, Maidenhead Heritage Centre Archive, 9-12-1942.

96 "No more 'Hiya Toots,'": Winnabelle Pierce, Diary, 9-18-1942.

96 "It had a rather odd effect on people": Ann Wood, Diary, 9-18-1942.

97 "Right now, I want to be as close to the front lines as possible": "Veteran Pilot Mary Hooper Wants to Raise Large Family After War," *Menominee Herald Leader*, 8-3-1943.

97 DEEPLY REGRET TO INFORM YOU: Mary Zerbel Ford Personal Papers, San Diego Air & Space Museum Library & Archives.

97 Mary wanted to scream into the night: Mary Ford, Journal, unnumbered, San Diego Air & Space Museum & Archives.

97 Wes and the Hudson's crew of five: Letter to Mrs. Hooper from Group Captain, Commanding, RAF Station, Sumburgh, 10-27-1942, Mary Ford Personal Papers, San Diego Air & Space Museum Library & Archives.

97 "It can only be presumed that the aircraft crashed": Ibid.

98 "But I can only offer a very slender hope": Ibid.

98 Two days after she received the telegram: Mary Zerbel Flight Logbook, Mary Ford Personal Papers, San Diego Air & Space Museum Library & Archives.

98 "keep busy as long as necessary": Mary Ford Personal Papers, San Diego Air & Space Museum Library & Archives.

98 "Keep your chin up, Baby" Ibid.

CHAPTER 12: COMING AND GOING

100 **Jackie was blindsided by scuttlebutt:** Much of the politics surrounding Jackie Cochran's appointment to the WASP appears in Landdeck, *The Women with Silver Wings*, 45–46 and 49–50.

101 **"No shape or form to anything":** Stratford, *Contact! Britain!*, 29.

101 **"Scuse me, scuse me":** Ibid.

102 **"She always thought of herself as a loner":** Author interview with Margaret Miller.

102 **"She was plain":** Ibid.

102 **"designated daughter":** Ibid.

102 **"Suddenly I was grabbed by a wonderful feeling":** Stratford, *Contact! Britain!*, 57.

102 **"Quit kidding":** Stratford, *Contact! Britain!*, 1.

102 **Nancy's fiancé forbade her to join:** Author interview with Nancy Miller Stratford.

102 **"I wasn't ready to settle":** Ibid.

103 **"She wasn't a particularly imaginative or introspective person":** Author interview with Margaret Miller.

103 **she was outspoken and independent:** Many details of Roberta Sandoz's background come from an author interview with her son, Mark Leveaux.

103 **"backwoods gal":** "Whitman Centerfold: Two Women," *Whitman Magazine,* 8-1985, 25.

103 **"country bumpkin":** Roberta Boyd Sandoz Leveaux, interviewed by Rebecca Wright, NASA Johnson Space Center Oral History Project, 3-25-2000.

103 **She climbed into the open cockpit:** Robert L. Shaffer, "Wartime Woman Pilot Designs Shakespearean Play Costumes," Associated Press Newsfeatures, as printed in the *News Leader*, Staunton, VA, 9-11-1954.

103 **"I was pretty young and wild and crazy":** Roberta Sandoz Leveaux, interviewed by Joan Hamilton, 5-2005, collection of Mark Leveaux.

103 **"I must have looked like a floozy":** Roberta Boyd Sandoz Leveaux, interviewed by Rebecca Wright, NASA Johnson Space Center Oral History Project, 3-25-2000.

104 **"What the blankety-blank is wrong":** Ibid.

104 **"I'm homesick":** Roberta Boyd Sandoz Leveaux, interviewed by Joan E. Hamilton, 5-2005, collection of Mark Leveaux.

104 **"She had a quiet tenacity about her":** Author interview with Mary Walton.

105 **"She definitely had a quiet strength and a sense of faith":** Author interview with Lauren Scott.

105 **"The training was difficult for her":** Author interview with Ann Smith.

105 **After a few weeks, a medical officer placed:** Mary Nicholson personnel file, RAF Museum Archive, courtesy of Terry Mace.

CHAPTER 13: THE FABLED MISCHIEF OF RATCLIFFE HALL

106 **"Took off with all my fear"**: Ann Wood, Diary, 9-23-1942.

106 **"Nelson Eddy atrocious as usual"**: Ibid.

106 **"Honestly, I believe if there is an inconvenient"**: Ibid.

107 **"If they serve that 1916 vintage champagne again"**: J. Gen Genovese, *We Flew Without Guns*, 109. The pilot who commented on the champagne was an American named Skippy Lane.

108 **"It was a pilot's heaven"**: Genovese, *We Flew Without Guns*, 110.

108 **The idea was "to rattle the windows"**: Genovese, *We Flew Without Guns*, 117.

108 **"When you open the throttle"**: Genovese, *We Flew Without Guns*, 118.

108 **"You better get that fixed, Captain"**: Genovese, *We Flew Without Guns*, 119.

109 **Ann sometimes popped up to help**: Ann Wood, Diary, 11-19-1942.

109 **"not something to dream about"**: Ann Wood, Diary, 8-6-1942.

109 **"A keen and competent pilot"**: Ann Wood personnel file, RAF Museum Archive, 10-15-1942.

110 **"It was definitely sticky"**: Ann Wood, Diary, 9-8-1942.

110 **Once she launched her Fairchild**: Ann Wood, Diary, 9-29-1942.

110 **"visibility completely nil"**: Ann Wood, Diary, 9-12-1942.

110 **And when she opened the hatch**: Ann Wood, Diary, 9-30-1942.

110 **"Couldn't see a thing"**: Ann Wood, Diary, 10-6-1942.

110 **a "complete madman but he manages"**: Ann Wood, Diary, 10-24-1942. All the descriptions of that day appear in this entry.

112 **"Where is my sunshine?"**: Stratford, *Contact! Britain!*, 72.

112 **Mary Zerbel Hooper was flustered**: Mary Zerbel Ford, Journal, Mary Ford Personal Papers, San Diego Air & Space Museum Library & Archives. Unnumbered pages describe this event.

113 **"Jesus Christ, what the hell is this stuff?"**: Author interview with Pam Ford.

113 **"Army boys took me home in a Jeep"**: Ann Wood, Diary, 8-18-1942.

113 **"Avery very easy—will do all the talking"**: Ann Wood, Diary, 8-29-1942.

113 **The officers who delivered urgent messages**: Ann Wood, Diary, 9-14-1942.

113 **"drunken brawl"**: Ann Wood, Diary, 8-7-1942.

113 **known as the "Crunchy Bar King"**: Mary Zerbel Personal Papers, San Diego Air & Space Museum, Library & Archives; unidentified newspaper clippings about Johnnie Jordan.

114 **On November 9, 1942, after a nearly three-hour flight**: Since Ann Wood was circumspect about this accident in her diary, I have reconstructed it from multiple sources. They include Ann Wood, Diary, 11-9-1942; author interview with Chris Wood Kelly; Ann Wood personnel file, RAF Museum, 11-9-1942; microfilm accident report, RAF Museum, 11-9-1942; ATA Accident Report, ATA Museum, Maidenhead Heritage Centre, 11-9-1942; Gloria Negri, "Ann Wood-Kelly, 88: Pilot Ferried War Planes," *Boston Globe*, 5-19-2006; and "Pilots: Ann Wood-Kelly," *AOPA News*, 3-5-1995.

114 "Crashed at St. Merryn, spent night": Ann Wood, Diary, 11-9-1942.

114 "I merely chalked it up to the mishap department": Ann Wood, Diary, 12-21-1942.

114 "Wasn't the least bit concerned": Ann Wood, Diary, 11-20-1942.

114 When her irrepressible buddy: Author interview with Chris Wood Kelly; and Whittell, *Spitfire Women*, 149–150.

CHAPTER 14: HER HEART IS INVOLVED

116 "The sirens are howling even as I write": Winnabelle Pierce, Diary, 8-12-1942.

117 "Great excitement": Winnabelle Pierce, Diary, 9-4-1942.

117 "I have such a supreme feeling of being able to get everything I want": Winnabelle Pierce, Diary, 8-16-1942.

117 Frustrated, melancholic, late at night: Winnabelle Pierce, Diary, 8-14-1942.

117 "If I am alive, I shall do my thinking tonight": Winnabelle Pierce, Diary, 8-23-1942, quoting *Flight to Arras* by Antoine de Saint-Exupery.

117 she "grinned" her way out: Winnabelle Pierce, Diary, 8-18-1942.

117 "English women don't, etcetera, etcetera": Winnabelle Pierce, Diary, 8-28-1942.

118 "The idea is for the plane to lift *me*": Author interview with Richard Poad.

118 "God, what a huge thing": Winnabelle Pierce, Diary, 10-1-1942.

118 It wasn't long after that when she resumed her affair: Winnabelle Pierce, Diary, 10-5-1942.

118 "Each year without living with a man": Winnabelle Pierce, Diary, 9-14-1942.

119 "He is so sweet and so much money": Winnabelle Pierce, Diary, 9-21-1942.

119 "I got very tight": Winnabelle Pierce, Diary, 9-26-1942.

119 "the usual talk of marriage": Winnabelle Pierce, Diary, 9-28-1942.

120 Louise's boyfriend, Ernest McGeehee: Winnabelle Pierce, Diary, 10-24-1942.

120 "Are you sure you're able to drive?": Ann Wood, Diary, 10-24-1942.

120 Some RAF boys had found Winnie unconscious: Ann Wood, Diary, 10-25-1942.

121 "A man does make a difference": Ann Wood, Diary, 10-25-1942. The man was an officer named David Coleman.

121 "Hey Squirt": Ibid.

122 "I never felt any animosity": William Clark, "A Glorious Adventure," *Santa Fe Reporter*, 8-9-1979.

122 "As the war went on": Rosemary du Cros, *ATA Girl: Memories of a Wartime Ferry Pilot*, 81–82.

123 They looked as sharp as they could: The story of Eleanor Roosevelt's visit to the aerodrome at White Waltham is drawn from the following: Associated Press, "Mrs. Roosevelt Talks on Despite Air Raid Sirens," in *Fort Myers News-Press* and other newspapers, 10-27-1942; Ann Wood, Diary, 10-26-1942; Stratford, *Contact! Britain!*, 51–52; Hazel Raines, letter to her mother, 10-27-1942, in Hawkins,

Hazel Jane Raines, 41; and Eleanor Roosevelt, Diary, 10-27-1942, Eleanor Roosevelt Papers Project, George Washington University Columbian College of Arts and Sciences.

123 **"All women must remove their trousers"**: John Webster, "Flag Down Remembrance Lecture," ATA Museum, 11-30-2020.

123 **"After being so used to wearing my long-handles"**: Hazel Raines, letter to her mother, 1-9-1943, in Hawkins, *Hazel Jane Raines*, 63.

124 **By now, it was becoming clear**: Landdeck, *The Women with Silver Wings*, 129–133.

124 **"What's going to happen when it's all over?"**: Martha Martin, "The Wings and the Women," *Daily News*, New York, 11-1-1942, 7.

125 **"Phooey"**: Winnabelle Pierce, Diary, 11-1-1942.

125 **"My mind is in turmoil"**: Winnabelle Pierce, Diary, 11-19-1942.

125 **"He made a remark about me having kids"**: Ibid.

125 **a "courting contract"**: Winnabelle Pierce, Diary, 11-25-1942.

125 **"I don't think you could put up with me"**: Winnabelle Pierce, Diary, 11-27-1942.

126 **"I was headstrong, wild"**: Winnabelle Pierce, Diary, 12-11-1942.

126 **"I loved him a lot as a good-bye"**: Winnabelle Pierce, Diary, 12-12-1942.

126 **was, in fact, a spy**: Author interview with Michael Beasley, and documents from the Beasley family archive.

126 **even though he'd mentioned to her**: Ann Wood, Diary, 8-26-1942.

126 **"Winnie is his gal, and he seems to love it"**: Ann Wood, Diary, 12-10-1942.

127 **"Her heart is involved"**: Ann Wood, Diary, 12-22-1942.

127 **"I found myself very scared"**: Winnabelle Pierce, Diary, 12-20-1942.

127 **"I hope I get over it"**: Winnabelle Pierce, Diary, 12-21-1943.

127 **"Heard Stubbs was killed"**: Ann Woods, Diary, 12-22-1942. The pilot's name was James Stubbs.

127 **"Peter was sweet"**: Winnabelle Pierce, Diary, 12-22-1942.

CHAPTER 15: STEPPING UP TO THE UPPER CLASS

128 **She strolled down the sloping High Street**: Dorothy Furey didn't leave behind her own detailed description of her encounter with the streets of Hamble, so this description is based on my own observations and the memoir by Alison King, *Golden Wings*, 38.

129 **"She couldn't stand it"**: Author interview with Adam Hewitt.

129 **"She said it was so bad"**: Ibid.

130 **"A complex character, difficult to assess"**: Dorothy Furey, personnel file, courtesy of Terry Mace.

130 **"She never liked being told what to do"**: Author interview with Adam Hewitt.

130 **A couple of times, she was blamed for taxiing**: Dorothy Furey, personnel file, courtesy of Terry Mace, 6-24-1942, 12-20-1942, and 5-27-1943.

130 **But when the undercarriage of a Hurricane wouldn't go down:** Dorothy Furey, personnel file, courtesy of Terry Mace, 11-9-1942.

130 **American Edith Stearns spotted a plane:** Stratford, *Contact! Britain!*, 111.

131 **"Oh hell, let's take a crack at it!":** Du Cros, *ATA Girl*, 67.

131 **another legendary beauty . . . Diana Barnato:** Sources for the background of Diana Barnato Walker include her book, *Spreading My Wings* (London: Patrick Stephens, 1994), and Diana Barnato Walker, *Oral History*, Archives of Imperial War Museums, London.

131 **"They said they exaggerated":** King, *Golden Wings*, 59.

132 **Joy Ferguson, a trained engineer:** Nina Baker, "Jonathan Ferguson's story—an update," Women Engineers' History, 2-4-2022, https://womenengineerssite .wordpress.com/2022/02/04/jonathan-fergusons-story-an-update.

132 **"Oh, the Polygon!":** Author interview with Adam Hewitt.

133 **Giving him the haughty treatment:** This first encounter with Lord Beatty is drawn from an author interview with Adam Hewitt and from Whittell, *Spitfire Women*, 179.

133 **"She knew I didn't approve of her":** Whittell, *Spitfire Women*, 181.

134 **"She always did exactly what she wanted":** Author interview with Adam Hewitt.

134 **"Oh, he was very romantic":** Whittell, *Spitfire Women*, 179.

134 **"She really turned her lights on":** Author interview with Adam Hewitt.

134 **The mission was poorly conceived:** Terrence Robertson, *Dieppe: The Shame and the Glory* (Boston: Little, Brown, 1962).

134 **He was otherwise handsomely fixed:** "Earl Beatty to Wed Mrs. Dorothy Sands," *The New York Times*, 6-15-1936.

135 **"For the upper classes," she said later, "it was like musical beds":** Lorna Duckworth, "Anthony Eden's Cleopatra," *The Mail on Sunday*, 1-26-1998.

CHAPTER 16: INVITATION FROM A LADY

137 **which called for the virtuoso skills:** Paraphrasing Curtis, *The Forgotten Pilots*, 165.

137 **"About three stories of hodge-podge":** Pyle, "Roving Reporter."

137 **"There she sat":** Hazel Raines, letter to her mother, 11-5-1942, Hawkins, *Hazel Jane Raines*, 47. A full description of the flight appears in this letter.

138 **"This job I am doing now":** Hazel Jane Raines, letter to her mother, 11-5-1942, Hawkins, *Hazel Jane Raines*, 47.

138 **"you'll never have to worry about me":** Hazel Jane Raines, letter to her mother, 8-13-1942, Hawkins, *Hazel Jane Raines*, 31.

139 **"I am slowly turning into a veritable old maid":** Hazel Jane Raines, letter to her sister Martha, 10-27-1942, Hawkins, *Hazel Jane Raines*, 40.

139 **"A pilot of above average ability":** Hazel Raines, personnel file, RAF Museum, 12-2-1942.

139 **"You young things!":** Curtis, *The Forgotten Pilots*, 223.

139 **"Where is that gal from Georgia?"**: This conversation derives from Hazel Jane Raines, letter to her mother, 12-23-1942, Hawkins, *Hazel Jane Raines*, 57-58; and "Experiences of Woman Ferry Pilot Told to Rotary," *Abilene Reporter-News*, 2-12-1944.

140 **"I'm pleased to meet another rebel"**: Hazel Raines quoted in "Former Ferry Pilot in Britain Is Speaker at Fifinella Dinner," *Ponca City News*, 2-26-1947.

140 **"Well, I'm Mrs. Roosevelt"**: This quote appeared in "Experiences of Woman Ferry Pilot Told to Rotary," *Abilene Reporter-News*, 2-12-1944.

141 **"the palatial mansion fairly reeks"**: This quotation and other descriptions of Hazel's visit appear in Hazel Jane Raines, letter to her mother, 12-28-1942, Hawkins, *Hazel Jane Raines*, 59-62.

141 **"Truly great works of art"**: Ibid.

143 **"That's a good thought on your part"**: Ibid.

144 **"There was festive spirit about"**: Ann Wood, Diary, 12-23-1942.

144 **"The skies were glorious"**: Ann Wood, Diary, 12-24-1942.

144 **"a horrible Christmas"**: Mary Zerbel Ford, Journal, unnumbered pages.

144 **Mary Zerbel Hooper had "a horrible Christmas"**: Ibid

144 **"we just sat in front of the fire"**: Stratford, *Contact! Britain!*, 53.

144 **other women "tried to make Peter"**: Winnabelle Pierce, Diary, 12-24-1942.

144 **"Peter slept elsewhere"**: Winnabelle Pierce, Diary, 12-25-1942.

CHAPTER 17: DICING WITH DEATH

146 **The southern pilot realized**: Hazel Raines, letter to her mother, 1-9-1943, Hawkins, *Hazel Jane Raines*, 64.

146 **The popular pilot Alan Colman**: "ATA Casualties by Date," www.raf-lichfield .co.uk, and Ann Wood, Diary, 1-17-1943.

147 **"burnt to cinders"**: Ann Wood, Diary, 1-21-1943.

147 **the American Kay Van Doozer was so shaken**: Ann Wood, Diary, 12-21-1942.

147 **"a gala hike—gloriously warm"**: Ann Wood, Diary, 1-17-1942.

147 **"dicing with death under leaden skies"**: Du Cros, *ATA Girl*, 79.

148 **Yet on January 3, 1943, Helen failed**: Helen Richey personnel file, 1-3-1943, RAF Museum Archive; ATA Accident Committee Report, Maidenhead Heritage Centre Archive, 1-3-1943.

148 **"but her nerves were shot"**: Winnabelle Pierce Beasley, Journal, 16.

148 **To the shock of her colleagues**: Helen Richey personnel file, RAF Museum, 1-20-1943.

148 **"Or is it is a question of nerve?"**: Ann Wood, Diary, 1-25-1943.

148 **under "considerable mental strain"**: A. Barbour, Chief Medical Officer ATA, letter to Jacqueline Cochran, 2-13-1943, Jaqueline Cochran Collection, Eisenhower Library. Quoted in Landdeck, *The Women with Silver Wings*, 182.

149 **"getting a long view of the war"**: "Personal Notes," *Rochester Democrat and Chronicle*, 10-10-1942.

149 "A sound, resourceful pilot": Virginia Farr personnel file, RAF Museum, 10-15-1943.

149 "A good officer and a sound pilot": Virginia Farr personnel file, RAF Museum, 1-22-1943.

149 Her British counterparts found it amusing: This anecdote appears in King, *Golden Wings*, 60.

150 "I knew it was someone rather fancy": Ibid.

150 "How the Duchess must have enjoyed": Ibid.

151 Flying too far into a narrowing valley: Cheesman, *Brief Glory*, 157, describes the Kirkbride environment.

151 Her colleagues believed: Ann Wood, Diary, 3-30-1943.

151 Had Kirkbride aviators not challenged the prohibition: Cheesman, *Brief Glory*, 157.

151 Frequently, when a plane seemed that it wouldn't make it: Author interview with Cristy Rodiger.

151 "she came under fire from German planes": Ibid.

151 "She would have done anything": Ibid.

CHAPTER 18: THE DRUMBEAT OF FATALITY

154 *I suppose they're all out to tea*, she thought: Hazel Raines, letter to her sister, 4-3-1943, Hawkins, *Hazel Jane Raines*, 67.

154 "What burns me up": Ibid.

154 "It's out of hoop skirts and into dungarees": "Dixie Calls the Roll," *Mademoiselle*, 2-1943.

154 "The aeroplanes are so different": Hazel Raines, letter to her mother, 2-2-1943, Hawkins, *Hazel Jane Raines*, 65.

154 "In God We Trust": "Macon Girl Ferries War Planes."

155 Still, there were consequences: Accounts of what happened in the village include an author interview with Laurence McGowen; www.collingbourne kingston.org.uk/history/spitfire-crash, undated; author interview with Steve Williams of the Spitfire Society; author interviews with local residents Andrea Palmer and Olive Bishop.

155 "London! Guard that plane!": "Macon Girl in Crack-up While Flying in England."

155 Hazel's injuries were so acute: Hazel Raines letters to her mother, 3-3-1943, 3-28-1943, Hawkins, *Hazel Jane Raines*, 70, 71.

155 describing "a funny experience": Hazel Raines, letter to her mother, 3-28-1943, Hawkins, *Hazel Jane Raines*, 71.

155 "a bump on my head and two beautiful blue knees": Ibid.

155 "I now look like a prisoner from Sing Sing": Ibid.

155 "darn lucky" to be alive: Hazel Raines, letter to her sister, 4-3-1943, Hawkins, *Hazel Jane Raines*, 73.

156 It sure is a tough blow for me: Ibid.

156 **"In difficult weather conditions she failed to maintain control"**: Accident Report, Hazel Raines ATA personnel file, 2-3-1943, RAF Museum Archive.

156 **But later, a fuller inquiry examined the aircraft**: Reconsidered Accident Report, 9-6-1943, Hazel Raines ATA personnel file, RAF Museum Archive.

156 **"well-disciplined" and "intelligent"**: Evelyn Hudson ATA personnel file, 11-3-1942, RAF Museum Archive.

156 **On March 16, she and Dorothy Furey Bragg**: The story of this crash is drawn from ATA Accident Report, 3-16-1943, and Gary Haines, "Posts from the Archive: Evelyn Hudson and ATA," Royal Air Force Museum, 12-25-2019, www.rafmuseum.org.uk /blog/posts-from-the-archive-evelyn-hudson-and-ata/.

157 **"The agony of getting from one position**: Ann Wood, Diary, 3-30-1943.

157 **In 1944, she applied to return to the ATA**: Stratford, *Contact! Britain!*, 35-36.

157 **"unlikely to become an efficient ferry pilot"**: Evelyn Hyam personnel file, RAF Museum Archive, courtesy of Terry Mace.

157 **determined to become a good doctor or a poor flyer"**: Ann Wood, Diary, 2-22-1943.

158 **The English pilot Honor Salmon**: ATA personnel database, ATA Museum, Maidenhead Heritage Center; https://atamuseum.org/personnel-database/; South Gloucestershire War Memorials, www.sites.southglos.gov.uk/war-memorials /people/honor-isabel-salmon/.

158 **"Poor weather is supposed—"**: Ann Wood, Diary, 4-21-1943.

CHAPTER 19: EYES WIDE OPEN

159 **A group of seven women**: Much of the description of the plan to deliver the Miles Masters comes from Winnabelle Pierce Beasley, Journal, 19, collection of Michael Beasley.

160 **Mary's background couldn't have differed more**: Details of Mary's childhood come from author interviews with her nieces Mary Walton, Lauren Scott, and Ann Smith, and documents in their collections.

161 **According to her petition, she claimed that her husband**: "Wife Seeks Divorce and Former Name," *The Portsmouth Daily Times*, 5-22-1928.

161 GIRL JUMPS OUT OF AIRPLANE. COME WATCH!: Unattributed clipping, collection of Mary Walton.

161 **An act of self-sacrificing heroism earned her more attention**: A full description of the accident appears in Walter R. Turner, "Mary Webb Nicholson: Blazing Sky Trails," *Carolina Comments*, 7-2007, North Carolina State Documents Collection.

162 **"she was on cloud nine to be flying full-time"**: Ibid.

162 **Mary took on Hurricanes**: "Daily Progress Report," Mary Nicholson personnel file, RAF Museum Archive, courtesy of Terry Mace.

162 **"She wasn't there to party"**: Author interview with Mary Walton.

163 **Mary's logbook showed barely more than an hour**: "Daily Progress Report," Mary Nicholson personnel file, RAF Museum Archive, courtesy of Terry Mace.

163 **A sudden revving of the engine, a loud bang:** What occurred with the oil leak and loss of the propeller of Mary's aircraft appears in various accident reports, including ATA accident report, Maidenhead Museum; Mary Webb Nicholson personnel file, RAF Museum Archive; and accident report, Imperial War Museums Archive, courtesy of Geoffrey Hudson.

163 **It was hard to tell that the prop was missing:** The descriptions of how Mary Nicholson would have reacted and what actions she took were drawn from the analysis of Geoffrey Hudson, an aviation historian and pilot who researched the crash and arranged a memorial plaque on the site in 2019.

The overall narrative of the crash is based on official accident reports, specifications of a Miles Master II aircraft, and author interviews with witnesses on the ground, including Eddie Collins, Murray Gill, Kelvin Gill, and John Waizeneker.

164 **"In my lifetime I cannot recall my grandfather with a smile":** Author interview with Ann Smith.

165 **"It is fitting to commend her courage":** "For the Cause of Freedom," *Daily Times-News*, 5-25-1943.

165 **"I thought it might easily have been me":** Gordon Gammack, "Ferry Pilot Will Return," *Des Moines Register and Tribune*, 5-1944, collection of Michael Beasley.

165 **Some RAF fighter pilots carried a loaded pistol:** Len Deighton, *Fighter: The True Story of the Battle of Britain* (London: Jonathan Cape, 1977), 255.

165 **"I didn't mind the idea of being bumped off":** Walker, *Spreading My Wings*, 36.

165 **"The service was simple and cold":** Ann Wood, Diary, 5-29-1943.

165 **"felt like a million dollars":** Ibid.

166 **"a staid, old-fashioned bachelor":** Ann Wood, Diary, 6-3-1943.

166 **"He has found his sea legs":** Ann Wood, Diary, 5-31-1943.

166 **"At first one wonders, then acts, and then a feeling of indifference":** Ann Wood, Diary, 5-27-1943.

166 **Mary was religious:** Whittell, *Spitfire Women*, 219.

166 **"If she thought she was going to die":** Ibid.

167 **"By the time he saw Miss Nicholson":** Author interview with Geoffrey Hudson.

167 **"a tremendous roaring noise":** Author interview with Murray Gill.

167 **"it suddenly went up in a big explosion":** Ibid.

167 **"She looked out. She looked straight at me":** Author interview with Eddie Collins.

167 **"She still had her hat on":** Ibid.

168 **"And the next thing, bang":** Ibid.

CHAPTER 20: THE BOMBER BOYS

169 **"Anything from twenty to thirty [ships]":** Ann Wood, Diary, 4-8-1943.

170 **The size and frequency of attacks gradually increased:** Baker, *The Aerial War*, 189.

170 **Two thirds of them would die:** Donald L. Miller, *Masters of the Air: America's Bomber Boys Who Fought the Air War Against Nazi Germany*, 7.

170 **Only one in four would complete:** Ibid.

170 **"should do well as long as she keeps her mind":** Dorothy Furey personnel file, RAF Museum.

170 **On the night of May 12, 1943:** Most of the account of this accident is drawn from "Halifax JBü924 Crashed at Wijnaldum," *Harlingen during the Second World War*, 1-15-2003, http://members.ziggo.nl/netuser/1943_HalifaxJB924.htm (site discontinued); a copy courtesy of Adam Hewitt.

171 **"Can you turn toward land?":** Ibid.

171 **"Hurry up! Get out!":** Ibid.

171 **The aircraft broke apart:** Ibid.

171 **In Bochum, the target of the bombing raid, 394 houses:** M. Middlebrook and C. Everitt, *The Bomber Command War Diaries: An Operational Reference Book, 1939-1945*, 273.

172 **Dorothy Furey Bragg later confided:** Author interview with Adam Hewitt.

172 **"I didn't even know how to contact":** Ibid.

172 **"She may have felt she made a mistake":** Ibid.

172 **By the spring of 1943, enough time had lapsed since Wes:** Mary Zerbel Ford, Journal, unnumbered.

173 **"I am all agog":** Ann Wood, Diary, 11-26-1942.

173 **"these little things that the average newspaper":** Ann Wood, Diary, 11-27-1942.

174 **"Little does he know":** Ann Wood, Diary, 6-26-1943.

174 **"Apparently loves telling you all about it":** Ann Wood, Diary, 3-1-1943.

174 **"It was one of those strange accidents":** Ann Wood, Diary, 5-29-1943.

175 **"Surely peace is a healthy, sane":** Ann Wood, Diary, 5-3-1943.

175 **"eying the Fortress-laden sky and wondering":** Ann Wood, Diary, 5-13-1943.

176 **He "impressed [her] no end":** Ann Wood, Diary, 5-22-1943.

176 **"a lovely dinner, glorious dancing":** Ibid.

176 **"pleasantly shy yet with so much savoir-faire":** Ann Wood, Diary, 5-23-1943.

176 **"He is as grand as I ever thought he might be":** Ibid.

176 **"still to be counted among those present":** Ann Wood, Diary, 5-25-1943.

176 **"volunteered for everything":** Willard Brown, 95th Bomb Group (H) Association, Oral History Project, 2000.

177 **"The majority to date find it most annoying":** Ann Wood, Diary, 6-7-1943.

177 **On June 17, she noticed that Bill hadn't called:** Ann Wood, Diary, 6-17-1943.

177 **"I am in a complete fever about going home":** Ann Wood, Diary, 6-22-1943.

178 **It also happened that the German propaganda:** I am indebted to this source for compiling this information and many other details about the Kiel raid: Andreas Zapf, "8th USAAF Mission #63: Attack on Bremen and Kiel, June 13, 1943," 9-4-2012, www.chronicles-of-the-luftwaffe.de/?p=299.

178 **Before the American B-17s could reach Kiel:** Other detailed information, including oral histories of survivors, appears in Ian Hawkins, "Aircrew Over Kiel: Excerpts from Courage★Honor★Victory," 95th Bomber Group Association, *Air Power History*, Summer 1989, 41–43.

178 "For the next fifteen minutes": Ibid.

179 "could not believe that anyone could possibly be alive": Ibid.

179 "There were B-17s out of control": Ibid.

179 A tail-gunner, Earl Underwood: Ibid.

179 Of the seventy-six ships: Zapf, "8th USAAF Mission #63: Attack on Bremen and Kiel."

179 Initial reports showed only 3 dead: Ibid.

179 The ultimate count would be: "VIII Bomber Command 63, 13 June 1943," American Air Museum in Britain, https://www.americanairmuseum.com /archive/mission/viii-bomber-command-63.

179 She couldn't fend off a feeling: Ann Wood, Diary, 6-25-1943.

CHAPTER 21: THE SHOCK OF THE FAMILIAR

180 "Those are girl?": "'British Are Wonderful People' Says Mary Zerbel Hooper, Home from Year's Service in England," *Daily Mining Journal*, Marquette, MI, 8-7-1943.

180 Some were shocked at the sight: Mary Zerbel Ford, Journal, unnumbered.

180 She finally got some: Ann Wood, Diary, 6-28-1943.

181 The *New York Herald Tribune* wrote: Patricia Strauss, "17 Americans Serve in A.T.A., Where Women Must Be Tough," *New York Herald Tribune*, 9-25-1943.

181 "doesn't have to be particularly strong physically": Ibid.

181 GIRLS TAKEN TO BRITAIN BY JACQUELINE COCHRAN: Ibid.

181 Jackie revealed that she was struggling: Jacqueline Cochran, letter to Grace Stevenson, Hazel Jane Raines, and Kay Van Doozer, 5-20-1943, Hawkins, *Hazel Jane Raines*, 81.

182 "If they would only realize that 'it can be done'": Hazel Raines, letter to her mother, 4-2-1943, Hawkins, *Hazel Jane Raines*, 75.

182 "It was good getting back on the job": Hazel Raines, letter to her mother, 6-18-1943, Hawkins, *Hazel Jane Raines*, 88.

182 "fairly marked post-concussion syndrome": Letter to ophthalmic specialist, Air Transport Auxiliary Headquarters, 7-10-1943, Hawkins, *Hazel Jane Raines*, 89–90.

182 Hazel Jane Raines was terminated: Hazel Jane Raines personnel file, contract terminated, 7-14-1943, RAF Museum Archive.

183 "I want a Coca-Cola and a hot dog": "Hungry for Cokes, Hot Dogs, Hazel Raines Returns Home," *Macon Telegraph*, 8-7-1943.

183 "Oh! I have slipped the surly bonds of earth": John Gillespie Magee Jr., "High Flight," 1941.

184 "This is certainly a rigid life and schedule": Hazel Raines, letter to her mother, 11-4-1943, Hawkins, *Hazel Jane Raines*, 103.

184 "an Amazon type": "'British Are Wonderful People' Says Mary Zerbel Hooper."

184 "I have hopes that someday": "Mary Zerbel Hooper Veteran Powder Puffer," *Herald-Leader*, Menominee, MI, 8-5-1943.

184 "Too many questions": Mary Zerbel Ford, Journal, unnumbered.

185 "extreme lack of desire to live": Ibid.

185 Which, she added, wasn't the same: Author interview with Pam Ford.

185 Roberta had mixed feelings: Author interview with Mark Leveaux.

185 "I wasn't much for dolls": Roberta Boyd Sandoz Leveaux, interviewed by Rebecca Wright, NASA Johnson Space Center Oral History Project, 3-25-2000.

185 "Mom kept trying to hammer out of solid granite": Ibid.

185 "It changes your perspective": Whittell, *Spitfire Women*, 141.

186 "I caught it like measles": Diane Lieberthal Wettstein Bolchalk, "WW II pilot still airborne," *Arizona Senior World*, 3-1986, 12.

186 "I was frightened at first": "A 'Forgotten Pilot' Remembers World War II," *TMC Focus*, Tucson Medical Center, date unknown, collection of Mark Leveaux.

186 "pleasing personality": Roberta Sandoz personnel file, RAF Museum Archive, 5-15-1943.

186 She saw puffs of smoke below: "A 'Forgotten Pilot' Remembers World War II."

187 "Peter was a knockout": "Whitman Centerfold: Two Women."

187 "I fell for his spurs": Roberta Boyd Sandoz Leveaux, interviewed by Rebecca Wright, NASA Johnson Space Center Oral History Project, 3-25-2000..

187 "I know America well": Author interview with Mark Leveaux.

187 "He was a guy who played with the truth a little": Ibid.

187 One distant aunt objected: Author interview with John Besford, nephew of Peter Leveaux, who provided information about the Leveaux family.

188 "Seems to me a bit hasty": Emily Chapin, Letters, collection of Hoover Institution, 8-9-1943.

188 "insists it isn't war hysteria": Emily Chapin, Letters, collection of Hoover Institution, 8-5-1943.

CHAPTER 22: A PARACHUTE OF FAITH

190 "I feel like I could tear down houses": Ann Wood, letter to her mother, 12-13-1943.

190 Only Bill himself knew: Three published interviews with Bill Brown made it possible to reconstruct the story of his survival of the June 13 raid on Kiel and subsequent imprisonment: Dan Hanson, "Willard W. Brown: Cleveland's own Colonel Hogan," https://www.clevelandseniors.com/people/willard-brown.htm, estimated date 1996; Zapf, "8th USAAF Mission #63"; Willard Brown, 95th Bomb Group (H) Association, Oral History Project, 2000.

190 "treated me with the dignity afforded an officer": Hanson, "Willard W. Brown: Cleveland's own Colonel Hogan."

191 the women had to strip off: Helen Harrison Bristol, "Flying when the Living Was Easy," *Airforce*, Summer 1982, 42.

191 "I am *not* peeing in a bottle": Author interview with Adam Hewitt.

191 Ann Wood encountered a more perilous dilemma: The story of this landing in Greenland comes from Ann Wood, letter to her mother, 9-19-1943.

192 Through twenty miles of narrow fjord: A description of this fjord appears in Miller, *Masters of the Air*, 59.

192 Once on terra firma: The story of the women at the Greenland base appears in Ann Wood, letter to her mother, 9-19-1943; and Mary Zerbel Ford, Journal, San Diego Air & Space Museum Library & Archives, unnumbered pages.

192 With no chance of anyone flying anytime soon: Mary Zerbel Ford, Journal, San Diego Air & Space Museum Library & Archives, unnumbered pages.

192 "What a stir": Ann Wood, letter to her mother, 12-9-1943.

192 "marooned without women": Ann Wood, letter to her mother, 9-19-1943.

193 "friendly enemies": This quote and the rest of the story of meeting Jack Ford and flying to Prestwick come from a partial unpublished manuscript: Mary Zerbel Ford, *Untitled Biography of the Flying Fords*, San Diego Air & Space Museum Library & Archives, 2.

193 "to check on the reputation for beauty of the local blond talent": Mary Zerbel Ford, *Untitled Biography of the Flying Fords*, 3.

194 "There's a difference between being afraid": Author interview with Pam Ford.

194 It was estimated that forty-five thousand: Miller, *Masters of the Air*, 182.

194 During a ten-day period, more civilians: Baker, *The Aerial War*, 195.

194 The cross-Atlantic allies produced 151,000 new aircraft: Miller, *Masters of the Air*, 203.

195 By early November, six weeks had passed: The story of Mary and Jack's speedy courtship comes from Mary Zerbel Ford, *Untitled Biography of the Flying Fords*.

196 "Mary is in a dither": Ann Wood, letter to her mother, 11-28-1943.

196 "obviously" she smoked and drank too much: Ann Wood, letter to her mother, 9-19-1943.

196 "Sometimes in life": Author interview with Pam Ford.

CHAPTER 23: GROUNDED

197 "She would do much better": Dorothy Furey Bragg personnel file, RAF Museum Archive.

197 By that time, she'd been held to blame: Ibid.

198 But in December 1943, Dorothy encountered a new difficulty: Author interview with Adam Hewitt.

198 One day in December: Ibid.

198 Eventually, she was diagnosed: Ibid.

198 The current Mrs. Beatty was supposedly: This and other details of Dorothy's living situation from Ann Wood, letter to her mother, 2-12-1944.

198 "I don't think she really cared": Author interview with Adam Hewitt.

199 "Dorothy always amuses me": Ann Wood, letter to her mother, 2-14-1944.

199 **"he commands your attention"**: Ann Wood, letter to her mother, 4-15-1944.

199 **a "former strip-tease artist"**: Strauss, "17 Americans Serve in A.T.A."

199 **She'd been a stay-at-home wife and mother**: "Aviator Sues Aviatrix," *Chicago Tribune*, 11-18-1937.

200 **"It got so you could sleep anyplace"**: "A 'Forgotten Pilot' Remembers World War II."

200 **"It helped everything a lot, that British courtesy"**: Diane Lieberthal Wettstein Bolchalk, "WWII Pilot Still Airborne."

201 **"This left me with my left hand, knees, chin"**: "Whitman Centerfold: Two Women."

201 **"Never stretch a glide"**: Roberta Sandoz Leveaux, Journal, 8, collection of Mark Leveaux.

202 **two days later, on February 11**: Roberta Sandoz Leveaux, personnel file, RAF Museum Archive.

202 **"When the love of your heart says, 'trust me'"**: Roberta Sandoz Leveaux, oral history, Flying Heritage Museum, 9-7-2006, collection of Mark Leveaux.

CHAPTER 24: FLYING UNDER A LUCKY STAR

204 **On New Year's Day 1944**: The story of Jack and Mary's engagement is drawn from Mary Zerbel Ford, Untitled Notes, 5a–6b, and Mary Zerbel Ford, *Untitled Autobiography of the Flying Fords*, 4–6, Mary Ford Personal Papers, San Diego Air & Space Museum, Library & Archives.

204 **"Would you marry me?"**: Mary Zerbel Ford, Untitled Notes, 5a.

204 **"This war is a job for all of us"**: "Veteran Pilot Mary Hooper Wants to Raise a Large Family After War," publication unknown, 8-3-1943, Mary Ford Personal Papers, San Diego Air & Space Museum Library & Archives.

205 **"I hope for your approval"**: Ann Wood, letter to her mother, 1-5-1944.

205 **"I can't see the marriage angle"**: Ibid.

205 **"I don't want Mary to have to take"**: Ibid.

205 **"You are too sensible to understand"**: Ibid.

204 **"lend some credence to the license I have taken"**: Bill Brown letter to Ann Wood, undated, quoted in Ann Wood, letter to her mother, 2-10-1944.

206 **"I am a misfit *par excellence*"**: Ann Wood, letter to her mother, 1-12-1944.

206 **"She is very continental in her outlook"**: Ann Wood, letter to her mother, 12-3-1943.

206 **Jack had returned from a bombing raid**: Jack Ford, handwritten account, Mary Ford Personal Papers, San Diego Air & Space Museum Library & Archives, unnumbered.

206 **"Bombs away!"**: Ibid.

206 **"Let's get married tomorrow"**: The story of Jack and Mary's wedding is drawn from Mary Zerbel Ford, Untitled Notes, 5a–6b, and Mary Zerbel Ford, *Untitled Autobiography of the Flying Fords*, 4–6.

207 **"If we can get the license"**: Ibid., 6–a.

207 "sparkling and bubbling": Ibid.

208 "miracle of miracles": Ibid.

208 "I'm so glad that you got married": Author interview with Pamela Ford.

208 Also known as the Baby Blitz: Baker, *The Aerial War*, 213.

208 6,200 sorties in one week, 248 Allied aircraft lost: Baker, *The Aerial War*, 210.

208 the Bloody Monday Berlin raid on March 5: Miller, *Masters of the Air*, 272.

208 his was the only one still intact: Mary Zerbel Ford, *Untitled Autobiography of the Flying Fords*, addenda.

208 OUT OF STOCK: Author interview with Pam Ford.

208 "the terror, anger, and fight": Mary Zerbel Ford, *Untitled Autobiography of the Flying Fords*, addenda.

208 but the stress showed in the wedding photos: Author interview with Pam Ford.

CHAPTER 25: HER FUTURE AT STAKE

210 "They were shot up in all kinds of ways": Author interview with Cristy Rodiger.

211 Colleagues like Winnie Pierce mentioned: Winnabelle Pierce, Journal, 12, mentions Virginia "picking up a chum among the British girls," and many colleagues and family after the war stated that they knew about her romantic life.

211 "not a frilly person": Author interview with Cristy Rodiger.

211 Virginia's stellar evaluations: Virginia Farr personnel file, RAF Museum.

212 Vivien often dreamed of living there: George Morton, "Woman Disproves Belief That There Wasn't Any 'Future in Flying For Women,'" *Los Angeles Times*, 10-25-1980.

212 "They take a house together . . . and all is ducky": Winnabelle Pierce Beasley, Journal, 17.

212 "just to get away from the rancid competitive atmosphere": Ibid.

213 "A two-hour flight has taken over three": Winnabelle Pierce Beasley, Journal, 18.

213 "Louise promiscuously moving from affair to affair": Winnabelle Pierce, Journal, 21.

213 She didn't bother to hide: The description of the Frankie Francis episode appears in Ann Wood, letter to her mother, 5-23-1944.

213 Unbeknownst to her: Author interview with Michael Beasley.

214 "Let's go home and get married": Winnabelle Pierce Beasley, Journal, 20.

214 "the marrying kind": Winnabelle Pierce, Letter to herself, 12-11-1941, collection of Michael Beasley.

214 "Her whole future is at stake": Ibid.

214 "but you get tired of being a professional flyer": Gordon Gammack, "Ferry Pilot Will Return," *Des Moines Register and Tribune*, dated approximately 5-1944, collection of Michael Beasley.

215 "it was one glorious adventure": William Clark, "A Glorious Adventure," *Santa Fe Reporter*, 8-9-1979.

215 she considered Winnie "one of the best": Ann Wood, letter to her mother, 5-23-1944.

215 even Pauline Gower, who had so often upbraided Winnie for carousing: Letter to Miss Winnie Pierce from Pauline Gower, 5-15-1944, collection of Michael Beasley.

215 she asked Jackie Cochran to write a cable: Ann Wood, letter to her mother, 5-23-1944.

215 "She mistakenly did believe": Author interview with Michael Beasley.

CHAPTER 26: THE WORLD-SHAKING DAY

217 Nancy Miller awoke to a steady roar: D-Day from Nancy Miller's perspective appears in Stratford, *Contact! Britain!*, 98.

218 "Everyone was filled with the awe and wonder": King, *Golden Wings*, 169.

218 She flew eighteen new types of aircraft: Author interview with Nancy Miller Stratford, and Nancy Miller Logbook, May 1944, Collection of Nancy Miller Stratford.

218 A few days before D-Day, Nancy: Author interview with Nancy Miller Stratford.

218 "Something was going to pop soon": Stratford, *Contact! Britain!*, 98.

218 "had a lot more ships in it": King, *Golden Wings*, 168.

218 "A new type of fighting man appeared": Du Cros, *ATA Girl*, 56.

219 a total of seventy-one thousand bombs on the French rail system: Miller, *Masters of the Air*, 291.

219 aircraft—more than ten thousand in all: Baker, *The Aerial War*, 218.

219 The Hamble airfield had been designated as a "prang patch": Walker, *Spreading My Wings*, 145.

219 "had romantic but vain thoughts": Stratford, *Contact! Britain!*, 98.

220 "I am ubiquitous": Ann Wood, letter to her mother, 6-8-1944.

220 "I'm off to D-Day!": Ibid.

220 "I was glad I was on leave": Ibid.

220 ten thousand Allied troops were killed: "Fact Sheet: Normandy Landings," White House, 6-6-2014, https://obamawhitehouse.archives.gov/the-press-office/2014/06/06/fact-sheet-normandy-landings.

220 "that in the face of momentous happenings [they] can do the commonplace": Ann Wood, letter to her mother, 6-8-1944.

220 The gala dinner made her feel guilty: Ibid.

CHAPTER 27: GOOD GIRL

223 The number of RAF sorties ballooned: Baker, *The Aerial War*, 225.

223 Her fiancé had left her only enough cash: Ann Wood, letter to her mother, 8-13-1944 and 7-9-1944.

223 "A capable pilot whose discipline": Dorothy Furey personnel file, RAF Museum Archive, 11-18-1943.

223 **"I enjoyed my time in the ATA"**: Dorothy Furey Bragg Beatty Hewitt, writing in the US ATA Veterans website, ATA Archive, Maidenhead Heritage Centre, Maidenhead, UK, https://atamuseum.org/us-ata-veterans/ (site discontinued).

224 **"which would probably happen with any man"**: Author interview with Adam Hewitt.

224 **"He made me look like a hardened bitch"**: Ibid.

224 **More than ten thousand V-1s**: Roy Irons, *Hitler's Terror Weapons: The Price of Vengeance*, 199.

224 **Ann Wood promised her mother**: Ann Wood, letter to her mother, 7-25-1944.

224 **"getting closer and louder until your eyes almost pop out"**: Stratford, *Contact! Britain!*, 133.

225 **she survived a spectacular crash**: Stratford, *Contact! Britain!*, 24; and Richard Poad, Lecture, "Thrills and Spills: The Story of the ATA," Maidenhead Heritage Centre, 9-21-2020.

225 **"It might have started as a lark"**: Stratford, *Contact! Britain!*, 193.

225 **"absolutely steady nerves"**: Strauss, "17 Americans Serve in A.T.A., Where Women Must Be Tough."

226 **She also shared the view**: Author interview with Nancy Miller Stratford.

226 **her first Hurricane solo**: Stratford, *Contact! Britain!*, 44.

226 **"Can never be given too much work"**: Nancy Miller personnel file, RAF Museum Archive, 1-3-1943.

227 **"one of the finest American machines in the world"**: Stratford, *Contact! Britain!*, 64.

227 **"USA? What does that mean, lady?"**: Stratford, *Contact! Britain!*, 71.

228 **"Don't let those eyes and that smile fool you"**: Margaret "Peggy" Lennox, "WHAT? A girl Training Men to Train for Uncle Sam?," Lehigh University Digital Collection, https://preserve.lehigh.edu/_flysystem/fedora/2023-12/38870.pdf

228 **"like the Devil waving his hand to come on through"**: Stratford, *Contact! Britain!*, 1.

228 **"was one of the hardest things I ever had to do"**: Stratford, *Contact! Britain!*, 92.

229 **"basic instrument flying, and a basic fight for survival"**: Ibid.

229 **Her covert lessons came to the rescue**: Nancy described this incident in *Contact! Britain!*, 107.

230 **"The training"**: Ibid.

CHAPTER 28: EAGER FOR THE AIR

231 **Peter had been reassigned**: Author interview with Michael Beasley.

232 **She "had some very close calls"**: Mary Zerbel Ford, Postwar Journal, San Diego Air & Space Museum Library & Archives, unnumbered.

232 **"We can learn a lot from dogs and cats"**: Author interview with Pamela Ford.

232 **"It would be a magical and unbelievable sight"**: Stratford, *Contact! Britain!*, 117. Nancy's descriptions of her leave appear on pages 113–153.

232 "What a joy!": Stratford, *Contact! Britain!*, 130.

234 "aerial dishwashing": Landdeck, *The Women with Silver Wings*, 162. I relied on this book's research on the struggle for equality for the WASP.

234 One pilot, Betty Davis, died in a crash when sugar was discovered: Olivia B. Waxman, "The Hidden Risk of Female Pilots During World War II, *TIME*, 9-7-2017.

234 "The women are mixed with men": Stratford, *Contact! Britain!*, 139.

235 "The fact remains that they are not as suitable": Landdeck, *The Women with Silver Wings*, 194.

235 gazing into the eyes of the "shapely pilot": Ibid.

235 "glamorous women flyers": Landdeck, *The Women with Silver Wings*, 211.

236 "All the jewels of the city's lights glittered": Stratford, *Contact! Britain!*, 147.

236 They killed an estimated: Stephen Henden, "V2 Rocket," undated, https://flyingbombsandrockets.com/V2_intro.html.

236 "a slight breach between those at home": Stratford, *Contact! Britain!*, 146.

236 "I wasn't fighting an actual war": Ibid.

236 *Aetheris Avidi*: Ibid.

CHAPTER 29: C'EST LA VIE

238 everything around it was smashed flat: Hugh Bergel, quoted in Cheesman, *Brief Glory*, 168.

238 "a leader of men": Walker, *Spreading My Wings*, 143.

239 "I wanted to sing": Walker, *Spreading My Wings*, 166.

239 "Nobody took a potshot at me": Ibid.

239 They decided to take off: The story of Diana Barnato Walker's flight home from Belgium appears in Walker, *Spreading My Wings*, 167-169.

239 *Where in heaven am I?*: Walker, *Spreading My Wings*, 167.

240 "How on earth did you get here?": Walker, *Spreading My Wings*, 169.

240 "The Fellow Up Top": Ibid.

241 "with an added Parisian twist": Ann Wood, letter to her mother, 11-10-1944.

241 "prepared with French cooks, which really takes it": Ibid.

241 "suggestion of heat, which is a colossal luxury": Ibid.

242 "the only life": Ibid.

242 "I continue to be unusually happy in my present state": Ibid.

242 "If that is to spur me on, you have failed": Ann Wood, letter to her mother, 2-6-1944.

CHAPTER 30: SPINNING INTO A NEW REALITY

244 The rapid progress made by Allied armies: I am indebted to Donald L. Miller, *Masters of the Air*, 370–375, for his description of the Allied air forces role in the Battle of the Bulge.

245 **Some 2,046 bombers:** Baker, *The Aerial War*, 230.

245 **They put 450 fighters out of action:** Miller, *Masters of the Air*, 374.

245 **The next day, she flew in a daze:** Ann Wood, letter to her mother, 1-3-1945.

246 **"I am green with envy":** Ibid.

246 **"A very quiet evening":** Stratford, *Contact! Britain!*, 160.

246 **"What have I done to deserve this?"** Stratford, *Contact! Britain!*, 155.

247 **She bucked around in 40-mile-per-hour winds:** Stratford, *Contact! Britain!*, 157.

247 **"amused but not frightened":** Stratford, *Contact! Britain!*, 158.

247 **"just as if a window shade was being drawn":** Ibid.

247 **"We saw you roll into the storm":** Ibid.

247 **"particularly ornery":** Stratford, *Contact! Britain!*, 109. The full story of this episode appears on pages 109-110.

248 **"Those houses are very vivid indeed":** Stratford, *Contact! Britain!*, 110.

248 **"I think I'm an average pilot":** Author interview with Nancy Miller Stratford.

248 **nineteen thousand Americans had been killed:** Miller, *Masters of the Air*, 375. I also relied on his account of Allied bombing of Germany after January 1945.

249 **The RAF dropped more bomb tonnage:** Baker, *The Aerial War*, 235.

249 **the month overall set a record for the volume of bombs:** Miller, *Masters of the Air*, 445.

250 **"They were not shooting *at* me":** Stratford, *Contact! Britain!*, 112.

250 **The pilot felt a powerful bang:** This story appears in Walker, *Spreading My Wings*, 178–180.

250 **"They all probably thought I was some lunatic":** Walker, *Spreading My Wings*, 179.

250 **"Why . . . are you bringing us only half an aeroplane?":** Walker, *Spreading My Wings*, 180.

CHAPTER 31: WHAT NOW?

251 **"Had quite a funny feeling":** Ann Wood, letter to her mother, 5-4-1945 (This is the date that appears on the letter, although it describes events that occurred several days later. It seems likely Ann continued the letter on those subsequent days without altering the original date).

252 **Ann Wood returned to Ratcliffe Hall:** Ann's VE Day experiences, including news of Bill Brown, appear in Ann Wood, letter to her mother, 5-4-1945.

252 **"So that was my VE Day":** Ibid.

253 **"We fairly went mad":** Ann Wood, letter to her mother, 5-4-1945.

253 **"puddle jumpers":** The source for this quotation and the trip to Brussels and Paris is Ann Wood, letter to her mother, 5-15-1945.

253 **"my tummy felt as though an electric mixer":** Ibid.

253 **The grand city hall stood undamaged:** Cheesman, *Brief Glory*, 188.

254 **Pauline Gower promised to look out for Ann:** Ann Wood, letter to her mother, 4-13-1945.

254 Doc counted eight women among his twelve best pilots: Ibid.

255 "To me the American girls": Curtis, *The Forgotten Pilots*, 146.

255 "I look like a country cousin": Ann Wood, letter to her mother, 3-26-1945.

255 "my dear, it's madly dangerous": King, *Golden Wings*, 109.

255 "infinitesimal amid such grandeur": Ann Wood, letter to her mother, 1-13-1945.

255 "I will be really sorry when I have to stop flying the world's loveliest airplanes": Ann Wood, letter to her mother, 4-13-1945.

256 "I wouldn't be keen on instruction": Ann Wood, letter to her mother, 4-2-1944.

256 "I have a horror of working behind a desk": Ann Wood, letter to her mother, 3-13-1945.

257 "It's difficult to consider, primarily the female angle": Ann Wood, letter to her mother, 3-26-1945.

CHAPTER 32: "THE SPITFIRE BROUGHT ME HOME"

258 British pilot Betty Keith-Jopp: This story appears in Whittell, *Spitfire Women*, 1–3.

258 "I can remember more or less accepting it": Whittell, *Spitfire Women*, 2.

259 "Hold on, Laddie!": Whittell, *Spitfire Women*, 3.

260 "was kind of chuffed": Author interview with Adam Hewitt.

260 "One of the most beautiful women": Lorna Duckworth, "Anthony Eden's Cleopatra," *The Mail on Sunday*, 1-26-1998.

260 "How did she out-aristocrat the aristocrats?" Author interview with Adam Hewitt.

260 "That takes considerable chutzpah": Ibid.

261 "desperately in need of everything": Dorothy Smith, "Women Ferry Pilots 'Call It a Day,'" *Montreal Daily Star*, 9-5-1945.

262 "The river made a shining spectacle": Stratford, *Contact! Britain!*, 176.

262 On her last taxi job: Stratford, *Contact! Britain!*, 188.

262 "just off the secret list": Ibid.

262 "I loved all the flying, the freedom": Stratford, *Contact! Britain!*, 212.

263 "I took the Spit you brought in": Stratford, *Contact! Britain!*, 195.

CHAPTER 33: ON TOP OF THE WORLD

265 "indescribably lovely": Ann Wood, letter to her mother, 6-25-1945.

265 "To see German people": Ibid.

265 "a grim sight trudging": Ibid.

266 "I am in a complete quandary": Ann Wood, letter to her mother, 6-6-1945.

266 "A thousand times, I thank God that you were generous": Ann Wood, letter to her mother, 6-10-1945.

266 She was willing to keep: Ann Wood, letter to her mother, 6-25-1945.

267 "employment at the moment was impractical": Ann Wood, letter to her mother, 7-17-1945.

267 "Your agency is failing miserably": Ibid.

267 "I often feel guilty that I seem to be enjoying myself": Ibid.

268 Her chief claim to the job: Ann Wood, letter to her mother, 9-6-1945.

267 for once felt inadequate: Ibid.

267 "I suppose if I were a get-your-man type": Ann Wood, letter to her mother, 8-18-1945.

269 For two days, she took the unusual ship: Ann Wood Logbook, ATA Museum, Maidenhead, UK.

269 Diana Barnato Walker dawdled: Walker, *Spreading My Wings*, 191.

270 "Already the days filled": Curtis, *The Forgotten Pilots*, 203.

CHAPTER 34: THE LOOK

271 There had been 1,246 pilots: Maidenhead Heritage Centre.

272 Her husband, Floyd Odlum, bought *Liberty*: Landdeck, *The Women with Silver Wings*, 276–8; also Landdeck, "Jacqueline Cochran: Pilot, Leader, Myth," Amelia Earhart Lecture in Aviation History, National Air and Space Museum, 5-10-2023.

272 enticed her to run up the score: Landdeck, *The Women with Silver Wings*, 275.

273 it would be "unnatural" for women to fly: Landdeck, "Jacqueline Cochran: Pilot, Leader, Myth."

273 "It isn't as exciting as England": "Helen Richey 'Loves' Job of Ferrying U.S. Planes," *Pittsburgh Sun-Telegraph*, 2-20-1944.

273 On January 7, 1947, her body: "Miss Helen Richey, Flier, Found Dead," *New York Times*, 1-8-1947.

274 "I wonder sometimes if Aunt Mary is up there laughing": Author interview with Lauren Scott.

274 As far as her family members knew: Author interview with Regina T. Hawkins.

274 She found career security in 1949: Paul Stephen Hudson, *Georgia Women: Their Lives and Times—Volume 2*, Hazel Jane Raines chapter, 273.

274 "The extra beat in my heart": ": Hazel Jane Raines, letter to her mother, 6-21-1956, Hawkins, *Hazel Jane Raines*, 210.

275 "It was not a marriage made in heaven": Roberta Sandoz Leveaux, oral history, Flying Heritage Museum, 9-7-2006, collection of Mark Leveaux.

275 "Without those girls": Roberta Boyd Sandoz Leveaux, interviewed by Rebecca Wright, NASA Johnson Space Center Oral History Project, 3-25-2000.

275 "how wonderful it was": Ibid.

276 "She just called herself Mrs. Beasley": Author interview with Michael Beasley.

276 Peter finally married her: Ibid.

276 At a reading of the will: Ibid.

276 **Peter left no assets:** Richard McCord, "Winnie: She Lived the Life She Loved," *Santa Fe Reporter*, 3-23-1983.

276 **"a living treasure":** Greg Toppo, " 'Living Treasure' Winnie Beasley Had Fun," *Santa Fe New Mexican*, 8-5-1997.

276 **His children eventually learned:** Author interview with Michael Beasley.

276 **His most notable mission:** Norman Beasley, "The Capture of the German Rocket Secrets," *Military Intelligence: Its Heroes and Legends*, compiled by Diane L. Hamm (Honolulu, HI: University Press of the Pacific, 2001). Reprinted by permission of the *American Legion Magazine*, 1963.

277 **"was a neurotic, insecure, social-climbing snob":** Author interview with Adam Hewitt.

277 **Every Friday night:** Ibid. Dorothy's son is the source for her postwar story.

277 **Dorothy's son by a later marriage:** Ibid.

277 **"It was thoroughly and completely condoned":** Caroline Davies, "American Widow Tells of Affair with Eden, Future Prime Minister," *The Daily Telegraph*, London, 1-27-1997.

278 **Shortly before her last marriage:** Author interview with Adam Hewitt.

278 **The two of them once came under machine gun fire:** Mary Zerbel Ford, Journal, unnumbered, San Diego Air & Space Museum Library & Archive.

278 **In Bangkok they picked up:** John Reese, "Lady in the Sky," *Frontline* magazine, 2-5-1980.

278 **"They had Lana Turner walk out of a blazing crash":** Illegible title, including . . . "Pilot," *Standard-Examiner*, Ogden, UT, 4-8-1990, Mary Ford Personal Papers, San Diego Air & Space Museum & Archive.

278 **"and he didn't say no very often":** Author interview with Pam Ford.

279 **Four years later, Jack took off:** Mary Zerbel Ford, Journal, and Steve Young, "A Pilot Shares her War Stories," *Argus Leader*, Sioux Falls, SD, estimated date 1988, Mary Ford Personal Papers, San Diego Air & Space Museum Library & Archive.

279 **She met a calamitous end:** Joel Kirkpatrick, "Pilot of Plane Found Dead in Crash at Scholes Field," *Galveston Daily News*, 4-29-1962.

280 **"She did her own thing":** Author interview with Harper Sibley III.

280 **"Those girls would take jobs that guys wouldn't":** Author interview with Tom Barlogio.

280 **Her body was placed on a boat:** Author interview with Nancy Kennedy.

280 **"I wasn't going to let marriage interfere":** Author interview with Nancy Miller Stratford.

281 **"but that was the kind of thing":** Author interview with Margaret Miller.

281 **"No!" she protested:** Author interview with Nancy Miller Stratford.

282 **Two close colleagues:** The other was Rosamund Everard-Steenkamp of South Africa, who died when a Spitfire failed in 1946. She was the last ATA fatality, part of a small group of British Commonwealth pilots who remained until that spring.

281 **The job called for her to fly:** Ann Wood-Kelly interviewed by Dawn Letson, Women Airforce Service Pilots Official Archive, 6-20-1997.

282 **"I'll fly over from Paris"**: Commentary from Ann Wood in Cochran and Brinley, *Jackie Cochran*, 186.

282 **"Don't make a move now"**: Ibid.

282 **"Look sharp!"** Author interview with Christopher Wood Kelly.

EPILOGUE

283 **"I came home with the feeling"**: Anne Hillerman, "World War II Women Pilots: Mavericks of the Sky," *Santa Fe New Mexican*, 8-26-1979.

283 **"We were unique"**: Ibid.

284 **"We were the thin edge of the wedge"**: Ibid.

INDEX

A NOTE ON THE AUTHOR

BECKY AIKMAN is the author of two books of narrative nonfiction: her memoir *Saturday Night Widows* and *Off the Cliff: How the Making of* Thelma & Louise *Drove Hollywood to the Edge*. Aikman was a journalist at *Newsday*, and her work has also appeared in the *New York Times*, the *Los Angeles Times*, and other publications. She lives in New York.